D0074860

The Return of Cosmopolitan Capital

Other works by the same author

Beliefs in Society: The Problem of Ideology, 1967

Competition and the Corporate Society: British Conservatives, the State and Industry, 1945–1964, 1971

India–China: Underdevelopment and Revolution, 1974

The Mandate of Heaven: Marx and Mao in Modern China, 1978

Economic Development, the State and Planning: The Case of Bombay, 1978

Of Bread and Guns: The World Economy in Crisis, 1983

The End of the Third World: The Newly Industrialising Countries and the Decline of an Ideology, 1986

Cities, Class and Trade: Social and Economic Change in the Third World, 1991

National Liberation, 1991

(ed.) *Cities in the 1990s: The Challenge for Developing Countries*, 1992

The New Untouchables: Immigration and the New World Worker, 1995

(with Sunil Kumar and Colin Rosser) *Jobs for the Poor: A Case Study in Cuttack (India)*, 1996

(ed. with Ida Fabricius) *Cities and Structural Adjustment*, 1996

Thinking the Unthinkable: The Myth of Immigration Control, 2001

The Return of Cosmopolitan Capital

Globalisation, the State and War

Nigel Harris

I.B. TAURIS

LONDON · NEW YORK

Published in 2003 by I.B. Tauris & Co Ltd
6 Salem Road, London W2 4BU
175 Fifth Avenue, New York NY 10010
www.ibtauris.com

In the United States of America and Canada distributed by Palgrave
Macmillan, a division of St. Martin's Press
175 Fifth Avenue, New York NY 10010

ISBN 1 86064 786 3

A full CIP record for this book is available from the British Library

Typeset in Minion by Dexter Haven Associates, London
Printed and bound in Great Britain by MPG Books, Bodmin

Contents

Preface

This book began life in many scattered forms, including some of my earlier writings. But the central argument was forced into a unified form during a course of ten public lectures that I gave in the autumn of 1998 at the American University in Cairo. There I tried to explore some of the implications of the emergence of a single global economy, of globalisation or, in its most extreme form, the fusion of national economies. One of the implications lies in the way we regard the economic history of the world, of economic development and the role of government; another, how we understand contemporary events and current trends.

In giving the lectures in Cairo, I was conscious that 42 years earlier, the well-known Swedish economist Gunnar Myrdal gave a set of lectures which came to constitute his famous little book, *Development and Underdevelopment* (National Bank of Egypt: Cairo, 1956). He there launched what was becoming known as development economics, a rejection of orthodox economics and an affirmation of the decisive role of the state in economic development. This book has no pretension to rival the immense influence of the earlier work, but it is pre-occupied with trying to understand why Myrdal – along with those of us that followed his lead over the ensuing two or three decades – was so wrong.

The argument here takes an historical form and, it might be said, this is a lazy, opaque, way to formulate an argument and a theory. This would be a valid criticism, but in the effort to cover so wide a field I have felt obliged – or my limitations have obliged me – to adopt this method. However, in another sense, history is crucial; the ahistorical approach of much social science, especially economics, is profoundly debilitating – in practice, circumstances change cases.

To cover such a wide swath of concerns is to risk treating sources without proper respect, perpetuating fallacies in the sources, just misunderstanding the record. This work has no presumption to provide a proper history, but it cannot, on the other hand, avoid giving some account of past events if we are to understand how we came to perpetuate such a profound misunderstanding of the nature of the system in which we live. The literature is vast, and I have no doubt missed much and misconstrued much, for which I can only apologise to the reader. This is a work of attempted synthesis and reconsideration, made possible now, I believe, only because of the way the world itself is changing – and in material terms, not simply in terms of ideas. Globalisation undermines the way we approach the present and thus forces us to reconsider the past as well as what we can understand of the future. It is especially important to start the task now because we forget so quickly the immediate past, and thus the striking novelty of the present is swiftly lost.

On the other hand, to try to identify long-term trends requires one to refrain from dealing with – or pontificating on – immediately current issues. The short term so often clouds our sense of trends. As the book is completed, the US economy, after one of the longest booms in its history, seems set upon recession; a new US President proposes to expand and change the direction of the American defence programme, both of which tendencies might test some of the propositions in this book. But no book can await events to test hypotheses – there would never be a time to draw the balance sheet; this is a task for the reader.

The central argument of the book on the relationship between war, the state and economic development – and why the relationship has become dislocated – is not new, although it has led only a subterranean life. Werner Sombart advanced a thesis on this theme before the First World War (*Krieg und Kapitalismus*, 1913). Charles Tilly has, with masterly scholarship, developed the story much further as an account of systemic warfare and the formation of the state system in European history; Michael Mann and many others have added to this story. On a much more modest level, Michael Kidron and Tony Cliff proposed an explanation for the economic growth of Europe and the US after the Second World War based on the return to war, a 'permanent arms economy'.[1] I have stretched this insight in the opposite direction, to cover the entire history of the modern state and of national capitalism. The greatest debt here is to Marx, even though my argument is quite inconsistent with what passes for Marxism, but the debts are clear in terms of a continuous argument with his historical work. From Charles Jones, I have borrowed the phrase 'cosmopolitan bourgeoisie'. These are far from exhausting the debts for ideas included here, even though some of the parents may no longer recognise their children in my presentation.

I have also a number of special debts. First, to Professor Enid Hill and the American University in Cairo for forcing me to spell out a case in a set of lectures; secondly to the audience in Cairo, who loyally persevered with my stumbling formulations, and cross-examined the arguments. A number of other people have been induced to read the manuscript and have both made some exceedingly important amendments and corrections, and – in some cases – disagreed fundamentally with the thesis: Colin Barker (of the Manchester Metropolitan University); Robert Brenner (of the University of California at Los Angeles); Robert Buckley (of the World Bank); Tirril Harris (of King's College,

London); Martin Khor (of the Third World Network); Krishna Raj (Editor of the *Economic and Political Weekly*, Mumbai); David Lockwood (of the University of Adelaide, South Australia); Alasdair McAuley (of the University of Essex); Desmond McNeill (of the University of Oslo); Sami Zubaida (of Birkbeck College, London); Ahmed Sehrawy (of the *International Socialist Review*, Chicago). Of course, these vital contributions – from many different perspectives – do not implicate anyone in errors; these are exclusively my own.

Finally, the book is written in the belief that xenophobia – and its ugly children: racism, religious bigotry, chauvinism and all the other varieties of chronic or mild patriotism, down to the tedious self-adulation and vanities of daily nationalism – is the cancer of a global civilisation, the AIDs of the new world order. It can lead to the common ruin of us all. This book, I hope, will suggest reasons not only why globalisation, despite its discontents, is not in principle to be feared, but actively embraced as allowing us to escape some of the age old tyrannies of a world of national states.

Acronyms

ACP	African, Caribbean and Pacific Countries (European Union preferential trade area)
ASEAN	Association of South East Asian Nations
Comecon/CMEA	Council for Mutual Economic Assistance (Soviet Union and its allies)
EBRD	European Bank for Reconstruction and Development
FBI	Federal Bureau of Investigation (US Government)
GATT	General Agreement on Trade and Tariffs
IMF	International Monetary Fund
MITI	Ministry of International Trade and Industry (Government of Japan)
NAFTA	North American Free Trade Agreement
NATO	North Atlantic Treaty Organisation
NEP	New Economic Policy (USSR)
NGO	non-governmental organisations
NICs	newly industrialising countries
NSDAP	National Socialist German Workers' Party
OECD	Organisation of Economic Cooperation and Development
RAF	Royal Air Force (UK)
RMB	Ren Minh Bao (currency of People's Republic of China; see also Yuan)
SA	Sturm Abteilung (stormtroopers, also known as brownshirts)
UN	United Nations
UNDP	United Nations Development Programme

1

Introduction

Half a century ago, it was taken for granted that the world economy consisted primarily of a set of interacting but autonomous national economies. The area of political authority, the territory of states, coincided exactly with the economic. Furthermore, states played the pivotal role in organising the economy, in directing capital and labour, as they did in society, defining the interests of society and undertaking the means to achieve those interests. A little earlier, in the inter-war years, opinion favoured economies organised as sets of monopolies, of corporations under the direction of the state, whether those corporations were also owned by the state or by private interests. The state plan was the central template of activity, and by implication the corporations were functionally organised relative to the state plan, not shaped by their responses to competitive markets, operating outside the determination either of any individual competitor or of government. There was a sneaking feeling that the then-Soviet Union constituted a superior form of society precisely because it had done away with markets and private ownership, had designed a 'scientific' economy under the rational direction of government. On the other hand, the Great Depression, it was widely felt, had shown that capitalism had reached the end of its potential and vindicated, if not the Soviet form of society, one or other of its state-dominated varieties.

The independence of the former empires married this intellectual inheritance to a sense of the limitless possibilities for development once the narrow interests of private capital, arbitrary and chaotic markets, and imperialist

1

governments could be thrown off. Experience of the war economies of Europe, like that of the Soviet Union, demonstrated for many people the scientific truth that the state could completely master the economy and society and direct them with scientific precision to whatever aims the government chose. The mood inspired the creation of a new branch of economic thought, the economics of development (with its associated technical branch, the economics of planning), combining the excitement of breaking the shackles of empire and of an economics founded supposedly to prosecute exclusively the greedy interests of capitalists and their creature, government. The new statist perception, in one or other modification, came to establish an orthodoxy that united the political right and left – from the World Bank or the United States State Department to the Social Democratic governments of Western Europe, most governments of the newly independent countries, to the Communists of the east. All agreed that governments had to direct the economy and to own whatever was required to do this. An American visitor observed the mood in Delhi during the heroic Second Five Year Plan (1956–61) –

> One element of the strategy – the proposition that it is the business of government to be the principal planner, energiser, promoter, and the director of the accelerated development efforts – is so fundamental and so little disputed in India that one would probably not bother to even mention it to an Indian audience (Lewis 1964: 26).

The intellectual position was part of a world in which one of its foremost economic inspirations, John Maynard Keynes, in the gloom of 1944, could reflect that there would never be a return to open world markets (in Harrod 1951: 567–68):

> I am, I am afraid, a hopeless sceptic about a return to the nineteenth century *laissez faire* ... I believe that the future lies with
> 1) State trading for commodities;
> 2) International cartels for necessary manufacture; and
> 3) Quantitative import restrictions for non essential manufacture.

It was a set of beliefs created in full only in the twentieth century in the period we discuss later as the apogee of the national state. Furthermore, it was more a summary of selected trends and aspirations, tidied up intellectually by proselytes, than an accomplished reality. We know now how far removed the reality of the Soviet economy was from the myth Western intellectuals chose to create, and chose to create precisely because they wished to insert key aspects of Soviet 'theory' into Western reality. In the late 1940s, conventional opinion, even among the more conservative, had become 'progressive', and had after much struggle and doubt come, depending on the place, person and time, to some approximation to the beliefs of social democracy or Communism at that time (the Communism was that of Stalin).

The statist orthodoxy was strikingly at variance with the history of the world, where world trade took place between geographically remote sources of production, only related to territorial governments as markets for what was traded rather than as themselves agents of trade or production. And it is strikingly at variance with our own orthodoxy with an emphasis on the necessary dominance of markets and private ownership, the reduction of the economic role of government, and the subordination of all sectors of activity, wherever feasible, to competition. There is no place here for the Plan, let alone the authoritarian power required to implement it.

The change is dramatic and profound. Indeed, we still do not have an adequate conceptual architecture to describe the new world – sets of interacting global sectors or networks of multinational corporations. By inertia, the world of states, territorially tethered to one place, still provides the common language to describe what is happening. More important, the statistical authorities which, in the main, decide what data should be provided to us to identify the world are paid and maintained by states, the data disciplined by the interests of government. Yet that picture of the world is increasingly misleading, askew of events.

This book is centrally concerned to understand how and why this immense intellectual transformation took place. For, unless one believes that governments and their economic advisers are guided by nothing better than random fashion, the change must suggest some profound change in reality, the decline of one kind of world and its chief conceptions. We need to understand the change not to make foolish fun of our errors in the past but both to understand what kind of world we are entering and to try to avoid confusing a temporary conjuncture with long-term trends. But then the question arises as to how the statist view was created and came to exercise such a universal influence, particularly in the context of the historical operations of capitalism. Only then can we understand the present and the continuing struggle of states to preserve their power against the forces of global integration.

Thus, the structure of the book begins with a brief – given the nature of the subject – account of the origins of capitalism, of business, and its relationship to territorial government. It is followed by an account of the creation of the modern state in Europe, the dynamic of a new kind of system which obliged rulers to identify an 'economy', to pay close and increasing attention to it, and hence to fashion simultaneously national centralised bureaucracies and a new type of society. The apogee of this system, the centralised-militarised state of the inter-war years and the period immediately after the Second World War, embodied the moment of greatest power for the state system in Europe. We then look at the transition in the years after the Second World War to our own times, the sources of the change which underlies the extraordinary transformation both of the world order and the intellectual climate, summed up in the word 'globalisation'. In particular, the idea of national economic development was transformed in the hands of the newcomers, Japan, and the newly industrialising countries (NICs); their experience was among the first indications of a new world economic order. The book then looks at three examples of resistance to the process, resistance to the erosion of national sovereignty – in Sub-Saharan Africa, in the former Soviet Union, and then, in the late 1990s, in the economic crisis of East and Southeast Asia. We then seek to gather together the threads of the arguments to consider what forms of governance appear to be emerging, what forms of social order may be appropriate to the new world. Finally, we consider some of the trends and countertrends in the world relative to the agenda of globalisation, before returning to the starting theme of the change in perception of the system.

The work is not a history, but a selection of some historical events to illustrate – it is impossible to claim anything stronger than that – a particular thesis about the peculiarities of European development which were both bequeathed to, and imposed upon, the rest of the world. The terms are, as historians are painfully aware, slippery. We use the term 'state' to describe territorial government, yet in reality there is such an immense variety of such forms of government, generalisation is not only rash, it certainly leads to false inferences when applied to all. We describe the 'modern state' (that is, the state initially of the European Great Powers, but subsequently covering the rest of the world thereafter) as centrally 'war-making', even though most governments call their weapons programmes 'defence'. The difference between the two is scarcely substantial, since in a system of competitive states, arming for defence is seen as an act of aggression. We identify the economic implications of the war-making state as 'the national capital project', as if it were exclusively war-driven; yet there have been states with capital projects but without armies – for example, today's Costa Rica – and states have moved between phases of war-making and dis-armament without this affecting the capital project. In the Marxist and Marxoid literature, the term 'capitalist state' is a notorious problem. In the propaganda of Moscow, it had some sense, contrasting the Eastern and Western blocs, but with the ending of the Cold War it is difficult to know what it could mean, except as a term of abuse, a kind of selfish state. If the adjective is to be more precisely used, we have to admit that any state operating in the modern world must reach some working accommodation with businessmen, domestic or foreign, to secure long-term survival, but to call it capitalist when there are no non-capitalists – in this limited sense – is to use a distinction which is either redundant or contrasted with only an hypothetical alternative (so it becomes not a description but an affirmation of political commitment). On the other hand, there are so many and varied relationships between private business and government (from the Venetian oligarchy to Nazi Germany), that a finer differentiation is required to serve any useful analytical purpose.

There are more difficult problems associated with reading concepts back into history. Once modern states were created, their historians tried to carve out a slice of history which could be presented as 'national', so that the brand new nation could – however implausibly – claim an origin in the most distant times and a continuity with that origin. Thus, we find the 'British' fighting against the Romans – where the geographical location of the tribes involved is merged into the idea of a much later political entity; or the 'French' are active long before any concept of France, let alone a political entity, was created. The same problem arises with 'international trade'. Trade between 'nations' implies transactions between political entities, agents living under jurisdictions which correspond to the modern idea of government, and therefore involves at some level inter-governmental relations, we assume, and the pre-eminent loyalty of the merchant to one or other government. Yet before the modern period, 'nations' rarely coincided with the boundaries of the political formations of the world, and inhabitants were required to obey government, not to be loyal to it. A Verona merchant in the fourteenth century in Cairo, buying goods from somewhere in the territories of India carries none of this political baggage. Yet we find the unwary still referring to 'Anglo–Italian' trade in the fourteenth century to describe wool exports by an Ipswich merchant, through a Flemish intermediary, to a Florentine buyer. To speak of 'international trade' here makes as much sense as speaking of 'inter-religious trade' (say between Christians and Muslims) when the religion of the merchants is, by and large, irrelevant to the transaction – or at most a subject to be verified rather than assumed. In practice, the social and political complexities are such as to defy easy inferences that fit the much later age of national states – if in 1611 an Armenian in Calcutta opens a line of credit for an Andalusian banker in Cairo for onward shipments to Genoa, we have to prove the relevance of the social categories rather than assume that they are self-evident. Without this, the past is colonised simply to reaffirm the eternal character of modern political arrangements – contemporary concerns are forced on the past.

'Globalisation' has become the popular term employed to escape from these problems. It has several demerits: it is a rather ugly word; it implies a degree of homogeneity in the integration of the world economy which is clearly lacking and may never occur. Furthermore, it seems to imply a unilinear process in which economic integration or fusion is accompanied by parallel processes of cultural, social and political integration which is clearly not the case and in no way necessary. On the contrary, economic fusion may produce political fission, as might be suggested in the case of the former Soviet Union or Yugoslavia (where political and social differentiation is not accounted for by economic processes). Nor need culture follow the flag; closer economic integration may lead to greater cultural diversity, a subject discussed later. We retain the term 'globalisation' here to refer to a tendency towards a wider economy – at one extreme the world – to supersede national economies; that is domestic economic activity becomes centrally determined by external factors (so that, indeed, the distinction domestic and external loses much useful economic meaning).

The word 'cosmopolitanisation' is used here to refer to what is happening to the world socially. It also has demerits – it is too long to be written often, too troublesome to say, and also rather inelegant. But it shifts the emphasis to the idea of a world of interacting polises, a set of defined social entities with linguistic, religious and cultural distinctions. While economic fusion – with great variation – seems possible, it is not possible to imagine a socially homogenous world. It seems more likely that people will not only preserve – indeed treasure – past social differentiation but will reproduce new forms, without those distinctions having any necessary economic (or political) implications.

There are no lobbies for globalisation. There is no noise to match the loud brash military music of the national, and even the ranks of the UN blue berets are there only because the national authorities grant them the right. Most governments understandably view economic integration with intense suspicion as undermining their authority. Since international organisations – from the United Nations to the World Bank – cannot go beyond the national interests of their leading members, there are no significant forces pressing for economic integration. The multinational corporations have no common agenda, and certainly no interest in the abstraction of global economic integration, only the conditions for them to maximise success (which may or may not coincide with globalisation). The process is being driven not by conviction but by the forces of markets, shaping all participant organisations in directions which are not clear until well after the event. Nonetheless, this book is written in the conviction that, compared to the old order of the first half of the twentieth century, what is coming about is strikingly superior to what went before – an occasion for considerable optimism rather than the reverse. The triumphs of the old state system and its culture are two world wars, and although the present order is still full of un-mastered dangers it will need to go a long way indeed to match the catastrophes of the past.

PART I

ORIGINS

2

The Origins of Capitalism

INTRODUCTION

From the beginning of recorded history – and possibly well before that – traders have been buying and selling for profit, have been moving goods from sellers to buyers. Out of the profits made, they have accumulated what we could, without distortion, call 'capital', enlarged assets in one form or another available for subsequent investment. As a by-product of this activity, merchants have had a direct and indirect role in the development of the production of goods: in farming, manufacture (artisan or handicraft workshops) and mining. Where traders have operated, commercial systems of production – production for sale rather than use – have developed. In fact, in many systems merchants have not been the precondition. Large operators have been conglomerates, combining the ownership and cultivation of land and livestock, the operation of manufacturing workshops, the exploitation of mines, and large scale trade and banking enterprises. The last, banking, was vital even if it was only in-house or simple money-lending; the credit base required for the extraordinarily risky and long-drawn-out business of long-distance and/or bulk trade required considerable financial backing.

Trade, the response to and the development of markets, has a stronger claim to being the essence of capitalism than any other activity. It was the shock of factory production which led theorists to identify the latecomer, industrial capitalism, as capitalism itself – 'Capitalism, that is, the modern industrial

9

system', in Gershenkron's words (1970: 4). Under the influence of Adam Smith, of Marx and other theorists of the nineteenth century – even when they did not use the word 'capitalism' – the factory system came to be identified as an entirely new type of society, uniquely created in the northwestern corner of Europe in the eighteenth century. Yet many of the more important features of that economy had occurred earlier in the richest regions of the known world – in Mesopotamia, in what was to become China, in parts of India and Southeast Asia, in Egypt. Research in the future may find even more extensive ancient networks and centres of commercial production in Sub-Saharan Africa and the Americas.

It is only now with the advanced decline of the factory system and of industrial capitalism that we can see this was only a particular form, and one which lasted barely two-and-a-half centuries. The decline of industrial capitalism today – as measured by the manufacturing share of total output or employment – hardly represents the end of capitalism. Even if, like Marx, we trace the origins of industrial capitalism to, say, the sixteenth century, even that is not enough to identify the history of the economic form. On the contrary, this period describes the period of the rise of the modern state rather than a unique economic system, the emergence, at most, of a national capitalism rather than its cosmopolitan version that had existed in some form for thousands of years. Nor is it any easier to identify a moment of time when 'capitalist society' – that is one dominated by commodity exchange – occurs. Such domination recurs historically, only to be defeated up to the arrival of the last, and the last, as we shall see, was by no means inevitable.

Throughout recorded history, those who mobilise physical power, the armies of the world as organised by territorial administrations, were almost always dominant. The imperatives which guided governments were usually political, not commercial, and only sometimes did these coincide with commercial interests; sometimes governments themselves initiated and controlled trade, but often they regarded merchants as subversive, with the power to escape territorial authority. In any contest between merchants and princes (if merchants were ever so foolish as to question the ruler), the territorial principle – the sword – invariably won. In the end, the immediate mobilisation of physical power could always defeat mere money. It has been equally so in our own times – the waves of nationalisations in the developing countries of the 1970s illustrate the real balance of power in such contests.

Perhaps this fear of subversion was why so many rulers favoured foreign minorities as their capitalists, favoured those who were by definition cosmo-politan and so, supposedly, not contenders for territorial power and more easily controlled. The tendency reinforced the inclination of the merchants themselves to form separate communities. In conditions where the law was weak and the

reach of the authorities limited, trust between individuals, without public guar-
antors, was the essence of trade. Traders were obliged to rely, where possible, on
those of the same background, family members, relatives, those of the same
geographical origin or religion, to rely on those whom they felt, often wrongly,
they could trust, backed on occasions by private force. As Pomeranz and Topik
(1999: 9) put it: 'trade was organised through networks of people who shared
the same native place – and thus a dialect, a deity (or several) to swear on, and
other trust inducing connections'.

Territorial rulers created clusters of concentrated demand, whether to supply
the ruler's household and entourage, to supply an aristocracy or, more often, to
keep armies (and sometimes populations) provisioned. In general, land taxes of
various forms financed such a system and were the basis for financing trade.
Often tax farming, the link between the two forms of power, land revenue
and commerce, provided another lucrative means by which the wealthy could
enhance their position. Accordingly, the capitalists of old divided into the often
immensely rich suppliers to rulers and their armies, and those who traded
between these clusters, from the masters of great caravans and fleets to the
humble peddler.

If the characteristic forms of government, founded upon land tax and
military power, were empire and kingdom, that of merchant trading and
commercial taxes were city-states. As we shall see, the 'nation-state' was a
peculiar and much later hybrid of these two forms. In practice, this division is
too stark, for city fathers owned and taxed land, and territorial rulers were
sometimes merchant princes. Sometimes, the profits of trade were pursued
by territorial rulers in order to fight their wars, if not to accumulate. But the
prototypical trader proper was subversive, since his occupation gave him the
power to escape any particular ruler. Furthermore, he expected to continue
trading regardless of wars, the endless squabbles of rulers, of their alliances and
enmities. He would continue to supply 'the enemy' with finance and arms or the
means to make arms. Rulers in their turn hardly expected merchants to behave
differently, although sometimes merchants were punished for the sins of the
rulers of their native place. But, in general, war and the rivalries of princes
inhabited a qualitatively different world to that of traders – they could be
catastrophic for the merchant, but in much the same way as a typhoon or storm
at sea.

But were not city-states also states? They were, but in general were built to
draw resources from trade, banking, ship-repair, the swapping of intelligence
and manufacture rather than land taxes. Here rulers often promised to levy no
unjust taxes to attract traders, even offered tax incentives to merchants to locate
their operations there, sometimes built fleets to protect them in the sea lanes,

created marketplaces and regulations to govern them, dredged harbours and built wharves and warehouses. They pioneered the creation of the infrastructure for capitalism. As Pomeranz and Topik observe (1999: xiv–xv):

> The market structures that are basic to our world ... are, for better or worse, socially constructed and socially embedded. They require a host of agreements on weights and measures, values, means of payment and contracts that have not been done universally nor permanently, plus still more basic agreements about what things should be for sale, who was entitled to sell them, and which people could haggle about prices (and settle disputes without drawing swords) without compromising their dignity.

The capacity of city fathers, whether single rulers or oligarchies of merchants, to create and sustain such a framework depended on not being overwhelmed by powerful territorial rulers. Insofar as cities survived, they did so within the interstices of a system of territorial power. They serviced a network of trading relationships that both linked the great territorial clusters and went far beyond them, drawing supplies from an immense diversity of sources and provisioning outlets far beyond the knowledge of the individual merchant or ruler. Long before globalisation was thought of, capitalism was, unknown to many of its participants, knitting together the territories of the world in commercial exchanges.

Alongside and interacting with relationships of exchange were many other social bonds of, for example, kinship, tribe and clan. There were quite different rules and values operative here, and where the two sets of regulatory imperatives overlapped, frequent conflict, out of which there was no preordained victor.

Insofar as history of economic exchange was recorded, it was most frequently done not by itinerant merchants but by scholars, secluded and supported by territorial rulers; this became the account of the history of civilisation. History has thus almost always been political history, the history of territorial rulers. We have, by comparison, precious few accounts of the travelling merchants and their transactions, and most of these do not date from much before the second millennium. Hence we are driven most often to see trade in the context of the territorial ruler, not the trader. Here there are many different types of relationship, from empires without commercial trade, empires that traded for the purposes of the state, merchant princes who traded for private profit and public purpose, to states that consisted in essence of private traders, and between them all, traders who operated on their own account, seeking insofar as possible to avoid relationships to governments.

In the case of the first, empires without commercial trade, two of the most famous are the great empires of the Americas, the Incas and the Aztecs. They seem to have combined vast territorial holdings and major distribution networks, but without markets, money or capital. This was most true of the

Incas. In the case of the Aztecs, a special caste has been identified as responsible for trade, but they were closely interrelated with territorial power: in modern terms, an arm of government. Parallels to the Aztec system seem to have occurred in the systems of some of the Assyrians, the Pharaonic Egyptians, even the Phoenicians, down to the twentieth century and 'state capitalism'. Merchant princes and commercial city-states were very much more frequent, as we shall see, and round these forms, perhaps, were independent trading networks, the earliest forms of 'free trade'.

However, this formulation is misleading, for it over-emphasises long-distance trade relationships, those in the distant past predominantly concerned with luxury goods. In what were for long periods the larger territorial formations, say China or one or other of the Indian Empires or Rome, the bread-and-butter of trade was 'domestic' – that is, within the political domains of a ruler: bulk movements of rice or wheat or timber. Here the availability of water transport was often a decisive factor facilitating exchanges: China's rivers (and canals), the Mediterranean Sea, the Ganges or the twin rivers of Mesopotamia. The development of such domestic trade was a powerful component in the creation of territorial units, in the emergence of rulers as capable – with bulk appropriations or purchase, granaries and secure transport routes – of, when needed, offsetting famine and ensuring food supplies.

To be sustained, commercial trade – and what it presupposed, specialised producers – required favourable social and political conditions, and for much of history these were lacking. The emergence of a private capitalist system from the complex of territorial and commercial forms is not therefore marked by a single moment of transition, much less a grand historical march of progress. Rather there were great surges of economic growth, of 'business', some of which occasionally established institutional forms favourable to further growth. But all, except the last, ultimately failed, either through natural disaster or more often a change in political conditions: the intervention of the territorial state to enforce other priorities. But the surges took place on a rising plane of productivity and innovation, of population and incomes, so that each fluctuation tended to start from a new technical and economic position and carry growth to a higher level, the whole process extending over very long periods of time. Even the last astonishing acceleration of the surge, to reach unprecedented heights of output – initially in the nineteenth century, but then spectacularly in the twentieth century – did not make capitalism secure from precisely the afflictions that in the past either destroyed or radically reduced it. However, now the present surge of capitalism, unlike its predecessors, seems to have attained the character of systemic self-perpetuation, to have created self-generating growth so that neither disasters nor the action of states can ultimately frustrate this drive. Insofar as the idea of a 'capitalist society' has a sense of permanency and self-perpetuation, it would seem to apply only to this very late stage. If this is so, then we can say of capitalist society – as opposed to capitalism – that it arrives only with globalisation in the last quarter of the twentieth century.

Thus, if we abandon a definition of capitalism as exclusively the industrial system, there is no historical moment when we can declare 'capitalism' has arrived – if we are to employ that term with any precision. Capitalism as a predominantly market-driven private and competitive system of accumulation occurs in some form at many points and times in the world. In many others, it is either entirely marginal or non-existent. In most times and places, the market system has been marginal or only indirectly important to the great affairs of state, the agenda of issues of war and peace of the territorial rulers. Even in our own times, when the business ethic has more intensively soaked into the fabric of daily life and even the affairs of government, the state still endeavours to make its agenda privileged – and if need be, governments liquidate business in pursuit of that agenda.

This chapter is directed to illustrate some of these themes, with particular emphasis on the sporadic emergence of a system of private commercial capital-ism. It is almost inevitably a superficial exercise, since it is impossible to go in depth into the historical detail concerned, even where the data is available. However, the preoccupation is not with describing each period, but seeking answers to a much narrower range of concerns. How far was commercial activity economically and socially significant in society at large in the pre-modern world? How far did the demands of trade, of market exchange, influence patterns of production – cultivation, manufacturing, mining – and hence patterns of innovation in those systems? We leave on one side the crucial question of how far social forms facilitated, impeded or were neutral in these interactions. How far in this pattern of exchange can we identify a private-competitive system, as opposed to trading in the interest of rulers and in accordance with what we have called the state agenda? How far, out of this process of exchange, can we identify the emergence of private businessmen as a separate class in society with some degree of class interest? How far is it possible to identify such a class developing an aspiration to determine the policy of the state in their class interest (as opposed to individuals acting as officials of state or as politicians, embracing the agenda of the state)? Thus it becomes possible to see what sense there might be in the phrase 'capitalist state'.

The next chapter examines the coterminous development over the past mil-lennium of the modern state, of the state agenda, and the nature of the ultimate marriage of state and capitalism. In this chapter, I hope to show that there are no defensible grounds for restricting the origins of capitalism to northwestern

Europe, nor to the birth of modern manufacturing, nor to the creation of the modern national state.

There is no qualitative distinction between the activities of traders, merchant capitalists, and those who farm, manufacture or mine. Trade has been transforming the scale and process of production for as long as recorded history, and has also been securing divisions of labour through the world's territories for similar periods of time. Far from globalisation being new, it is most ancient; what is peculiar is the occurrence of the much shorter period of 'national capital'.

Following this idea of globalisation as intrinsic to capitalism, the class of 'businessmen' (to use an anachronistic term for want of a better one) who created and sustained this system has normally been cosmopolitan, composed of networks of people of different ethnic, cultural, linguistic and religious origins, threading their way between the murderous rivalries of the territorial rulers. They are thus, if true to their calling, intrinsically subversive in terms of the state agenda. However, businessmen are also pragmatic, and if their profits can be secured by a monopoly – the reward for accepting a special relationship to authority, the state, which grants monopoly – they will happily do so.

A cosmopolitan trading system, rooted in defined but changing geographical areas of production, produced a territorial pattern of trading cities, a necklace of points of exchange (Braudel's 'archipelago of cities'). Territorial princes created empires and kingdoms. The merging of the two is the creation, very late in the day, of 'nation-states'.

ANCIENT TRADE

So far as the Eurasian land mass is concerned, the earliest civilisations were accompanied by the growth of extensive trade, drawing goods from surprisingly distant sources to service the emerging complexes of city-states (even when these were politically organised as federations or empires) – in the Yellow River region of north China, the Indus Valley, Mesopotamia, the Nile Valley (and, around the same time, in Central America). There is evidence of trade between Egypt and the rest of the Mediterranean from 7000 BC and, slightly later, between the Indus Valley and Mesopotamia. This, however, concerns recorded trade, and records only occurred with the emergence of a literate class (and a need for records was often closely related to the revenue needs of territorial rulers, whether taxes or profits, as well as the needs of traders to record their transactions), itself closely related to the development of territorial power. Hence there is no account of trade before the territorial entities of which we have records emerged, nor of trade networks outside these clusters of development, of what may have been even then itinerant pedlars, trading on and beyond the fringes of civilisation, particularly along watercourses. Conditions of great insecurity, sheer physical obstacles and the limited surplus for trade may have severely limited this, but on the other hand goods do indeed seem to have been distributed outside the perimeters of what was known as civilisation.[1]

At present, the best documented cases of ancient trade networks are from the Middle East and east Mediterranean, and it is with these that we therefore start. But future research may reveal – for example, along the Chinese or Indian coasts – even earlier or more developed systems.

The Assyrians

Much of the trade in ancient empires appears to have been related to the needs of government, and particularly conditions of endemic warfare – the supply of copper and bronze, of weaponry, of leather and timber. So overriding was the preoccupation with war, Diakonoff (1992: 17) observes, that in 2000 BC Babylonia, there was no word for 'abroad' or 'foreign country' except 'enemy country'. Nor were the results of trade, of peaceful exchanges, necessarily distinguished very clearly from plunder, the result of warfare and official theft. Similarly, no trading class appears to have been clearly distinguished from the rulers. In the Assyrian cities and trading colonies, for example – Babylon, Aram, Anatolia – in the middle Bronze Age (2300–1600), palace, temple and market were integrated in sustaining trading. Trade was strongly encouraged to acquire the goods for, and raise the revenues of, the state (insofar as one can employ that word), although there seem also to have been 'private' clients. There was also trade in bulk necessities to supply armies and perhaps, on occasions, the population at large. We are perhaps misled by the modern conception of a clear distinction between the public and private.

Trade linkages extended westwards from Mesopotamia to the Mediterranean and Egypt (handling wheat, barley, cattle, silver, gold and textiles) and eastwards to what were to become Persia, Afghanistan and India (the first evidence of trade with India dates from 3000 BC). The Akkadean Empire constituted one of the first known hubs of trade, linking the Indian Ocean and Anatolia on the Mediterranean (exchanging wheat and textiles for copper, tin and jewels), with further links to Egypt at one end and the Indus and Hwang Ho civilisations at the other. With the collapse of the empire, there was a period from 1950 BC – some accounts suggest – when independent traders and trade networks emerged from official control, regulated by merchant guilds – 'in modern terms', Lewy (1971: 58–59) boldly declares, 'the first experiment of free enterprise on a large-scale'.

The Phoenicians

From 1200 BC or so, a set of trading cities emerged on the Levantine coast of the east Mediterranean, perhaps the by-product of the trade demands of Mesopotamia and Egypt. Aradus, Berytus (Beirut), Ugarit, Sidon, Tyre, Sarepta and others constituted the competitive centres of a Phoenician trading network that reached the height of its commercial and territorial power between 1100 and 850 BC. The trade colonies – with associated mining, smelting and manufacturing – were spread through the Mediterranean, some of the more famous ones being established in North Africa (Carthage), Cyprus (and its famous copper mines), Sicily, Sardinia, peninsular Italy, coastal France and northwestern Spain. The network now linked the Atlantic and the Indian Oceans, and once the Straits of Gibraltar was breached, links stretched southwards along the African coast and northwards to the mines of Cornwall in England and to Ireland. The trade networks created and sustained important centres of mining and manufacture – metals, glassware, textiles, dyes, furniture, jewellery. From Egypt came gold, from Africa ivory.

Trade again seems to have been powerfully shaped by rulers of the cities, directed by an aristocratic class of merchant warriors, enforcing mercantilist policies, with a key role – as bankers and warehouses – for temples. Warfare and trade were not clearly distinguished – the Phoenician fleets were armed (particularly against Greek pirates), and cities maintained navies. One trading colony in particular, Carthage on the North African coast, came to supersede its parents, creating, by the standards of the time, a major commercial hub in the central Mediterranean area, handling gold, incense, iron, copper, silver, tin, African animals, dates.

The Greeks

Some historians (for example Moore and Lewis 1999) have argued that some of the Greek city-states went well beyond the form of state-supervised trade, manufacture and mining to forms of market-driven 'free enterprise'. However, there appears to be a wide range of different forms, and the distinctions are of degree rather than kind. At its peak, there are said to have been 1300 independent cities, poleis, 200 of them around the Aegean but the rest spread round the shores of the Black Sea, the Mediterranean (particularly Egypt and North Africa), Sicily, peninsular Italy, the French coast (Massilia, later to be Marseilles) and Spain. In the Aegean, not all of them allowed private trade – Sparta notoriously so. Others had major relationships with, for example, the metallurgical

manufacturing cities of Etruria in northern Italy, making and exporting
weaponry, bronze and iron utensils, tools, as well as pottery and amphora.

Many of the Greek cities were dependent for their survival on trade. The
warships that guarded the seaways (and, as well, preyed on passing ships) to
protect giant fleets (it is said the peak number of vessels was not surpassed
before the nineteenth century) were built from timbers hauled from Macedonia
and Asia Minor. Grain to feed the home populations was a key element in trade
– 800 voyages per summer were made, it is said, from the port of Athens to
secure the means to feed the population of the city (2–300,000). The port of
Rhodes, which emerged as a key junction point for east Mediterranean trade,
was linked to the Phoenician cities on the Levantine coast, the points where the
caravans from the East (and ultimately to the Indian subcontinent and, by the
Silk Route, to China) arrived; other key links were to the Egyptian coast (to a
city which took finally a name of Greek origin, Alexandria), and thus to the Red
Sea, Arabia, Somalia, the Indian ports and beyond to south China.

Many of the institutional means to facilitate trade were developed in the
leading Greek cities – coinage, from the sixth century BC, replaced barter (or the
use of ingots as a medium of exchange), a legal framework to underpin the
repayment of debts, rights to property, a city capital market and a credit system.
The growth of commerce stimulated production of cash crops in agriculture
(grapes and wine, oranges, olives and olive oil, honey, wool, cheese), and of
mining and manufacture (marble, fullers earth, pottery, pitch) (Casson 1964:
72–73). Indeed, the commercialisation of farming made necessary the grain
imports to feed the farmers as well as the non-farmers.

The Athenian basis of political power and of citizenship (and hence access
both to the rights of self-government, to land and the obligation to bear arms)
was vested in land-ownership, not trade or wealth in general. Commerce, artisan
manufacture and the ownership and management of ships were in the hands
of non-Athenians, slaves and others (*metics* or foreigners, recruited from
Marseilles, the Black Sea and Asia Minor). By the fifth century BC there were
possibly a quarter of a million inhabitants, including perhaps 40,000 resident
aliens and 150,000 slaves. Trade – and thus both foreigners and part of the slave
population – was vital for the survival of the city both in terms of daily foodstuff
and in the capacity of the city to defend itself. Traders were therefore generally
treated with respect, offered incentives to settle, legally protected and their
representative consuls treated with dignity. Successful slaves, acting as managers
and agents in commerce, could become freedmen, and so earn access to land,
to marriage with Athenians, to political participation. However, the basis of
the Athenian state, landownership carrying the obligation to bear arms, defined
a clear class of outsiders, or cosmopolitans, those concerned with trade,

manufacture and mining. Being foreigners, they could escape the political preoccupations of the citizens – 'Traders were,' Macdonald (1982: 113) observes, 'usually seen as part of an international business class who followed markets with little regard to their citizenship or residency'.

The two millennia of fluctuating development between Mesopotamia, Egypt, the Levantine coast and Greece interacted with other important – and possibly even more important – changes in the Indian subcontinent and in what became China. To take the second as an example, little is known of the very distant history of China (that is before 2000 BC), and the specific features of commercial activity are equally obscure even after that time. However, they must have been considerable, since by the time when the evidence becomes clearer, about 600 BC, already significant advances had been made in cultivation and irrigation techniques, in the casting of iron (the first known in the world, 513 BC) and the making of iron tools, the beginnings of mass production, the use of harness etc.

However, it is in the period of warring states (453–221) that technical progress seems to have accelerated, spurred by the competition and warfare between states, a condition not unlike that which occurred in Europe two millennia later. Rulers endeavoured to expand output, particularly agricultural output (in the valley of Wei, Shansi, the central plain, and the Ch'engtu basin, Szechuan), and to exploit new resources in order to build their military power, creating a period that was, according to Gernet (1996: 72), 'one of the richest known to history in innovations'. The instruments of this drive to expand royal power was a new class of merchants and a vast increase in trade, now of everyday goods rather than luxuries for rulers – cloth, cereals, salt, metals, wood, leather, hides. Some of the trade reached outwards to the northern peoples, to Manchuria and Korea, and to the southern tropical regions. Chinese silks are said to have reached northern India by the fourth century BC. Large scale industrial enterprises (for example iron mines and foundries) emerged, and major transport undertakings, river fleets and mass carts, to carry the commodities. Important administrative centres became trading and manufacturing cities – and the conquest of those cities by rival rulers combined military and commercial motives. Metal coins were in use from the fifth century.

By the time of the Western Han (206 BC to 9 AD), when China's population was about 58 million (the first census of taxable heads of households was held then), a new surge of commercial growth carried China's merchants to Southeast Asia and the Indian ocean. By the first century AD, commercial relations had been opened with the 'Indo-Iranians', with significant imports from the west of glass, amber, agate, cornelian and slaves. Funan port in the old Cambodian kingdom of the Mekong delta became a crucial hub for trade distribution in Southeast Asia, linking China to the north and Java in the south.

Embassies from the Indian subcontinent are said to have arrived between 89 and 105 AD, and merchants from the eastern regions of the Roman Empire are reported in central Vietnam in 166, and in China proper by 226. Glover (1990: 73) notes of this time: 'By the early Christian era, these trade routes reached out to bring together the previously rather separate south-east Asian exchange systems, linking them with a vast network stretching from western Europe, via the Mediterranean basin, the Persian Gulf and the Red Sea, to India, south-east Asia and China.'

In the north and northwest, Han armies probed into Central Asia, followed by the merchant caravans that opened the route for the supply of silk to the Middle East and to Rome.

Military penetration was softened by gifts to the rulers of the territories of Central Asia, particularly silks from the great state silk factories – enormous quantities of silk were distributed in this way. With direct production, the state also instituted monopolies in particular goods, 119 in all, governed again by state production but with the participation of non-state producers – for example, in iron and steel (China made the world's first steel in the first century AD), in salt and in silk. Production flourished in farming, in manufacturing (with cloth mills, foundries, lacquer factories), in commerce and banking, and in trade. However, already the rulers showed a traditional suspicion of wealth outside the direction of the state – there were sporadic attacks and campaigns against trade, particularly external trade (and a ban on the export of 'strategic goods' – iron and weapons). But the wealth of innovation in this period rapidly raised the conditions of both production and transport. For water transport, the invention of the rudder, the anchor, the drop keel, the capstan, canvas sails and advanced maritime cartography launched China's sea power well ahead of any rivals.

Chinese silk and other goods (including ebony, ivory, textiles from India) became important in Mediterranean Europe in the heyday of the Roman Empire.[2] The Silk Route through Central Asia was initially important, although often restricted by the growing burden of taxes levied by the principalities controlling the land routes. Persian and Roman traders (usually Syrian from the eastern provinces) favoured the sea route through the Persian Gulf. Arab traders operated routes down the Red Sea (a trade which is said to have developed well before the first millennium). The first Greek maritime manual (in Latin translation) on the Red Sea route to India (*Periplus Maris Eythraee*) dates from the first century AD. The relics of this trade – Roman coins, amphorae for wine, Spanish oil jars – have been found at a number of sites in India (particularly Arkamedu and the Coromandel coast). Roman business agents are known to have settled on the Indian seaboard, and some south Indian rulers are said to have employed European mercenaries; Tamil merchants traded with Egypt. Some Roman exports reached China and Korea.

However, although this long-distance trade has received most scholarly attention, it was a minor part of the goods traded within the empire. The massive concentration of population in administrative centres (some estimates put Rome's population, at its height, at over one million), the dispersal of population in colonies on the perimeter of the empire, and the servicing of large and mobile armies necessitated large-scale movement of cargo, particularly 'interprovincial maritime commerce' (Rostovtzeff 1957). Part of the bulk trade was state appropriations, tax and tributary deliveries of grain, handled by government agents (Hopkins 1973: xii), but the larger part appears to have been private trade (even if to government orders) and in the hands of merchants and contractors who were usually freed slaves or foreigners. However, knights (*equites*) were important in financing trade, and even more in manufacturing, financed from the profits of land cultivation and tax-farming (and profits from trade flowed back into land purchase and improved cultivation, as well as into manufacture). Tax farming was an important element in building private fortunes and thus other business activity. Rome was an important trader in wine, pottery, metalware, glassware, in tiles (with mass production), bricks, tableware, lamps, stoneware and marble. Commercial demands increased the size of ships and led to advances in navigation techniques. Trading was concentrated in particular commercial centres – Ostia, Alexandria, Palmyra and a scatter of townships in Gaul and other imperial territories. Some companies and workshops were of substantial size with large slave-labour forces; company shares were issued, and some measure of limited liability introduced, with partnerships and agencies.

India, as we have seen at various points, is one of the most ancient hubs of trade between East and West, China to Mesopotamia and westwards. Given the costs of movement, this was mainly trade in luxury goods, but internally India developed major trade networks in basic commodities. Some see the decline in the Western trade (through the Gulf and the Red Sea) with the crumbling of the Roman Empire as precipitating the opening up of Eastern trade, to Southeast Asia (with Indian trading colonies) and thence to China. However, the traders of Arabia, Egypt and Persia in the Gulf kept open east–west trade links through much of the first millennium, creating merchant colonies (and from the seventh century colonies of Islam) along the littoral of western and southern India, the Southeast Asian seaboard to Southeast China. The communities of those trading townships showed at any one moment the geographical spread of trade – Gujeratis, Fujianese, Persians, Armenians, Jews, Arabs – and, over time, the changing communities involved. Gokhale (in Pollet 1987: 43) has given us a portrait of one such trading settlement early in the first millennium, Broach on the western coast of India. Many of the merchants then were 'Indo-Greek', and there were many Greek settlements along the coast. The mariners' manual mentioned earlier describes the route from Egypt to Broach, and Arab cargoes of wheat, rice, ghee (clarified butter), sesame oil, cloth and honey. The merchant groups of Broach included, as well as Greeks and Arabs, Persians, Sindhis, Gujeratis, Mahrattis, Konkanis, Malabaris, Tamils and Romans. The bulk of the goods traded in the city's markets included wine, copper, tin, lead, coral, cloves, glass, gold and silver, perfumes, musicians and girl slaves (from the Mediterranean). Broach remained important until the eighth or ninth century before declining. By the fourteenth century, Surat had replaced it.

Long before then, the Arab and Persian land and maritime trade networks had become immensely important across the whole Middle East, with a dominant junction point in Abbasid Baghdad (founded in 762). As we have seen, Arab traders were present in the trading cities of southeastern China and Southeast Asia even in the early centuries of the first millennium. There are records then of Muslim merchant communities (and later mosques) on the Cambay, Malabar and Coromandel coasts of India; in Southeast Asia in the Sriviyaya Empire of eastern Sumatra and Java between the seventh and tenth century; and by the fourteenth century, in the Madjapahit Empire of eastern Java, in Sumatra, southern Malaya, Borneo and the Philippines; and on to the Chola Empire in southern Vietnam. Some historians estimate that by the twelfth century bulk production for export was taking place in South and Southeast Asia – in textiles, metals, utensils, weapons, semi-precious stones and raw materials (raw silk and raw cotton), horses as well as food grains (rice, sugar, butter, salt, dried foods) (for references, see Abu-Loghod 1989: 271).

Parts of Sub-Saharan Africa were also included in this growing network of commercial activity. From at least the tenth century, Arab traders established colonies along the East African littoral (with particularly important centres at Zanzibar, Malinda etc). These exported to India and beyond slaves, ivory, gold, iron, rhinoceros horn, tortoise shell, amber and leopard skins. Gold mines in ancient Zimbabwe were said to be already deep (100 feet or so) by the ninth century, and gold was traded through Kilwa to Mogadishu and Malinda to the Persian Gulf. Chinese sources record the import of African slaves, and some claim that by the twelfth century most rich Cantonese families possessed black slaves (Mathew 1963: 108). Remains of seventh century Chinese porcelain in Africa show an important element in imports; other commodities came from India, Burma and Vietnam. On the other side of Africa, the trans-Saharan trade routes from West Africa were even more important – it is claimed that two thirds of the gold employed in the northern hemisphere in the late Middle Ages derived from West African mines (in particular Bambuk and Bure) (Hopkins

1973: 82). In Sub-Saharan Africa, however, the main medium of exchange was not gold but Indian textiles (India, it is claimed, produced about a quarter of the known world's cloth up to the eighteenth century). By the fifteenth century, West Africa had become 'an integral part of a web of relations that connected forest cultivation and miners with savanna and desert traders and merchants and rulers of north Africa' (Reader 1998: 107).

It might have seemed that, from the eighth century or so, the scattered surges of capitalist growth in various parts of the Eurasian land mass were at last beginning to come together in a mutually reinforcing process. Simultaneously, the growth of the economies of southeastern China, the western and southern Indian littoral, Southeast Asia, the Arab–Persian lands and, on the perimeter, the Mediterranean and west African clusters of economic activity accelerated, transforming both domestic sources of production and the closely interrelated external commercial exchanges.

Perhaps the strongest commercial growth occurred in south China in the period of the T'ang dynasty (618–907) and, after a pause, in the principalities of the south, particularly the Southern Sung dynasty (960–1279). Just prior to the T'ang period, there had been a major expansion in the area irrigated and sown with rice, and a substantial extension of public works (587–608) – canals and river embankments to create a major interconnected water transport system, and parallel roads. The state created public granaries (both to offset crop fluctuations and supply military movements), and this stimulated a great growth in rice trading. Silk manufacture and trade generally boomed. External trade expanded between the seventh and ninth centuries, creating significant colonies of foreign merchants in the southern metropolis of Yang-tu. Colonies of Arab and other merchants settled at what was then the most important external trading city, Canton, with some 200,000 inhabitants, as in other port cities like Quangzhou (Zaitun, its Arab name), Fuzhou. Canton is said to have contained merchant colonies of Malays, Iranians, Indians, Chamars, Vietnamese, Khmers and Sumatrans. At its peak in the eighth century, the T'ang capital, Ch'ang-an, had become a great cosmopolitan city with possibly a million inhabitants (which would have made it the largest city in the world at that time), and a continuous movement of population: merchants, students and pilgrims. Large privately owned factories are reported, employing up to 500 workers, with significant labour disputes (in 782 for example).

Furthermore, the demands of commerce seeped into the countryside, stimulating both the conversion of crop lands and livestock herds to commercial production, and the creation of rural manufacturing. Indeed, Eberhard 1977: 195) reports a saying of the people of the Lower Yangtze that they displayed 'so much interest in business that they paid no attention to agriculture'.

Merchants, especially foreign traders, were permitted, but with regulation and occasional persecution. For a period, they were not allowed to own land, paid special taxes, and at times were obliged to pay forced loans – as for example, when the emperor died in 782. In 879, a massacre of foreign merchants took place in Canton (it is said some 120,000 were killed: Eberhard 1977: 194) and shops and warehouses were looted.

In the late T'ang period, military rebellion undermined both the dynasty and the regime of trade regulation. For a time, rapid commercial growth further stimulated urbanisation and rural manufacturing – to produce wine, charcoal, paper and textiles. Commercial crops expanded in silk, sugar, tea, vegetables, oranges, timber, bamboo, oil seeds and hemp. So strong was the growth that it survived the disintegration of the dynasty, and grew more vigorously in the group of principalities – the period of 'five dynasties' (900–960) – that replaced the empire.

The period of the Sung dynasty, particularly its southern component, is probably the most sustained period of the growth of capitalism seen in the world to that date. Agricultural innovations – in seed-planting technology and tools for cultivation – increased the productivity of rice cultivation to unprecedented levels, releasing labour for manufacturing and trade. Large-scale workshop and mine production (the largest in the world before the eighteenth century in Europe) emerged, partly in the hands of the state but with a growing private component – in metallurgy (especially the northern Sung), ceramics, textiles (silk, hemp, cotton), paper, printing, dyes, vegetable oils, tea. Again, innovations accelerated the growth of output – hydraulic bellows, for example, were employed in foundries; explosives were used in mining (gunpowder was invented in 1044; the first rockets in 1132; mortar projectiles in 1280), water-powered machinery appeared, and pit coal came to replace charcoal. The introduction of moveable type allowed a major growth in the output of the printing industry to reach a mass audience created by the growth of literacy – perhaps 30 per cent of the population of 1000 AD were, to some degree, literate. The output of books, posters, advertisements, documents, paper money, wrapping paper, lifted the industry in successive phases. In heavy industry, the growth was, by the standards of the time, remarkable. The output of metallurgical goods by 1078 reached possibly more than 125,000 tonnes per year, a six-fold growth over the eighth century. Cast-iron output, produced in blast furnaces (using coal, not charcoal), is said to have reached 114,000 tonnes in the same year – by comparison, it took another 700 years for England's output to reach 68,000 tonnes (1788). The use of iron spread to many other processes – tools, nails, weapons, bridge chains. By the early eleventh century, Chinese arsenals are reputed to have been producing 16 billion iron arrowheads annually.

The growth of output took place with a great expansion in domestic trade, facilitated by the unique network of navigable waterways, possibly 50,000 kilometres in length. China's then political area constituted easily the largest market in the world. Trade was no longer simply in luxury goods – indeed, as incomes rose, some former luxuries became items of everyday consumption. Growth was also greatly facilitated by the move to monetary means of exchange, coins. As early as 997, it is said, 800 million coins were issued annually, and by 1085 over 6 billion (Ebrey 1996: 142). In addition, certificates of deposit, cheques, promissory notes, bills of exchange came to be employed in the eleventh century, and in 1024, the first bank notes were issued in Szechuan (which avoided the weight problem involved in the use of iron coins).

External trade remained mainly in luxury goods – high value and low weight. Merchants delivered to China incense, precious stones, ivory, coral, rhinoceros horn, ebony, sandalwood. Exports remained dominated by silks and ceramics. Supporting maritime trade, important advances were made in technology, and the size of ships grew (with crews numbering several hundred men) along with the size of the fleets – the visitor Marco Polo marvelled at the number of vessels plying the Yangtze, greater, he thought, than in all of Christendom. It is thought that for much of the period the principalities had a combined trade deficit, and to cover this paid in precious metals and coin – copper coins from China spread through Southeast Asia and into the Indian Ocean. In this period, important Chinese trading communities were established in Southeast Asia – great Fujianese merchant families sent indentured servants as agents and managers of their shipping; if they were successful, they could be freed and perhaps adopted by the families of their patrons (and found a wife of higher social status). The Chinese communities created in Southeast Asia became important for subsequent European trade settlements, particularly in Manila and Batavia.

Over time, the preponderance of trade increasingly engaged the attention of the governing orders, even to the point of creating what has been called a 'mercantile state'. Government regulation shifted from price and market controls to taxes on trade – and by the end, it is said, commercial taxes and the yield of state monopolies produced more revenue than taxes on land and agriculture. However, even these last taxes represented a shift from traditional dues to market-oriented taxes – labour dues (*corvée*) of the peasantry and artisans were commuted to taxes.

The state participated in trade and production and maintained monopolies in particular commodities in order to finance and supply its armies – the military forces of the Southern Sung tripled in size between 979 and 1041 to one-and-a-quarter million men; military spending was said to take three quarters of public revenues to cover this.

In population and settlement terms, this period of sustained economic growth is said to have doubled the population to 100 million or so by 1100 (on the 750 figure). The density of towns increased, particularly along the major trade route, the Yangtze river, on the borders and coasts. It is said of Khaifeng (capital of the Northern Sung) that it was the first city not dominated by the state, the military and administration, but rather by commerce, production and consumption. It may have contained one million inhabitants (compared to the then leading European city, Venice, with possibly 50,000). Hangchow, the later capital of the Southern Sung was said to be even larger. Quangzhou (Ch'uan-chou, Arabic Zaitun) in Fujian province, the leading port of southern China after the decline of Canton, attracted numerous foreign visitors, and some of the Arabs and Europeans have left us accounts of their astonishment at the scale of trade and the wealth of the city, larger than any other in the world (indeed, Friar Odoric of Friuli says that the ships in the harbour were greater in number than in all of Italy, at the time economically the most advanced area of Europe). Jacob D'Ancona (1997: 114) has left us a vivid portrait of the city[3] and its cosmopolitan character:

> a man may go about the streets of Zaitun as if it were a city of the whole world and not of Manci [South China], in one separate quarter being the Mahometans, in another the Franks, in another the Armenians who are Christians, in another the Jews…and in another, those of Greater India, and in each quarter, separate parts again, as in the quarter of the Franks, there is a part for the Lombards, a part for the Germans…

The scale of private business activity – and its ramifications through all sectors of production – suggests something that had hardly been seen before, the percolation of a form of capitalism throughout society. It is hardly surprising that Eberhard (1977: 241) should comment that by the end of the twelfth century all conditions for 'real capitalism' had appeared. A clearly distinct and dedicated working class had been created, working in relatively large concentrations. A territorial pattern of specialisation had occurred. 'The basic reason,' Gernet (1996: 321) observes, 'for the economic expansion of China in the eleventh to thirteenth centuries must be sought in the development of an urban bourgeoisie consisting of landowners and rich merchants'. And this 'wealthy, self-conscious urban middle class' (Twitchett 1983: 30) seemed increasingly to have come to dominate society – the *hong* or guilds of merchants and craftsmen slowly began to take over from the official authorities in administering those elements of the economy of concern to them. They also came to constitute important lobbies on government on taxation and requisitions.

Growth did not stop with the destruction of the regimes by the Mongol conquests – merchants accommodated to the new order of the Yuan dynasty

(1271–1367). Under the Ming dynasty (1368–1644), there was a further surge of growth – of trade, large-scale production in manufacturing and mining and in maritime technology. Agriculture continued up to the eighteenth century to be the most advanced in the world, with levels of soil productivity far ahead of most other places. Large-scale manufacturing – in porcelain, paper, sugar, steel and ironware, silk, lacquerware and furniture – now came to supply world markets. In the late sixteenth century, there were said to be 50,000 workers employed in 30 paper factories in Kiangsi province. At the same time, domestic traders shipped rice from state and private granaries for possibly one million people on the 1400 miles of inland waterways, one thousand miles up the Yangtze river.

China was by the fifteenth century the greatest maritime power in the world. At its height in the late fourteenth century, the imperial order could mount 1700 warships and 400 armed transports. Its fleets now probed into the Indian Ocean and as far as the East African seaboards – the most famous example being those of the political expeditions of Admiral Zheng (1405–33). The largest fleet consisted of 62 junks of unprecedented size, with 225 support vessels, carrying, it is said, 28,000 men.

The peak of economic activity under the Ming emperors is said to have been the Wan-li era (1573–1619). Gernet (1996, 429) enumerates some of the important elements of the economic order:

> the formation of a proletariat and of an urban middle class, the transformation of rural life, which was permeated by the influence of the towns, and the rise of a class of important merchants and business men. The money changers and bankers of Shansi who had branches in Peking, the rich traders of Lake Tung-t'ing in Hunan, the shipowners, enriched by sea-borne trade, of Ch'uan-chou and Chang-chou in southern Fukien, and above all the great merchants of Hsin-an (the present She-hsien in southern Anhwei) formed a new class calling to mind the businessmen of the early days of capitalism in Europe.

The faction that won power over the imperial bureaucracy turned official China away from its external orientation and in favour of a concentration on domestic affairs – there were no more giant fleets to impress the foreigners. The Chinese trading communities of Southeast Asia were abandoned. Foreign trade was banned and the coast cleared to guard against pirates. It did not stop foreign trade but it became smuggling. In retrospect, this proved to be an important obstacle to the growth of Chinese capitalism, particularly when it came to confront the competition of the Europeans, but it did not end economic growth in the domestic market. Indeed, in the eighteenth century China was almost certainly richer than other areas at that time. Maddison (1995) estimates that as late as 1820 two thirds of the world's gross domestic product was accounted for by China and India together. Ultimately, regardless of the degree of significance of domestic capitalism, the decisive role of the state in China controlled the ambitions of the merchants. By the nineteenth century, the Europeans had advanced so far ahead that they could raid China with impunity; it took almost a century of wars for China to establish a political order capable of defending itself.

This, however, is to run well ahead of the story. Parallel to the great surge of growth beginning about the eighth century in China is the simultaneous rapid economic growth of the newly unified Arab and Islamic lands under the Abbasids, who took over the lands and administration of the former Sassanian Empire of Persia and displaced the Byzantine Empire. Somewhat like China, the new empire unified for a time an immense area of relatively rich lands – from Persia westwards as far as Morocco – with much of it accessible to water transport, linking the two trading areas of the Mediterranean and the Indian Ocean. Of all the great religions, Islam is perhaps the most favourable to trade (Buddhism may be a close rival), and once land areas were linked, commerce flourished. The partial results in terms of civilisation were expressed in the architectural glories of Cairo, Baghdad, Damascus, and far to the west Cordoba and Granada. In particular, in terms of the minor part of trade, the external, it included the ancient trade lands of the Levant, the rich production centres of Egypt (with Alexandria the access point to the Mediterranean and the trade with northern Italy), the land routes to China through Central Asia, and the sea routes (the Gulf and the Red Sea) to India, Southeast Asia and thence also to China. Like the ancient trade networks of the Mediterranean, the Arabs endeavoured to create an Islamic sea, linking the east Mediterranean, Muslim North Africa, Muslim Sicily and Muslim Spain. In the East, Arab and Persian shipmasters dominated the Indian Ocean, linking the three main sectors of Aden–Hormuz in Arabia, Cambay–Calicut on the Indian coast, and Malacca–Guangzhou in Southeast Asia and China. The traders combined exchanges in luxury goods (especially silk, porcelain, spices), with bulk ballast of basic goods (dried fruit, leather, rock salt, dried fish, raw cotton, alum, alkaline ash for soap etc). By the twelfth century, Indian Ocean trade was dominated by the famous Karimi merchants under the patronage of the Ayyubid dynasty of Egypt; their main centre was in Fustat (Cairo); from Alexandria, they shipped cargoes to Genoa, Pisa, Venice, Salerno, Amalfi, Prato, Lucca, Barcelona.

Trade stimulated the specialisation of production in different localities. Sugar plantations were developed around the Shatt-al-Arab marshes of lower Iraq – the African slave-labour force rose in armed rebellion in the ninth century. The Egyptian linen weavers, like the cotton weavers of western India, rose to prominence. In the richer areas, land was cultivated to produce saleable crops – foodstuffs like wheat, barley, sugar, vegetable oils, dried fruit, as well as industrial materials, cotton, wool, dyestuffs, timber. And the commercial demand forced technical innovations in the design of ploughs, irrigation works, transport.

The trade with the advanced Muslim civilisation was crucial in the development of north Italy, and through Muslim Spain with France and the rest of Europe. This is best known in terms of the transmission of ancient Greek texts – the Arabic translations of, for example, Aristotle and other classical writers that circulated in the Middle East, again translated, this time into Latin for circulation in Europe's monasteries (much of the transfer taking place through Jewish merchants and scholars of Baghdad and Spain). But there were perhaps more important technical transfers – of Cairo's cloth-knitting methods through Spain to France and beyond; or the medieval cloth, fustian, from Fustat to Italy; the Italian cloth of the time, *baldacchini*, was a copy of the Baghdad original, and enterprising cloth-makers copied Islamic designs for exports back to the Muslim world (as the Chinese silk-makers copied Islamic motifs for sales to Persian or Arab buyers in the Middle East).

Europe's warrior merchants

The North Italian cities traded with the initially much richer Islamic civilisation from at least the eighth century, and some of them were already becoming wealthy by the middle of the ninth. Ferociously competitive with each other, warfare was an intrinsic element of their commercial maritime life, and indeed it was finally the Venetian mobilisation of military power which led to its domination of the trade of Byzantium, the Levantine coast and Alexandria. Venice early established this position. In 1082, the fleets of the city were able to blockade the lower Adriatic and save the Byzantine fleet from destruction by the now Norman kings of Sicily (the Venetians thus paid back a debt: the Byzantine fleet had saved Venice from destruction by Charlemagne). The Venetian merchants thus won singular privileges over their rivals within the Byzantine Empire, including their own walled quarter in Constantinople (the old relationship did not prevent the Venetians diverting a Crusade to ransack the city in 1203–4, ultimately, though much delayed, the death blow to the Byzantine Empire).

The wealth created was not simply in trade. Manufacturing developed from an early time. The Florentine economy in particular was based upon the manufacture of woollen goods in a vast network of workshops, employing a hired labourforce. In 1378, in what is rated as possibly the first industrial working-class rebellion in Europe (and a temporary conquest of power, lasting until 1382), the rising of the Ciompi against the ruler, the *gonfalonier*, the textile workers took over the city.

Florence and Genoa were the first cities to issue their own coins. Florence and other cities of Tuscany pioneered modern banking practices – with cheques, holding companies, double-entry book-keeping, maritime insurance, letters of credit etc – partly through handling the collection and management of the Papacy's finances.

Venice emerged as the dominant maritime power of the eastern Mediterranean, with almost a monopoly of the trade from South and East Asia. The city was a prototype for the European form of capitalism, the union of state power, the sword and commercial enterprise, the means to pay for the sword, where trade necessarily involved armed rivalries and overseas conquest. The governance of the city-state, although varying at different times, was perhaps, the closest to what one might call a 'capitalist state', an oligarchic order uniting merchants, land and the great families of the city. The city pursued a policy not of free trade, but of mercantilism, a public and private attempt to fix the market, by force or manipulation, in favour of the city. Government backed its merchants with armed force, and obliged them to travel in publicly organised convoys (both in order to control them and to defend them against pirates), to carry cargoes in Venetian ships, to handle it in Venetian port facilities, to buy from Venetian sources – regulated to minimise competition between Venetians interests. Pearson (in Tracy 1991: 76) observes that in the Italian cities generally, there was

> almost an identity between trade and government. In the Italian cities, traders were forced to collaborate, forced to pay taxes, forced to trade, forced to use local merchants and sell their goods, and the role of foreigners was very clearly regulated so that the natives would make the profits. The State-merchant connection in the Mediterranean was perhaps most clearly seen in the case of Venice where indeed there was little difference between the State and merchants.

For Venice, naval protection, like the possessions seized throughout the Mediterranean to foster the city's commercial interests – 'a trading post empire' as Braudel (III 1984: 119) calls it – was state backing for private and public commerce. The 'heart of the state' (as the Venetian government called it in 1509) was a great complex of state capitalism, the famous Arsenal. Here an immense concentration of skills were devoted to a self-contained cluster of activities to build, equip and arm the galleys of the fleet, backed with immense stocks of raw materials and machine capacity. The Arsenal had a monopoly in constructing ships, made ropes, cast artillery, made sails, refined saltpetre and made gunpowder, even retaining lumberjacks to cut the forests for ships' timbers. At its peak, financing the Arsenal took between a quarter and a third of the revenues of the state; it employed 28,000 workers (Ruggiero in Pullan 1968: 59). The Venetian system – in Tilly's words (1990: 147), 'an exceptionally supple and predatory state' – was, in its heyday, immensely successful. Braudel (III 1984: 119) calculates that in the fifteenth century the 150,000 population of the city (and 1.6 million with its other Italian and overseas territories) produced a revenue nearly as large as the kingdom of France (with a population of 15 million).

Although the cities of northern Italy, relating to the rich trade in luxury goods of the Arab Empires, were the first in Europe and for long, the most advanced in the continent, the cities of northern Europe, particularly those in the low countries began to develop in bulk cargoes (grain, butter, cheese, timber, wool, fish, wine, textiles, salt, copper, tin, lead: see Steenegaard in Tracy 1990). Indeed, it was the dominant position of the cities of Flanders, controlling the trade of the Rhine and east and south along the West European seaboard, that provoked the 1158 creation at Lübeck in north Germany of the defensive Hanseatic League of self-governing northern cities (Mauro in Tracy: 1990). They operated between the four geographical extremities of Novgorod in Russia, Bergen in Norway, London and Bruges. The League was finally unsuccessful in keeping the merchants of the low countries out of the Baltic. Amsterdam merchants and others tried to establish a monopoly in the Baltic, developing Sweden's iron mines to supply an internationally famous arms industry.

In the thirteenth century, the leading areas of economic growth in northern Italy, with its linkages to the east Mediterranean, became directly connected with Flanders, with its links to the Baltic and along the Atlantic seaboard. The Champagne fairs in France – in the towns of Troyes, Provins, Bar-sur-Aube and Lagny – effected the junction of the two advanced wings of the European economy, exchanging textiles from the north for spices and silk from the south. This also offered the opportunity for the advanced banking services of the Italian cities to spread to the northern centres. The Champagne towns prospered with tolls, fees, rents and sale of land to the traders. The trade had become important enough by 1285 for alternative methods of transaction to be created when the King of France appropriated the territories and closed the markets. One set of merchants shifted the market to Lyons (where there was a stronger attraction in access to the mining and manufacturing cities of south Germany). Others, chiefly those from Genoa and its ally Barcelona, opened the commercial sea route to Lisbon and on to Bruges and Antwerp. Venice followed (in 1314), also expanding direct links to south Germany.

Thus, by the time of the 'calamitous fourteenth century' and the devastations of the great plagues, a significant part of the Eurasian land mass was dotted with the junction points of a maritime and inland waterway trading system, stretching from Northeast Asia to Northwest Europe. The threads from this trading system stretched deep into the settled agricultural areas, changing patterns of production to support growing bulk movement of raw materials (grain, raw cotton, wool, timber etc) to distant manufacturing centres. Thus, Ulm in south Germany in the late fourteenth century produced cloth for Venice that was then shipped to the Levant to compete there with textiles made locally or imported from India. Silver and copper, mined in the Harz Mountains, in Bohemia, Tirol and later Bosnia (much of it with Venetian investment) also flowed to the Levant and beyond.

The agents of this vast interaction, domestic and external trade, were the colonies of foreign merchants – of Venetians in Aleppo, Genovese in Cairo, Arabs in the cities of Cambay or Coromandel or Java, Chinese at Malacca. Enterprising city rulers wooed foreign merchants to call at their ports, offering a framework of legal and physical security to their goods, warehouses and means of exchange, as well as the physical infrastructure required – wharves and go-downs, dredged harbours and pilots, as well as walled quarters with local mosques, temples, churches or synagogues, administered through the privileges of self-government and consuls. The development of the Malayan port of Malacca was a well-known example of an entrepreneurial city. Founded by pirates in the twelfth century, by 1480, when the Portuguese traveller Tomé Pires wrote of the city, it had an estimated population of 40–50,000 with 61 'nations' represented.

Some of the princes of the Indian Ocean principalities auctioned the right to collect taxes, inspect cargo and collect customs and harbour dues, so favouring particular merchants and building their financial assets to the point where they could act as bankers and financiers to princes (much as the Rothschild fortunes were created in Hesse four hundred years later). Some moved on to become officials of the state, generals and admirals. Many operated not as merchants but as capitalists in land, manufacturing, mining, transport, banking and commerce, as well as working as tax-farmers for government. Many rulers of coastal principalities in Asian waters frequently came to depend on the revenues of trade, but regarded commerce with disdain (with the exception of the Omanis and a few others), dedicating themselves exclusively to what we have called the state agenda, or in Barendse's phrase (1998: 34), preferring 'the stirrup to the ship'.

As the scale of Asian trade with Europe grew – as incomes and productivity grew – it was increasingly restricted by the shortage of goods produced in Europe that Asian markets were willing to take. As we noted earlier, West African gold had played an important role in lubricating transactions, and from the sixteenth century an immense inflow of silver from the new Spanish colonies in Latin America to Europe and East Asia (the first Spanish treasure ship from

Acapulco in western Mexico arrived in Manila in 1572) lifted the scale of demand and applied great stimulus to Asian producers and traders and European buyers (Chaudhuri 1990: 455; Tracy 1990: 3). Between 1500 and 1800, it is estimated, nearly half the silver produced in the world was being fed into the Chinese money supply in return for silks and porcelain (the Mexican silver peso became the first world currency, and persisted for two centuries, often employed as a local medium of exchange).

The Europeans were initially entirely dependent upon this pre-existing system of commerce. But their strength lay not simply in the means to buy. As we have seen in the case of the Italian cities in the Mediterranean, warfare was a key component in European trade, and warfare with a quality and range of equipment and a design of ship that gave the Europeans immense initial advantages over Asian traders (without the backing of state naval protection nor a comparable scale of armaments on board). The European approach, armed trade, made no sense in the competition with Asian traders unless the heavy additional costs of carrying the capacity to make war could be met by establishing a monopoly position in buying commodities and in their distribution and sale without the rewards of piracy and booty from lands seized. Hence the almost necessary by-product of the European mode of trade was empire, particularly in the first instance, maritime trading-post empires.

In the Mediterranean, the supremacy of Venice – particularly over Pisa and its closest rival, Genoa – was achieved by force of arms and the attempt to create monopolies in particular commodities rather than the quality of entrepreneurship, let alone an adherence to free-market principles. The Pisans employed military force along the North African coast to secure a trading monopoly. The Genovese (Airaldi 1997) aimed to follow a global policy of opening commercial markets and fighting to do so by creating the special form of capitalist-seafarer-soldier (Pearson in Tracy 1991: 76). It was this peculiar marriage of the physical and military power of the state with commerce which initially marked out the rise of European power.

The kingdom of Portugal set out to break the Venetian military, and hence commercial, monopoly of the east Mediterranean (the Levant coast and the Alexandria–Cairo route to Asia). They aimed to achieve this by pioneering the route to the Indian Ocean round the coast of Africa and the Cape of Good Hope. Portuguese sailors were the first to attack the principle outside Europe that the high seas belonged to all. Starting with the assault on the trading centre of Ceuta in Morocco in 1415, they explored southwards round the coast of Africa and finally broke into the Indian Ocean – Vasco da Gama arrived in Calicut in 1498. They came as armed interlopers rather than as simple merchants, with new heavy cannon – as, from the perspective of the existing traders, essentially pirates. Their arrival constituted, in Robinson's words, a 'gunpowder revolution' (1996: 134). But they were not pirates. Their aim was not merely to prey on other traders (they did that as well), but to enforce a monopoly of all the key junctions between the sources of spice and the European market, a monopoly to which all traders must conform – and pay heavily to do so (so that Portugal could control the supply to Europe). They took control of the Straits of Hormuz, the mouth to the Gulf, and of Bab-el-Mandel at the mouth of the Red Sea; by 1507, they had captured Aden and Oman. Within two decades of their arrival, they had gone some way to creating a monopoly, with a line of fortresses from Hormuz at the head of the Persian Gulf to Malacca in the Malay peninsula. 'The Portuguese elaborated a complex system of compulsion' (Brady in Tracy 1991: 117) whereby, behaving as the instruments of an armed state, they used conquest to destroy their trader rivals, to force treaties on rulers that conceded trade privileges that were enforced with armed power, to institute a pass system at sea to force all trade through Portuguese-held ports (pre-eminently Goa and Cochin on the Indian western seaboard, Malacca in Malaya etc). The battle with the Venetian monopoly in the eastern Mediterranean was fought out in the Indian Ocean. As Tomé Pires famously observed, 'whoever is lord of Malacca has his hand on the throat of Venice' (*Suma Orientale* in Tracy 1991: 7).

The Portuguese monarch tried to ensure that the exports of Asia to Europe flowed through Lisbon and thus were accessible to royal taxation. Initially, there was considerable success. By 1518, nearly 40 per cent of the royal revenue came from trade (a share larger than that which was raised from the domestic taxing of Portugal itself).

However, Portugal could not ultimately mobilise sufficient armed power to control the Asian seas. Only with imperialism proper, under the British, the French, the Dutch and so on, would it have been possible to employ local armies to achieve this result. Indian and Malay merchant ships began to carry arms, including heavy guns. The rulers of the trading principalities developed protective warships. By 1540, the Sultan of Aceh and the ruler of Cambay had reopened the route from Southeast Asia to the Red Sea (and the Portuguese fleets failed to recapture Aden at the mouth of the Red Sea); Malacca was boycotted by Asian traders. The Asian traders evaded the Portuguese maritime guards, bypassed the Portuguese enclaves and resumed the flow of goods through the Persian Gulf and the Red Sea to Venice. 'Asians were less dependent upon their states,' Pomeranz and Topik (1999: 5) observe, 'and hence could persist, even thrive, in the face of European cannon'. Furthermore, the Ottomans consolidated their new empire, taking Egypt in 1517 and Baghdad in 1534, unifying and making secure once more the land and sea trade routes between Europe and Asia. Finally, the brief if remarkable moment of Portuguese dominance was swiftly challenged by new and larger sharks in Asian waters: the Dutch (arriving in 1602), the English and the French. A joint force of English and Persians took Hormuz and once more opened the Gulf.

The growth of European demand, combined with growing markets elsewhere, must have had a substantial effect on Asian producers, on the organisation of production, but the evidence is at best fragmentary. Reid (1993: 186) concludes that, in the case of Southeast Asia, these effects were indeed substantial:

> The entire period 1400 to 1630 was one of rapid monetisation and commercialisation of the economy, with the most rapid expansion in the period 1570 to 1630. A large proportion of the population, by any contemporary standard, was drawn into production and marketing for the world economy and came to rely on long distance imports for such everyday items of consumption as cloth, ceramics, utensils and coinage.

Even if this is true of the smaller economies of Southeast Asia, external trade must still have been a very small part of the great land mass economies of China and India. Here domestic trade was always very much more important. The *banjaras* trading caste (within which the Marwaris, famous in modern times as a leading Indian business community, were the most important) managed very large-scale movements of freight, collecting produce from the villages to distribute throughout the subcontinent. Some of the caravans were very large, according to Habib (in Tracy 1990: 376): he reports Roe's observations of 1615 of 19,000 bullocks carrying wheat, 14,000 oxen with rice, and 20,000 with sugar. Tavernier also claims caravans of 10–20,000 oxen, carrying rice, wheat and salt. Habib himself estimates that possibly 1.14 million tonnes of cargo were in this way shipped in stages over 720 miles (or 820 million tonne-miles), compared to the 2500 million tonnes carried by Indian railways in 1882. Whatever the actual scale – and these claims seem exaggerated – this bulk land transport was interwoven both with external trade (for example bulk exports of textiles to be made up in the Gulf) and the coastal trade of India – in fish, salt, sulphur, ghee, paint, iron, fruit and gram flour. The trade created substantial fortunes and families of wealth and land that survived well into the British period. Indeed, in the seventeenth and eighteenth centuries British trade and industry relied on Indian finance; not until the 1860s did British finance start to become significant, pushing Indian wealth into land and the sons of the former Indian business groups into the civil service and the professions.

Close behind the Portuguese royal warrior-merchants were the Dutch, determined to exercise even greater ruthlessness to tear the monopoly of the spice trade away from Lisbon in favour of Amsterdam and the cities of the low countries. Now the power of the state was embodied in the monopoly corporation of merchants, the VOC (the United Dutch East India Company), with official powers to wage war in the name of Holland, to make peace, parley and treaty with other states. A leading representative of the VOC advised his masters in Holland in 1614: 'From experience, your lordships ought to know very well that in India, trade is driven and maintained under the protection and favour of your own weapons, just as the weapons are furnished from the profits of trade, in such wise that trade cannot be maintained without war, nor war without trade'. (Jan Pieterszoon Coen, Bantam, 27 December, to Heren XVII, Board of Directors, VOC in Tracy 1991: 1)

To the commercial interest of the merchants, the crown married its national policy to attack the pre-eminent position of Spain and Portugal in overseas possessions. By 1669, the Dutch had 150 trading ships, the majority of them armed, with 40 warships and 10,000 troops in the Indian Ocean. They sought to sweep through the Portuguese possessions on the route to the spice islands in the southeast of what is now the Indonesian archipelago – Malacca fell early (1641), then Makassar (1667), and Bantam (1682). However, ultimately, the only way of excluding foreign competition was by appropriating the whole of the archipelago and establishing political control of the producers. Trade became subsidiary to the exercise of armed and finally – territorial – power.

The Dutch were among the more extreme Europeans at this stage in the struggle to exclude competition through the closure of territories to competitors. However, as with the Portuguese, they were successful only insofar as local rulers could be compelled to accept their power, and even then temporarily. The ruthlessness of the Dutch in seeking to control production – and destroy alternative sources – provided opportunities to their rivals to seize the initiative from them by offering a less oppressive regime. Furthermore, once the Ottomans restored the unity and security of the Middle East, trade through both the Persian Gulf to Aleppo and Istanbul, and the Red Sea revived, so that the Dutch could not monopolise commerce through the route round the Cape of Good Hope.

Wherever the territorial rulers were strong, they could repulse the Europeans. Indeed, the great land empires mobilised a scale of forces that could not be confronted by however many troops the puny ships of the Europeans carried. For example, the Mughal emperor Akbar is said to have put armies in the field in the 1590s numbering 343,000 horsemen and 4 million foot soldiers, many of them armed with muskets (Parker 1988: 276–77). Only when the Europeans abandoned the role of merchant and became territorial powers – with their own locally recruited forces – could they fight serious wars. But then, like the Asian powers themselves, they acquired the interests of the state, not the concerns of the lowly trader.

Traders in Asia were no less appreciative than the Europeans of monopoly if it could be secured, but they rarely had access to the scale of armed power required to achieve it, and then only on a comparable scale to that of the Europeans in the smaller principalities of Southeast Asia. By default, free trade was for them the outcome of this position. Pearson notes (in Tracy 1991: 74) that 'A crucial element in the encouragement [to merchants to call at a particular port] was the very existence of free markets which were precisely not embedded in any political system but rather operated free from political interference'.

Thus, what was taken for granted in Europe in its long history of princely rivalries, the marriage of business and the preoccupations of the state, was what was peculiar, uniquely European, in Asia. As Chaudhuri (1985: 14) puts it: 'the phenomenon that is in need of explanation is not the system of peaceful but of armed trade'.

In Europe, this fateful marriage would ultimately entail the defeat of precisely those who employed it first, the city-states of northern Italy and of Flanders. Once the contest was not the market competition of merchants, operating solely on their own account, but of the physical power of states, then the relative weight of the state determined the outcome – and the stronger and larger states came to dominate the system.

There were differences of emphasis among the Europeans in the relative balance of armed power and trading. Elizabeth I of England endowed her East India Company with powers of monopoly comparable to those of the Dutch, but the directors were forever reproving their officials with wasting money on military ambitions rather than sticking to trade (and the officials were equally irritated at the myopia of their directors in failing to allow the company to match the military efforts of the Portuguese, the Dutch and the French). 'All war is so contrary to our constitution as well as to our interest', the directors write plaintively in 1681, 'that we cannot too often inculcate to you an aversion there to'. And seventy years later, they again reproach their officials who 'seem to look upon yourselves as a military colony than [as] the factors and agents of a body of merchants' (in Parker in Tracy 1990: 280). Under such accounting, as late as 1740 the British had forces of only 2000 in India, a corps of basically security guards. Only in the confrontation with better-armed French were the British forces pushed up to 5000 sepoys (Indian troops) in 1758, and 9000 in 1765. By then, some officials were beginning to glimpse a quite different agenda, a territorial empire with the power to raise taxes on the land (and so escape part of London's control) rather than the profits on trade and the puny ambitions of traders.

The fusion of interest between merchant and state power remained for long ambivalent. For example, in the case of Amsterdam, the city which most obviously inherited in Northwestern Europe the position of Venice or Florence in the Mediterranean, there were throughout the seventeenth century continual struggles between the territorial ambitions of the House of Orange, the *stadtholder* of the United Provinces and the commercial interests of the city fathers. When the Prince of Orange wished to ally with the English Stuarts to seek to recover the southern Netherlands from Spanish rule, Amsterdam merchants were set upon breaking the stranglehold of Copenhagen on the straits that led into the Baltic. Even more wilful, Amsterdam financed the *stadtholder*'s enemies, the Spanish, diverting pirated Spanish silver to pay the troops of Spain and even building ships for Spain's Philip II (as they did later for another 'enemy of Holland', Louis XIV). Meanwhile, it was Amsterdam capital which financed the development of Sweden's iron mines and the resulting arms industry to defeat Denmark. The issues fed into the civil war of 1650, but the Prince ultimately only won in 1680; then his subordination of Amsterdam accrued to the benefit of the rising power of London and Paris, creatures of far larger territorial powers than the Netherlands.

A COSMOPOLITAN CAPITALISM

Commercial exchange is, as we have seen, as old as recorded history, trade between geographically distant economic clusters of demand and production. But also merchants trawled the world well outside these centres. The largest of these clusters existed within empires, and the relationship between these territorial political entities and a world trading system has often been remote. Runciman's (II 1952: 95–96) comment on Byzantium might equally apply to many of these empires: 'Byzantine foreign trade ... received very little encouragement from the imperial authorities whose interference in it was only concerned with questions of revenue and the acquisition of raw materials needed by imperial factories'. Trade continued regardless, it seems, of the wars of the rulers, of who might be allies or enemies of the territorial princes. The Geniza documents of Cairo (Goitien I 1967: 60), dating from the beginning of the second millennium to the early medieval period and covering Jewish commercial and other affairs, show that it was easy to forget 'that political boundaries existed at all'.

Of course, princes were often the largest consumers – of war materials, of building materials, of agricultural goods and luxuries. But this final demand was crucial only for the traders who dealt directly with this consumption. On the other hand, rulers were dangerous for traders. They seized goods arbitrarily, insisted – as in Mameluk Egypt – on the right of first refusal (in precious goods, textiles, lead and wax), their officials most often required extensive bribery, and commercial fortunes depended often on the value of currencies rulers issued. Sometimes rulers barely distinguished between regular taxes and tariffs and straight theft, and while they possessed overwhelming superiority in physical power, their right to steal could not be challenged. Merchants were wise, if possible, to avoid rulers and their legion of officials, or at least treat them as fearsome – 'a bottomless chasm', Goitien (I 1967: 348) comments, 'divided the rulers from the ruled. The former were half-gods with standards of morals and conduct differing from all that was regarded as decent or even permissible'. The only justification for accepting the debauched, sadistic and corrupt behaviour of princes was that the lack of any government was even worse.

Some of the larger political authorities were, as we noted earlier, tempted by the view that business and its links beyond the boundaries of the state were intrinsically subversive. They were tempted to order the closure and destruction of external commercial relationships. While the southern Sung dynasty, as we have seen, might tolerate and sometimes even encourage trade, for a time, both the Ming and Qing dynasties tried to close China, as did Tokugawa Japan, the kings of Korea and of Siam. Like the Ming rulers, the early Mameluks of Egypt laid waste parts of the coastline to destroy the possibility of external trade and contacts (to make more difficult the penetration of foreign political influences).

Trade, however, created networks of independent cities, the stepping-stones along the watercourses and coasts which constituted the highways of commerce. There were associated land routes that penetrated deep into the heartlands of continents – Nelly Hanna's Cairo merchant (1998) of the sixteenth century had an agent in Kano in what became northern Nigeria, handling gold, feathers, ivory and slaves. The city-states, unlike the empires, often did not have access to much land revenue, and were therefore dependent on the revenues generated by trade. The more farsighted rulers, as we have seen, managed policy to attract and keep the traders. This seems to have been as true of the city-states of Southeast Asia and littoral India as of northern Italy. Rulers also on occasion themselves financed trading expeditions to raise revenues – some Indian princes and even Mughal notables, for example. In the late thirteenth and early fourteenth centuries, some of the Egyptian Mameluks traded on their own account, and taxed smaller merchants to guard public monopolies. In 1432, Sultan Barbay laid down a monopoly of the Red Sea trade, rendering the merchants who filled the royal warehouses agents of the ruler. The rulers of the Ottoman Empire, in improving routes for pilgrimages to Mecca, in creating the security of fortresses and khans where pilgrims could stay, encouraged merchants; a common administration facilitated the standardisation of law and thus the recognition of deeds of mandate, records of sales and powers of attorney. Political authorities were under a religious obligation to help pilgrims travel to Mecca, and merchants joined their caravans; during Haj, they were exempt from customs duty, so that virtue and profit could be won together.

The Ottoman pashas, initially uninterested in trade, came in time to own ships and invest in cargo. According to Palmira Brummett (1994: 176), this led them to encourage and shelter commercial wealth. Even the dynasty and its *askeri* (the official class) participated, particularly in the long established grain exports. Thus, sometimes, territorial rulers, even in empires, engaged in trade as quasi-merchants, and followed policies directed at encouraging trade. It would be absurd, however, to suggest they were the creatures of the traders.

A COMMUNITY OF MERCHANTS?

Some successful merchants, as we have seen, acted as officials of the princes, from tax-farmers to financiers to contractors. Yet again this did not imply that territorial rulers were the agents of business, much less that businessmen, as businessmen, were wedded to the purposes of the state. As Origo (1957: 43) notes of the late fourteenth century in north Italian Prato, merchants were normally engaged in government only insofar as it directly touched their interests. Like their Geniza forebears, they regarded their rulers as an alien stratum, and the interests of trade took precedence over those of their city. 'Did merchants really care about nationality and regional dominance when deciding what regions and commodities they should invest in?' asks Eleanor Congden (in Aguis and Nelton 1997: 171) of her fourteenth-century merchants. Four hundred years later in British India, a comparable doubt about loyalties is noted by Ludden (in Bose 1990: 164): 'in their (unorientalised) world categorical opposition, [they] did not separate the "Indian" and "European". Alliances formed and opposed one another for reasons that made sense in that world; and they fought for the fruits of merchant capital'.

Certainly, merchants formed – and were obliged, as a condition of survival to form and sustain – groups of their own 'nation', physically embodied often as a quarter of a foreign trading city; but this had few implications for the political aims of the rulers of their homeland. No doubt, networks of collaboration – in trade and, even more, in marriages – were predominantly within this 'nation', but it did not prevent commercial alliances between 'nations'. Nor did it prohibit the constitution of a multi-nation community of trade – 'the idea,' Congden puts it (Aguis and Nelton 1997: 171), 'that international merchants at the turn of the fifteenth century formed a "community", or even a "culture"'. Goitien argues that his Cairo merchants, centuries earlier, formed a 'free trade community'. Dotson (Aguis and Nelton 1997: 123), examining merchant manuals of the fourteenth century, concludes that they 'suggest the existence of a true business community reaching across cultural differences perceived as barriers'. Among his evidence is the opposition of Christian merchants to the embargo placed on trade with Egypt and Syria in the crusades of the second half of the fourteenth century.

The existence of 'community', of a common interest, did not rule out the most ferocious rivalries – the Venetian treatment of the Genovese in Constantinople or the Pisans on the Levantine, or the Dutch treatment of their rivals in Southeast Asia. But then this was not much different to the mutual treatment of rivals within each 'nation'. The Medicis destroyed and banished their Florentine rivals in much the same spirit. Thus, if 'community' includes as part of its norm savage civil war then merchants could be a community, certainly for many centuries before the warrior merchants of Europe made market competition an issue of armed power and thereby added a much sharper cutting edge to commercial rivalry.

More normally, before the arrival of the Portuguese and other Europeans in the Indian Ocean, free trade – without arms – guaranteed the cosmopolitan community of merchants. In the heyday of Malacca, say in 1500, with possibly 2000 ship movement annually, Tomé Pires reports that 84 languages were spoken in this, the largest port in the world on his account. The imposition by force of a Portuguese monopoly in 1511 killed the city – its population dwindled, its markets died. As we have seen, Broach on the western mid-Indian littoral boasted a similar diversity. In Hormuz in the mid fifteenth century, 24 nations were recorded (including merchants from China, Russia, Java, Siam, Abyssinia and Zanzibar (Jackson and Lockhart 1986: 422). Bruges in the fifteenth century counted 16 nations, and by the seventeenth century (according to Murray 1972: 52) Amsterdam had become the 'most cosmopolitan city in Europe'; it was predominantly and firmly Protestant, but nonetheless allowed open worship for at least all Christian denominations – 'the commercial life of the city was strictly regulated by the ruling oligarchy which in many ways was a guild of merchants, tolerant of foreigners, regardless of their religious beliefs or the animosities of local guilds towards them'. Lyons in 1571 (Mauro in Tracy 1990: 263–64) was a city of foreigners, though the citizens of each Italian city were counted as a separate nation. Some stayed several generations. Merchants from Lucca were in Lyons from 1466 to 1629 – 'The Italians of Lucca,' Mauro notes (*ibid.*: 266) 'were tempted to become citizens of Lyons, subjects of the King of France, which would have given them a source of power. They were restrained from doing so only by other potential loyalties: to Europe, on the one hand, which was a real economic entity in the sixteenth century, and to their home country of Italy on the other'.

Sometimes, the expatriate community became cut off from its homeland – as happened to the Chinese in Manila and Batavia under the Ming. They then became merchant communities without a homeland, much as the Jews and Armenians were at this time. The Chinese operated on their own account, and then worked for the Spaniards, the Portuguese and the Dutch. The Armenians, having pioneered trading linkages on the frontiers of the known world – in the ninth century to northern Russia and in the early middle ages to Mongolia – were driven out of what was then their homeland; the aristocracy were settled by the rulers of Persia in New Julfa, from where they recreated their commercial networks linking Venice, the Ukraine, India, Burma, Siam, Batavia, Manila and Canton (even, bravely, to Lhasa) (Aghassian in Tracy 1990).

Often the special quarter in a foreign trading city in which each 'nation' lived was self-governing, with a consul recognised by the local ruler. Inhabitants were governed by the laws of their religious denomination – or one of its schools – rather than by the territory at large. Judges were thus able to travel the known world as itinerant skilled workers, giving judgements – and earning their keep – as they went from city to city (Goitien 1967: 77). Thus, the famous Islamic judge, Ibn Batuta (1304–68), travelled from Morocco to China and back, dispensing Maliki law.

The movement and residence of merchants was not at all unique. Cosmopolitan interchanges were much greater then than in the later heyday of the nation-state. Churchmen travelled the length of Christendom, as Muslim divines travelled the world of Islam, and learned rabbis carried their wisdom between Jewish communities. Princes by the accident of inheritance came to be rulers of foreign lands, and regarded themselves as unimplicated in local cultures and languages. Mercenaries fought for whoever promised to pay. Though merchants might travel further and cross the boundaries between different predominant religions, they were not unusual in moving between 'nations'.

The shifting location of prosperity induced those with capital to beat tracks to where it was more likely that a living could be earned. Indeed, the 'fluidity of movement', Hanna (1998: 25) notes of Cairo's merchants, 'clearly indicates that the political events of the time did not necessarily affect such matters as migration and trade'. Italian merchants created Lyons as an important market centre, Venetian and other banks created the bourse and banks of Bruges and Antwerp. Dutch capital, as we have seen, in defiance of the Prince of Orange, developed the iron and munitions industries of Sweden, invested in the English East India Company, in the wine industry of the Loire, in tobacco cultivation in Maryland and Virginia, in sugar in the West Indies. By and large, as in the Amsterdam example of religious toleration, there was tolerance – Goitien notes the close integration of Jewish, Christian and Muslim merchants in Cairo under the Fatimids and early Mameluks; the Jews operated in all sectors of the economy, including manufacture and agriculture, and there were many

Christian–Muslim partnerships, and Muslim–Jewish alliances (particularly in tax-farming).

Those with skills to sell also migrated towards centres of prosperity. Cairo attracted silversmiths from Ceuta (in Morocco) via Sicily; some moved on via Aden to Sri Lanka (Goitien I 1967: 50). Syrian–Palestinian dyers and silk-weavers in the eleventh and twelfth centuries moved southwards to escape war, and 'Rumanian' tailors, cobblers and goldsmiths followed in their tracks.

The movement – of traders, capital and skills – changed the technology, the types of cropping, the organisation of production. This is most clearly illustrated in the migration of types of cultivation, in the endless process of import-substitution (and the reduction of transport costs). For example, sugar refining moved from Southeast Asia and India to Mameluk Cairo and Syria, thence to Italy, Spain and Portugal, and so to the Netherlands. By 1605, Amsterdam had three refineries, and 81 years later, 60. 'Capital laughed at frontiers,' Braudel comments (II 1982: 528). 'It flowed towards safe investments.' Sugar cane cultivation followed the same route westwards – to Palestine in the eleventh century, to Venetian Cyprus and Crete, to Sicily, Malta, southern Spain and Portugal, and thence to Portuguese Madeira, the Azores and São Tomé (Tracy 1990: 25). Cotton manufacture migrated from the Indian subcontinent to Egypt, to Milan, and then Italian merchants developed it in south Germany at Ulm, Augsberg and Nuremberg (so displacing Italian exports) and then on to the northwest. Silk was such a valuable product it was a natural candidate for transfer. However, for 800 years, the producers in China were able to defend their monopoly of supply – until, it is said, two Persian monks carried silk-worms home. From there cultivation spread to Syria, Anatolia and Lebanon. The north Italian cities – Lucca, Florence, Venice – became important centres, exporting back to the Levant coast manufactured silk, before Lyons, and then Zurich, Cologne, and later Holland and England became important (the Huguenot silk weavers, expelled from France for their Protestant confession, carried their skills to Norwich and London).

The transfer of crops created manufacturing industries – in fourteenth-century Cairo, cotton spinning and weaving, sugar refining and confection, flax weaving etc. The Mameluk officials and the merchants invested in sugar refining – there were 66 refineries in the early fourteenth century (Abu-Lughod 1989: 232). They built paper-making factories (many are said to have belonged to the Sultan and his officials). By the sixteenth century, the export of cash crops was important – rice and other grains to Arabia, Anatolia, sugar and linen to the rest of the Ottoman Empire and Europe. It was financed with merchant capital. In sixteenth century Anatolia, merchant and banking capital financed village weaving in both cotton and silk. By the seventeenth century, thousands of cotton weavers, silk winders and cloth workers in Indian villages were producing for export and living on traded foodstuffs.

With the migration of crops and of manufacturing capacity went innovations, the introduction in Europe in the early medieval period of wind and of water power for example. All manner of mechanical innovations arrived well before steam power. Indeed, one historian (Laurent 1935: 45) sees the mechanical innovations following the introduction of wind power in the thirteenth century as 'an industrial revolution only a little less advanced than that at the end of the XVIII and the beginning of the XIX centuries'. The same would be true in many other fields, not least the development of financial instruments, for example letters of credit.

The system enforced interdependence over long distances and elaborated patterns of geographical specialisation. In this, there was nothing at all new in the twentieth century. Thus, when Edward III of England (1312–77) defaulted on his debts in 1339, the three great banking families of Florence (the Peruzzi, the Accianoli and the Bardi) were bankrupted, and much misery was inflicted upon the city. The bankruptcy of the King of Spain in 1622 in similar fashion devastated Genoa.

In sum, then, it becomes impossible to say with precision when 'capitalism' began. The surges of growth which we have noted here included both measures of self-reinforcing progress and defeats, retreats and declines. Many of the elements of an exchange economy occurred very early in the story – as Chaudhuri (1978: 207) observes: 'division of labour, industrial production and long distance trade were part of the social community from pre-historic times. It will be difficult to find a society in any age or place which did not have some of the features of the exchange economy, based on the concept of relative values, money use and the market.'

Second, the relationship between this competitive capitalist system and the state, the territorial rulers, was only a necessary one where the officials of state or the rulers themselves traded on, as it were, public account (as opposed to their private benefit, admittedly a difficult distinction to defend for much of the past). So far as private traders were concerned, the relationship was contingent. Businessmen were delighted to have a monopoly if the rulers offered it (and policed it), but left to themselves they were obliged to accept the equality of free trade as the least bad option. Capitalists accommodated the territorial rulers, adjusted to them. Sometimes they were able to exploit state power, more often they were exploited by it, but there was no necessary connection and therefore, politically, no necessary loyalty. Rightly, therefore, capitalists were seen as potentially subversive of the political order, unpatriotic, not committed to the state agenda (this disassociation of business and the state was, as we have seen, sometimes enforced by only permitting trade and manufacture to be undertaken by foreigners). The spirit – that capital is an alien – is reflected in the 1790 declaration of the Comte de Custine in the revolutionary Assembly of France: 'Will the Assembly which has destroyed all kinds of aristocracy flinch before the aristocracy of capitalists, these cosmopolitans whose only fatherland is the one in which they can pile up their riches?' (25 November, in Braudel II 1982: 47) In later years, the internationalism of business was a constant reproach, reflected in attitudes to international finance, the City of London or Wall Street, to antisemitism, the response supposedly to the notoriously cosmopolitan Jews, in the persistent stories of businessmen financing the enemy, conspiring to profit from war or the manufacture of arms with which the sons of the native soil would be slaughtered.

We are in some position to give provisional answers to the questions with which we began. Commercial activity was economically and socially significant for long periods before modern history began. The demands of market trade propelled continuous changes in innovation and in the forms of production, in technology and organisation, in agriculture, manufacturing and mining. We can certainly detect the emergence at various points in time of private capitalism, and indeed of a class of private capitalists with, presumably, some sense of a common interest. However, it is very difficult to see that class as having serious aspirations to take over the territorial state, to adopt the agenda of the state as its own. The partial exception to this is the creation of the mercantilist city-state at various times, a case of which Venice or Florence are the prototypes. However, not only did this order not prove viable in the long term – it was defeated both by internal mutations towards princely rather than merchant rule but also by being overwhelmed by a quite peculiar and modern political formation, the nation-state.

3

The Modern State

A prince should thus have no other thought and aim than war, nor acquire mastery in anything except war, its organisation and discipline; for war is the only art expected of a ruler

Niccolo Machiavelli (1952)

The word State is identical with the word war. Each State tries to weaken and ruin another in order to force upon that other its laws, its policies and its commerce, and to enrich itself thereby

P. A. Kropotkin (1902)

INTRODUCTION

The capitalism described in the preceding chapter depended for the stability of transactions – the reduction of risks to manageable proportions – on reliable territorial administration, on government. The dependence might vary; the solitary peddler relied least on government, but the moment the cargo became large, bulky and valuable, security was essential. The more the system advances, the greater the dependence on government – for security and reliability of trans-actions, for accepted forms of exchange, for laws that enforce contracts, protect cargo and assets, and ensure redress; reliability requires that these rules are ultimately backed by the threat of the exercise of force.

However, government is Janus-faced. The capitalist – the merchant, the manufacturer, the cultivator, the miner – in requiring administrative order and reliability, thereby exposes his (and it was usually his) vulnerability to that official force being turned against himself, turned to expropriation; his only defence is flight. It is with princes as with bandits. The capitalist, like the peasant or the handicraftsmen, has no defence except in those rare circumstances where equivalent physical power can be created in the armies of rebellion. The condition of a stable low-risk capitalism at the same time contains the threat of the destruction of any economic activity, the threat of laying waste by the state and its armies. Straight theft replaces taxes.

The logic of territorial power does not conform to the logic of capitalism, nor vice versa. In the last chapter, we suggested one feature of this – competitive markets in the past seem to sustain a peculiar settlement pattern: junctions in flows of commodities, finance and information, externally oriented open cities scattered along the trade routes. The trading and producing system is not territorially bounded, and waxes and wanes as the economy changes (reflected in the rise and fall of cities, the migration of capital and labour between them, the extension or shrinkage of cultivated area and habitation). Territorial rulers are under no such discipline, but rather in conditions of endemic warfare, they build for periods empires and kingdoms, sometimes fiercely bounded patches of territory that have no necessary relationship to any 'natural' economic geography. Territorial states also wax and wane, but by means of warfare and appropriation (and sometimes through marriage or inheritance), through the use of physical power, not commercial power: the opening of new economic resources or abilities. The mobilisation of this physical power is financed, in the prototype case, from land taxes – hence the territorial ruler is, unlike the merchant, tied to a particular piece of land and a particular cultivating population. Ibn Khaldun recognised the logic of territorial power in the fourteenth century when he quoted the Iranian king, Anushirwan (Khusraw I, 531–70 AD): royal authority rests on the army; the army on money; money on taxes; taxes on cultivation; cultivation on justice, the quality of officials and political rule, on royal authority (Chaudhuri in Robinson 1996: 127)

Territorial rulers also, as we have seen, relied to varying degrees on trade to sustain their armies and their consumption. Put simplistically, the yield of land tax – from landowners and peasants – went to pay for the prince's purchases and so into the profits of merchants and to remote producers. As a consequence, around each territorial ruler, there was often a cluster of traders, of markets, whether some of these were also state officials or simply private merchants. This city was, in the prototypical case, at the same time the centre of royal power and administration, of the consumption services of the prince, aristocracy and armies, as well as a market, a set of commercial locations, and often of manufacturing (although this also took place in rural households). The great and glorious merchant princes and bankers, close to the emperor or king or his court, no doubt looked with contempt upon the solitary peddler or the scruffy caravan, plodding the long routes to Xanadu, but ultimately the one depended on the other for the luxuries delivered to the ruler or the necessities provided to his armies and his people.

The different territorial logic indicates different objectives, different institutional structures, above all different systems.[1] This stark dichotomy, between a territorial/political and a commercial/economic logic, needs, as we have seen, to be qualified – some merchants were armed, even with private armies, some became officials of state, generals and admirals; some princes, even within empires, traded, their estates produced commercial crops or operated great workshops and mines. But the logic of the dichotomy is not affected by the cases which combine characteristics of both, and particularly is this so when we note that as we approach contemporary times the intermediates tend to become more rare – the division of labour between state and commerce becomes exclusive.

The story of this chapter is how one logic, that of the state, the territorial ruler, came to subordinate and completely reshape the other, that of capital. The imperatives of the state system carved out economically 'irrational', even if politically expedient, patches of territory, creating politically defined economies; the political order forced its coherence upon the fragment of a wider economic system. The process was costly in terms of capital – for example, in the later nineteenth century the networks of trade and production which historically linked the cities of German-speaking Central Europe eastwards and on to Russia had to be violently reshaped to invent a German economy, the economy of the new reich. A similar process occurred in reverse with the end of the Austro-Hungarian Empire after the First World War, of the European empires after the Second World War, or in the 1990s with the break up of the former Soviet Union (in these last cases, the reorganisation was of an economy defined by a former political entity rather than of an unbounded system). 'Natural' economic geography, that defined by natural features (rivers, seas, deserts, mountains, resources) was sacrificed to the interests of the political order: ultimately cosmo-politan capitalism was sacrificed to the creation of a set of national capitalisms in the interests of states.

However, historically what we have called, somewhat clumsily, 'territorial administration' has had no standard format, nothing we can reasonably call, as we can today, the state. The justification for identifying a modern state is that this form of administration, of territorial political power, with its sociological shadow the nation, became so standardised, encompassing the entire world. Because of its generality, its historical peculiarity and the recentness of its creation often escapes us.

A school of historians trace the origins of the state system to the north-western corner of the Europe of the eleventh and twelfth centuries. This sometimes leads to the omission of all the other paths that might have occurred, identifying our account of the past simply by present concerns; at worst, this produces a kind of inevitability about what evolved, and thus a false justification – trying to prove why Europe came, even if temporarily, to dominate the world. But Europe's position was not secure, in terms of world power, until the second half of the eighteenth century, so we cannot read its inevitability into the eleventh. Nor are the other regions of the world yet well enough researched to test with any rigour the thesis of Europe's uniqueness before the eighteenth century. There may have been elsewhere many false starts that need to be explained before we can understand Europe, and Europe's development may have many more elements of accident than are accounted.

However, to return to the central theme, what identifies this 'modern state'?[2] Some of the key attributes include its durability, independent of the person of the ruler, its spatial fixity and impersonal character, but above all its claim to absolute domestic power, to complete sovereignty within its domains. The institutional form is characterised by unusual bureaucratic centralisation, by the elimination of thousands of other loyalties to authorities both within and beyond the national territory. The state invented not only an economy to fit its territories but also a society, supposedly characterised by what was the result of the process rather than its cause, a common culture, language and mores (and, for many people, a genealogical descent). Of course, none of these supposed common elements is in practice shared equally by all modern states. Where this degree of 'homogeneity' was achieved, the obverse was a high degree of subordination to one authority; it involved an extremely long-drawn-out and brutal process extending over centuries, with almost ceaseless resistance and occasional rebellions that on rare occasions produced revolution.

What was the dynamic which produced this strangely standardised form? The sheer universality of the institutional form and the character of its power suggests that it was not the product of an internal essence (the soul of the nation), by domestic factors, but rather was imposed upon states and their peoples through the external creation of a state system. This is not to deny the important differences between modern states, a product of different histories, geography, position, weight and role within the system, but for all this, compared to the past, the world is governed by a remarkably uniform order. The dynamic of this system, created in Europe and imposed upon the rest of the world, is one of competing states driven by the imperative of military defence and of warfare – at a minimum, the defence of national independence.

The thought is not at all new – as Van Creveld (1996: 4) observes of the state in general, 'The prime function of the State, as that of all previous forms of government, has always been to fight other States, whether defensively in the attempt to defend its interests or offensively to extend them'. Nor is war and warring states peculiar to Europe. What is slightly peculiar is the stability of the system of warring states, the impossibility of establishing a durable imperial hegemony throughout the continent as occurred in China, India and elsewhere. It was touch and go, and at times a number of imperial aspirants nearly secured this outcome, but in the end, to use the Chinese phrase, the period of warring states persisted into the modern world and became the established form. As Walter Dorn (1963: 1) comments,

> It is [the] very competitive character of the State system in modern Europe that distinguishes it from the political life of all previous and non-European civilisations of the world. Its essence lies in the co-existence of independent and co-ordinated States whose expansionist drive provoked incessant military conflicts ... and above all, the prevention of any single power from reducing the others to a state of permanent subjugation.

However, this outcome came late in the day, formally embodied in doctrines of the 'balance of power' following the two Treaties of Westphalia (1648) that closed the Thirty Years War. Even then it did not rule out the heroic Napoleonic endeavour to dominate the continent, nor the complete liquidation of Poland. There had been many earlier examples of a briefly stable system of warring states – in Southeast Asia, in India, in the pauses between Chinese dynasties, and perhaps also in Africa and the Americas. It was therefore not simply a stable system of competing and war-making states which was peculiar, but rather the relationship that this system forced on the domestic economies of each participant, summarised in Tilly's succinct comment (in Evans et al. 1985: 172): 'War-making, extraction and capital accumulation interacted to shape European State-making'.

In sum, then, in the second millennium after Christ, Europe's history was marked by endemic warfare. Writing of the eleventh century, Howard (1976: 1) observes '"peace" in Europe, that peace for which congregations in Christian churches so sincerely prayed, existed only in exceptional and precarious oases of time'. And Nef (1950: 155), writing of a period eight centuries later, notes that 'For Western Europe as a whole, years of war were still the rule, years of peace the exception'.

A system of permanent war – or war punctuated by periods of preparation for war – entailed that, in normal circumstances, the central obsession of the civil arms of government was with raising the means to wage war. Furthermore, the costs rose dramatically as the competitive scale of warfare increased and innovations in military technology escalated the burden of what was required. This in turn led to a preoccupation with the methods by which rulers could extract from the ruled adequate resources – with taxes, loot, expropriations – and so therefore with the instruments to achieve these ends: the bureaucracy, the tax-collectors, the police, the courts and the bailiffs. Hence the external imperatives of a war-making system compelled continual attempts to reshape the internal regime and its domestic environment, impelled by the apparently never-ending escalation in costs of equipment and the scale of manpower required in warfare. There was never a point of rest. Between wars, meeting the debts incurred in past wars dominated public revenues; each ruler was 'compelled by the constant tension and rivalry among themselves repeatedly to exert all their forces so as not to be dislodged from their place' (Tilly 1975: 185). In poorly managed states, princes lived from hand to mouth, from year to year, attempting to pull together by any means the required sums, wildly conceding privileges to extract contributions at one time, abolishing them with the same end in another, while facing sporadic rebellion, peasant war and noble revolt, resistance to squandering the social patrimony in deadly waste. If the prince was unlucky or imprudent, the demand for 'ship-money' to finance his fleet, could – as in the case of the England of Charles I – set off events that led to civil war; or – like the case of the Seven Years War and the Bourbons of France, or the wars of 1905 and 1914 and the Romanovs of Russia – lead to revolution in which the old regimes were swept away.

The loot of war offered some relief. War then became a struggle to capture the means to wage war. But only exceptional control could ensure that the troops themselves did not make off with the booty. Bankers offered another exit by postponing the need to meet present costs to some distant future date. But in the frenetic drive to war, the borrowings could swamp the borrower. The English wars against the Scots and the French between 1542 and 1550 cost two and a half times the revenues of the crown; selling off crown lands, levying higher taxes and expanded borrowing briefly closed the gap. But in the case of the Spanish king a little later, only bankruptcy – both of monarch and his bankers – saved the day. For those bankers lucky enough to be offered the privilege of lending to kings, it was a recurrent nightmare – 'Such complacent bankers as the Fuggers, the Welsers and the Hochstetters who had made possible the campaigns of Charles V and Francis I, had been dragged by their defaulting royal debtors into spectacular bankruptcy' (Howard 1976: 38). The risk was high, but the rewards of success immense – 'Behind every successful dynasty stood an array of opulent banking families. Access to such bourgeois resources proved crucial to the prince's State-building and centralizing policies' (de Vries 1976: 79).

Juggling with short-term ruses to raise money quickly might be required in the event of crisis, but a prince with an intelligent chancellor might be led to consider how, in the longer term, to escape this ruinous and dangerous hand-to-mouth life. If the king's income depended upon the taxing of land, the prosperity of agriculture and the means to tax the crop, backed by solid powers of enforcement, were the vital determinants of adequate royal revenue. If trade generated wealth, facilitating trade and instituting the means to expropriate part of the revenues were similarly vital. Thus, the infant study of economics and the creation of an economic policy became important ways to enhance the capacity of the ruler to fight. Princes acquired an interest in promoting capitalism and, to ensure its growth, often invented a class of national capitalists, a client instrument. This was a rather more distinctive European feature of the system of warring states: a system of warring national economies or of national capitalisms.

Thus, over the centuries of its development, the logic of the European state system both developed and refashioned, for the first time, a set of national economies, the tail, as it were, of the battlefields. The interest in war-making shaped what the constituents of those national capitalisms should be, with an emphasis on delivering the giant projects the state required – from the great siege works of the fourteenth century, the castles, walls, cannon and warships, to the immense output of the iron and steel and capital goods industries of the nineteenth and twentieth centuries – the tanks, the artillery, the steel warships, the shells and chemicals. It also bent the national economy towards economic self-sufficiency, at almost any cost, in the interests of being free from the possibility of external trade embargo by an enemy power.

The demands of the state accelerated the accumulation of capital in a national form. From the point of view of the national capitalist, war-making, public expenditure, formed a crucial intermediate stage between public revenue raising and the private accumulation of capital. It was an alliance of convenience between the king and his creature – 'If Colbert saw commerce as an instrument of State power,' Howard (1976: 48) comments of the famous French chancellor, 'the merchants saw State power, especially naval power, as a necessary means of increasing their commerce'. Rulers thus transferred resources from taxes on the population at large, from consumption, to the profits of those who supplied the means to wage war. However, as the scale and costs of war-making rose, rulers were obliged increasingly to involve the population at large, or its dignitaries, in voluntarily accepting the burden, encouraging the people even to rejoice, if possible, in being allowed the privilege of paying to fight the king's enemies, of making a contribution to the heroic national enterprise. By these means, the mass of the inhabitants came to be invited to join what had hitherto been a privileged minority, the 'nation'. As we shall see, the induction involved not just contributing taxes, but in becoming soldiers and in the militarisation of civil society, a perverse reversion to an archaic form, the Sparta of ancient Greece – 'perhaps,' Keegan observes (1993: 243), 'no society known to historians has ever better perfected the warrior system'.

This chapter seeks to describe how the war-making system created in Northwestern Europe forced each ruler into a particular mode of rule, how the external context obliged each prince to reorganise the domestic regime of the state and create a separate national economy with the capacity to generate not only the resources to sustain the changing scale and quality of the drive to war, but also the equipment and supplies to do so. These were the two ends of the spectrum, war-making and capital accumulation, but in between came the inhabitants, the victims and the subjects of these violent processes, often consistently opposed to the perpetual changes required and the apparently limitless appetites of the state. To achieve the final end, rulers had finally to invent a nation out of the inhabitants, to imbue in each mind a loyalty which would deliver up the resources to fight and the soldiers to do it, to make apparently unlimited sacrifices to the state. From this beginning, the whole world was conquered by the standard form of the modern state.

ORIGINS

In the year 1000, European governance was composed of a wide variety of competing and overlapping jurisdictions – princes of immensely different standing and powers, from emperors to petty local potentates, religious foundations and orders, associations (urban and trade leagues), military orders, city communes and more. Loyalties for secular rulers were usually divided in many different directions and personal to particular lords. For the mass of the population, loyalty was not required, only obedience. The princes thus ruled with ambivalent and qualified powers, shaped by complex and contradictory custom and changing practice as well as by the particular personality of the ruler concerned, rather than any institutional attributes. The land ruled was virtually a personal possession – 'A kingdom,' writes Rosenberg (1958: 5), 'like any estate endowed with elements of governmental authority, was the private concern of its owner'. In the royal domains, the officials of the ruler – what was to become the nucleus of the bureaucracy of government as well as the personal servants of the palace – pursued first and foremost the interests of the prince (and his private interest was coterminous with – if such a separate distinction could have even been conceived – the public interest). By contrast, in the city-state, the citizens and staff of the city authority owed loyalty to an institution, a communal entity.

Carving out of this complexity single unified and sovereign regimes, independent of the changing person of the ruler, with a complementary institutional structure and a systematic financial basis, was an extraordinarily long and tormented process. The character and will of particular rulers played a decisive role, interacting with the responses and initiatives of rivals at home and abroad, the domestic balance of power and the vagaries of harvests, of flood and famine, not to mention a great deal of luck.

England in the eleventh century, by the 'accident' of a conquest (and its island isolation) which overrode the complexities of inherited rights and privileges, was fashioned by its Norman conquerors as one of the most centralised kingdoms in Europe. Within a century, another group of Normans went even further in this respect in creating the Kingdom of the Two Sicilies of Frederick II (1194–1250) with a bureaucracy and a tax basis to sustain it. These rationalisations took place fortunately on the margins of the European system and in relatively small principalities, so the full effects in terms of war-making in the heartlands of the continent were damped down. The casualties were felt in neighbouring France and southern Italy. Nonetheless, domestic rationalisation – and permanent reform – was sooner or later forced upon the more important contenders for power. Yet to rationalise the tax take on a poor agrarian population enhanced revenues but still produced a poor yield.

There were other sources of revenue. Parallel to the territorial princes, there had already emerged, as we have seen, concentrations of private wealth in the trading city-states, pre-eminently at this time in northern Italy. Often the revenues generated from trade were, relative to the income of kings, enormous. For example, the freight charges levied by Venice to carry the Crusaders to Constantinople in 1203 were double the size of the then annual revenues of the King of England. By the mid-fifteenth century, the annual income of Venice was said to be 60 per cent higher than those of the French Crown (at a time when the size of the population of France was ten times that of Venice) (Tilly 1990: 143n.).

The wealth of the Italian cities flowed into the hands of bankers and thus was put to the task of financing the territorial rulers. But the capacity to borrow, the costs, partly related to how far the monarch could guarantee servicing and repayment, how far the tax system was effective and under direct control (as opposed to dispersed among tax farmers). By the fourteenth century, Western European rulers had undertaken to put the fiscal basis of the state under their direct control and create a nascent bureaucracy to organise revenue collection. In this they copied the pioneer – and rival – in raising dispersed revenues, the church.

In comparable fashion, rulers found it necessary to supersede their dependence upon the private recruitment of troops by subsidiary lords, and create forces directly loyal to the monarch. With this process came the long struggle to eliminate or subordinate all other centres of armed power – to establish the exclusive royal monopoly of arms. To seal the relationship between the troops and the ruler, they had to be paid, vastly expanding the role of the public exchequer. Since the rhythms of war rarely followed the cycles of tax-collection (and harvests), borrowing became important to negotiate the gaps in income flows. Some princes supplemented their incomes from taxes through charges on trade – as we have seen the counts of Champagne did this in holding their great fairs.

Making taxation effective required uniformity and transparency, knowing who owned what and what the relative yield of land and the income of cultivators was. This required a codified legal system under the exclusive direction of the crown. The standardisation of coinage through the lands of the rulers was a similar necessary reform, creating a single tax area; under Louis IX of France, the number of separate currencies was cut from 300 to 30 between 1265 and 1300 (Spruyt 1994: 162). The same is true of the standardisation of weights and measures – as North (in Tracy 1991: 22) comments: 'The way weights and measures will be devised will be with the objective of maximising the ruler's income. The history of weights and measures makes sense only if we recognise the priority of the ruler's interest.'

THE MILITARY REVOLUTION

In the fifteenth century, a series of innovations in military technology and the organisation of warfare immensely increased the pressures on rulers to raise resources. New forms of artillery, using cannon balls, began to make city walls and castles vulnerable to destruction, one of the important factors in making possible the unification of France and the swift military progress of Charles V through Italy (1494) – 'a true revolution in war-making', according to Keegan (1993: 321). There were other innovations – socket bayonets replaced pikes, the matchlock musket the flintlock, with the development of a pre-packaged cartridge – all of which raised the firepower of infantry and the vulnerability of cavalry. Armies and navies were much larger, the concentration of massed firepower much more deadly – provided the unruly troops could be drilled to move in massed formations. But it was not worth drilling an army of changing peasant lads, only for a cadre of regular soldiers with some measure of technical proficiency, a standing army. Accordingly, 'we find rulers striving to exact payment rather than military service from their vassals and other subjects in order to prepare themselves for war. This became a prime cause of the development – or at least the more frequent convocation – of assemblies of the estates, parliaments, *etats-generaux* and *landtages*' (Hintze 1975: 193).

As the costs rose, so more innovations in royal tax organisation took place and increased sums demanded. The growth in trade of the merchants in some of the leading countries offered new sources of revenue. From the fourteenth century, in England under Edward III, levies on trade became significant sources of royal revenues – by 1500, nearly half of government revenue came from this source. As we saw in the last chapter, the Portuguese crown went very much further in seeking to exploit trade to this end, only to be outpaced by the Dutch warrior-merchants.

The English monarchs, as we have seen, also granted monopolies to their selected merchant companies – making them targets for royal taxes and levies. This empowered the trading company to exercise royal prerogatives of naval power at sea, as armed privateers. On the other side, the granting of royal privilege bound the merchants into some national loyalty, offsetting for some (depending on the profit rate) the temptations of cosmopolitanism. It might be cheaper and more efficient to buy from foreign merchants, but they were less accessible to taxation, more mobile in escape.

Monopoly was thus a key means to try to keep traders loyal to the crown, to subsidise the high risks of trade, particularly of armed trade. Merchants, insofar as they agreed to these arrangements, now became important instruments of royal power and national military ambitions. Royal monopoly, however, was only one of several means to seek to shift the balance of international economic advantage to the crown and to its favoured merchants, summed up in the doctrines grouped under the label 'mercantilism'. All were driven by the needs of royal revenue and warfare – in the words of the famous statesman to the king of France, Jean Baptiste Colbert (1619–87) 'trade is the source of finance, and finance is the vital nerve of war' (Carr 1983 in Held 1985: 137).

Mercantilism embodied no coherent vindication or theory of the economy. It was simply the 'common-sense' of those who identified with the crown, identifying the strength and prosperity of the state as the same as, insofar as anyone considered the matter, that of the welfare of the population. Indeed the state was made the object and the subject of economic policy, sacrificing, if need be, the wellbeing of the population at large to the accumulation of the power of the prince. It defied the logic of capitalism, of a world economy, seeking to discriminate consistently against foreigners even – indeed, especially – if their goods were cheaper. The approach is ancient – as we saw in the complaint in the last chapter from Pliny the Elder at Rome's imports from the east. William Stafford in the England of the sixteenth century reacts with similar sentiment concerning English wool exports to Europe, which were turned into cloth and then exported back to England (an early version of the vindication for import substitution): 'What grossness be we of, that see it and suffer such continual spoil to be made of our goods and treasures...They must make us pay at the end for our stuff again...whereas with working the same within our Realm, our own men should be set to work at the charge of strangers' (1581 in Ruben 1979: 44–45).

Political rulers thus defied both the logic of a world division of labour and the interests of capitalism at large, favouring a particular selection of national capitalists, an alliance between state and, to use a modern term, 'crony' business. They discriminated against imports (as the attack of foreigners) and foreign business. It was assumed that there was a fixed supply of wealth in the world, embodied in gold and silver, and the aim of exporting was to get as large a share of this as possible and to hoard the precious metals as the embodiment of economic power – in the conclusions of Mun (1664 in Irwin 1996: 35): 'The ordinary means therefore to increase our wealth and treasure is by foreign trade, wherein we must ever observe this rule: to sell more to strangers yearly than we consume of theirs in value'. Armed power was a supportive instrument to help the traders of one's own nation to secure a favourable outcome. England's Navigation Acts of the mid-seventeenth century (supported, incidentally, by that supposedly free trader Adam Smith) embodied the ambition to expand English exports and cut imports from all territories except English colonies (backed by adequate naval power to enforce the will of the state) – the 'twin goals of strategic power and economic wealth through shipping and colonial monopolies' (Wilson 1967: 520–21). This is the programmatic origin of the first frontiers with their customs posts, of periodic bans on exports (to conserve domestic resources) and on imports (to protect local production, even if at higher cost), and the core concern, to maximise the inflow of gold into the exchequer of the king. As France's Henry IV put it, the control of trade was 'the only way to stop transporting out of our Kingdom gold and silver to enrich our neighbours' (in Braudel II 1982: 545). Running through the strategy was the attempt to secure self-sufficiency, an invulnerability to foreign economic attack. It was not something in which merchants, left to themselves, would have had an interest, since they lacked the power to enforce a monopoly, the other side of the coin to self-sufficiency. They would care only for the market with the highest rate of return. England's Chancellor Robert Cecil in 1599 explained the motive for his ban on the export of copper and bronze: 'principally...that Her Majesty and the Realm might be served in that commodity to make ordinance and necessaries rather than stand to the courtesy of strangers [to supply them]' (Hale 1985: 215).

The justification of the programme was not the accumulation of capital of those capitalists selected for favour – that was an incidental by-product – but the building of state power. As Schmoller (1931: 43) notes, in its innermost kernel, (mercantilism) is nothing but State-making. The essence of the system lies not in some doctrine of money, or of the balance of trade; not in tariff barriers, protective duties or navigation-laws; but in something far greater, namely in the total transformation of society and its organisation, as well as of the State and its institutions.

Free trade would have increased aggregate wealth faster, but not necessarily in the hands of the state and its immediate clients.

The heart of the national industrial system was the making of arms and naval vessels, what ultimately became heavy industry. These were made to government order and under government supervision, sometimes in government factories. The inputs to arms-making were similarly controlled, from heavy industry to mining to growing and cutting the trees for raw material; exports were prevented and the price of purchase fixed. Thus, the French kings developed the first of the largest arms factories in the early sixteenth century at Nancy, with furnaces, forges, cannon foundries, gun-powder mills and saltpetre shops. We have noted earlier one of the most famous examples of this in the Venetian Arsenal. Rivals imitated the initiative – Sweden, Russia's Peter the Great, the United Provinces and England. By 1642, it is said, Sweden and England produced nearly half the iron made in Europe (Nef 1950: 80). Yet even with this autarky, so great was the demand for arms, an important international trade grew up, supplied especially where the nationalism of the territorial princes was weakest, from the north Italian cities and from the cities of Flanders.

Nonetheless, the cost inexorably grew, driven by the scale, the frequency and the longevity of wars. Take as one example the dimensions of armies. Between the eleventh and fifteenth centuries few armies were larger than 10–12,000 men in size (the Spanish armies that tried to reconquer the Netherlands in the 1560s were about 9000 foot soldiers and 1600 horsemen). Henry V of England at his famous victory at Agincourt fielded barely 6,000 men (Nef 1950: 91). By the time of the French Huguenot wars of the sixteenth century, there were perhaps 10–15,000 on each side (Van Creveld 1977: 5) – 'the price of independence was becoming very high indeed,' according to Howard (1976: 22). During the Thirty Years War in the seventeenth century, the combatants started out with armies of about 30,000, but in the bitter and increasingly brutal struggle for mastery – laying waste much of Germany – sizes rose to the extraordinary level of 100,000 on each side (Nef 1950: 92). Furthermore, the technology and training of troops required that they be professional, not peasant conscripts, and only mercenaries met this need quickly, but again the costs were vastly increased. By the 1670s, Louis XIV, the most powerful monarch in Europe, put in the field against the Dutch 120,000, and began to develop a standing army of 150,000. In the words of Tallett (1992: 199), the State consistently fielded numbers of men larger than it could support and administer, provoking frenetic administrative innovations, including the use of intendants and commissaries to speed the collection of taxes, and *intendants d'armee, commissaries de guerre* and *controleurs* to supervise the supply of troops, their payment, discipline, billeting and movement.

Furthermore, there were expensive problems of supply. By the early seventeenth century, armies of mercenaries on the march were too large to live off the land. Even more, troops who were obliged to forage for food or steal it were poor fighters. They occasionally starved and thus were prone to mutiny or to desert. To guarantee the fighting capacity of the warriors required the ruler to guarantee food supplies and clothing as well as arms and ammunition. That required draught animals – horses or oxen – to haul the supplies from warehouse to field, but then the animals themselves had to be fed if the war efforts were to be sustainable. Van Creveld (1977) estimates one wagon, pulled by between two and four horses, was needed to supply every 15 men. With heavy artillery, the costs were even higher: the largest cannon, five-and-a-half tonnes, required 30 horses to pull; six half cannons with 100 rounds of ammunition each needed 250 horses. On a long march, stocks had to be sited along the route, except that where mobility and surprise were a key to success this gave away the battle plan. An extended season of hostilities exaggerated the logistic problems – Louis XIV's 1672 army of 120,000 had to be supplied in central Germany and the Netherlands. Van Creveld calculates that the typical army of the seventeenth century – 60,000 men and 40,000 horse – required two pounds of bread per-capita, or 120, 000 pounds per day, with 60,000 pounds of other foodstuffs, and 20 pounds per horse (or 800,000 pounds for the army), a total of 980,000 pounds to be delivered daily if the soldiers were to fight with a will. Long sieges were a nightmare for the quartermasters.

They were not a nightmare for the suppliers, but an opportunity to excel and to profit. Provisions for the military (or, at this time, the more important navy) offered a vastly enhanced and concentrated demand that was decisive in the growth of the businesses involved. With standing armies and permanent garrisons, demand became increasingly stable, a source of permanent enrich-ment for that cluster of private interests privileged enough to be selected by the ruler. Thus a whole complex of elements came to constitute the core of the nascent national capitalist class – bankers, receivers of interest on loans to the crown, providers of transport and horse, of bulk purchases of textiles (uniforms, blankets, tents, pennants), of horse equipment (leather, harnesses etc), of arms and ammunition, of food and drink; and beyond them, those manning heavy industry, shipbuilding and servicing, mining. Orders for supplies had an exaggerated effect on particular localities – for example, orders for shoes on

England's Northampton, or for bricks and quarried materials for fortresses (Lille in the late 1660s provided to the French Crown 60 million bricks and three-and-a-half million quarry stones [Tallett 1992: 38]). The effect of government purchases on the marketed surplus and on the expansion of capacity would have been much greater. Supplies to the crown, particularly in time of war, constituted a major force in expanding the economy and in the process of capital accumulation, and on a narrowly restricted national basis. Furthermore, they affected the capacity for large-scale production and management – 'military organisation was,' Steensgaard (in Parker and Smith 1978: 38–39) observes, 'one of the century's most advanced forms of enterprise: fortresses, navies and royal palaces constitute the century's biggest efforts in planning and organising, and its most precious investment'.

The gains were not simply those recorded, for there was also immense corruption in the transactions and transfers. For example, a fifth to a quarter of the monies transferred to pay armies in the field in the fifteenth and sixteenth centuries disappeared in the 'networks of peculation' (Hale 1985: 209) – 'shots, cries, the trudge of marching feet: the sound most prominent in the economic historian's ears is that of the greasing of palms' (Hale 1985: 210).

To reverse this loss required a programme of civil-service reforms to create a dedicated cadre of professional officials, not available until late in the nineteenth century. But before then those close to the crown might, without immense effort, become immeasurably wealthy. When England's Henry VIII nationalised the monasteries, part of the project of building national royal power, he made available an immense swath of rich lands with which to reward his supporters (thereby creating a powerful new social interest in defence of the king and his new national religious order), much as did the waves of nationalisations in the twentieth century in post-independence developing countries – both implementing the 'national project' and creating a class of loyal clients. More broadly, the actions of the prince created immense opportunities for private advancement (Ertman 1997: 321–22):

> the creation and expansion of administrative and financial institutions represents a unique opportunity for personal and familial enrichment and social aggrandisement because it inevitably involves the extraction of wealth from the population at large and its concentration – ostensibly for the public good – in the coffers of the State organisations. Once amassed, such wealth presents an inviting target to rent-seeking groups, be they government officers, financiers, the military, political bosses or the employees of subsidized State enterprises.

Indeed, so powerful was the economic role of the state that whole new social strata were created, reshaping the appearance and culture of society, reshaping the composition and demands of clients and lobbies.

Rulers might strive to create a national system of provision and a loyal group of capitalists to provide it, but the supply of manpower was for a time much less self-sufficient. As we have noted, the growth of the size of armies and the length of time they were required to be in the field forced the need for increasingly professional troops. When the ruler depended on peasant levies, raised by subsidiary lords, the numbers had been available, but with difficulty and between harvests – Henry VIII of England raised an astonishing 120,000 in 1548, and Edward VI made explicit the obligation on all males, aged 16 to 60, to undertake military service. To make that effective, as also the taxable capacity of the population, required an accurate record of the population, a national census; in 1544, the Swedish crown introduced an annual census to force parishes to deliver up the required number of young men. But numbers, for given seasons, were not enough. A ruler risked defeat with untrained forces facing professionals.

However, the more frequent the wars, the more warfare itself created its own manpower. The demobilised soldiers of one war became available as mercenaries for the next, much as soldiers of fortune were available for civil wars in Sub-Saharan Africa in the last quarter of the twentieth century. They were more technically qualified in the sciences of war and more experienced than most of the prince's subjects. They were usually organised by mercenary colonels acting as private contractors. In particular, the Swiss earned fame after the ending of their domestic wars for their special tactics (the pike phalanx). There were others: former soldier-citizens of the Italian city-states (organised by contractors, the *condottiere*), former troops of the royal armies of France and England who, between wars, were highwaymen and bandits, preying upon travellers; or the *landsknecht* of the German lands, a force of *ronin*, warriors without a lord, who would have been recognised in Japan after the establishment of the Tokugawa peace. Thus, for the moment, the growing nationalism of the territorial states of Europe was accompanied by dependence on both cosmopolitan banking and cosmopolitan armies.

Through an extended period, the rivalries of a number of powers led to the establishment – by force, subterfuge, fraud and bribery – of centralised orders, elements of an enforced national unity, an embryonic bureaucracy and a system of taxation. A number of rulers were particularly associated with the process – Louis XI of France, Henry VIII of England, Charles VII of Sweden, Isabella and Ferdinand of a newly restored Christian Spain, Maximilian of Austria. It was not at all inevitable, and some failed. The nobles of Poland blocked the emergence of a powerful crown, leaving the country exposed to the lamentable partitions of the eighteenth century. The principalities of Germany and of Italy resisted unification until the nineteenth century. Nor was the outcome inevitable for those powers which were apparently most wealthy – Spain might have access to the riches of its American empire but could still be defeated by the tiny Netherlands; France might bestride the continent, but Prussia and England, far smaller and poorer, might still challenge it. In the early eighteenth century, the British economy was half the size of the French, but it was able to commit nearly as much money and manpower, and raise them with much greater ease. Partly, superiority came from relatively easy access to capital – in the mid-seventeenth century, the Dutch republic raised a million florins on the domestic money market in two days, something impossible for, say, Prussia (Tilly 1990: 90 ref.). Partly it came from enthusiasm – the English Civil War demonstrated that those inspired with politico-religion, the meritocratic New Model Army, were superior to mercenaries (though this showed also the dangers of a politicised army). Partly it was organisation and discipline, creating the Prussian ideal of a military automaton, a 'clockwork army' based upon an educated officer cadre (military schools were being established throughout Europe). Partly it was the result of the organisation of the whole of society to support the army and navy – in relatively impoverished and unpopulated Sweden, the kings militarised society (and inspired both Prussia under Frederick I and Russia under Peter the Great to follow suit). The country was divided into eight military regions, each responsible for raising and maintaining one or more regiments, to reach an army of 40,000 (or 2.7 per cent of the 1.5 million population). Later in the century, farms were grouped to support one fighting man, to farm his land while he was absent – and to be punished if he deserted. The economic burden on a poor agriculture must have been barely tolerable.

Up to the seventeenth century, there is perhaps nothing unique in the developments of Northwestern Europe, nothing in which there are not parallels elsewhere in the world. But the outline of something peculiar was beginning to appear, and it was embodied in the relationship of private capital to the state, and in particular in the economic role of the state. The relationships are most perceptively summarised in a famous formulation in the middle of the nineteenth century by the founder of economic history, Karl Marx (1996: 739):

> The different moments of primitive accumulation can be assigned in particular to Spain, Portugal, Holland, France and England, in more or less chronological order. These different moments are systematically combined together at the end of the seventeenth century in England; the combination embraces the colonies, the national debt, the modern tax system, and the system of protection. These methods depend in part on brute force, for instance, the colonial system. But they all employ the power of the State, the concentrated and organised force of society, to hasten, as in a hothouse, the process of transformation of the feudal mode of production into the capitalist mode, and to shorten the transition. Force is the midwife of every old society which is pregnant with a new one. It is itself an economic power.

As we suggested in the last chapter, Marx was wrong to see what was emerging as the capitalist system, but he was most perceptive – and hardly consistent with other of his formulations – in identifying the decisive role of the state, rather than the class of private businessmen.

However, despite all, the cosmopolitan temptations of the system were not defeated. Merchants, as from time immemorial, continued to trade where profit led, to stimulate manufacturing, mining and commercial agriculture wherever they landed and, insofar as they could, evaded or cheated on the regulations of a mercantile state. The Spanish crown could not defend its monopoly of trade with its American possessions – dozens of foreign traders regularly traded illegally (and the Spanish American subjects of the king traded with equal enthusiasm). The British found it no less impossible to keep their American colonists to themselves. Freebooters ran rife in British India, despite the official monopoly of the East India Company, shipping their earnings in the late eighteenth century through Copenhagen and other clandestine routes into Britain.

Furthermore, despite the efforts of rulers to keep population and capital within the emerging borders, many escaped the economic straitjacket that the state sought to weave. Skilled workers, particularly in armaments and shipbuilding, fled or were wooed by the agents of foreign rulers. And capitalists who felt unjustly treated could also move. Hall (1986: 132) comments on the apparently immensely powerful Spanish king: 'time and again, Phillip II wanted to behave like an autocrat but the mobility of capital defeated him... and [the capitalist] could go elsewhere to a stable State, that is, from a rapacious State to a long-lasting and organic State somewhere in the larger society'. As in so many things, the Jewish community provided a model for the wandering capitalist.

A NEW WORLD ORDER

In the eighteenth century, some leading European governments were beginning to emerge as world powers, based now upon a national capitalism. This had institutionalised systematic innovation and thus the capacity to revolutionise the forms of production and unlock virtually unlimited wealth. But it was wealth devoted at its core to the enhancement of national sovereignty and the armed power of the state.

In this period, the ruler's armed forces came to constitute a separate warrior society, with its own living quarters, religion, health services, law, judiciary, military supply system. It remained, however, like the nation, the creature of the ruler – as Hintze (1906/1975: 200–201) describes it:

It was an instrument of the monarch, not an institution of the country. It was created as a tool of power politics in the foreign sphere, but at the same time, it served to maintain and extend the sovereign's power at home. Any resistance to this vast royal instrument of power became impossible in the country. The army embodied most clearly and palpably the new idea of the State – that of the powerfully centralised absolutist State.

The century also saw emerge, more sharply perhaps than ever before, two prototypes of the warring state. The first, unquestionably the most popular among Europe's rulers up until the Napoleonic wars, was founded upon the extraordinary military authoritarianism of Prussia. The second, for those with eyes to see, was founded upon the idea of a popular war – of the urban Nederlanders against the restoration of Spanish imperial rule; of the New Model Army in England's civil war; and, above all, of the irregular warriors, the guerrillas on horseback, of the American colonists against British imperialism (the War of Independence, begun as a rebellion by the colonists against paying for the wars of the British crown). Those in the future, with the benefit of hindsight, might also have inserted in this roll of honour the guerrilla warfare in Corsica against the French in 1768–69 (all fit male Corsicans, aged 16 to 60, were pledged to fight the French to the death), perhaps the stuff of the inspired dreams of the Corsican child, Napoleon.

For much of the eighteenth century, however, Europe's princes were dazzled exclusively by the Prussian model. This involved, as we noted earlier, the complete militarisation of society, creating an obedient well-drilled military machine, ever prepared to die for the king. The model was a tribute to the power of organisation and culture rather than resources, for the territories of Brandenburg–Prussia were poor compared to their rivals.

The Prussian Model

As we noted earlier, the social-military model of Sweden preceded that of Prussia. The Swedes under Gustavus Adolphus occupied Prussia (during the Thirty Years War), a founding demonstration for the Prussian ruler, the Great Elector of Brandenburg–Prussia, Frederick William (1620–88) of the military, administrative and financial unpreparedness of his lands. Equally, it demonstrated the efficacy of those reforms that Prussia won a great victory over Sweden at Fehrbellin in June 1675. The Elector's programme involved the reform of the army, of the economy and of Prussian society. One of his first targets, pursued by him and his successors, was to turn the Prussian gentry, the Junkers, into a pliable military instrument: 'I win the authority of the Junkers,' he proclaimed, 'and build my sovereignty like a rock of bronze' (Hintze

1906/1975: 48). Exploiting their temporary weakness, he rode roughshod over their rights, tying them effectively to their lands. Their sons were removed at an early age to undergo full-time military education. They were forbidden to serve a foreign government (a treasonable offence) or, without permission, travel abroad – on pain of the confiscation of their property (Corvisier 1979: 90). Any who acquired an education abroad was prohibited from working for the state. The rewards of reform were bequeathed to his successors – through army service from a young age, the aristocracy was turned into a state cadre as effective as, centuries later, the Communist parties.[3] By the second half of the eighteenth century, one in four of the Prussian nobility had served in the armed forces, and military uniform had become the daily mark of noble status – and obedience to the crown. Indeed, in almost all armies – in Russia, in Austria, in France – the male aristocracy had now moved to wearing a standard uniform, the sign of a drilled collective and of obedience, as compared to the sixteenth century warrior, who gloried in the diversity of his clothes, seized as loot (the outer garments slashed to reveal the expensive silks within).

A parallel programme of reform was the reorganisation of society, again riding roughshod over the prerogatives of local government to institute, on the original Swedish model, cantonal conscription and permanent and effective taxation to support the military. The creation of a standing army was the central aim here, as an 'iron hoop' to hold together the scattered dependencies of the crown (Hintze 1906/1975: 46). There was considerable opposition – 'The Ständestaat politicians regarded regular regiments as the continuation of war in time of peace, as the core of an emerging dynastic-military dictatorship and hence, as a monstrous innovation'(Rosenberg 1958: 36–37). Once created, the army, its bureaucracy and finance, became the heart of the state – 'Prussia,' Minister von Schrötter observed, 'was not a country with an army but an army with a country which served as the headquarters and food magazine' (Rosenberg 1958: 43). Powerful war commissars, with associated tax officers and regents of the central government, dominated the country. Their role was to sustain the militarisation of society, ensuring obedience to the chief drillmaster, Frederick William and his successors. He bequeathed to his successor the simple message: 'Have money and a good army; they ensure the glory and safety of a prince'(Gaxotte 1942: 18).

'The institutional framework,' Craig (1955: 14) notes, 'the economic activity and even the social organisation of Prussia was determined in large part by the needs of the army'. And under Frederick the Great (1688–1740), 'The army now moulded the State to its needs; it was now the principal obstacle to political or social change of any kind' (Craig 1955: 19). The crown promoted arms manufacture, foundries and engineering works on the basis of local iron ore deposits.

However, the overall system did not have the same effects as occurred in Britain and France: there was only a weak local business class to exploit the opportunities. Many other powers were, at the same time, seeking to reshape the domestic economy for the purposes of warfare – promoting the manufacture of arms and shipbuilding (best known in the case of Russia).

However, the demands of military service threatened to deprive the civil economy of manpower and thus the resources to sustain the army. In the eighteenth century, the king became increasingly dependent upon mercenary troops, on impressing prisoners of war and kidnapping foreigners in order to protect the domestic labour supply – 'useful hardworking people should be guarded,' the king decreed, 'as the apple of one's eye, and wartime recruits should be levied on one's own country only when the bitterest necessity compels' (Werke VI 1913–14: 226–7 in Craig 1955: 23). By 1804, half the army consisted of mercenary troops.

The immediate military effects were impressive. Not only was the size of the Prussian army – based on a relatively small and poor population – pushed up to what would have seemed earlier insupportable levels, its offensive power was spectacular. The number of troops rose from 4650 in 1640 to 45,000 in 1672 (Black 1994: 100), and then in the next century to 83,000 (the fourth largest in Europe, for a country the tenth largest in territory and thirteenth in population). Furthermore, the discipline and drill of the army made it the object of envy of all Europe's rulers – it possessed a collective flexibility and precision never before seen.

However, the army – like Prussian society – depended upon peasant bondage, a quasi-serfdom, sustained by ferocious Junker domination and savage punishments. It created a 'fearful obedience to authority' (Rosenberg 1958: 49). At its peak, the armies raised more than 4 per cent of the population for military service. As firepower rose and became more accurate, the casualties increased, so that recruitment had to be intensified; in the one year of 1759, during the Seven Years War (1756–63), Prussia lost 60,000 men. With such a cruel regime and the increasing risk of death, the rate of desertion was accordingly high – 30,216 between 1713 and 1740. The penalty for desertion was death, so those in flight were obliged to emigrate.

More decisively, at its moment of test the army and the Prussian model failed. Napoleon inflicted a terrible defeat on Prussian arms at Jena and then at Auerstadt in 1806. More terrible still for the ruler was the fact that the populace and the local officials in Berlin and other Prussian towns welcomed the French conqueror as a blessed relief from the Hohenzollerns, and agreed to work for him. Under the settlement reached with Napoleon at Tilsit in 1807, Frederick William III lost half his territory and citizens, paid a heavy indemnity and was obliged to pay for the French army of occupation. Terror had failed before revolutionary enthusiasm.

The lessons were not lost on the officials advising the king. Indeed, the experience of the Napoleonic defeat transformed military thinking, nowhere more so than in the mind of the military theorist who laid down the principles of warfare for the next century and a half, the Prussian officer von Clausewitz. The reformers who came to power in Prussia in 1807 wanted to create a popular state and army, to secure the voluntary adherence of the population. Minister Baron von Stein, writing after his first audience with the king in August, reminded himself that 'The chief idea was to arouse a moral, religious and patriotic spirit in the nation, to instil into it again courage, confidence, readiness for every sacrifice, on behalf of independence from foreigners and for the national honour, and to seize the first favourable opportunity to begin the bloody and hazardous struggle' (Craig 1955: 40). The lesson was correct, but carrying it out required a radical transformation of the social structure to establish an order which was worth defending – one not based upon serfdom, on the exclusive and unchallengeable civil rights of the nobility, on an absence of any participation. Indeed, perhaps the agony of this crisis led to Prussia producing some of the leading philosophers of nationalism – from Herder to Hegel.

As for the reforms, the military resisted, and Napoleon, recognising the danger, obliged the Prussian king to abandon Stein not much over a year after he was appointed. By the time of the defeat of Napoleon, the panic was over and the reformers could be driven out. Prussia would have to await the revolutions of 1848 to make even some gestures at reform towards a popular monarchy and army.

In its time, however, the Prussian model was immensely influential – in France, Russia, Austria – even down to the systems of drill and tactics. Between 1764 and 1785, the British sent observers each year to report on Prussian manoeuvres, and the 1786 British military drill regulations were based upon the Prussian version.

Meanwhile, the size of the contending armies grew. Thus the military forces of Austria increased through the eighteenth century – from 157,000 in 1740 to 307,000 in 1783 – with an effective peacetime strength of 171,000. The emperors were obliged to initiate financial and administrative reforms to underpin this expansion. Reforms in the military establishment ended the private ownership of regiments, enhanced the professionalism of the officer cadres, and opened its ranks to those without aristocratic birth (creating a 'service nobility', those who acquired titles through military service).

Until the nineteenth century, control of water routes – navigable rivers, canals or the high seas – was as crucial for the movement of troops as for commerce. Thus, for much of the later medieval period, power – and commerce – depended upon naval firepower. The greatest powers sought to command the seas – as the Venetians had done in the Mediterranean, the Portuguese had tried to do in the Indian Ocean. By the eighteenth century, the growth and reform of land forces was paralleled by the expansion and improvement in sea power. England and Britain, which aimed, with ultimate success, to create the largest fleet in Europe, expanded its navy from 24 ships (with 6290 men) in 1578, to 156 (with 19,551) in 1660; 313 (and 48,072) in 1710; 432 (and 84,797) in 1762; to over 1000 (and 142,098) in 1810 (Duffy 1980: 82). It was not simply the growth in numbers. Ships grew in size. In 1720, only two warships operating were of more than 3000 tonnes; by 1815, a fifth of all ships over 500 tonnes were in this class (Black 1994: 197). Furthermore, the firepower per ship, and its accuracy, were immensely expanded and improved. By the later years of the century, only Britain, France and Spain could face the escalation in costs. When the French finally dropped out of the race, the British attained a position of unrivalled supremacy (with, it is said, half the European fleet). Seapower was to be the key to territorial empire in the following century.

The military competition of the eighteenth century was financially ruinous unless the national economy was already robust and the administration capable of identifying and capturing revenues. The size of armies and navies came to exceed what was considered to be either financially tolerable or logistically manageable. Three quarters of the revenues of France's Louis XIV had gone to finance present wars or past war debts. His successor, with a considerably expanded income, paid an even higher proportion – 26 per cent of public expenditure was devoted to current military spending and 49 per cent to service debts on past wars (Goubert 1973: 137). Ultimately, the credit of the state was ruined, forcing the king to summon the Estates General to secure some financial settlement – thus setting in train that sequence of events that not only destroyed the monarchy but released the genie of popular national power (Tilly 1990: 74).

France was one of the largest and richest powers in Europe. By rights, that should have settled the military issue in terms of resources – Quesnay (in Milward 1977: xii) puts it like this: 'It is wealth … which upholds the honour of armies … it is in the constant affluence of a country's tax payers, not in patriotic virtues, that the permanent power of the State is to be found'.

But Quesnay omitted here the capacity of the state to lay hands on the affluence, to tax and do so without appearing to be intolerably unjust or arbitrary. It is here that the English (and subsequently the British), despite being poorer and, in population terms, much smaller than France, had an advantage. But still the costs rose fearfully – between 1700 and 1815 public spending increased fifteen times over, and the armed forces (army and navy) share (to pay for current wars and debts on past wars) varied between 78 (1700) and 95 per cent (1801) (Mann 1988: 107). In the 127 years between 1688 and 1815, the country was engaged in major wars for roughly 70 years.

At the end, the Napoleonic wars obliged the British to maintain in 1801 350,000 men under arms (and at various times finance its allies: Portugal, Savoy, Denmark, Hesse-Cassel, Austria, Prussia, Saxony, Trier), and half a million men in 1811 (that is equal to nearly a tenth of the domestic labourforce). Many more were engaged in supplying the forces with arms, clothing, foodstuffs, transport, ships and so on. The cost to the public exchequer was accordingly high – perhaps equal to half national expenditure. Indeed for the half century up to 1830, government consumption, the overwhelming bulk of which went to the armed forces, was larger than the value of exports, suggesting that the transition made in Britain in terms of national economic development was powerfully war-led.

However, the costs could be met and, despite much grumbling (British tax revenue rose from £18 million in 1793 to £77.9 million in 1815), without undue strain. The exchequer was not bankrupted, the monarchy not overthrown. On the contrary, the business class boomed. In particular, raising money for the state, through the miraculous mechanisms of the national debt, the Bank of England and the City of London's capital market, created a coalition of forces to back the state. Between 1786 and 1819, the national debt tripled in size to £844 million. The mechanism provided a new means of raising money from, and guaranteeing the future income of, the wealthiest classes, a vast increase in banking and financial transactions available to finance trade, manufacturing and agriculture. But it also created a rentier class that underpinned the position of the landed and the leisured classes of the nineteenth century (providing a means by which a newly wealthy business class could enter the nobility) and a growing market for the output of the new economy.

Furthermore, it sustained a period of the most rapid economic expansion and transformation – the creation of the world's first 'developed' national economy. As Hobsbawm (1965: 147) notes, but without pinpointing the economic role of war,

> The industrial revolution was generated in these decades – after the 1740s when this massive but slow growth in the domestic economies combined with the rapid – after 1750, extremely rapid – expansion of the international economy; and it occurred in the country which seized the international opportunities to corner a major share of overseas markets

The economy developed – through the expansion of empire, courtesy of the armed merchants and imperial power, increasing agricultural productivity and the incomes to purchase the output of farmer and landlord, increasing trade. All were elements, but there was also the unprecedented growth of the state and the economic effects of its military and naval spending.

The military economy also forced the rate of technical innovation as well as generating scale production and economies. The Wilkinson cannon-boring machine made possible Watt's steam engine. The military demand for high-grade iron ore affected the output and quality of the metal fabricating industries. The demand for military uniforms stimulated the creation of the spinning jenny and of mass production of standardised cloth.

There were also social implications. The Prussian method of war led inevitably to high desertion rates. Between 1755 and 1757, of the 70,000 recruits to the British army 12,700 (or 18 per cent) deserted, compared to 142 who were killed and 13,000 who became sick. In the American War of Independence, of the 175,990 recruited (1774–80), 1243 were killed, 18,545 died of disease and 42,069 (or 24 per cent) deserted. Only with the galvanisation of popular incentives and an improvement in pay and conditions (treating the soldier as a patriotic adult) could the desertion rate be reduced.

Some of the first efforts to preserve those who were recruited to the colours went to trying to reduce the sickness rate. Illness could disband an army or a navy without a shot fired. A third of the British force invading Havana in 1742 went down to yellow fever and malaria. Scurvy, typhus, yellow fever, malaria and dysentery decimated armies much more effectively than cannon and shot. The first large-scale attempts to remedy this came in the second half of the eighteenth century, the first large hospitals for naval ratings and the introduction of the first preventive measures (for example varying the diet of sailors). For the king's soldiers and sailors, it was necessary to begin to introduce something of a small welfare state, at least while they stood to the colours, to guarantee their fighting capacity. When whole peoples came to constitute armies, the state would extend protection to all.

In sum, then, the reaction of the rulers of Europe to systemic competition forced the reorganisation of domestic taxation and finance to sustain perpetual warfare on land and at sea. All to some degree embarked on this enterprise, to create national economies with the domestic means to wage war. The wisest – or luckiest – created or fostered the social means to achieve this end, a national business or capitalist class with the capacity not only to exploit the opportunities provided by the state but the means to make it more effective than it would have been if left only to the state (as in Prussia). However, the Napoleonic case shows the weakness of even the creation of a reformed army and a national capitalism in social isolation. The means might be there to fight, to buy and bribe allies, but the Prussian model could not defeat the French, a nation willingly under arms. Iron discipline, based upon terror, could not defeat iron self-discipline based upon revolutionary commitment. A national society needed to be invented to back a national capitalism.

NAPOLEON: A NATION AT WAR

The American War of Independence might provoke rejoicing among Britain's enemies (particularly Louis XV of France), but it could not affect the balance of power in Europe, nor the principles of military tactics and strategy. These were revolutionised at this stage only by events in Europe, and specifically by nearly two decades of French revolutionary and Napoleonic wars (1793–1815). Here for the first time in a great power – perhaps in the eighteenth century the greatest power in Europe – the monster of popular nationalism was released both to terrify the crowned heads of the continent and to inspire the more thoughtful to glimpse the immense military strength of a mobilised nation. 'France' was no longer just a monarch and his nobles, a small minority of the inhabitants of the country, but an entire population. War was no longer a matter of rulers and their officers scrabbling for taxes or being obliged to stoop to the indignity of borrowing, nor of bullying sullen peasant lads or indifferent mercenaries to fight. The national state could now in principle penetrate every pocket and every heart. The change was explosive, and it transformed how people understood society as well as the nature of warfare, the logistics and the finance, making possible the astonishing sacrifices of the French soldiers and citizens.

Such mass enthusiasm for the purposes of the state reflected an unlikely popular trust in the justice of those purposes. Governments were to become adept at creating and managing such enthusiasm for their own ends. Thus, paradoxically, popular nationalism both liberated the state to pursue its agenda with greater efforts, but also limited its capacity to manoeuvre, to compromise before a mass audience. But dissimulation could do much to disguise betrayals. In war, 'the great lie factory... turned out war propaganda,' as Finer (in Tilly 1975: 162) puts it. 'All was now swallowed in the extraction-persuasion cycle; not just the entire economy but the press and mass media.'[4]

The politics of revolution made it possible to overcome with ease the historic constraint on warfare, raising the men. Citizens were supposedly proud to be called upon to fight and did so in unprecedented numbers, but at costs that could be met with relative ease. The Edict of the Committee of Public Safety of August 1793 (Ellis 1974: 97) is typically uncompromising:

> until the enemies have been driven from the Republic's territory, all Frenchmen are permanently requisitioned for the service of the armies. The young men will go to fight, the married men will forge arms and make army supplies; the women will make tents and uniforms, and will serve in the hospitals; the children will shred old clothes; the old men will be taken to the public squares to excite the courage of the combatants, the hatred of royalty and the unity of the Republic.

The 'whole nation had become nobility' (Vagts 1959: 34) – or rather nearly the whole population had become the nation (there were many exclusions, not least much of the aristocracy). Von Clausewitz (1835/1968: 384–85), observing this astonishing spectacle from his Prussian barracks, could only marvel at the strange resurrection of ancient clan loyalties – full citizenship was now accorded only to those who bore arms or had done so – in a modern context:

> War had again suddenly become an affair of the people, and that of a people numbering thirty millions, every one of whom regarded himself as a citizen of the State... Henceforth, the means available – the efforts which might be called forth – had no longer any definite limits... the danger for the adversary had risen to the extreme.

By September 1794, France had 1.2 million men under arms.

The scale of warfare had changed shockingly. But also the aims and the style. The European wars of the modern period since the fourteenth century had had limited aims, to defeat the enemy, and limited effects, usually on the distribution of territory, the payment of indemnities, the acquisition of privileges. Napoleon's aim, however, was to destroy the enemy, to remove his capacity to fight again. The secret of warfare was not mobilising set-piece confrontations like rituals, but employing secrecy, surprise and mobility – which, with such giant armies, was an extraordinary accomplishment, relying wholly on the willing participation of the troops. To protect the element of surprise, there could be no obvious preparation (but rather a state of permanent preparedness), no advance supply dumps in the forward areas, and great capacity to change direction on the march. Thus the unprecedented number of troops had to forage for supplies as they moved (but now they did not desert) and avoid any delays so that supplies were not exhausted before they moved on. The armies did not bother to take the fortresses which marked Europe's frontiers since that took time, during which supplies ran out. The *élan* of the troops seemed to make such sacrifices easy to achieve – again, von Clausewitz (1835/1993: 258) marvelled (especially at the contrast with his Prussian levies):

> What an enormous contribution the heart and temper of a nation can make to the sum total of its politics, war potential and fighting strength. Now that governments have become conscious of these resources, we cannot expect them to remain unused in the future, whether the war is fought in self-defence or in order to satisfy intense ambition.

There had of course been earlier examples both of conquest to destroy opposition and of the committed dedication of the troops (the Arab armies which spread Islam from Iran to Spain were comparably inspired). The Assyrians, the Mongols, the Timurids inflicted devastation when faced with opposition. The Romans were famous for it – 'almost every year, the Romans went out and did massive violence to someone – and this regularity gives the phenomenon a pathological character' (Harris 1979: 48). But the French armies did not lay waste, only seek so to disable that an enemy would not try to fight again.

The effects of this new type of warfare would echo down the nineteenth century, the source of those radical populist reforms – from the ending of serfdom, land reform, mass education and the introduction of measures of electoral suffrage – undertaken by almost all powers to try to create nations that would be ever ready for war. Even during the wars with France, rulers were obliged to invoke popular resistance – without fundamental reform – and in defence of the crown and the old order (as in Spain, in Austria in 1809, in Russia in 1812). Administrative reform and centralisation was also implicit in the need to mobilise unprecedented resources for warfare. But above all, inventing the nation was the heart of the endeavour – to achieve the power to arm the people without, as had been understandably feared for countless generations, them turning those guns on their rulers.

However, inventing the nation turned for some more on exclusion than inclusion – the French excluded much of the aristocracy, but also minorities with other languages or dialects (Aquitanians, Bretons, Normans, Gascons, Provencals), who were obliged to become first and foremost French to be citizens. The exclusions linked the antisemitism of the Castilian monarchs to that of the Russian Tsars in the late nineteenth century and the great ethnic cleansings of the twentieth century to invent homogeneous nations, to instil some sense of unity.

However, Napoleon not only demonstrated the immense potential of popular war but also its limits. In the invasion of Russia, the Grand Army of France was pushed far beyond its enthusiasm, and there was a considerable underestimate of the popular commitment of the ordinary Russians to the defence of their country (that is, popular nationalism was possible without revolution). 600,000 were mobilised for the invasion of Russia (200,000 Frenchmen, 100,000 drawn from territories annexed by France, and the rest from elsewhere, mainly Germans). In this case, supplies were organised on an unprecedented scale, since it was not thought possible to live off the poor Russian countryside. Subsistence stocks were created for 400,000 and 50,000 horses for 50 days (one million biscuits were stored at Stettin, with immense shot and powder stocks in East Prussia). However, the armies took 82 days crossing the 600 miles to Moscow – with an average speed of 7 miles a day. The supply trains could not carry the 300 tonnes required daily. Napoleon's custom of travelling swiftly to reach supplies early failed – the Russians endeavoured to ensure that there were none. Neither enthusiasm nor staff planning could defeat the Russian winter.

Towards the end of the wars, Europe – society and economy – had been partially mobilised. The numbers of belligerents were unprecedented – in 1812 both the Russians and the Germans put in the field over one million men. The losses were equally spectacular – the French lost, all told in two decades, between 1.3 and 1.5 million men, enough to dent the country's demography in the following century. Furthermore, the domestic economies were reorganised for war. In France, production for war was concentrated to achieve the economies of standardised mass output. A giant powder factory was created to produce 300,000 pounds of powder per day, and the mass output of shells; at the end, there were immense stockpiles (Black 1994: 57). The British manufactured at least 3.2 million small arms, and ended with a stock of 743,000 serviceable muskets. New areas of heavy industry were developed – in the Ukraine, in South Wales and the West Midlands.

The Napoleonic wars appear now as the first modern conflict, of nationalism and of whole peoples rather than of simply a warrior class. They required the mobilisation in France of almost everyone for some military or military-related task, and some measure of reorganisation of the whole society and economy. The costs were immense. At the end France no longer dominated the continent. French development was retarded for long into the future. The wars knocked France, for a time, out of the contest for world domination, leaving the way open – even if only briefly – for the British.

THE WAR STATES

'A people and nation can hope for a strong position in the world only if national character and familiarity with war fortify each other by continual interaction' (von Clausewitz 1835/1993: 226).

In the century after the Napoleonic wars, there were in Europe apparently decreasing constraints on the development of a militarised society. An overwhelmingly dominant state, increasingly fortified by the guided output of sophisticated weaponry, directed rapidly industrialising national economies. With the benefit of hindsight, it seems as if the horrors of the trenches of northern France in the next century are already implicit in the settlement of the Napoleonic wars.

It did not seem so to the Europeans of the time. There was the illusion that at long last war had been banished from the continent, that now domestic affairs – and particularly the rising tempo of the class struggle – had displaced the conflict between states. Yet the surface calm concealed a bitter reality: Europe had exported its wars to the rest of the world; now they had become world powers, the Europeans fought globally. Some of the century's bloodiest collisions were fought in the Crimea, in Mexico, in Paraguay, in India (to suppress what the

British called the Mutiny), in the Taiping rebellion in China (with between 10 and 20 million dead), in the long settlement of Africa, north and south, in Burma, in Indo-China, in the struggle between Austria and Prussia, between Prussia and France and so on. One of the most horrifying was the American Civil War – with 620,000 deaths (more than American losses in either of the World Wars or the Vietnam war) – the first fought with railways, telegraph, steamships and Gatling guns. Events in the US – with nearly one million men under arms in the South, and two million in the North (out of a pre-war population of 32 million) – were the auguries of 1914.

Just as the shock of European maritime arms swept through the Indian Ocean when the Portuguese arrived to do battle with Arab and Persian merchants, the same shock, now of land warfare, swept through Africa, fought to the Napoleonic norms of destroying, not defeating, the enemy. 'There are no traditions of devastating warfare among the mixed farming people in Southern Africa before the nineteenth century,' Leonard Thompson (1990: 27) writes. The imperialist Lugard observed in East Africa that 'when the Wakikuyu fight a man gets his skull cracked perhaps at most. If the British fight, and bring guns, many many men die' (31 October 1890 in Perham 1956: 47). The Europeans fell upon Africa like Tamburlaine or Gengis Khan swept through Central Asia.

In Europe itself, the rivalries grew inexorably, fuelling an increasingly intense arms race. With the unification of Germany, now the largest single power on the continent of Europe, they were immensely exacerbated. Peace or not, vulnerability to war grew: 'during the second half of the nineteenth century, [the rivalries],' Van Creveld (1996: 5) writes, 'reached the point where much of the world had been turned into an armed camp'. Howard (1976: 110) concurs:

> By the end of the nineteenth century, European society was militarised to a very remarkable degree. War was no longer considered a matter for a feudal ruling class or a small group of professionals, but one for the people as a whole. The armed forces were regarded not as part of the royal household but as the embodiment of the Nation.

A contemporary observer, Friedrich Engels, makes much the same observation in reflecting on the Franco–Prussian War (1870–71), in a statement both so significantly wrong in one respect but so perceptive in the broader case as to be worth citing at some length (1887/1990: 158):

> [the war is] a turning point of entirely new implications. In the first place, the weapons used have reached such a stage of perfection that further progress which would have a revolutionising influence is no longer possible...all further improvements are of minor importance for field warfare. The era of evolution is therefore, in essentials, closed in this direction. And second, this war has compelled all continental powers to introduce in a stricter form the Prussian *Landwehr* system,

and with it, a military burden which must bring them to ruin within a few years. The army has become the main purpose of the State, and an end in itself; the peoples are there only to provide soldiers and feed them.[5] Militarism dominates and is swallowing Europe. But this militarism bears within itself the seed of its own destruction. Competition among the individual States forces them, on the one hand, to spend more money each year on the army and navy, artillery etc., and this more hastens their financial collapse; on the other hand, to resort to universal compulsory military service more and more extensively, thus in the long-run making the whole people familiar with the use of arms.

The observation on the limits of arms technology is delightfully wrong, given the immense technical fertility that was to come after Engels (not least, flight, radio and radar, nuclear weapons etc). There are also, interestingly, two other errors: the growing financial burden, which was growing absolutely, but also simultaneously declining as a share of the extraordinary output now possible. The stupendous escalation in costs of the First World War would still not ruin the European states. Productivity could support an almost unlimited militarisation now. Then there is the point about arming the people: Engels did not see, as the rulers of Europe did, that this was a decreasing threat – nationalism generally swept armed populations into, and kept them in, an unbelievable loyalty to their rulers. More generally, the accuracy of Engels's view of the domination of society by the military seems to be inconsistent with what passes for Marxism. Engels presents a supposedly capitalist society in which the army rules society in its own interest, rather than in the interest of capital.

Thus a remarkable transformation had occurred. For hundreds of years, the majority of the population of Europe had rightly regarded its rulers with fear, not to say terror. People felt relief, self-congratulation, if they escaped involvement, since any involvement would almost certainly leave them the loser – at worst they might be idly killed, at best imprisoned, maimed, abused, robbed. The proto-state, the nobility, could be distinguished from bands of armed robbers only by the quality of their clothes and equipment. Given a history generally of unrelieved cruelty, greed, fraud, it was astonishing that now, regardless of its character or personnel, the state had become endowed with the benevolence and moral infallibility of God. Individual leaders might be abused or ridiculed – it was the privilege of wayward children to mock indulgent parents, and the abuse of the election platform or a free press might pass for that – but the institution itself acquired a sanctity untouched by such criticism. Nor had social conditions by the mid-century advanced so far as to persuade the mass of the population that their rulers were benevolently disposed towards them. Hippolyte Taine, visiting London in its glory in 1872, observed, 'the lanes which open off Oxford Street, stifling alleys thick with human effluvia, troops of pale children crouching on filthy staircases; the street benches at London Bridge where all night whole families huddle close, heads hanging, shifting with cold ... in abject, miserable poverty' (Ackroyd 2000: 600). Yet still, the state had become, in Van Creveld's words (1996: 5), 'an end in itself, an earthly god in whose honour festivals were celebrated, monuments erected and hymns composed or sung'.

Many regard the induction of the citizens into the club of the nation as a bargain, an implicit social contract. The citizen agreed to be loyal to the state (with the implication that, if need be, the citizen would fight to defend the state and risk death) in return for admission to the nation, the right to vote and participate, and gain access to a range of social services in health, education and social security. As Gollwitzer (1969: 90) puts it, 'Conscription, compulsory education and the right to vote form the three pillars of the democratic State'. We might go further to suggest that the programme represented a partial extension to the population at large of the privileges of the armed forces – the civilians had become, as it were, the resting part of the military. In reality, the contract was not a bargain. It could be withdrawn unilaterally by the state as it had been granted.

The change in the attitude – from subjects to citizens – was not simply external conformity, although there was much of that. The state needed to ensure that, in general, citizens willed what it willed; they behaved as if they owned state policy, and did so by instinct, by attitude, rather than by thought and cogitation. As Poggi (1978: 101) puts it, government strives to ensure that 'citizens ... comply with its authority not from inertia of unreasoning routine or the utilitarian calculation of personal advantage, but from the conviction that compliance is right'. Schumpeter (1927/1958: 12) observed in London that 'At the time of the Boer War there was not a beggar ... who did not speak of "our" rebellious subjects'. Of course, in the capital city popular identification with the monarch is much older than the nineteenth century – there is evidence of this in Elizabethan London, but it would be difficult to see this as equivalent to modern nationalism.

However, despite appearances, the state only partially succeeded. There were always those who resisted, even if the terms of the resistance were laid by the state.[6] Even in time of war, governments had to pay attention to the possibility of mass strikes and riots. But they were sufficiently successful to help drive the war machine on its suicidal trajectory. And when the state failed – as the Japanese emperor failed in 1945 – it led to a palpable crisis of the psyche among the citizens.

The commitment to the purposes of the state had to override not only the economic calculation of the individual's advantage but also the moralities taught in home, school or place of worship. The security of the state required its officers, and on occasions its citizens, to lie, cheat, torture or kill, to find guilty without trial or even elementary enquiry, and to execute. Little wonder that those who demurred and embraced pacifism were treated not as people with a different opinion but – like homosexuals in the recent past – as creatures arousing such moral disgust, guilty of the unspeakable, no argument was possible, only outraged rejection. Schumpeter (1927/1958: 11) notes the peculiar character of 'the appeal to national sentiments':

> All other appeals are rooted in interests that must be grasped by reason. This one alone arouses the dark powers of the subterranean, calls into play instincts that carry over from the life of the dim past … the irrational seeks refuge in nationalism – the irrational which consists of belligerence, the need to hate, a goodly quota of inchoate idealism, the most naïve (and hence the most unrestrained) egotism.

When war came, in 1914, it was greeted by many not with the appropriate gloom at all that would inevitably be lost, but with a sense of liberation. At last, it seemed, the talk, the deals, the slippery negotiations and compromises were over, and now the line of clear duty was revealed – 'immense frustrated energies were released' (Howard 1976: 111) and, at least in theory, daily adventure could lift male spirits. The widows and parents might grieve, but for many men it was the time of their life.

At the core of the new religious cult of the state stood the military. The history of each newly invented nation was also invented to achieve an heroic saga of war, of victories won against impossible odds, of atrocities awaiting revenge. Nations now acquired the possibility of 'remembering' events in the past that no person could remember, or 'wishing', 'demanding', 'daring', 'raging', 'mourning'. But nations were bizarre personalities – 'If the nation as organiser has a personality,' Ehrenreich (1997: 203) observes, 'it is that of the mounted warrior of old: impetuous, belligerent, touchy about all matters of "honor", and in a state of readiness at all times for war'.

Indeed, war was the very *raison d'etre* of the nation, the sacred affirmation of its existence and superiority, its historical validation, beyond all calculations of accident, let alone profit and loss. Those slaughtered in agony on muddy battlefields were not to be objects of grief but rather 'glorious martyrs', embracing with joy the splendour of being killed as validating the nation. Van Creveld (1991: 166) comments that 'So elemental is the human need to endow the shedding of blood with some great and even sublime significance that it renders the intellect almost entirely helpless'. There may be such a need, but the state has an even more pressing requirement – to divorce wives, children and parents from the terrible loss lest they be driven to reflect on the meaninglessness of war and the futility of the purposes of the state.[7]

The incorporation of all (except 'foreign' minorities) into the nation was also a process of militarised discipline of all institutions – from the village church and memorials to the dead (nationalism now expropriated a supposedly universal religion), to prayers in primary and secondary schools, to standing to attention in the prescence of the flag or the anthem, to the high decorative rituals of state – 'No important State function can go forward without the accompaniment of drum rolls and soldiers at attention,' Vagts (1959: 21) writes. 'The inauguration of presidents, the coronation of monarchs, the celebration of national holidays – all these events require everywhere the presence of the soldier as "ceremonial appurtenances"'. From the late eighteenth century until the 1950s, rulers tended to appear in public in military dress – from the King of Prussia to the General Secretary of the Communist Party of the Soviet Union.

The mythic role of the armed forces as the sacred embodiment of the nation was completely, indeed risibly, at odds with the reality. Real armies in real history were chaotic, bureaucratic, blundering, often starving and ill-supplied, subject to the often wonderful absurdities of generals, and far removed from the fictions of efficiency, honour and heroic self-sacrifice. In the myth, they alone were incorruptible, and thus contrasted with, say, capitalists, who were venal and unpatriotic. In societies with a claim to be socialist, it was the army – like the party – which supposedly alone embodied honesty and hostility to greed, a welcome adherence to poverty. Reality was again startlingly different, with military corruption a perpetual problem. The officer cadre frequently demanded and were granted lavish privileges – in housing, clubs, subsidised shops, transport, all the appurtenances of a *nomenklatura*.

In the late nineteenth century, as the culture of war spread throughout European society, so the economic, social and technical sinews of popular war were developed. For example, in economically backward Russia the defeat of the Crimean War led not only to a rapid upgrading of the armed forces but general industrialisation and social reform – from the ending of serfdom to the opening up of higher education. Building industry required the creation of the appropriate social order – in the words of Engels (1890/1990, 27: 34): 'the government set about breeding a Russian capitalist class ... The new development of the bourgeoisie was artificially forced as in a hot-house, by means of railways concessions, protective duties and other privileges.'

The state inventing a national capitalist class was an innovation in Marxism, but one which much more closely fitted the reality of national development in Europe generally, not just in backward Russia. Indeed Hintze (1902/1975: 176) goes further and asserts that 'without this era of economic promotion through the State [the mercantilist period], the development of the bourgeoisie would have been impossible'.

WORLD WAR

For the leading powers, the output of manufacturing and of the means to make war accelerated. Once again the size of armies lurched upwards, on the military assumption that since equipment on all sides was roughly equivalent, sheer numbers now held the key to victory. In 1870, the French called on nearly half a million men, and in 1914 over four million. At the outbreak of the First World War, the French mobilised 62 divisions (with 15,000 men per division, a total of around 930,000); the Germans 87 divisions (1.3 million men); Austria 49 (735,000) and Russia 114 (1.7 million). Several million horses moved immense quantities of supplies from railhead to front, but the largest item of cargo was still fodder for horses.

Firepower increased even more rapidly. Napoleon's artillery at Waterloo consisted of 246 guns, firing 110 rounds each per battle. But at the Somme in July 1916, the British fired 100,000 guns and 20,000 tonnes of shells per gun. The nineteenth century saw an immense increase in weaponry, in the intensity of firepower (symbolised in the machine gun), in the speed of firing, and the protection of the guns (for example, in the next century, the tank). Modern mass-production manufacturing opened up an almost unlimited capacity to provide the means to fight.

Other innovations vastly eased the problems of supplying armies in the field, for example the invention of canned meat (1845), evaporated (1860) and dried (1855) milk, margarine (the result of a competition set up by Napoleon III in the 1860s to find a durable butter substitute). Medical services now made possible the protection of the troops and the treatment of the wounded to restore them to combat. The South African War (1899–1902) was the last, it is said, where there were more deaths from sickness than from action.

Durable foodstuffs and medical supplies were only elements in sustaining armies in the field. Much more impressive was the extraordinary increase in mobility. As we have seen, in the eighteenth century the problems of supplying armies severely limited the capacity to move (unless there were convenient water-courses). Only late in the century was there serious road engineering, and even then there were no all-weather roads until the early nineteenth century. The coming of the railways revolutionised the potential to move armies and armies of a size that could never have been centrally directed earlier (now telegraph transformed communication). It also made possible centralised government (the capacity for public officials to reach swiftly all cities of the territory). Between 1825 and 1900, 175,000 miles of rail tracks were laid, crossing most natural barriers to bind territories into a single national system (with gauge changes at the border to prevent military trains crossing). Between 1870 and 1914, the mileage nearly tripled. In 1870, single lines could carry eight trains per day, double lines twelve; in 1914, the equivalent numbers were 40 and 60. The increase in speed was astonishing – the march from, say, Rome to Cologne had remained at about 67 days since the time of the Romans; it was now reduced to 24 hours.

The military potential of railways was recognised early. The Russians demonstrated this in 1846 when they moved 14,500 men and their horses 200 miles to Cracow in two days. Prussia – and later Germany – was particularly innovative here, driving to achieve the standardisation of gauges between the German principalities. The Prussian army created military railway units to construct track as the armies advanced in order to provide reinforcements, replacements and supplies. To make military control of the rail network effective, Prussia nationalised nearly half the railway system in 1860, and all of it by 1880. In 1866, Prussia moved the Prussian Guards to the Austrian border in one week, with 12 trains per day. Moving the armies to France in 1870 was even faster. In 1876, a railway department was created in the High Command to develop new track at strategic points for military purposes – for example to villages along the borders with France and Belgium (with platforms up to one mile long to unload troops and supplies with the greatest speed). The innovations proved their worth in August 1914 when a German army of over one million men was moved to the western front in days. To the great surprise of the German commanders on the eastern front, the Russians were able to do the same thing.

If railways revolutionised European warfare, they also pulled together empire. The great railway schemes of Africa and Asia were the instrument for continuous military penetration. In India, there was much emphasis on the commercial potential of railways – and Bombay's businessmen were particularly persistent in demanding tracks through to the Ganges valley which would check the position of Calcutta. But until 1891, only the state was willing to put up 60 per cent of the cost, and that was for the military control of India (and, it was claimed, the shipment of emergency grain to famine areas).

Steam power and the steel ship similarly revolutionised both naval power and mobility, and the sinews of empire. To put such fleets to sea placed a premium on global territorial possessions. Warships consumed prodigious quantities of coal; in the middle of the nineteenth century, the stock carried on board was exhausted in five days steaming at 20 knots. The British control of most of the world's coaling stations gave it a position of great power in controlling ship movement. In 1905, when the Russian Baltic fleet was required to move from its home base to support Russian forces fighting the Japanese in East Asia, Britain was an ally of Japan and refused access to British coaling stations. The fleet was obliged to pack every possible space, including the decks, with coal, making it incapable of combat until much of this had been burned.

In sum, the second half of the nineteenth century saw the leading states of Europe emerging as a set of unified military powers, backed by demarcated national militarised economies. National capitalism had shown extraordinary rates of growth and self-transformation, as had the armed forces of Europe. The costs of the process of war-making rose equally dramatically – for example, the national debt of Britain, standing at £599 million in the late nineteenth century, reached £7460 million in the period 1910–19. But the state found much greater ease in raising these sums than the much smaller sums raised in the eighteenth century – there were no tax revolts or bread riots. A national society had been dragooned into support for war, the ancient sport of kings, which had now become what seemed the doom of civilisation. Engels (1990: 451) in 1887 described the apocalyptic future:

> world war of an extent and violence hitherto unimagined. Eight to ten million soldiers will be at each other's throats and in the process they will strip Europe barer than a swarm of locusts. The depredations of the Thirty Years War compressed into three to four years and extended over the entire continent; famine, disease, the universal lapse into barbarism, both of the armies and people, in the wake of acute misery; irretrievable dislocation of our artificial system of trade, industry and credit, ending in general bankruptcy; collapse of the old States and their conventional political wisdom to the point where crowns will roll into the gutters by the dozen, and no one will be around to pick them up; the absolute impossibility of foreseeing how it will all end and who will emerge as victor from the battle; only one consequence is absolutely certain: general exhaustion and the creation of the conditions for the ultimate victory of the working class.

EMPIRE

This account of how the European state came to create a particular form of national capitalism, subordinate to its interests, casts a different light on the nature of European imperialism. The European warrior-merchant class indeed had an interest in creating safe territorial enclaves for its exclusive use as sanctuary, ship servicing centres, warehouses and markets – much as Venice, the prototype merchant-state, created a network of commercial centres for the exclusive use of its merchants in the eastern Mediterranean, or as the Portuguese, and then the Dutch tried to create a string of exclusive commercial principalities on the route to the spice islands. But creating such commercial 'empires', financed out of the profits of trade, was quite different to coming to rule the more normal empire, inland territories financed out of land taxes on the inhabitants. The first could be lightly armed to minimise the costs; the second necessarily adopted all the prerogatives – and arms – of a sovereign territorial power. Merchants continued to favour the first – and indeed to try to force their governments to offer public sanction to such acquisitions – but were far from aspiring to shoulder the quite different tasks – and immense costs – of the second. That required states. Of course, some did well in the colonies: adventurers, exiles, mercenaries. With a settled order, some businessmen followed the lead of the state to profit through the exploitation of raw materials, to contract to build infrastructure, to supply the public authorities, but these were the things they had done at home and were in no way peculiar. In practice, this share of business was small. It did not demonstrate that territorial empire was acquired in the interests of capital. As Schumpeter (1927/1958: 5) notes, 'The fabric of social interests is so closely woven that scarcely ever can there be any action on the part of a State that is not in keeping with the concrete interests of someone, an interest to which that action can be reduced without manifest absurdity'.

The tensions between the commercial and the territorial interest ran through the history of British imperialism. Adam Smith, with many others, opposed the extension of empire as entailing heavier taxes, distorted investments, a high risk of war and corruption. As we have noted, the directors of the East India Company vainly tried to curb the enthusiasm for conquest of their factors in India and its implied need for a significant military and territorial establishment which wiped out the profits of the company. The arguments in favour of parsimony persuaded the British cabinet in the early years of the nineteenth century (when, during the Napoleonic Wars, Spain and Britain were at war) to reject the pleas of the creoles to expropriate Spain's possessions in Latin America.

The contradictory attitude to empire partly explains why it is difficult to show the relative profitability of empire and therefore its economic justification. A number of historians have examined the questions at stake (see for example Jobson and Arruga 1991; Sherwood 1965, 1969, 1970; Thomas 1968; Coelho 1973; O'Brien 1988, 1990). O'Brien covers the ground for the British Empire systematically, endeavouring to construct some element of a cost–benefit analysis of imperialism, with some useful conclusions. Despite efforts to increase self-sufficiency, Britain still imported 90 per cent of its raw materials (excluding coal) in the 1890s, but only a third of these came from the empire (and about a quarter by 1930). Between a quarter and a third of British exports were shipped to markets in the empire (the peak, in 1902, was 39 per cent), but these became decreasingly important. Of British investment abroad, about a quarter (at its peak) went to the empire (but on the private account, under a fifth). What funds did go were heavily biased to the self-governing dominions rather than the colonies. In terms of rates of return (Davis and Huttenbeck 1986), for much of the period the empire yielded not much better than domestic rates (overseas non-empire returns tended to be better); Davis and Huttenbeck (1986) suggest investment in empire was 67 per cent better than outside the empire before 1884, 40 per cent worse afterwards. About two thirds of emigrants from Britain went to destinations outside the empire, particularly to North America.

Thus, for private business – without accounting for the supporting public investment that made private profits possible – empire was important but the rest of the world was generally very much more important.

However, this leaves out of account the interests of the state. After all, it is unlikely that any half-way realistic cost–benefit analysis of military spending would give a positive rate of return. The economic analysis omits the elements at stake in the competition of states. This was far more important in the occupation of territory than economic calculation. The British government, like the French, did not know what economic advantage might follow from seizing parts of West Africa, but neither could it afford to let the other find out first. Once acquired, the territory had to be administered much as if it was part of the metropolitan holding, its population and resources then accrued to the power of the imperial state. India may not have been immensely important for Britain's capitalists (and much of the capital employed there up to 1860 came from Indian sources, not British), but it was important for the British state, for its military needs and for those classes who depended upon employment in the state – the officials of the military and civil administration in England and India. Lord Salisbury, as British Prime Minister (1882 in Johnson in Bose 1990: 238) focussed more narrowly on the significance of India for him: 'an English barracks on the Oriental seas from which we may draw any number of troops without paying for them'. It is difficult to overestimate the significance of this for a global power, one capable of dominating the rest of Asia and of Africa. Thus, if we look at imperial India, it is first and foremost as a key constituent of British global military power, not as crucial for British business. Nearly half the public revenues of British India were spent on the army, and the military interest was paramount in most infrastructure investment (railways, roads, industry, medical services). '[In] this era,' Washbrook writes (in Bose 1990: 42), 'the British empire was the principal agency through which the world system functioned; the Indian army was, in a real sense the major coercive force behind the internationalisation of industrial capitalism'; or, we might suggest, of the domination of the world by the British state.

It was a brief moment, a time when it was possible to mimic the ancient cosmopolitanism of world capitalism within the framework of a nationally governed empire. However, the semblance of cosmopolitanism was, for the most part, temporary. Once the Great Powers of Europe found it necessary to draw the lines of loyalty much more tightly to face the intensifying contest in Europe, it was not enough to be a citizen of the British Empire. It was necessary to be British (and preferably English) and white. Such a narrowing revision suddenly made the subjects of empire immensely unequal. It became vital to have one's own state, not to shelter within a cosmopolitan empire. The first independence movements – or at least movements for self-government – began in the 1870s at the same time as the most ferocious contest for empire between the Great Powers, the long run in to 1914. By the time of the First World War, empire is already under sentence of termination.

THE PERSISTENCE OF COSMOPOLITANISM

If the primary motive for European imperialism was political, not economic, it might have provided, as we have suggested, a half-way house to a cosmopolitan economy, a system of trade and production within much larger territorial areas. However, in practice this was not so because the world economy expanded much more rapidly. Thus, for a time the themes of increased nationalism in the political sphere and increased cosmopolitanism in the economic appeared to coincide. Of course, in the nineteenth century, a cosmopolitan economy persisted even if unrecorded – Conrad's solitary tramp steamers plied the Rio de la Plata or the Niger, networks of Chinese junks straddled the East and Southeast Asian seas, Javanese traders slipped between the labyrinth of islands, whole systems of distribution connected world markets and peasant cultivators, peddlers, village and town craftsmen, weavers and miners, apparently untouched by the great dramas of war between the leading powers. Traders from Shikarpuri, a small city in Sind, western India, set out to become small money-lenders, merchants and agricultural brokers in the Tsar's Central Asian possessions, in Northwestern China and in Iran, all largely unnoticed by the British Raj; another group from Sindhi Hyderabad built a global network, from Cairo to Panama to Morocco, selling handicrafts to Victorian tourists, again with hardly more than a nod at the territorial powers involved (Markovits 2000). Sometimes these layers of interaction were affected – as imperial maritime policing extended controls, as wars briefly swept the seas clean, or, as with the arrival of cheap British spun cotton in India, the spinners were decimated (although the weavers expanded). Markets were regulated, pirates kept at bay, routes patrolled, currencies and weights standardised, taxes and tariffs levied; but the dynamic was remote from the issues of national power. Merchants still often did not know or did not choose to know who were supposedly the enemies, and who the friends, of the governments from which they derived their citizenship.

On the other hand, the British historically depended much more on trade than many of their European rivals, and therefore almost necessarily on a greater degree of cosmopolitanism. As empire was consolidated, this bias, as it were, was institutionalised and provided a kind of core for that period, 1840 to 1870 (and in some respects extending on to the end of the century and beyond). Indeed, in the case of some imperial cities, the extension went much further, even through the years of the most extreme national power – in Alexandria until 1956, in Shanghai until 1949, in Hong Kong until 1992, and in Singapore even now. Even in the City of London, at the heart of British national power, the demands of finance ensured the persistence of some measure of cosmopolitanism until the onset of the Great Depression.

The British Empire embodied the contradiction since it was both the political enclave of a national territorial state and the heart of a global capitalism, more of its external activity operating outside the empire than within it. Elements of the national economic state agenda, embodied in protectionism, persisted until the 1840s. Then free trade, the explicit embrace of cosmopolitanism, overwhelmed both the old agenda and the firms associated with it. The City of London was transformed – 'the potentially harsh truth was that the City was now playing in a different ball game, one that internationally minded merchant banks would find it easier to adjust to than old-style merchants whose interests tended to be bound up in a particular geographical area' (Kynaston I 1994: 166). For Europe, free trade arrived slightly afterwards, but was beginning to crumble from 1879, although the British persisted until the Great Depression. The US remained solidly protectionist, with tariffs between 20 and 40 per cent until the Second World War (Bairoch 1989).

For three decades or more, the system expanded with unprecedented speed – the volume of world trade increased five times over. Within this period, Kynaston (I 1994: 167) notes for Britain, 'In retrospect, the 1860s marked a unique decade: capital, goods and labour flowed almost unhindered round much of the known world in unprecedented quantities, the nearest we would ever come to a fully liberal free trade system' (that is, we might add, until our own times). The cosmopolitanism seemed to promise a world without nationalism, provincialism and racism, a world in which trade harmonised all. The period was sufficiently misleading to beguile its greatest theorist, Karl Marx, into believing that an international liberation would, and quite soon, parallel and overwhelm the internationalism of capital.

Furthermore, in the 40 years up to 1914, not only trade continued to expand, along with capital movements (by 1913, a third of British wealth was invested overseas), but also migration. The US labourforce grew by a quarter between 1870 and 1910. No wonder it might feel that nations were disappearing along with the possibility of war.

Even when the change of direction came – with the Franco–Prussian War and the unification of Germany and Italy – the first reactions were cosmopolitan: the flight of European financiers to London (bringing the famous names of Emile Erlanger, Credit Lyonnaise, Deutsche Bank). Kynaston reports an 1887 survey of City firms showing that 35 per cent were managed by foreign-born directors, many of German extraction. In the ensuing years, however, the steady growth of the fears and insecurities which fashioned nationalism, the fruit of both the increasing clashes between the Great Powers and the rising tempo of the domestic class struggle, undermined the surface appearance of harmony in Britain. When the great cosmopolitan and free-trade party, the Liberals, split in the 1880s, 'that was the moment when with mid-Victorian reforming zeal finally exhausted, there emerged in its hegemonic form, a social-cum-political compact devoted to the defence of property against the threat of socialism … a compact of land and finance, of white collar workers in the proliferating slums of "villa Toryism"' (Kynaston I 1994: 368). It was simultaneously a mighty affirmation of Britishness, against the thefts and cunning greed of the French and Germans in Africa, the Russians in Central Asia and China and a multitude of other threats in other places. Yet many in the City, like, no doubt, manufacturers exporting to the Americas or Europe, retained a hope in a broader world. The 'profound paradox' was explicit in the tension in the City, 'between on the one hand, an almost crude patriotism, and on the other, an earnest desire not to destroy the wonderful global money-making machine built up over the previous century' (Kynaston II 1995: 493).

The government was increasingly concerned to ensure British capital was indeed British: that is, it favoured Britain's 'friends' and did not lend to 'enemies', for example financing the German-built railway from Istanbul to Baghdad. Many of those in the City – albeit a dwindling band – regarded such official interference as impertinent and market-distorting. On the other hand, the officials smelt a whiff of treason in the single-minded pursuit of profit; Arthur Henderson at the Foreign Office (Kynaston III 1995: 514) believed that

> we cannot rely with certainty on any of these financiers being animated by disinterested and patriotic motives. They look solely and simply at the profits which they may derive … It is a matter of perfect indifference to them … whether the ends which they pursue are or are not in harmony with the interests of the country.

It was characteristically disingenuous to see 'patriotic' as 'disinterested', and 'the interests of the country', that is the interests of the government, as defining the standard of moral excellence. After all, was not the point of capitalism that businessmen assessed commercial issues on the basis exclusively of profit, without fear or favour on other questions? And if they did not do so, how could the system be intellectually justified as directed to optimise the welfare of the majority? Already a case was emerging that distinguished between financiers as bad capitalists – cosmopolitan traitors (with often more than a hint of antisemitism and the implication that Jews owed loyalty to no state) – and manufacturers as good capitalists, natives and patriots, who demanded that 'British' capital should be employed exclusively by British companies, not lent to foreigners. It helped the Labour Party soften its critique of capitalism by concentrating its fire on unpatriotic finance and in defence of patriotic manufacturers.

THE MODERN STATE AND CAPITALISM

In sum then, what we call modern capitalism is defined as a set of national economies, and as such is the creation of the modern state. This state was developed in essence long before modern capitalism and expropriated and reshaped parts of a long pre-existing cosmopolitan capitalism. The state was fashioned to meet the needs of a war-making system, activated by the persistent – systemic – military rivalries of the leading powers of Northwestern Europe. In turn this created the forms of national civil government with its accompanying taxation system, bureaucracy, and finally the preoccupation with forcing economic development on a national basis and a unified social structure. In part, rulers constructed the industrial economy directly in the interests of war-making – in the arms industries and associated raw material extraction, capital goods industries and infrastructure. In part they achieved these ends through the manipulation of private business, through providing incentives and punishments to further the state's priorities. The coercive – physical – power of the state, enforcing taxation and other means of extraction of resources from the population, was employed to force the transfer from popular consumption to state spending on war and the servicing of debt incurred by past wars, and thereby through the hands of the instruments of the state, private capital, manufacturing, banking and the rentier class. The central preoccupation of the ruler accounts for the peculiar features of national capitalism: the development of contiguous bounded geographical areas, politically not economically defined; the enforcement of social 'homogeneity' (even to the point, in some cases, of expelling the business class if it could be portrayed as 'foreign'); the development of a peculiar industrial structure biased towards heavy industry and the production of weaponry and appropriate raw material inputs; the pursuit of self-sufficiency in both agriculture and heavy industry; the dominance for a long period of mercantilism in economic policy in the interests of state economic power, even though this reduced the welfare of the population – in essence, the politics of the predatory state invariably dominated the economics of the market. This peculiar model led to the progressive exaggeration of the differences between what were becoming the countries of the world, differences which had little relationship to original natural resource endowments.

Was there then no 'bourgeois revolution'? There was certainly a progressive extension of suffrage (and the rights associated with this) and a steady increase in the constraints on the prerogatives of the crown (leading in some cases to the establishment of republics), but this process was far from establishing business control of the state. The importance of the lobby for great bankers and merchants long predates the changes in suffrage; they did not need the vote. The vote did not confer special access to government on the mass of smaller business. The importance of this process is perhaps looked at more accurately from the opposite end – as the extension of the means to penetrate successive layers of the population with the state agenda so that, at the end, there was no limit to the sacrifices that could be demanded of the population. In this enterprise, king or not, the change was brilliantly successful.

War has been endemic in the world throughout recorded time. In the ancient period and in modern times there were military states – from the Empire of Dahomey in West Africa to the Incas, Pharaonic Egypt, Sparta, Prussia – where both economy and society were organised to support warfare. But this was not married to deliberate economic development, seeking constantly to expand the taxation base to fuel the war economy. Rulers, as we have noted, sometimes did engage in trade and production for trade, and the proceeds were sometimes employed to finance war – some of the Egyptian Mameluks, Moghul nobles, princes of Southeast Asia (for example the rulers of Burma before the arrival of the British (Taylor 1987: 47)), rulers of the Ottoman Empire or Safavid Persia, the gentry of Sung China. But in general the link was loose, and more commonly, as in Mughal India, rulers depended on – and were preoccupied to sustain – land taxation, and were, as a result, remote from the concerns of commerce, expressing at best the 'indifferent neutrality of the State towards merchants' (Habib in Tracy 1990: 67). It was the obsessive drive of the competing European powers over several hundred years – although only decisively so in the eighteenth century – which created peculiar national capitalisms which in turn propelled efforts to become rival imperial capitalisms.

By implication, an agenda of 'state issues' existed in the war-making system over and above the interests of the economic classes of society. It might be that merchants ran the Venetian state or landowners directed policy of the Latin American states of the nineteenth century, but this was not the norm within the competitive system which emerged in Europe (and, indeed, was ultimately incompatible with that system). The state here could not be a 'capitalist state' even if its interests in warfare lay in fostering the interests of some capitalists (as opposed to others); if indeed it were so directed by the interests of its capitalists, it was liable to fail in the competition with other states, since capitalists as capitalists had no special competence in the pursuit of the state agenda. The separation of state and business was achieved most sharply where the capitalists were foreigners – the Chinese in modern Southeast Asia, Indians in modern East and Central Africa, the English in Argentina, or more generally, Jews, Armenians, Lebanese etc. The 'foreign-ness' of the businessmen symbolised their origin in a cosmopolitan world, and the continuing temptation that they would sacrifice the interests of the national rulers to profits in that wider world.

The history of Japan provides a fascinating example of a powerful state without the systemic imperative to war-making and related national military industrialisation. In the late sixteenth century, the civil wars were fought with massed firepower – Oda Nobunaga in 1575 employed 23 ranks of musketeers to fire continual volleys of 1000 rounds for twenty seconds (Parker in Tracy 1991: 17). Japan's weapon-makers were famous exporters throughout East and Southeast Asia. But after the settlement of the clan wars (1587) and the dispersal of Kubla Khan's invading fleet from China, the shogunate was sufficiently free of external conflicts to ban the use of firearms (having appropriated all manufacture in 1607). By the end of the seventeenth century, firearms had died out, and the samurai relied exclusively on the sword. Japan, like China, Korea and Siam, went in the opposite direction to the Europeans, to closure against the rest of the world, thus deliberately offsetting any systemic imperative. It could do so because, unlike the Europeans, it was not embedded in a system of endemic rivalry and warfare. The comparable drive in Europe to unification and centralisation along with national industrialisation was neutralised. The shogunate, despite establishing an absolutism, did not seek to establish a mono-poly of the legitimate use of violence, a uniform system of law, a bureaucracy and a national system of taxation. All that awaited the arrival of a world of systemic warfare at Japan's doorstep.

The Northwestern European states pursued a national capital project, the heart of which was industrialisation. Having established its domination of capital, the state, as it were, expropriated society to create 'nation-states'. Over an extended period of time, with major struggles of popular opposition to this process, the state finally succeeded in socialising the major part of the popu-lation, establishing the strongest possible basis for warfare and, incidentally, the purposes of national capital. The Europeans were then ready for the most unrelenting and total struggle for dominance, to the point where self-destruction faced them.

4

The Apogee of the Modern State

INTRODUCTION

All the long years of preparation came to fruition in 1914, with the outbreak of another Thirty Years War, germinated in Europe's bitter rivalries but settled now in the world at large. The potion – Prussian organisation and discipline, the Napoleonic spirit and nationalism, and the astounding power of modern industrialism – was more destructive than anyone could have imagined. Yet those not required to face directly the enemy ranks had been most schooled to applaud the necessary slaughter, to experience the liberating joy of patriotic self-righteousness[1] in the face of catastrophe. To make a festival of murdering foreigners had been ground into the minds of children from the earliest age, ages when the very notion must have seemed misty. The idea was nurtured by parents, by teachers, by schoolbooks and by newspapers – in complete but unnoticed defiance of the official Christian doctrines of universal love for all. 'By 1914,' Keegan (1993: 355) observes,

> an entirely unprecedented cult mood was dominating European society, one which accepted the right of the State to demand and the duty of every fit male individual to render military service, which perceived in the performance of military service a necessary training in civic virtue and which rejected the age old social distinction between the warrior – as a man set apart whether by rank or no rank at all – and the rest.

'[N]othing in the history of the modern State,' Van Creveld notes, 'is more astonishing than the willingness, occasionally even eagerness, of people to fight for it and lay down their lives for it'.

91

Those in authority were not heedless of the risks. Germany's Chancellor Von Bulow (1900–9) knew that 'an unsuccessful war would mean the end of the dynasty'. The same foreboding in Vienna, St Petersburg and Istanbul could not be kept at bay. Those with eyes to see in London and Paris could also detect that the disastrous invalidation of European civilisation embodied in the world war would ultimately spell the end of empire. And the gloom that a whole way of life was about to be destroyed affected the more perceptive in the governing classes of most countries. Yet what is surprising is that despite the sustained madness of the war, all the partial rebellions, mutinies, strikes, the disintegration of armies and so forth, so many regimes held fast – keeping the loyalty of enough citizens to hold revolution at bay. Only in Russia, where the socialisation process and the resources to make it possible were so poor, did the Tsar's war produce full social revolution, and then, only in *extremis*.

The First World War was a triumph of the efforts of the state to organise its resources, economy and society, for the task in hand. It was part of the most belligerent century on record. Tilly (1990: 69) records that from 1900 to 1990, there was 234 wars (civil or international) where at least 1000 people were killed. The total number of deaths, on a conservative basis, may have been as many as 115 million military personnel, and possibly an equal number of civilians. Despite the long history of warfare, past centuries now seem pacific. There were 205 wars in the nineteenth century (with possibly eight million dead), and 68 in the eighteenth century (with possibly four million dead). Per thousand of the population of the belligerent powers, five died in the eighteenth century, six in the nineteenth, and 46 in the twentieth. These were the triumphs of the creation of the modern state.

The scale of deaths in the First World War was a function of the size and exposure of forces and the density and accuracy of firepower, since in most other respects the contending armies were equally balanced. In the July of 1914, Europe had four million men under arms; by the end of August, 20 million. A total of 65.8 million men fought (Ferguson 1998: 436), one in eight of whom (or 9 million) were killed – or an average of over 6000 per day. Within the average were spectacular occasions – at Verdun in 1916, the French lost half a million men, the Germans 400,000. By November 1918, 1.7 million Frenchmen had died. The French, British, Germans, Russians and Austrians lost in slaughter a generation of their governing classes. In some cases, the losses were heavily concentrated – by October 1914, most of the former university students from Bavaria who had formed the 22nd and 23rd corps of the German army were dead, 36,000 of them tipped into a common grave after just three weeks of fighting.

This was the arrival of the mass production of death, the military parallel to contemporary industrialism. It was matched by the escalation in the expenditure of ammunition. At Hooge in 1915, the British fired 18,000 shells; in the battle of the Somme in 1916 two million, and two million again at Arras in 1917; in the third battle of Ypres, 4.3 million.

Even more astonishing was that nothing was settled. The 'war to end all wars' turned out to be no more than the preface to intensified Great Power rivalries, culminating in an even more destructive – indeed suicidal – war. To some observers after the First World War it seemed that to continue the militarisation of Europe would be to destroy what was left of what Europe supposedly stood for. In the early 1920s, C.M.H.Lloyd (1924: 321) reflected on the implication: 'Another great war will plunge the world into a sort of military communism in comparison with which the [state] control exercised during the recent war will seem an Arcadian revelation. Personal freedom and private property are condemned by the exigencies of war.'

For Lloyd, the fear was not of revolution or Bolshevism, but of that 'military communism' which each regime was obliged to introduce to match the murderous rivalries of its neighbours.

This chapter looks at selected cases of the final outcome and the theory of the drive to develop national economies for the purpose of making war. First, we look at one of the more liberal examples, Britain. Then at what was in effect a developing country, Japan. Finally, at one of the most extreme forms of the modern warrior-state, Nazi Germany. A later chapter considers the nearest rival to Germany in this respect, the USSR. Finally, the chapter draws out some of the key features of the war itself.

BUILDING THE WAR ECONOMY: BRITAIN

As we noted earlier, from the 1870s the process of reorganising economies to fit the needs of war followed from increasing Great Power rivalries. Some of the changes appeared simply to be reactions to markets, some consciously linked to the needs of military supply, but all fashioned to continue to separate out a national economy from the international, and to organise industries as functional monopolies rather than competitive markets. Contemporaries noticed the tendency to increasing cartelisation of industry, each dominated by one or a handful of very large companies, or the 'self-reorganisation' of industries led by industrial trade associations (often with international agreements with competitors abroad on the division of markets).

In 1910, Rudolf Hilferding, part of Austrian social democracy, now at the height of its intellectual influence, advanced an analysis of what he saw as a new form of capitalism, *Finance Capital* (1981). He drew his model largely from

Germany, but the essence was a system of functionally, rather than competitively, organised national industries, directed by leading banks as monopolies, working in alliance with the state to control markets at home and abroad. It was an account Lenin drew upon heavily for his famous pamphlet on imperialism.

War subordinated civil government to the needs of the front – in Roy Jenkins's words (1969: 387), 'the jobs of the politicians ceased to be that of looking for strategic alternatives and became concentrated upon supplying men and munitions for slaughter'. In ensuring that supply, the state now immensely enhanced the growth of monopoly and cartels, to a unified and centralised national economy under the direction of the state. The Ministry of Munitions or of War demanded single suppliers, even if this entailed forcing all competitors into one producing group (or forcing their elimination altogether). In the British case, still relatively cosmopolitan for reasons explored elsewhere and with an industrial structure not dominated by banks (as in the German case), similar trends in terms of industrial organisation were apparent. The war coalition directed state trading organisations in key commodities, reorganised and central-ised the railways, directed insurance, shipping and food supply. By 1918, the Ministry of Munitions had become the largest employer in the country. The government purchased about 90 per cent of all imports, and marketed about 80 per cent of the food consumed domestically, controlling most prices (MacIntyre 1979: 64). In dim outline, the model – a centralised functional economy, with state-selected suppliers (the rest excluded) and state-determined production, quality and price – simultaneously corresponded to what seemed to match the needs of the armed forces for unlimited supplies and to the ideal of the socialists. Implicitly, the whole required a national enforceable plan.

However, after the war, while free trade persisted in Britain, it was impos-sible to force all producers into moderating competition in order to raise prices (so exposing the domestic markets to import penetration), let alone accepting planned targets whether set by businessmen or the state. The Conservative Party became committed to protection against imports just after the turn of the century (even if disguised as 'empire free trade'), but the party leadership feared to submit such a policy – which implied increasing the price of imported food – to electoral decision. There were some concessions (for example the 1921 Safeguarding Duties), and governments were willing to nationalise new industries for reorganisation where there were relatively few entrenched interests as in electricity generating, in civil aviation, in broadcasting, and later on London transport. Not until the Great Depression drove Britain off the gold standard (1931) was it possible to end free trade, control imports and thus create the precondition for 'industrial reorganisation' in favour of the largest companies (implemented in steel, shipbuilding, cotton etc). By 1938, the Prime Minister,

Neville Chamberlain, was beginning to toy with the idea of an economic statistics agency as the core of a state planning system.

What of the City of London, the shrinking enclave of cosmopolitanism? As we noted earlier, the capacity of the City to lend to all creditworthy borrowers regardless of the attitude of British governments turned on the existence of the gold standard, free trade and, in Britain, a balanced budget (assuring borrowers and lenders that local political issues would affect neither the commitment to the gold standard nor the activities of the City). The First World War suspended all three. Waging the war severely damaged the finances of the government and hence the City, allowing New York to dominate the world financial market (by 1920, New York's foreign issues were roughly double those of London). It was understandable that the City was dedicated to a return to the gold standard as soon as possible and thereby to the restoration of its fortunes against New York.

However, the old 'automatic mechanisms' of financial activity had, in the new order, become politicised, subject to political discretion. The question was not now what was good for world finance and its City core, but what was good for British business and employment. Furthermore, the City itself, faced with the challenge of national power, became divided. In the midst of war, strong hostility had developed among some of the City firms towards those run by people of German origin. Nationality or national origin now loomed larger than the cosmopolitanism which had made the City's fortunes. The creation of a voice for manufacturing, the Federation of British Industry (set up in 1916), raised the demand on the City that 'British' finance should be invested in British industry, not loaned to foreigners. Indeed, some alleged that 'British' finance had been used by German firms in the City to finance 'German economic penetration' of British markets (Kynaston III 1999: 45).

After the war there was no return to normal, even though the City managed to secure a restoration of the gold standard. The leading economist of the time, Keynes, attacked this precisely in defence of national political discretion – 'it made the market supreme over the industrial system ... [and] prevented the encroachment of the political government on the industrial system' (1925: 23). The high bank rate necessitated by restoring the gold standard at its pre-war exchange rate (to reassure foreign borrowers) now, it is said, hit British domestic investment and raised unemployment. '[S]o long as unemployment is a matter of general political importance,' Keynes (*The Nation*, 14 July 1923 in Kynaston III 1999: 104) declared, 'it is impossible that the Bank rate should be regarded as it used to be as the secret *peculiam* of Pope and Cardinals of the City'. Money should be managed to facilitate business in Britain, and if it were not, the City's 'days may be numbered'.

Matters only got worse. A disastrous slump in the coal-fields in mid-1925 was attributed to the increase in costs produced by the return to the gold standard at pre-war parity. The reluctance of the City to finance British industry if the rates of return were poor exacerbated matters. The Labour opposition demanded the nationalisation of the Bank of England, and later of all major banks in order to make finance subject to political priorities and a relatively low-cost input to manufacturing. The financial collapse of the late 1920s and the ensuing slump overtook all these issues. It was the final end of the old cosmopolitanism. Now government priorities, not market outcomes, were to determine the economy, with a policy of cheap money (the bank rate remained at 2 per cent from 1932 to 1939, the first time the rate had been so low since 1897) to finance British manufacturing. Both the political left and right agreed that there was a 'bankers' ramp': the City had brought Britain to within an ace of destruction in the interests of foreign borrowers: greedy and unpatriotic finance had sold the nation short. The same idea did good service in the US, leading to the Glass-Steagall Act of 1933 (not abolished until 1999).

Economies were now closed. It had happened earlier for migration, as each country increasingly regarded the foreign-born as agents of hostile governments (with catastrophic effects, as the Nazi expulsion of the Jews of Germany began). Now, closure affected both trade and finance. The government had made itself supreme within a unified and corporatised national economy. National planning became a popular issue, particularly among the largest businessmen. It was crystallised in an ambitious scheme for the reorganisation of the entire economy with large-scale nationalisations and planning, presented by a rising Conservative politician, Harold Macmillan (1938). In the Second World War, the passion for planning became universal. Businessmen chosen to help produce for war became enthusiastic converts to planning – witness the November 1942 National Plan for Industry, signed by 200 of the leading businessmen of the country. After the war, a new Labour Government persisted in the endeavour, nationalising a set of basic industries and public utilities to ensure the creation of an economy which could be directed by the state.

In the inter-war years, Keynes himself was an important theoretician of these changing trends, and above all prophet of the national political economy and the abandonment of cosmopolitanism. As early as 1925, he welcomed government by experts, as opposed to 'sterile' party politics – that is a functional rather than a competitive model of politics. He stressed the need for self-sufficiency (rather than optimal welfare): 'I become doubtful whether the economic cost of national self-sufficiency is great enough to outweigh the other advantages of gradually bringing the producer and consumer within the ambit of the same national economic and financial organisation'. Free trade and free capital movements, he felt, were more likely to cause wars, and the foreign ownership of assets was dangerous – 'let goods be home spun ... and above all, let finance be primarily national'. 'We do not wish to be at the mercy of world forces,' he declared, with an echo of the contemporary demands on the World Trade Organisation in Seattle, 'working out, or trying to work out, some uniform equilibrium according to the ideal principles of laissez-faire capitalism'. Even as late as 1944, as we noted earlier, just before the Bretton Woods conference to design a liberal world trading order, we find him considering it impossible to think that there could ever be private market-driven international trade, only state trading and domestic cartels (Treasury memo 1943 in Harrod 1951: 290). It was a long way from the cosmopolitan world market economics of his youth.

With the onset of the Second World War, the government assumed, with relative ease, draconian powers to direct the economy and the labourforce. The public interest was now to supersede all private claims for the period of the war. The system, in essentials, hardly differed from that of the Soviet Union. C. M. H. Lloyd had predicted 'military communism' in the event of a Second World War, and the reality came precious close to that, much as was recommended in a secret 1936 memorandum within the Bank of England on what preparations were required for war: 'a total mobilisation of resources, without any consideration of the rights of the individual ... official interference in practically every aspect of personal and institutional activity'(in Kynaston III 1999: 441). It seemed the end not only of a cosmopolitan City, but also of a liberal Britain, replaced with authoritarianism and a war economy.

Other Great Powers, as we shall see, were usually in advance of the British in these trends. Still perhaps the clearest exposition of the comparative picture is Brady's classic of 1943. German military planners were at work in the 1890s on what kind of civil economy needed to be developed to support war. Walther Rathenau, a major businessman (head of the electrical engineering giant corporation AEG), urged in 1914 (and subsequently in his book, *Things to Come*, 1917) the renunciation of competitive individualism in favour of a quasi-socialist system, corporatist unification of industry and a national plan.

Even in the US, with a market much larger than the European and therefore with, in principle, a higher level of domestic competition and less potential for reorganisation, some of the same trends could be seen (see Hawley 1966: 541), particularly when provided with the framework of Roosevelt's New Deal. Even there planning was becoming not Bolshevism and utopia but the 'common-sense' of the largest businesses. Left and right converged on some common progressive consensus, corporatist and statist.

JAPAN, ECONOMIC DEVELOPMENT AND WAR

We saw in the last chapter how war and war finance played a key role in forcing national economic development in Britain in the eighteenth century. If there were doubts as to how far this process could be reproduced in the twentieth century, two hundred years later (with an entirely different type of industrial structure and military demand), the Japanese case was a striking confirmation that it could.

Japan was at war for half the years between 1886 and 1945, and this period included 10 major wars (two of them world wars). Indeed, it was the military unpreparedness of the country – exposed in the bombardment of the American naval commander Commodore Perry in 1853 – which inspired the seizure of power of the outer samurai clans in 1868. The systemic imperatives, so long held at bay by the closure of Japanese society, had arrived with a singular and highly symbolic act of violence: the Meiji Restoration was the domestic response. The rationale of breakneck industrialisation which followed the political coup was explicitly to make the country militarily robust. At the beginning, the country had no modern military capacity (as we noted earlier, the shogunate suppressed the firearms industry), yet it was able in an astonishingly short time to emerge as a Great Power – with an empire in the 1890s (confiscating Taiwan and Korea) and able to inflict a crippling defeat in East Asia on a European Great Power, Russia, in 1905. Thus, from being the victim of systemic imperatives – in the shape of Commodore Perry – Japan had itself become in less than half a century the hammer of those imperatives on ill-prepared Korea and China. By 1925, Japan had become the third-largest naval power in the world and the fifth-largest military power.

Military spending averaged 10 per cent of the gross national product in these years (and over 12 per cent in the three decades before 1945). From the early 1930s, this military drive was guided by ambitions as heroic as those of the 1890s – for the domination of Asia, whose first stage was the seizure of China's Manchuria. Steps were taken to force the rapid growth of the heavy and chemical industries to support this drive. The older *zaibatsu* (larger private business corporations, traditionally instruments of state power) resisted efforts to make them subordinate to the war economy, but conformity was the condition for growth and opposition crumbled – speeded by the murder of the head of Mitsui in 1932.

Along with growth in output, measures were taken to centralise the economy. The state took powers to control foreign exchange, imports, capital investment, prices, labour and what industry was to produce. The measures were haphazard and gradual, responses by the military to particular supply problems rather than part of a general scheme. However, from 1936 the military pressed for a fully planned economy – 'to adapt all national activities to war conditions, to place manpower, materials and all other visible and invisible resources at the disposal of the Government' (1937 army document in Bisson 1945: 206–207). The physical direction of the economy was to be accompanied by close attention to civilian morale, employing 'thought warfare' to 'instil strong national thought in the minds of the people in times of peace'. The model was the military administration of Japan's puppet state in Manchuria, Manchukuo, with a 'unitary control system covering the production, distribution and consumption of important goods' (*Tokyo Gazette*, September 1940: 89–91 in Bisson 1945: 17). These efforts were formalised in a Six Year Plan for the economy (1937/8 to 1942/3), and a Five Year Plan for armaments (1938/9 to 1941/2), and in 1940 a grand Outline for the Establishment of a New Economic Order.

As we noted earlier in the case of Britain, the institution of central state control required industrial reorganisation – systematic cartelisation of industries, dominated by the largest firms, and the suppression of the rest (or their absorption in centrally directed guilds). In this way, by 1941 it was estimated that only 72 firms exercised control – under military supervision – of all major sectors of the economy. The cartels, under public direction, were endowed with quasi-public powers to enforce discipline. For example, the Japanese Cotton Spinners' Association of Osaka proclaimed the change of direction in July 1940: 'The JCSA which has hitherto had an important mission as the central influence of the textile industry, must hereafter aid positively the execution of national policies, reorganising itself into an institution for carrying out State affairs' (Bisson 1945: 35). Overall national direction was to be achieved through a Council of Key Industrial Control Organisations, 'based on the guiding principle of "State Interests First", designed for a complete execution of a planned economy'.

The national direction of agriculture and of labour were established separately, with controls on worker mobility to try to prevent firms poaching each other's workers. The Finance Ministry assumed powers to direct banks to finance munitions production, and this was rationalised in September 1940 in a National Finance Council to organise the distribution of finance according to government priorities. Of course the practice was, as everywhere, something different, with continual rivalries within the different parts of the bureaucracy, service infighting, waste and corruption. But insofar as it was feasible, the Ministry of Munitions established some overall direction of output and distribution.

Japan was economically, with Italy, one of the weaker of the belligerent powers in the Second World War – with some 4 per cent of world output (compared to Germany's 13 per cent) and, in 1938 6 per cent of world steel production (compared to Germany's 20.7 per cent). Furthermore, it faced severe shortages of vital raw materials: as late as 1936, it relied for two-thirds of domestic oil consumption on imports from the US; the country produced only 16.7 per cent of the iron ore consumed in its steel mills (and 62 per cent of the steel used), 41 per cent of aluminium, a quarter of its oil needs, a third of its salt consumption; it possessed no nickel or bauxite (Hara in Harrison 1998: 239). As in Germany, much effort and investment was devoted to trying to find synthetic substitutes, but it was accepted that the country could never be self-sufficient for war. This conclusion inevitably impelled imperial expansion to capture sources of supply in Southeast Asia, under the control of the European colonial powers – the French, British and Dutch. Thus the reorganisation of the domestic economy was part of a military plan for an international division of labour within Japan's 'co-prosperity sphere' as it was called in Tokyo – bringing rice and coal from Korea, iron ore and coal from Manchuria, coal and cotton from China, sugar from Formosa (Taiwan), oil and bauxite from the Netherlands East Indies (Indonesia), tin and rubber from what was then Malaya.

Nonetheless, the growth in capacity and in output was phenomenal even if less than in more industrially advanced rivals and allies. The fighting strength of the army increased three times over between 1936 and 1942, and munitions capacity by between seven and eight times. In the three years and nine months after the Japanese assault on the US fleet in Pearl Harbour, Japan built 15 aircraft carriers, 6 cruisers, 126 submarines, 63 destroyers, 70 transport ships, 168 coastal defence ships: 682 naval ships in all, along with 720 cargo ships, 271 oil tankers, and 60,000 military aircraft. And beyond this, expansion of overseas and domestic raw material and manufacturing required to support these efforts was equally extraordinary.

Without the urgent necessities of war, it is impossible to see how such a rapid and sustained industrialisation could have occurred, based upon the spectacular sacrifices extracted from an impoverished labourforce. It was the economic launching of Japan, achieved by war not by markets. Morishima (1982: 96–97) concludes on the period from the early 1930s,

> Economic growth was certainly not achieved through using the mechanism of the free operation of the economy; it was the result of the government or the military, with their loyal following of capitalists, manipulating and influencing the economy in order to realise national aims ... the price mechanism scarcely played an important role, and the questions of importance were how to raise capital and to meet the government's demands and the nature of the demand generated from the enterprises at the receiving end of a government demand.

The losses were huge. In 1945, the gross domestic product was only just over half what it had been in 1941. There were three million casualties. Most naval shipping and planes were lost, 80 per cent of civil shipping, 35 per cent of the national machinery stock, a quarter of the building stock. Perhaps a quarter of the national wealth was destroyed, and the government's debts increased 10 times. But the economy had still expanded enormously and created a workforce capable of supporting spectacular growth, the basis ultimately for Japan's emergence half a century later as the second-largest national economy in the world.

EUROPE'S LAST WARLORD: NAZI GERMANY

Remarkable as Japan's economic development was, it was the capacity of military Prussia – in its German guise – which, with a Napoleonic inspiration of the German people (but without a German revolution), astonished, confused and terrified the world. Hitler took the logic of the European state system and the stunning economic power which it had released to its final absurdity, to self-destruction.

The First World War, far from ending the drama, proved only a rehearsal. It seemed as if, in the years of peace, governments and people were, unknown to themselves, only being trained for what was needed for total war, for the complete mobilisation of the entire resources of countries in unremitting and pitiless mutual destruction. Of course, unknown to all, new horrors lay beyond the rim of the Second World War, but never again would they call upon the totality of society. Total war required totalitarianism, whether in its extreme or its moderate forms, and the pinnacle of the totalitarian orders was the Second World War.

The build-up was slow. Stern (1960/1961) sees the 1890s as the time when the German High Command returned to considering the direct integration of the civil economy with the needs of warfare. The military planners estimated what immense production modern war would require and inferred that to extract this output would require making the economy a single supply system, a 'socialist system', not a set of interacting markets, let alone one determined by consumer demand. But these were still hesitant conceptions, lacking both precision and economic sophistication, even if they recognised that the whole of society was engaged in war, and that the outcome was a partial function of the level of economic development, of technical innovation and economic reserves. '[M]odern war', as Colonel Georg Thomas (in Carroll 1968: 40) of the German High Command expressed it, echoing Clausewitz, 'is no longer a clash of armies, but a struggle for the existence of the peoples involved. All resources of the nation must be made to serve the war.'

In 1924, the German High Command established an Economic Staff Office in the General Staff (with Georg Thomas as its chief) to develop preliminary economic plans. The office also had responsibility to retain links with former

Wehrmacht officers now working in industry and therefore identified as possible economic instruments of military purposes. With the 1926 departure of the Allied Control Commission (supervising Germany's continued disarmament under the Versailles Treaty) and the beginnings of Germany's rearmament, Defence Minister General Gröner instructed the Office to begin working on guidelines for the conversion of industry to war production, with a matching plan to ensure adequate supplies of labour and raw materials, and means to stimulate and sustain the morale of the population. This would require general government intervention in the economy to supersede the profit motive and control employment, prices and output. Such an approach would need to en-compass the whole of society and the entire allocation system as well as the psychology and emotional condition of the population.

These concerns produced a new subject, *Wehrwirtschaft*, the study of the means to reshape the peacetime economy to fit the needs of warfare, or as Count Alexander Brockdorff (in Volkman in Deist et al. 1990: 492) put it in 1935, 'the remoulding in peacetime of the economy for war on the basis of military considerations'. This later produced a *kriegswirtschaft*, a war economics (Stern 1960/1961: 274). Both subjects were established in the Prussian War Academy and the Academy of Military Technique at the Berlin Technical University. The creation of these subjects was based upon the judgement that war was not an exceptional state of modern society, but part of the norm, and furthermore an important developmental opportunity (indeed, a necessary feature of a dynamic economy). Colonel Thomas (in Overy 1994: 178n.) summarised this view: 'the frontiers between war and peace, State and economy, politics and the conduct of war, have disappeared and the defence-based economy has become the definite economic trend of our time'. The view that war was normal and acceptable was something that both Hitler, privately, and Mussolini, publicly, were concerned to establish: 'The distinction between a war and a peacetime economy,' in Mussolini's words during an address to the Supreme Committee for Self-Sufficiency (18 November 1939, in *The Times*, 30 November 1939 in Stern 1960/1961: 275),

> is simply absurd. There is no such thing as an economy of peacetime and an economy of wartime. There is only a war economy because in history, on the basis of the number of years of war, it is proved that the state of warfare is the normal state of the peoples, at least, of those living on the European continent, and because, even in the years of so-called peace, other forms of warfare are practised which in turn, prepare for armed warfare.

However, these concerns did not encompass merely Germany's domestic economy at that time. They were integrated in the main lines of foreign and international commercial policy. A common inference from Germany's loss of the First World War was that it had been overwhelmed by far larger economies – the US, the

British Empire, Russia. For Germany to stand a chance of winning in any future conflict, it must become also a *grossraum*, a large economic territory or empire. Hitler in his *Secret Book* (1928) announced that the First World War had brought to an end the old bourgeois order of capitalism and the nation-state; henceforth the struggle would be between empires. Germany must thus take up the central military task of conquering an empire – 'We National Socialists,' he proclaimed in *Mein Kampf* (1943: 654), 'consequently draw a line beneath the foreign policy tendency of our pre-war period. We take up where we broke off 600 years ago. We stop the endless German movement to the south and west, and turn our gaze towards the land of the east'; and again (Hitler 1943: 131), 'the new German Empire should set out on its march along the same road as was formerly trodden by the Teutonic knights, this time to acquire soil for the German plough by means of the German sword, and this to provide the nation with its daily bread'. Hitler's archaic – peasant – imagery coincided, however, with entirely modern military preoccupations with securing exclusive access to the raw materials required for arms. The Führer might speak of clearing the Ukraine to settle hundreds of thousands of German farming families, but it was the iron ore of eastern Ukraine and the oil of Romania which had more concern for the High Command. Hitler had also a guiding fantasy that the world was being strangled by a Jewish conspiracy, the heart of which lay in Russia, Poland and the Ukraine (as well as the US), so that the two missions – land for German farms and the destruction of the global conspiracy – coincided (Kershaw 2000: 68).

Perhaps the vision of land for farms, of new colonisation, had some appeal as an archaic rural idyll to the mass of unemployed Germans, many of whom might still have parents or grandparents who farmed, even though the supply of 'daily bread' was, at this stage, hardly one of the most important problems facing Germany. The later years of the Weimar Republic witnessed the devastation of the economy in the worst slump in the history of industrial capitalism, at its most severe in Germany. Between 1929 and 1933, eight million workers lost their jobs, industrial output fell to the level of the 1890s (by 43 per cent between 1927 and 1932), and agricultural production declined by 37 per cent. Political instability and growing insecurity produced, for many, a longing for order, for the direction of business to prevent layoffs, for centralisation and an imposed discipline. The first autarkic controls were introduced to offset slump and predate the Nazi ascent to power – indeed Wette (in Deist et al. 1990: 722) concludes that '1933 [when the Nazis came to power] did not represent a break; rather the National Socialist regime was able to exploit the favourable climate of opinion in its practical work'.

Opinion among many of the ruling order favoured national autarky and central planning, even without the preoccupations of the military planners.

Indeed, Gregor Strasser of the Nazis presented a project to the Reichstag in May 1932 for an autarkic and state-directed economy, with an agriculture capable of feeding the population, and a level of exports only sufficient to purchase necessary imports, organised through bilateral state agreements (Volkman in Deist et al. 1990: 177). Autarky promised for the farmers protection and so high prices, but for the Nazi strategist (Wilhelm Deist in Deist et al. 1990: 181), it expressed 'the vital right of every people and every nation so to shape its economy that it becomes a fortress within which, in the event of trade policy, currency policy, or indeed, warlike complications, it cannot be brought to its knees by hunger or by thirst'. It also captured supreme power for the state to dominate the economy, and prevented Germany's capitalists escaping through their linkages with foreign markets.

However, at the outset of Nazi rule, Germany not only depended upon a considerable body of imports, it was a major exporter. Any long-term policy of autarky collided directly with the interests of a significant section of big business. Indeed Germany's breakneck pace of expansion in the mid-and later 1930s, the results of the massive rearmament efforts, required a rising volume of imports and thus increasing exports.

Once in power, Hitler proceeded on the question of autarky, as on so many issues, with circumspection. Nonetheless, there was a drive to try to increase agricultural self-sufficiency – the agriculture *führer*, Darré, launched a 'production battle' to achieve self-sufficiency in food and limit imports to vital raw materials for armaments (it failed – the regime was not willing to pay the farmers enough). In 1933/34, Georg Thomas, on behalf of the German High Command published a five-year plan to co-ordinate military supplies, and achieve some measure of food and raw material self-sufficiency. Concrete steps were, however, limited at this stage.

In 1933, the German economy was mired deeply in the Great Depression, at its lowest point. Industrial production was not much over half the level of 1928, investment barely covered a third of depreciation, a third of the workforce (or some six million workers) was without work. Gross national product had declined by over 7 per cent per year since 1929. There was little sign of recovery as Hitler assumed office. However, the central priority of the new government was to develop national military capacity – 'The future of Germany,' Hitler told the cabinet in February 1933 (in Overy 1994: 4) 'depends exclusively and alone on rebuilding the armed forces'. But in the immediate period to 1936, the priority was to develop infrastructure (to support the military drive) and to lower unemployment. The new government was – perhaps to its intense surprise and relief – immensely successful in these two complementary endeavours. Public funds pumped into infrastructure (particularly the *autobahns*, as well as

housing and military spending), ran at three times the level of industrial investment and led to double digit-growth (to 1938). The effect on unemployment
seemed little short of magic: 4.8 million (1933); 2.7 million (1934); 1.7 million
(1935). By 1937, the six million unemployed at the beginning of the decade had
found jobs and there was evidence of labour scarcities. Industrial production
had exceeded its previous peak, 1928–29, and real gross national product was a
tenth higher. By comparison, US unemployment was still around 20 per cent,
British over 10 per cent (Abelshauser in Harrison 1998: 122–76).

Parallel to this performance, the share of the armed forces in public expenditure advanced from 4 per cent (1933); to 18 per cent (1934), 39 per cent (1936);
and fully a half by 1938 – 'Everything to the armed forces' as Hitler put it in
February 1933. The army was expanded to 21 divisions (three times the size
permitted to Germany under the Versailles Treaty). However, there was less
success in the other military priority, the minimisation of the dependence of
Germany on imports to sustain this overall growth.

In 1934, under military pressure, Economics Minister Hjalmar Schacht was
made 'economic dictator'. He prepared a new plan to centralise the preparations
for war, its central aim being the radical reduction in external economic
dependence. A virtual state monopoly of foreign trade was introduced, with
the control of imports to priority needs (arms and food), export subsidies and
a series of bilateral treaties with governments in Eastern and Southern Europe
to guarantee supplies from militarily controllable sources.

The plan failed in this respect, as did the Four Year Plan that replaced it, with
vastly increased powers of intervention under the Party direction of Herman
Göring (rather than that of a former private businessman like Schacht). This
created, in the view of Georg (now General) Thomas, 'a war economy in its pure
form'. (Volkman in Deist et al. 1990: 277). Hitler's commentary on the Four Year
Plan reiterated the aim of achieving total autarky (but 'wherever possible'). But
it was impossible to force foreign governments supplying Germany with raw
materials to accept terms of sale which favoured Germany; on the contrary,
under the bilateral agreements, Germany could only secure priority materials
(oil, bauxite, chrome, iron ore) by buying the supplying countries' agricultural
surpluses at 20-40 per cent above world prices, a premium level to include also an
allowance for the fact that Germany did not pay in freely convertible currencies.
Economic imperialism could work only with bayonets.

If a section of the military promoted the reorganisation of the peacetime civil
economy to support a future war effort, Hitler had little interest in economic
questions. Like most of the historical rulers of Europe, he was concerned only
with the grand strategy of domination – he felt, in Carr's words (1972: 1), that
'the conduct of foreign affairs was the supreme art of the statesman and an activity

which must take precedence over all other aspects of policy'. The economy – and its agents, private businessmen – were there to solve the problems thrown up by foreign policy (and keep the population properly soothed) – 'Hitler's own view of the economy,' Overy (1994: 2) writes, 'was as primarily an instrument of power. For him, the economy was not simply an arena for generating wealth and technical progress; its *raison d'etre* lay in its ability to provide the material springboard for military conquest'. Or again (Overy 1994: 235): 'He was happy for the economy to perform the political tasks which he set it to do – the creation of employment before 1937, preparation for war afterwards; but he left Schacht and big business to achieve the first, and unwisely expected Göring to achieve the second'.

Hitler's indifference to the economic questions did not help to relieve the external dependence. The problems grew increasingly severe: the shortage of raw materials and the foreign exchange to purchase them (because of the relative decline in exports). There were severe balance-of-payments problems in the second half of 1936, and thus an inability to purchase the imports required to sustain growth. Furthermore, agricultural output was inadequate – harvests were poor, partly because of a price freeze and rising demand because of full employment: the government considered bread rationing. An embargo by Russia on oil exports to Germany led to a fuel crisis at the same time. The Fuhrer was unrelenting: 'If we do not succeed in developing the German *Wehrmacht* within the shortest possible time into the finest army in the world... Germany will be lost. The principle applies here that the omission of peacetime months cannot be made good in centuries' (memo to Göring in Carr 1972: 57).

From 1936, workers became increasingly scarce, a situation made worse in August of that year when the period of military service was doubled to two years (publicly this was supposedly in response to the same change in France and Russia) to create a peacetime army of 36 divisions (with 800,000 men under arms). The expansion of the economy stripped the country of labour reserves, leading to controls, and finally direction of labour to ensure national priorities were met and a scarcity of workers did not produce wage inflation.

A quarter of the gross domestic product (and over half of government spending, leaving aside indirect spending on arms and materials) was now devoted to the armed forces (1939). In the last three years of the decade, two thirds of industrial investment is said to have been directed to war and war-related expenditure. Yet still the pressure grew to increase output for war. This produced a relative decline in production for the civilian population. While heavy industrial output increased (by 170 per cent), investment in consumption goods production did not reach the 1929 level (consumption as a proportion of an admittedly growing national income declined from 71 per cent in 1928 to 59 per cent in 1938).

The growth in war output was spectacular. Take, for example, the airforce. In 1933, the *Luftwaffe* was said to have possessed 80 aircraft with 450 staff, and little manufacturing capacity. By 1936, 180,000 were employed in manufacturing aircraft, and Germany was already a technical leader in the field. The 1938 plan now proposed building the means to manufacture 16,000 combat aircraft within two years (a five-fold increase in capacity).

In November 1937, Hitler outlined to his service chiefs his immediate plans: to undertake a European war sometime between 1943 and 1945 to conquer a resource-rich area in Central Europe as the economic basis to sustain world war. This entailed subsidiary plans for a vast increase in, for example, investment in air power and in naval armaments (to be completed by 1949).

By 1939, the accidental opportunities of foreign policy – and Hitler's exploitation of the main chance without provoking Great Power armed opposition – had gone a considerable way to creating a manufacturing core to the new German Empire. The Reich had absorbed the Rhineland, Austria, Sudetenland–Bohemia. Through bilateral agreements it had achieved the capacity to draw on raw materials from Eastern Europe – Romania, Hungary, Slovenia, Greece, Bulgaria – with further links to Spain and Italy. The next targets were the coal and iron ore deposits of Polish Silesia, and the agricultural output of Poland proper. By then, the Fuhrer assured his service chiefs in May 1939, Germany would be invincible. But, as it happened, so great was the demand for raw materials that some sectors of arms production were operating at 70 per cent of capacity. Although pursued entirely on grounds other than those of raw-material supply, Hitler's masterstroke of a pact with the Soviet Union incidentally acted to relieve the difficulties of domestic war production. The Nazi–Soviet Pact of 1939 brought the supplies Germany needed; the Führer, with some jubilation, was able to assure his generals, 'we need not be afraid of blockade [in the west] as the east will supply us with grain, cattle, coal, lead, zinc' (Volkman in Deist et al. 1990: 358). Germany had paid for two-thirds of what was supplied before the *Wehrmacht* launched its fateful invasion of the USSR.

The plan targets for achieving the full complement of armaments might lie in the future – some were scheduled to be complete only at the end of the 1940s – but Germany by 1938 had become a war economy. Its central principle was now to devote all possible resources to the aim of achieving military preparedness. For the civilian population, this entailed a kind of civilian military mobilisation. Consider this 1939 injunction, with its echoes of the spirit of the edict of the French revolutionary Assembly in 1793 (see p. 71):

> All German people, wherever they are and whether they are at present in uniform or not, are soldiers ... Each one must serve the community and subordinate himself to it, since he depends on it and cannot exist without it. In the event of war, the

whole nation, from children ... to the most aged, and including women as well, are
part of the defensive struggle (SA Hauptstürm Führer Simon in Der SA Führer 4/39
in Volkman, ibid: 149).

More pithily and with more qualification, Göring, after the outbreak of war
with France and Britain, repeated the point to the Reich Defence Council (18
November 1939): 'Every German, male or female, aged between 14 and 65, must
in effect have a mobilisation order in his or her pocket, indicating where they
are wanted'.

Hitler had moderately good grounds for assuming that Britain and France
would not react to the invasion of Poland, particularly given that he had
succeeded in neutralising the Soviet Union (partly by agreeing to share the
spoils with Moscow). This miscalculation was, as it subsequently turned out,
fateful. French and British opposition gave him the pretext to overrun Western
Europe and Scandinavia, to eliminate France and chase the British off the
continent. It seemed now that very little could stop him.

Full war also gave the regime the occasion for full economic mobilisation of
the country. In the winter of 1939–40, Hitler increased the output targets well
beyond what had seemed entirely unrealistic before. He now sketched in the
material requirements for his long war, a war of 10–15 years' duration. The targets
were spectacular: a five-fold increase in aircraft production (with an annual
peacetime target of 20,000, and wartime production of 30–40,000); in 1940,
Germany produced 10,000, itself a remarkable achievement on the past but only
half the peacetime target, a third to a quarter of the wartime aim.

In passing, we can note that *grossraum* did not, at least in the form Hitler
envisaged it, work. The Ukraine did not provide land for German farmers nor
supply the Reich with bread. On the contrary, it was from developed France and
the Benelux countries in the west that this came. The French were forced to
supply far more food and industrial raw materials than were available in the
occupied but impoverished Soviet Union. The productivity of labour in a
developed country was far more important than mere land.

For the average German, the choices, insofar as there were any, were between
volunteering for war and risking death, or a life of unremitting and poorly
remunerated civilian toil to sustain the Führer's ambitions. It was not just that
Hitler called the bluff of the state-making system, he called the bluff of German
xenophobia – how much was the average German prepared to sacrifice for the
fantasies of his leader? In 1940, on the record, it might have seemed that the
Führer could not fail. The unbound German Prometheus could, with impunity,
cry defiance at the gods. Yet two of his decisions pulled him back to earth: to
plunge into the quagmire of Russia, in which he would lose his thousands of
warriors, and to declare war on the US with its awesome economic might.

Hitler and Capitalism

Nazi Germany tests to the limits the thesis that capitalism as a system, in the 1930s, controlled the state, that Germany was in any sense a 'capitalist state', dedicated to the purposes of the growth of capital. Much work, particularly in the former East Germany and the Soviet Union, has gone into identifying the evidence that Hitler and his comrades came to power in order to 'represent' the capitalist class of Germany, particularly big business. Indeed, in Brecht's famous play, *The Resistable Rise of Arturo Ui*, the relationship of the Nazis to business is represented in the fable of a quasi-Hitler and his gangster friends being invited to run the town by the shopkeeper in order to defend him against the workers. The approach contradicts the central thesis of this book and so requires some examination.

Before Hitler came to power, the lack of a single coherent political position by big business is more striking than support for one party or another. Indeed, under the terrible blows of the Great Depression, the political views of business tended to fragment across the spectrum of options, albeit tending to avoid the Social Democrats and the Communists, but also the Nazis (or NSDAP, the German National Socialist Workers Party, as it officially called itself) as being no better than the left. On the other hand, once in office, the Nazis presided over a sustained economic boom (in conditions of world stagnation), and many businessmen were prime beneficiaries of this process. After 1936, the divergence of interests as Hitler's war plans became better known became extreme, even though business in general had no means to oppose the trend – certainly no means as powerful as that of the armed forces, no less concerned to avoid self-destruction and yet no less captive to the Nazi state.

In the run-in to power, there is no solid evidence of big business support for the NSDAP, and for obvious reasons. The Nazis, seeing themselves as competitors of the left for the popular vote, called for revolution, the destruction of capitalism and the formation of a 'workers' and soldiers' state'. Party propaganda demanded the nationalisation of cartels, trusts, monopolies and the largest companies, covering much of Germany's big business of the time. It would have been perverse in the extreme for big business to contribute to such a party – without the benefit of knowing what was to happen in the future.

Hitler's general approach was entirely pragmatic on the issue of private business, not believing that it was either a serious political threat or that it could contribute to the ascent to power, particularly given the need to appeal to the popular, anti-capitalist feeling in the country. Bullock (1952: 141) illustrates the point: 'When Otto Strasser asked him what he would do with Krupp [the best-known and largest family business group in Germany] if he came to power,

Hitler at once replied, "Of course, I would leave him alone. Do you think that I should be so mad as to destroy Germany's economy?"' Anti-capitalism dominated the tone of popular opinion, so no party with an aspiration to power could be anything other than that. Small business and farmers, an important potential base of support for the Nazis, were also universally hostile to big business.

There is no evidence, it seems, of big business contributions to the finances of the NSDAP. The party, up to 1932, appears to have financed itself out of subscriptions and collections, although in 1933, as members of the National Front (with the German National Party and a veterans' organisation), the coalition received some business funds. But in general, 'Most [leading businessmen] remained frustrated politically, having discovered that economic potency did not translate readily into political effectiveness in a democratic polity, where ballots weighed more than money and where blocs of disciplined interest-group voters counted for more than did financial contributions' (Turner 1985: 340).

Hitler seems to have avoided meeting businessmen publicly for fear that it would compromise the appearance of Nazi anti-capitalism. His one publicised encounter was a speech to the Industrial Club of Dusseldorf (26 January 1932); it occurred because the club – to protests – had earlier invited a Social Democrat speaker, and Hitler was put up supposedly to balance this. People in the audience reported that he said little specific and nothing on his party's intentions for the economic future of the country, except to stress the urgent need to defeat Marxism. There were no questions. In the audience, apart from the well-known Nazi supporter Fritz Thyssen, there were none of the great names of the Ruhr, but rather managers and owners (with some 207 lawyers) of medium-sized companies; no one from Krupp or I.G. Farben, later associated with the Nazi government, was in attendance. When, at the end, Thyssen identified his commitment, about a third of the audience cheered. However, with some jubilation, the left-wing press highlighted the occasion as showing the junction of the great barons of capitalism and the Nazis, but it was a far-fetched thesis. Nonetheless, perhaps it discouraged Hitler from any other meetings with business – he refused to address the Hanover Business Club shortly afterwards.

Hitler did encourage the creation of a circle of business advisers, the Keppler Group. But only two of the twelve participants were thought to be of any substance in the business world (the best known was Hjalmar Schacht, ex-President of the Reichsbank and to be Hitler's first Minister of the Economy). At this stage, one person from I.G. Farben joined the NSDAP before it came to power, but he was a 38-year-old executive rather than one of the senior owners or managers.

Once in office, however, matters changed, and business and government were necessarily interdependent. Indeed, Hitler crushed not only the left of the

NSDAP, the people who had mistakenly taken his anti-capitalism seriously, but also the trade unions and the Social Democratic and Communist Parties, in order to establish his public credentials. Now national economic policy restored the capital markets, stabilised the economy, expanded public investment, and set in train a boom bigger and longer sustained than anything that had happened since the First World War. Business had come so close to being destroyed, economically and politically, that it is hardly to be wondered that there was universal gratitude for the restoration of profits and growth.

The solid basis of growth underpinned greater business tolerance of 'left excesses' by the Nazis. When the SA occupied the headquarters of the employers' association at the time of the suppression of the trade unions, Krupp volunteered to collect funds from firms for the NSDAP if the campaign of violence against business was ended. The offer was accepted – 'this financial backing', Schweitzer (1964: 36) comments, 'was not a payment for services expected or received; rather, it was a form of protection money, voluntarily offered and readily paid, for being exempted from the violence of the SA as well as from the spy system and concentration camps of the Gestapo'. On the other hand, the government was willing to make concessions when needed – when the party called for the compulsory reorganisation of business into corporatist groups in 1934, Schacht used his influence to ensure that the proposal was dropped.

There was business resentment that the government so consistently favoured heavy industry (and hence the Ruhr), rather than the major part of the economy, the consumer industries. However, heavy industry after 1936 was hostile to the orientation on autarky, since many of the bigger businesses were highly competitive exporters, did not trust the Nazis' capacity to stay in power, and were unwilling to risk expanding capacity without being able to export to diversified markets. By 1935, there was a growing recognition that business objections carried little weight with the regime, and indeed might carry the risk of punishment. Hitler indicated the correct balance of power in his view of the relationship in a 1935 memorandum (in Abelshauser in Harrison 1998: 145): 'The Economic Ministry has merely to set national economic tasks, and the private sector has to implement them. If, however, the private sector believe that it is unable to do this, then the National Socialist State will know how to solve these tasks itself.'

The emphasis on autarky in the Fourth Plan exacerbated the hostility, but expansion soothed business resentments, binding firms into the projects of the state. Public funds consoled for the sacrifices, even if it was a most inefficient outcome, as Overy (1994: 200) notes: 'The "military-industrial" complex was a very one sided arrangement, creating through military priorities and technical ignorance, a high cost, wasteful and poorly organised armaments economy'. Businessmen willing to accept public direction and close regulation established secure patron–client relationships and made profits, combining in Overy's words again (1994: 18), 'a defensive opportunism' with an 'unavoidable complicity'. Even the mighty Krupp could not deflect the regime – in the end, the group accepted the shutting off of its export markets in return for extraordinarily large army orders, locking the Krupp companies into state priorities (not the state into Krupp priorities). I. G. Farben, the group most close to the regime (and one of the largest beneficiaries), the group whose officials manned part of the public structure and shaped policy in the fields of closest interest to them, was unable to influence the priorities of the regime outside the sphere of its technical competence (Hayes 2001).

The real balance of power was illustrated when the Ruhr business magnates, supposedly the most powerful group of big businessmen in Germany, dared to seek to challenge the state on the issue of autarky in the steel industry. Despite all the efforts, Germany by 1936/37 could still only meet 18 per cent of the steel industry's need for iron ore from domestic sources. The bulk of the rest was imported from France and Sweden. Göring, now boss of the Economic Plan, instructed the industry to reduce imports by relying on low-quality domestic ore (where the ferrous content was only 30 per cent) from Salzgitte. The Ruhr steel-makers argued that to use this ore would require the expensive reconstruction of their blast furnaces and a doubling of capacity, and the high cost of the resulting output would make it impossible for them to supply their customers abroad. Hence the steelmakers would lose their long-term markets and Germany's export revenues would decline, making it more difficult to import vital supplies for the rearmament programme. There was some give – the steelmen admitted that they might use local ore if steel prices could be raised by 50 per cent. Hitler's response (February 1937 in Volkman in Deist et al. 1990: 307) made no concessions: private industry must solve the technical question of using domestic ore or forfeit the right 'to continue as a free industry'. Again, there was some flexibility, since the government made it known that it would be willing to consider covering any increased costs.

The proper reply, in July 1937, was somewhat more brutal. Göring set up, within the public sector, the Reichswerke Herman Göring to bypass the barons of the Ruhr heavy industry. The Reichswerke compulsorily purchased the private mineral rights of Salzgitte with a view to producing public-sector steel. In August 1937, the Ruhr steelmen met to draft a defiant rejection of this innovation in what became known as the Dusseldorf Memorandum. This rehearsed the arguments for rejecting Göring's change of direction and defending *gewerbef-freiheit* (business freedom). The change of policy was seen as fatally compromising 'the businessmen's independence of action and the maximisation of profit and economic advantage which that independence permitted. Nazi political hegemony in the end prevented German capitalists from acting as capitalists' (Overy 1994: 94).

It was a pathetic gesture, showing how little Ruhr heavy industry understood the balance of power and the state. The Gestapo were monitoring the meeting, and for a time Göring considered arresting the whole group. He was dissuaded, and instead sent a warning telegram to the nine leading participants (and a letter to Krupp, promising great and exclusive benefits if he co-operated). Seven of the nine withdrew their support, and the memorandum was not sent. The two rebels were summoned to meet Göring, and the Gestapo tape recording was played back to them, with warnings of the concentration camp. It was the end of the rebellion. Schacht, still President of the Reichsbank, had lent the group some support, so he also was sacked. Ruhr steel had learnt the lesson. The car industry was taught the same when it demurred at starting the people's car project – the Volkswagen factory was opened by the state at Fallersleben (later Wolfsburg).

The Reichswerke then began a process of spectacular growth. In the control system – under Göring's economic dictatorship – it was favoured with scarce raw materials, labour and plant. It expanded wherever the state needed supplies and regardless of private interests – into aviation, aluminium, synthetic oil and rubber (in collaboration with I. G. Farben), chemicals, military equipment, as well as iron and steel. It took over assets expropriated from Jewish families (for example the industrial group of Count Louis Rothschild) and from renegades (from Thyssen after he fled from the Nazis and Germany in 1939). It was the heir to industrial assets in the occupied territories: Austrian mines, steel works, factories in engineering, armaments, operations in construction and shipping; Czech heavy industry; coal mines in Polish Silesia, Soviet Ukraine and the Donetz basin; a mass of private ownership rights in associated companies and subsidiaries. Within 18 months of its foundation, the Reichswerke had become the third-largest enterprise in Germany, and by 1941 the largest economic group in Europe, symbolising in its scale, diversity and growth the unification of the economy and war in the hands of the state, of profit and theft.

As the Reich extended, the Reichswerke followed as an economic jackal. Göring was careful always to assert pre-emptive rights to the spoils of war; in Poland, he warned private German business, 'Any wild confiscations and any profiteering of individuals will be prosecuted ... The essential point is that Polish property liable to confiscation shall be utilised in the interests of the Reich, i.e. of the community but not for the benefit of individuals' (19 October 1939 in Overy 1994: 332). No private German interests were allowed to lay claims to property in Poland and East Prussia (lost to the Reich under the Versailles Treaty), and there were specific exclusions of German business from priority areas – for example the iron mines of Lorraine.

Göring failed. His gigantic enterprise was ultimately broken up in 1942. The new economic dictator retained such sections as were required. However, the exercise demonstrated the real balance of power between the state and private business – business was reduced to being an instrument of the state, not at all the reverse. Only the shell of private enterprise remained under state direction and, as in the Soviet Union, those who managed industry were subject to state instructions, backed by the use of terror and the threat of the concentration camp (and, as in the Soviet Union, economic failure by business was 'economic sabotage', treason): 'The first 18 months of Nazi rule...,' Hayes (2001: 122–23) writes, 'established in the Third Reich, for individual businessmen and everyone else, that terror was the greatest of political realities'.

Thus, in sum, the case that Nazi Germany was directed by German capitalism is as plausible an argument as that the Soviet regime embodied an alliance of the workers and peasants of the USSR. The evidence is sufficient to have led one of the leading non-Communist Marxists of the post-war period, Timothy Mason, to acknowledge that 'both the domestic and foreign policy of the National Socialist Government became, from 1936 onwards, increasingly independent of the influence of the economic ruling classes, and even in some essential respects, ran contrary to their interests' (1966: 54). Or again, 'The political leadership of the Third Reich was able through means unforeseen by anyone to maintain their independence from the old ruling class which it had gained in the crisis of 1930–31' (1966: 59). It 'is in fact very difficult to demonstrate the participation of economic leaders or organisations, even in an individual way, in the formation of overall policy in the Third Reich' (1966: 61). Mason sees the circumstances as almost unique, and therefore the Nazis as *sui generis*. Yet, just as there was nothing special about the year 1936 in terms of the formation of state policy in Germany (only a change of direction), so Hitler behaved in principle no differently to the historic leaders of Germany in his relationship to business, and no different to the rivals he faced abroad. Capital and its interests did not direct the state anywhere at this time.

THE SECOND WORLD WAR

The war brought the European war-making system to perhaps the highest point it would ever achieve, the collision of completely unified militarised national states, now put to the task for which they were designed, unremitting mutual destruction. Mussolini might boast, 'All in the State; nothing outside the State; nothing against the State' (in Rosenberg 1958: 2), but it was true to a greater or lesser degree in all the belligerent countries. Furthermore, the system was now so strong that it is hardly surprising that, after the exhausted cessation of hostilities in 1945, the best that could be hoped for was a return to a further phase in the perpetual war, albeit a Cold War, to domestic orders of Lloyd's 'military communism', or Orwell's slightly more realistic picture of 1984. Even during the war, observers saw as much. The distinguished American sociologist Harold Lasswell (1940) brooded gloomily – like Engels in 1878, but without the American being able to derive Engels' ultimate optimism from the picture of catastrophe – on the emergence of a world of 'garrison States', enshrining 'the supremacy of the soldier'. Popular psychology had now to be continually managed to ensure confidence and morale: 'concerted action depends upon skilfully guiding the minds of men; hence the enormous importance of symbolic manipulation in modern society' (1941: 320) in order that they will work willingly in whatever activity the state requires, to obey whatever is ordered. 'From the earliest years, youth will be trained to subdue – to disavow, to struggle against – any specific opposition to the ruling code of collective exactions'. All other associations would be disallowed, 'no economic, religious or cultural life outside the duly constituted agencies of government' would be permitted.

The gloom at the total militarisation of society, anticipated in times of peace as of war, was paralleled during the Second World War by the most extraordinary economic expansion in the history of industrial society. It produced an immensely enhanced output dedicated to the laying waste and the slaughter of the other side. The 'sides' were not now the immense serried ranks of warriors, but whole economies, the great engines of warfare. The five Great Powers in the leading position put 43 million men in the field (perhaps over a third of their male working population), with each economy fully mobilised to sustain them. In the end, it was the greatest combined economic weight, that of the Allies, pre-eminently the Americans, which won the contest. Two thirds of the troops, in the end, were Allied. Not that the largest number predetermined victory – Russia showed that. It was the economic muscle to sustain those men (and to control the seas and the air through which supplies from the world at large travelled) which now counted: nearly 50 million rifles, automatics and machine guns were produced by the Allies (1942–1944); over two million guns and mortars; over 200,000 tanks; over 400,000 combat aircraft; nearly 9000 naval vessels (Harrison 1998: 13). By 1944, the Allies were producing three times as much war material as the Axis powers.

Thus, in this kind of warfare the superiority in absolute economic weight of the US could not be defeated (of course, this was not true after the war for other types of warfare). Under the lash of war, an already giant economy grew with stunning speed. Between 1939 and 1940, the US gross national product increased by 52 per cent, and total manufacturing output by 300 per cent

(1940–1944);[2] on the volume index, this represented an annual average increase of 15 per cent (compared to 4 per cent from 1896 to 1939). By sectors of war production, the picture was even more staggering – on an index for 1939 of 100, aircraft production reached 245 in 1940, and 2842 in 1943; in explosives and ammunition, 140 and 3803; in ships, 159 and 1815. In five years, American industry produced nearly 300,000 military and special purpose aircraft (compared to Germany's 111,767 in ten years, or Britain's 123,818, also in ten years; let alone Japan's 69,900 in five years, and the Soviet Union's, 138,800, also in five years). In tanks, the US produced 86,700, compared to Germany's 44,857 (but the Soviet Union's 138,800). For sheer production, it seemed, war could not be matched as a stimulus, certainly not by mere markets.

In the American case – unlike those of its allies or its enemies – this prodigious increase in the output for war went also with a tangible increase in the popular standard of living: it was a real boom. Average hourly wages increased by 50 per cent in the war years, and pre-tax profits by 350 per cent (post-tax profits, however, by 120 per cent).

Growth was fuelled by a growing utilisation of capacity (there were still three million unemployed in December 1941); an increase in the size of the workforce; a diversion of workers and investment from agriculture, domestic service and those not in paid employment (for example housewives) to industry; by increasing the productivity of those in work (in industry, averaging 25 per cent per year); an increase in hours worked; new investment, and by the unprecedented economies of scale and of continuous mass production. The great advances in modern production, after all the years of dispiriting slump, now came into their own. They allowed the US to subsidise its allies worldwide – from the Kuomintang in China (or the Vietminh in former French Indo-China) to the Soviet Union and Britain; US aircraft supplies, for example, met nearly half the allied demand.

For all the others, output and capacity also expanded with miraculous speed, but the costs were much more apparent. For all except the Americans, the popular standard of living was forced down as resources were redistributed from consumption to war production. In Britain, the richest of the European rivals before 1939, the value of consumption was reduced by a quarter to a fifth between 1938 and 1944. But this was nothing compared to the losses of the Russians. By November 1941, the German forces had occupied 63 per cent of the pre-war coal mining capacity of the USSR, 58 per cent of the steelmaking, 60 per cent of aluminium production and 41 per cent of railway track. The physical assets lost to war reached perhaps a quarter of those existing in 1940 (Harrison 1998: 292). Russia's vulnerability was as much part of Stalin's grotesque strategic errors as German military prowess, but nonetheless it led to the rapid implementation of the long-standing aim of shifting the Soviet economy eastwards to the Ural mountains and beyond. For the much abused Soviet consumer, 1943's agricultural output was 37 per cent of 1940, 1945's 54 per cent, famine levels; the output of consumer goods was 54 per cent of 1939 in 1943, 59 per cent in 1945. Indeed output did not again reach the 1939 level until 1949. By 1945, Russian real wages are estimated to have been 40 per cent of the 1940 level.

The human losses in Russia dwarfed all else, with deaths through war, illness, starvation or malnutrition reaching possibly 27 million. In 1959, there were, in the age group 35–50, still seven women for every man.

People everywhere paid for this heroic economic expansion. The British aimed to cover 53 per cent of war expenditure from taxes, Canada 55 per cent. The Americans aimed for 42 per cent, but by 1943 had achieved only 20 per cent. The Germans looted the occupied territories: between 1943 and 1944, 38 per cent of German public revenues came from these. For all, the gaps were covered through borrowing (against taxes on their future citizens). The British sold off their assets in North America, the cumulative savings of the past, as well as running up extraordinary debts, mortgaging the future, with both the Empire and North America. Thus, both the savings of the past and the income of the future were poured into the abyss. What medieval prince would not have marvelled at this spectacular mobilisation from all his traditional sources, but now on an unbelievably enhanced scale?

Paying for the war, even starving for it, was, of course, not at all the worst of it for non-combatants. America (and for a time Japan) might be protected by distance (the German Amerika project to produce a bomber that could cross the Atlantic and return did not arrive in time), but elsewhere the war of economies made the civilian populations a vital target from the beginning. The vast fleets of bombers now tried to destroy the enemy's economy and demoralise the civilian population. The Luftwaffe attempted both in Britain at the beginning of the war. By 1943, when the RAF sought deliberately to target the German civilian population, to maximise what in our own times has become 'collateral damage', there had been an immense increase in the power to inflict damage. Between 24 and 30 July 1943, 30,000 of the inhabitants of Hamburg were said to have been killed (and 80 per cent of the bridges damaged). Nine months later, the Allies laid waste with fire an area of 1600 acres in the centre of the city of Dresden, with 25,000 dead (mainly women and children) and 35,000 missing. In Japan, incendiary bombs from American bombers in 1945 left 60 per cent of the area of the 60 largest – wooden – cities burnt out. Finally, in an appropriate crescendo to this story of horror, at Hiroshima on 6 August and at Nagasaki three days later over 100,000 were burned to death in the first two atomic bombings.

These murderous assaults on the 'innocent', assumed guilty by reason of their accidental membership of the enemy nation, did not work, or did so, so marginally, that they were hardly worth the effort – unless as acts of fearful revenge. Populations had no power to influence or change their governments. Nor, it seems, did such privations demoralise them. They gave little sign that they were persuaded that their leaders had been or were wrong. The enemy bombers remained less frightening than their own regimes. To the bitter end, it seems, the glue of social – national – solidarity in the main held, and indeed may have been strengthened by the unbelievable hardships and dangers inflicted on Germany. Nor did the bombing seriously damage the military economy. In 1944, 6.5 per cent of Germany's machine-tool industry was destroyed, yet it was repaired or replaced by the end of the year, a 'testimony to the extraordinary productive capacity which a highly developed economy seems to retain in the face of every difficulty' (Milward 1977: 80).

The relative invulnerability to destruction was not simply a product of productive capacity, but of the dedication of the workforce and the central direction of the state. Each government stumbled from immediate problem to problem, endlessly innovating to create a single unified economy and society as a military supply system. Markets were suspended, the price system dispensed with in favour of physical allocation systems and controls, directed by officials. Some of the officials directing the system would be economists, cheerfully abandoning their market paradigms for forms of rigidly enforced mercantilism, even Soviet-style material planning, in the name of the collective. There was little or no attention to costs, only to what was needed, based on the assumption that 'The cost of war was virtually limitless and virtually irrelevant' (Milward 1977: 102). Civil society, the legal system, the defence of rights, were in suspense before the unlimited discretionary power of the state to do as it wished. Furthermore, the *Führerprinzip*, one-man management, had virtually unlimited power. '[W]hat emerged [in Britain],' Milward (1977: 111) writes, 'was almost as far from democracy as the government of Germany or Italy'.

As in 1918, many of the innovations of war persisted into peace. Indeed, Europe's embrace of planning and large public sectors – in heavy industry and mining, in transport, ports and telecommunications, in energy, and in some cases in steel, shipbuilding, aviation, military equipment, and in banking and insurance – could be seen as the completion of the programme of creating national military economies. Of course, the reforms were championed either as instruments of popular liberation or as the necessary technical means to make possible national planning. But they would have been understood in the old Prussian High Command as having a quite different significance.

In the war, there were variations. Military communism was undertaken more comprehensively in Britain than in Germany. The British intervention in the lives of its citizens was paradoxically – in legal terms – more draconian than in the Axis countries, giving total power to the state over private interests to pursue its aims. For example, unlike most governments, the British took powers to conscript women and direct them to whatever work it required (the German government imported between seven and eight million slave labourers to meet a similar severe shortage of workers). There were paradoxical effects: the British enforced a standard consumption level for the population through rationing (and allocation of supplies), leading to an unprecedented degree of equality in consumption (and a measurable narrowing in physical and health differentials). The German order tolerated the growth of, in Milward's words (1977: 284) 'savage inequities'.

In 1914, the decision to go to war by the Tsar, the Kaiser, the Emperor of Austro-Hungary and the Ottoman Sultan ultimately cost each his empire. Similarly, the decision of the European governments to go to war in 1939 and 1940 cost them not only their empires but also their position of political domination in the world. It was an unbelievably costly act of folly.

Furthermore, the Second World War demolished the myth that countries needed *lebensraum*, needed space for people and new raw materials. The productivity of the workers of the US was far more important than the vast acres and millions of the Soviet Union and the British Empire. Of course, it would take a good few more deaths and brutalities before the Europeans were forced to admit this, but the economic rationale was already becoming clear – in the new economy, empire was an economic burden.

For the next half century, the US – with, in some areas, the Soviet Union – exercised a competitive dominion of the world: military, political and economic. It was from a position at the outset of overwhelming economic superiority: by 1944, the US produced 40 per cent of the world's armaments (its output per man hour was about double that of Germany, five times that of Japan). Whereas the fleets of the British Empire were more than twice the size of those of the US in 1939 (the US navy was 43 per cent of the size of the British); by 1947, the British navy was 65 per cent of the size of the American.

THE APOGEE OF THE STATE SYSTEM

The Second World War exposed the inner contradiction of national capitalism and its master, the sovereign state. On the one hand, it led to spectacular increases in production and productive capacity; on the other, to immense destruction. In peacetime, governments defended their failures on the grounds that economic necessities, the outcome of 'blind markets', determined what could be done; in war, the primacy of politics ruled all, the apparently unlimited voluntarism of the state.

Whether in Nazi Germany or the Soviet Union, the state and its powers narrowed to the individual leader, who seemed thus to have the power in his own hands to override all material necessities, all institutions and classes. In Germany, Hitler – with increasing confidence – destroyed or overrode the political ruling class of the country, the trade unions and the left, the Nazi Party, the army, the barons of the Ruhr or German business in general. The closer to war, the more extreme the dictatorship became, until, single-handedly, Hitler could will the self-destruction of Germany. The old ideas of the state – among Marxists, that capital directed the state; among liberals, that the population at large was 'represented' by the institutions of government – were clearly as absurd as the idea that the people of the wards of Chicago directed or were represented by the local Mafia. The state, like the Mafia, had its own agenda, and for those who might disagree the choice was limited to silence or self-destruction. The individual conscience that was supposed to check tyranny could survive such a context of terror only among people so eccentric as to knowingly court suicide: civil society was dead, or just shadow-play like the mass organisations of the Soviet Union or Nazi Germany, controlled by their governments, stamped with the image of the military, the loyal brotherhood of arms.

The voluntarism of the state, the supremacy of politics and what the Nazis and fascists called 'the will', had spectacular successes. Germany in 1933 was economically prostrate, yet within three years the new regime had achieved full employment. Within seven years, it was capable of decisively defeating France and Poland, chasing the British off the continent, seizing the Benelux countries and Scandinavia – and then inflicting devastating losses on the Soviet Union. It was a close-run thing. If the US had not entered the war (or Hitler had not, following Pearl Harbour, declared war), it is possible that Hitler could have secured his domination – and the Europeans might now have to know German. If the German occupation of part of the Soviet Union could have been held, Stalin might have been driven to a compromise settlement, leaving the British marooned on their islands until Germany was ready to deal with them.

Thus, the record for much of the time seemed to demonstrate that the state could achieve anything, that there was no limit to what could be extracted from populations and the marvellous productivity of the modern industrial economy. If the material potential was so dazzling, even more impressive was the capacity of states to persuade the population of the singular merits of self-destruction. The state, as it were, sucked dry the population and raised itself as pure ego, a monstrous instrument of collective vanity and aggression. Populations had been so suborned that they were defenceless before the fantasies of their rulers – for example before the astonishing and absurd delusion that those Germans claiming Jewish descent constituted a conspiracy that controlled the world, and it required a world war to break this control. Why were people no longer defended against these fantasies by elementary common-sense? The state, like the good doctor who identifies an invisible virus as the source of the ailment, could point to an invisible conspiracy and be believed – or at least lead judgement to be suspended. Even self-interest could not stand against the deluge, the desire not to die nor to allow one's family to die. Like those strange religious cults which lead to the collective suicide of the participants, Germany seemed to be in the grip of a longing for self-destruction.

Not all, of course, were convinced. But apart from the opposition in Germany and Italy, only the Russians, Byelorussians and Ukrainians rebelled in any number against their government and welcomed the invading German armies – as ordinary Prussians a century and a half earlier rejected the Prussian military system and welcomed Napoleon. Napoleon was not so cruel as Hitler – the pitiless savagery of the German invaders turned the Russians and Ukrainians, against all odds, into passionate defenders of the Soviet Union. It took pitiless Nazi repression to make the Soviet Great Patriotic War.

Governments acknowledged some residual civil society insofar as they felt obliged to lie, to conceal what they were doing from their domestic audience. In the state-making system, rulers were obliged to pretend that what they did was in the interests of their populations, and the more subject to democratic votes they became, the greater the pretence. So they pretended that domestic policy was all-important, when their behaviour demonstrated that foreign policy was the *raison d'etre* of government. The Weimar regime undertook secret rearmament to defeat the provisions of the Versailles treaty. Just over two decades later, Britain's Winston Churchill developed the atomic bomb without reference to the British House of Commons lest the MPs or the British electorate protest. Pursuing the state agenda required deceit, secret budgets and expenditures, secret services and secret outrages.

However, in the end, the catastrophes of Europe led to an American world. While much of the world proceeded to construct brand new states, to complete at a world level the European state-making system, in Europe itself something different began. Without anyone intending it or foreseeing it, for the first time for more than half a millennium in Europe, the modern state system began to unwind.

PART II

TRANSITIONS

5

The Great Transition

INTRODUCTION

By 1948, it seemed, as little had been settled by the Second as by the First World War. The apparently inexorable logic of the war-making competitive state system had not been dislodged. The Great Powers, scarcely free of the blood-letting and devastation of the second war, returned obediently to the old obsession with planning each other's mutual destruction in a third, now however on a quite extraordinarily enhanced scale of destructiveness.

The economic agenda – building war economies – was now virtually complete, or completed in Europe by the extensive post-war reforms to achieve planned economies and welfare states (all were now to be included in the social framework of the armed forces). What private business survived was heavily corporatist, managed by cartels and monopolies with quasi-public powers, essentially instruments of state. So pervasive was the change that it was taken as part of the normal order of things – the champions of free enterprise approved 'industrial self-government'. Those who favoured competition and free markets were dismissed as marginal, even idiosyncratic to the point of being dangerous. The corporatist–statist right (the liberal Right hardly survived) joined hands with the left in the tasks of organising national state-capitalism. In Britain, this was symbolised by the Conservative Party's embrace of an Industrial Charter in 1947 and its acceptance of 'social democracy' (Harris 1972: 79–84). Of course, the programme of post-war reforms was for most people less the rationalisation

125

of a war economy, more a fortification against the expected post-war slump and stagnation (the sequence that followed the First World War). In Europe, it was assumed that the national economies would remain autarkies, trading as between states, despite the brave American thoughts embodied in the new Bretton Woods regime for international economic relations.

However, it was a quite different world to that of 1918. First, the arena of contest between the Great Powers of Europe had disappeared. One non-European power, the US, now dominated both Europe and the world. What had once been the absolute sovereignty of the European powers was now granted, licensed by Washington – as if the US President had become a new Holy Roman Emperor. There were those in the US who favoured a joint world condominium with Russia, but the partner was for long broken-backed by the war, its people and its economy more harshly savaged by the hostilities than any other. The paramount position of the US – in military, economic and political terms – was unique and perhaps would never be repeated. Indeed, there could be nothing more than a relative decline in the American position in the following years. The symbol of that moment of supreme power was Fort Knox, holding in 1949 three quarters of the world's gold stock. Indeed, knowledgeable Europeans feared US economic domination would paralyse the rest of the world – Europe was being strangled by the lack of liquidity (Balogh 1949). The technological gap between North America and Europe seemed equally unbridgeable – Europe, now shattered by war, could never hope to catch up.

From the American side, the picture was different. The capacity of the economy had been, for the purposes of peace, vastly over-expanded. It had been the same for all the belligerents in 1918, and had been a source of slump and long-term stagnation. Despite the destruction in Europe, the main contestants ended the war with fixed assets not less than 1939, and in some areas, for example machine tools, greater (Harrison 1998: 28). But equipment was technically antiquated (by American standards), and the reduction in the consumer-goods industries, in social infrastructure (especially housing) and transport (vehicles, shipping etc) was, unlike the US, immense. Thus, a peacetime economy in North America seemed to spell slump and stagnation; and insofar as it did, Europe's recovery would be slow and halting. War alone had made possible the great American boom, and without war the world might return to the dispiriting stagnation of the 1930s.

The Americans tried to establish a new order in the face of intense European suspicions that this was merely a cover for American economic domination. As with the British adherence to free trade in the preceding century, seen as simply an intellectually dubious defence for forcing British manufactured exports on everyone else, the US promotion of liberalisation was also seen, perhaps rightly, as a manoeuvre to make space for the prodigious output of the American economy. In 1946, the British parliament – with strong Conservative rage – was bludgeoned into opening the empire to American capital and exports. On the other hand, Churchill's warnings of the threat in Moscow seemed no more than an expression of British self-interest to monopolise Washington's attention. Yet it was Churchill's military–political option which resolved the economic question. On the one hand, Congress – despite fury at having to reward with finance the European warmongers, those who had led to the death of so many Americans – resolved that Europe must be restored rather than punished. Marshall Aid (from June 1947) began to pump modest sums of hard currency into Europe to relieve the gold shortage. On the other, the descent of an 'iron curtain' across Europe (as Churchill put it in his famous speech at Fulton, Missouri) led to the general rearmament of the US and its allies and clients – including Germany, Italy and even Japan. In particular, West Germany, the fragment of the country not occupied by the Soviet Union, was seen as a weak link that might, in exchange for neutrality, accept Soviet proposals for the reunification of the country. It had to be wooed – in an astonishing turnaround in attitudes so recently since the war. Economically, the change in political strategy led to the US financing a quarter of Europe's imports in the three years to 1950 (and two thirds of Europe's imports from the dollar area).

War – or the threat of war – had once more played its wonderfully therapeutic role in creating economic growth, in saving capitalism. It seemed, yet again, politics was all, the state determined the economy. As the European economy moved into rapid growth, the strategic pieces fell into place – the Czechoslovak Republic fell to Moscow; the Soviet Union tested its first atomic bomb; the Chinese Communist Party came to power in Beijing; and in 1950, 'hot war' broke out between on the one hand, the US and its allies, and on the other the North Korean regime, backed by the Soviet Union and China. American military spending rose from $13 to $50 billion (1949–53).

The strategic change promoted an unprecedented period of sustained rapid growth in Europe. It restored growth in the US but without the same level of boom – the annual growth rate in the first half of the 1950s was around 3.5 per cent, in the second half 2.3 per cent. But Europe produced a set of economic 'miracles' – the combination of very low-paid skilled labour, starved markets, imported US technology, pushed by a war boom, propelled a headlong 'catching up' process.

Buoyant profits on the European side of the Atlantic, compared to more modest ones on the American, along with continuing restrictions on imports, began to induce US companies to cross the water. Investment abroad ran at double the rate of investment in the American economy from the late 1950s, and at 16 per cent annually between 1957 and 1965. European fears of an American economic invasion intensified.

The fears were understandable, but with the benefit of hindsight as misplaced as Europe's subsequent terrors of immigration, a remnant of the old political order of competing empires and territorial expropriation. The US ruled the world, insofar as it did, by reason of its economic weight at home and the resources that weight generated, not the reach of its capital (or rather companies owned in the US) nor its exports, let alone that of its armed forces. Indeed, with the benefit of hindsight, the transatlantic migration of US capital has a quite different appearance – it was the first escape of US companies from the embrace of the American government. The new strategically defined Atlantic economy offered, quite unintentionally, the possibility of flight from the over-lordship of Washington, the first small measure of 'globalisation' in its modern sense. One of the few to note this context was Schurmann, writing in the early 1970s (1974: xxvii):

> a complex struggle between government and business has made for much of the political history of the United States. In that struggle, the government has become more and more powerful, and business has reached further and further into the world. It is the international economy that poses a counterweight to the might of the American State much more than national American business.

Thus, at the very pinnacle of its power in the world, the American state unknowingly was creating – or allowing the recreation – of a cosmopolitan world economy where capital had no necessary relationship to any particular state, but relationships to all states where it operated. What the Americans pioneered, the Europeans followed, and later, in the 1980s, companies from the leading developing countries. The capitalists had to retain their nationality, like the culture of their origin and language, but capital was set upon a return to its normal condition of having loyalty exclusively to the making of profit.

Furthermore, even in strategic terms, the world, despite appearances, was quite different. The Cold War was not a reaffirmation of Europe's ancient national egotisms, of absolute sovereignties. On the contrary, the conflict required the continual curbing of sovereignty in a far more integrated coalition than ever before, NATO. Membership of the alliance required the effective merger of national armed forces, certainly under American direction but also requiring close multinational collaboration. The twentieth-century conflict between France and Germany was now smothered in alliance, the stepping-stone to the economic and political merger of Europe in the European Union. Thus a new kind of political order was emerging, not simply an American Empire nor yet a federation with the US but a military association and then a European political project that entailed severe limits on the very substance of state power, its armed forces. Each accepted that they could no longer defend themselves alone, and that therefore the idea of a self-sufficient economy made no sense. It took a long time for this to emerge – indeed, so great are the continuing suspicions and rivalries that fusion is still far from accomplished. The instincts of the politicians are still very much captive to the old agenda. But in substance it has gone.

There was another remarkable innovation that enhanced these trends: the arrival of nuclear weapons and other major innovations in warfare. Any attempt to employ nuclear weapons in the hostilities between nuclear powers was in effect suicidal. As Keegan (1993: 48) puts it, 'a State, if required to defend its own existence, will [have to] act with pitiless disregard for the consequences to its own and its adversaries people'. Thus the central purpose, the foundation of the multiplicity of other purposes and of agencies of the modern state, the perpetual drive to dominance through war or its threat, now led to stalemate, to the creation of destructive capacity so great that it could never be used except at the price of self-destruction. It was the end of unlimited war, of what Clausewitz drew from Napoleon's innovations, total war to destroy the enemy. The fear of self-destruction now forced the Great Powers to accept the status quo in Europe, and for a remarkable – albeit periodically frightened – half century, there was stability on the edge of the division of Europe, 'down the line of the eastern marches of the Carolingian Empire,' as Howard (1976: 230) puts it.

THE GREAT BOOM

However, many of these major changes would not have been effective without the other remarkable and unexpected occurrence, an extraordinary boom in the Atlantic core of the world economy, ultimately spilling over to East Asia, to Latin America and beyond. The quarter of a century of growth expanded world output at growing speed – by 250 per cent between 1950 and 1972, and with an unprecedented geographical spread of growth. Take steel, such a vital though declining component of the national war economy. It took 57 years to produce the first 100 million tonnes (to 1927); 24 years to reach the second (1951); eight to produce the third; and by 1973, the world was making 700 million tonnes. By then too, Brazil, China, India and other newcomers were significant producers, and South Korea was laying down the domestic means to become in the following decade, no doubt briefly, the world's most efficient steelmaker.

The boom lifted almost all the boats, transforming the living conditions, the style of life and the psychologies of millions of people. It was most obvious in North America and Europe,[1] but much more dramatic in Japan; yet it was even more powerful in developing countries, as reflected in the figures for the average expectation of life at birth – from perhaps around 32 in 1950 to about 50 in the mid-1970s, an addition of a remarkable 18 years, or more than half a 1950 life. It was a result of the radical decline in infant deaths, itself a summary measure of many different changes – from improved protein intake of mothers, a reduced burden of work, improved security of water supply and waste disposal, improved medical care and the control of epidemic diseases.

Trade was the initial key to this process of spreading growth. Throughout the period since 1950, trade has almost invariably grown faster than production, so that the average country exported a growing share of national output (and imported a growing share of consumption). Such periods of rising trade had existed before, but unlike, say, the nineteenth century, when trade and capital movements were, relatively, equally or more important, it was intra-industry trade (the exchange of goods between national segments of the same industry) rather than inter-industry (exchange between different industries) which grew most rapidly. The significance of this was the shift from arms-length exchanges between separate national economies (exchanging, say, coffee for manufactured consumer goods), to exchanges between specialised subsectors of the same industry – the beginnings of a global division of labour. No country could any longer pretend to self-sufficiency, to produce exclusively for a home market; all, to a greater or lesser extent, came to produce for the world. Governments which historically managed an autonomous or relatively independent national economy now found themselves managing a fragment of a world economy where the sources of growth and the destination of output were beyond both their power and their knowledge.

However, participants rarely saw this at the time; it is only apparent with the benefit of hindsight. The unexpected boom from 1947 impelled the slow reduction of those controls directed at managing a slump (and in directing a war economy). But the basic structure – corporatism, state enterprise and state direction – did not seem to change. The old state agenda seemed to dominate centre stage, and there was much opposition to each step in the opposite direction (for example, to the convertibility of currencies in the late 1950s). Indeed, in the British case, a poor economic performance in the 1950s (now exacerbated rather than helped by high military spending) led under a Conservative and a following Labour government to a return to planning and a rehabilitation of corporatism in the 1960s. Not until 1975, under a different Labour government, was monetarism briefly embraced. The ending of capital controls, like privatisation of parts of the public sector (a full assault on the war-making state and its capital project), had to await the years from 1979; full capital liberalisation came only with the financial 'big bang' of 1987. Thus, 'structural adjustment' through the initiative of the state in Europe, unlike what was to come in, say,

Sub-Saharan Africa, was long, slow and hesitant, without a clear overall logic, let alone an understanding by those who executed it. In private business, the changes were faster in unwinding corporatism under the impact of declining barriers to imports and intensified competition – in integrating domestic and world markets.

Thought lagged well behind the process of change. Corporatism as an explicit doctrine was long discredited by its association with Italian fascism, but the practical outcome of corporatism and state direction remained for long dominant. Galbraith (1967: 296) in the 1960s described the American economy as essentially a corporatist one: 'In notable respects, the corporation is an arm of the State' and 'the State in important respects [is] an instrument of the industrial system'.

Furthermore, the long boom was itself attributed, perversely by subsequent standards, precisely to the reorganisation of society, the creation of state-directed national economies. Large public sectors, with intelligent management of economic policy, had, it seemed, stabilised demand so that economies could sustain full employment and steady growth almost indefinitely. Shonfield (1965: 231) summed up the supreme confidence here: 'The State controls so large a part of the economy that a planner can, by intelligent manipulation of the levers of public power, guide the remainder of the economy firmly towards any objective that the government chooses'.

The doyen of orthodox economic opinion, Harvard's famous Paul Samuelson, expressed the same confidence: the business cycle at last had been conquered (in Zarnowitz 1972: 167). In the late 1960s, Arthur Okun (former chairman of the President's Council of Economic Advisers [1970: 33]), proclaimed that recessions, 'like airplane crashes' were now preventable. Indeed, the cult of planning, plans and planners seemed to reach its crescendo just before the 1970s and world recession revealed a quite different and unplannable world economy.

Of course, by later standards, the 'world' of the world economy was basically the Atlantic economy and Japan. Between 1955 and 1973, two thirds of world trade in manufactured goods took place here. In 1974, this area had 40 per cent of the world's manufacturing labourforce, 66 per cent of the output and 85 per cent of manufactured exports. The real world economy was still to emerge, after the end of the Atlantic boom.

The system, then, appeared to be one of fortified national economies, amended on the margins by elements of liberalisation. But cosmopolitanism was undermining this appearance. We have noted the case of trade, creating a dispersal – and hence a technical integration – of manufacturing (so few products could be said to be wholly made in one country). There was also finance. As we saw earlier, in the British case this was one of the last items to succumb to the state and to nationalism. And yet, despite what had seemed to be its destruction, it was one of the first to revive as a cosmopolitan element. The City of London almost disappeared with exchange control, a protected economy and the war. For almost three decades to 1960, the City languished, reduced simply to financing the British corner of the old world economy. Indeed, it seemed there could never be a return to a global financial system where currencies and external trade were not monopolised by governments as instruments of national power. If it were to return, it would surely be in the hands of the largest centre of finance in the world, New York.

An accident of London's situation offered a route back to the old order. During the war, the British government could only persuade its imperial dependencies and dominions to lend if it offered the facility for them to withdraw their funds at will. The facility to cover this allowed the funds to be 'offshore', outside the control of the British financial system. The US failed to match these advantages from depositing funds in New York, and even, at a later stage, increased taxation on such funds. In the late 1950s, the Moscow Narodny Bank, fearing that funds it held in New York might be seized by the US government in reprisal for some act of Soviet foreign policy, withdrew them and deposited them 'offshore' in London. There were lowered charges, profits escaped tax, so many others came to deposit their funds – including the profits of US companies operating in Europe. Thus was born an extraordinarily dynamic component of world finance, initially the Eurodollar market, but then the Euromark, Euroyen and other offshore supplies of liquidity. By the late 1970s, the offshore funds had become larger than the combined reserves of the developed countries, the OECD group. It was a real market, without official supervision – and it could and did break fixed exchange rates (as the dollar was driven to float under President Nixon). Now the world's banks flocked to London to trade in offshore funds, providing the nucleus for the beginning of international company mergers and acquisitions, for leasing work, financing world trade and manufacturing, futures and commodities, and foreign-exchange transactions. Thus, well before most governments were moving to decontrol national finance, the offshore financial markets had created a powerful cosmopolitan determinant of national finance – indeed, national reform was driven now by the demands of this global market.

THE REVOLT OF THE 1960s

The trends were not simply of a global economic order undermining the national economic fortresses. There was also rebellion at home, within the citadel. It was in the field most central to the old form of the state, war-making, and affected overwhelmingly the most powerful state in the world. From a position of what seemed indisputable dominance, the US launched a war against a rebellion by ill-armed irregular troops, guerrillas, in a small and impoverished country of Southeast Asia, Vietnam – and lost. It was as if the well-drilled Prussian field army were once more swamped by the enthusiastic masses of Napoleon's Grand Army; or, better still, given the context of American power, as if the mighty lumbering Hessian forces of the British met the lightly armed, fast-moving irregulars of the American War of Independence and were driven out. However, there was another component – the rebellion of Americans against the war. Hitherto, the prototype war-making state had programmed the responses of the population, and invariably, opposition to a war constituted high treason, a crime so unspeakable that it was barely possible to defend publicly those who disagreed – as the treatment of conscientious objectors in both world wars illustrates. Now, not only did a generation of young Americans openly oppose the war (including one, Bill Clinton, who was to become President 30 years later), they did so on such a massive and determined scale that it was impossible for the authorities to contain it. Furthermore, thousands of young men fled the country to escape military conscription. The troops themselves could not escape and retreated into demoralisation. It was a quite extraordinary decline, noted by a contemporary witness (Heinl 1971):

> Our army that now remains in Vietnam is in a state approaching collapse, with individual units avoiding or having refused combat, murdering their officers and non-commissioned officers, drug-ridden and dispirited where not near mutinous ... [C]onditions exist among American forces in Vietnam that have only been exceeded in this century by ... the collapse of the Tsarist armies in 1916 and 1917.

The protest movement that began in the US, spread globally – American embassies assumed the battle-scarred image of Vietnam itself. The ferment spread to the American soldiers in Vietnam, sapping the very fibres of the military apparat of the US. The political geography had profoundly changed – civil society had returned with a vengeance.

Once the war had been conceded to the Vietnamese, the American establishment rushed to cover the tracks, to pretend that the old disciplines were still intact. But military intervention by the US had, in comparison with the old order, become fatally flawed – it now required popular permission, by no means given lightly, and, according to the US government, no American deaths. Later the qualification would acquire an even greater limitation, to no 'collateral damage' – that is, no casualties among the civilian population of the 'enemy nation'. Wars had, it seemed, dramatically narrowed once more to conflicts between governments, not peoples or nations. In practice, no one knew how to isolate governments in order to punish them, so that in practice armed forces

fell back on the old reflex. However, a great impetus was given to the development of accurate weaponry in order to try to pinpoint targets more precisely
and so avoid unintended deaths.

The opposition to the Vietnam War was crucial for the future of the system
of war-making states, but it was only one thread in a remarkable abandonment
of those ancient social disciplines, carefully instilled for generations, to inculcate
loyalty to the purposes of government, loyalty in war and a ready acceptance of
the slaughter of war. The anti-war politics tended to become submerged in
broader social concerns, in general liberation – of black Americans, of women,
of students and free speech, of China's young in the Cultural Revolution and,
under an older agenda, of Africa and the Third World. The slogans raised
continued long after the movements had died, reforming the relations between
black and white, and men and women, and instituting a more general democratisation. Black liberation had its most significant triumph not in America but
much later in the collapse of Apartheid in South Africa.

Perhaps never before has there been such a widespread popular rebellion
without a central political focus, a social movement without a revolutionary
programme. It was a vindication, so late in the day, of an anarchist revolt, directed
at changing society rather than conquering state power (even though there were
traditional political components: political demonstrations, trade-union strikes,
including a French general strike, the 'May events' in 1968).

It is difficult to assess the impact of such a relatively diffuse set of movements, but they began changes which were to continue for a long time, creating
societies that seemed remote from the old state form – above all, the granite
inscrutability of the male warrior began to disintegrate. War for the developed
countries no longer required the whole of society and the economy and therefore no longer required the drilling of the psychologies of all. Even when agreed,
it became a matter for professionals, and therefore for everyone else a 'spectator
sport' (in Michael Mann's phrase [1988: 183–87]), where there were neither blood
nor corpses. Indeed, wars for the developed countries tended to join the world
sporting events as one episode in friendly rivalries, remote from the old agenda.
However, in many developing countries the old agenda remained firmly intact
and in sharp contrast to the frivolous approach of the developed.

A THIRD WORLD

With the benefit of hindsight, then, the 1960s in the developed countries can be
seen as marked by a popular rebellion against the disciplines hitherto demanded
by war. It coincided with the earlier changes of the political world, the forced

unification of the European Great Powers, and in the economy, the reversal of the drive to separate national economies, governed by mercantilism. But the agenda of the revolutionaries of the 1960s was far too radical (and unspecific) to be achieved by the weapons they had to hand: peace, flower-power, 'make love not war', an amiable and gentle anarchism before the world's scowling samurai.

The revolt connected, however, with a quite different agenda in the rest of the world, covering the majority of the people, the 'developing countries'. The student revolutionaries of Berkeley or Nanterre might see themselves as allying with those of Beijing in China's Cultural Revolution – parading professors round the campus in dunce hats – or the leaders of new Africa, proclaiming a new African socialism. But the two were aiming at quite opposite targets. The one might seek to break the oppressive disciplines of the war-making society and the national capital project, but China witnessed a rebellion against the Communist Party, led by its Chairman, directed to restore the disciplines of the old order; and Sub-Saharan Africa was throwing off colonialism in order to put in place just those disciplines, to create strong states – backed by strong national economies – in the name of the defence of national independence.

The national economic agenda was not new in developing countries – Atatürk in inter-war Turkey had initiated the process of building a strong unified and militarised state with a large public sector; Chiang Kai-shek had tried to do something similar in the China of the 1930s, and so had the great populist dictators of Latin America in the 1930s and 1940s: Cárdenas of Mexico, Vargas of Brazil, Péron of Argentina. But memories are short, and for the newly independent countries of the post-war world it seemed what they had to say was not only strikingly new but an alternative to the sterile options emanating from Washington and Moscow. A generation of heroes bestrode the world: Sukarno of Indonesia, Nehru of India, Chou En-lai of China, Ben Bella of Algeria, Nasser of Egypt, Castro of Cuba. Messianic energies seemed to be released, symbolised by China's Great Leap Forward in 1958, a new leadership for the world in contrast to the old leadership of the Great Powers which had led to two world wars, the Great Depression and now the Cold War. Consider the exaltation of Indonesia's Sukarno, opening the 1955 Bandung Conference (Abdulgani 1981: 88) of what was to be known as the 'Third World':

> What can we do? We can do much! We can inject the voice of reason into world affairs. We can mobilise all the spiritual, all the moral, all the political strength of Asia and Africa[2] on the side of peace. Yes, we! We, the peoples of Asia and Africa, 1,400 million strong, far more than half the human population of the world, we can mobilise what I have called the 'Moral Violence of Nations' in favour of peace.

The relationship between the capacity to defend national independence, to participate in the competitive state-system, and the growth and development of the national economy was now perfectly understood. As in Stalin's Russia and Mao's China, the growth of heavy industry (steel and capital goods), supposedly the source of modern armaments, was the criterion to assess national economic progress, and the success of 'the plan'. A galaxy of economists rebelled against the eternal verities of orthodox economics, to create a new 'development economics' – Myrdal, Hirschman, Baran, Singer, Balogh, Kaldor, Streeten, Seers and many more. Drawing on the path-breaking work in the 1930s and 1940s of the Argentine economist Raúl Prebisch, the development economists rejected the idea that open markets, free enterprise and private ownership could any longer develop economically backward countries. The state, modelled on the European war-economy or some modification of the Soviet order, was the sole agency independent enough to mobilise savings and investment, if necessary by force, sufficient to break the inertia, the debilitating logic of economic backwardness at the same time as igniting the enthusiasm and dedication of the millions to back the process. Charles Issawi (1963: 49) had a more astringent comment on Nasser's version of the old national capital project, citing a 1918 comment on Bismarck's 'State Socialism' of the 1880s – 'it was the renaissance of the mercantilism of the seventeenth century, adapted to the benevolent and illuminated despotism of the eighteenth century and the conditions of a militarist state, remodelled by the phenomenon of modern industrialism'. Or, we might say, the historical references showed no more than the continuity in the economic policies made necessary to create the national economic basis for a war-making state in the modern state system.

The new economic consensus assumed an extraordinary role for the state, for the political, in establishing mastery of the economic world and the capacity to create the level of development needed for the 'defence of national independence'. The belief became a kind of religion, an exaltation of 'national liberation' (which rarely involved much real liberation of the mass of the population). Consider the 1961 Biblical litany of Nkrumah (1961: 32), who led the independence movement of black Sub-Saharan Africa in securing the first independence, that of Ghana, and advised the national liberation leaders of the continent: 'Aim for the attainment of the Political Kingdom, that is to say, the complete self-determination of your territories. When you have achieved the Political Kingdom, all else will follow ... '

Hindsight allows us to see how far these heroic ambitions depended on world boom, rising commodity prices and expanding markets for the raw-material exports of Africa. The 1960s saw simultaneously the crescendo of the movement for national liberation, symbolised in armed struggles (Angola, Mozambique, the then Southern Rhodesia) and the arrival of African socialism (famous in the hands of Senghor, Nyerere and Kaunda), and the beginning of its disintegration.

Elsewhere, the old agenda also failed. Between 1960 and 1963, China went through possibly the worst famine in the history of the world (with perhaps 30 million deaths), partly attributable to the relentless pursuit of the old policy agenda, albeit disguised as a popular campaign (MacFarquhar: 1997, 3). India's Second Five Year Plan ended in defeat, sunk by the failure of the rains to produce the food and of exports to pay for the imports to underpin industrialisation. The Sukarno regime in Indonesia collapsed in 1965 in an appalling bloodbath. Egypt's Nasser was defeated massively by Israel, and other leaders, Ben Bella, Nkrumah and so on, were driven from power. The attempt to forge nations and build independent national economies seemed everywhere to have ended in failure.

Yet even if the old agenda had failed, there were major improvements in the livelihood of people. As we have seen, the survival of infants throughout most of the developing countries showed improved diets, the spread of infrastructure and of health facilities. Educational figures improved remarkably. The old agenda had been both to build the war economy and, to this end, to incorporate the population in the drive to war, partly by extending to them the privileges of the armed forces. The association of welfare and militarisation still had some validity, nowhere more so than in Israel, as Migdal (1988: 171) notes: 'The Israeli State has created an extensive policy network, simultaneously making it one of the most militarised States in the world and among the most extensive welfare States'. However, failure did not end the attempts to create an independent national economy to parallel an independent polity. The steel industry of, say, Egypt, India, China, Argentina or Nigeria remained a priority, even though people were beginning to forget why. Indeed, the first major post-war recession (1973–74) in the world economy spurred many developing countries to increase the defence of the old agenda through a wave of nationalisations and enhanced state intervention (Little et al. 1993). Externally, this was financed not through enhanced export revenues (these were declining in the slump in world trade) but increased borrowing of recycled petrodollars. Only the debt crisis of the early 1980s brought that phase to an abrupt end and forced a radical change of direction.

'Structural adjustment' was the name given to the attempt to shift from the old agenda to a new one, with open economies, balanced budgets, the exploitation of existing advantages rather than forced industrialisation that defied global patterns of specialisation. It was a long and complex process, far longer than those who initiated the reforms understood when they began. State domination was so ubiquitous, stripping it was like peeling an enormous onion without knowing what leaves remained. In doing so, the old national economies were steadily and forcibly incorporated in a global system.

FROM WAR-MAKING TO WELFARE AND DEVELOPMENT

In sum, in the period of transition a series of new and major strategic and economic factors came together cumulatively to force, for the first time, the breaking of the ancient systemic logic of Europe's war-making states. The development was slow, sporadic, with sudden reversals, but ultimately locked into the much wider strategic global logic of the contest between Moscow and Washington. Underneath that umbrella, people hardly noticed the slow changes – they were only revealed when the Cold War came to an end.

One of the important indicators of the break with the past was the changed pattern of state spending. The decline of the war-making state was not simultaneously a decline in the role of the state, but rather a shift away from defence spending to social spending, to income transfers, to solidifying social support in conditions of opening the economy to the markets of the world. Income transfers in the leading states steadily increased up to the 1980s, then stabilised for a short time before declining, but only slightly. At its peak, the state was choosing to appropriate and distribute between 40 and 50 per cent of the gross domestic product (and in Sweden, 68.8 per cent). For the smaller powers of Europe, the growth in the share of the state paralleled increasing economic integration in Europe and the world (Katzenstein 1985). The burden of taxes required to sustain this shift provoked considerable opposition, particularly in the US; some believed that the new world economy allowed the mobility of capital to escape taxation, thus increasing the burden on the immobile inhabitants (a theme taken up later).

Thus, war-making for the first time began to go into relative decline among the Great Powers – in terms of expenditure, but more in terms of the involvement of whole populations. Total war was not at all required for the kind of 'police operations' now becoming common. Some governments nonetheless persisted with the old symbol of total war, universal military conscription, but where it continued it was now justified in terms of its benefits for civil society, a training in social disciplines and responsibilities, rather than through any connection to the needs of warfare.

By contrast, the old forms of war preparation became increasingly a matter for developing countries. And actually going to war was increasingly a matter of civil war in some of the poorest countries. The technology of orthodox war had become remote from the material, technical or social resources of the poorest countries. Unlike for the Europeans in the eighteenth or twentieth centuries, war in poor countries now had no beneficial economic effects – it looted or destroyed economic resources, not expanding them. Countries were thus driven backwards by war, robbed of the most elementary means to maintain unity, let alone protect their populations from want.

The old system – the national capital project – seemed to deliver not only an astonishing enhancement of the capacity to slaughter but scarcely believable increases in national wealth (and thus much greater inequalities between countries), in the productivity of labour and in standards of living. The opening of the system now intensified many of these trends. Perhaps the most important single summary measure of that progress was the increase in the average expectation of life at birth – for the world, from under 40 in the late nineteenth century to 67 a century later (and in the US, for men, from 50 to 77). In the last 40 years of the twentieth century, for the 614 million inhabitants of the 48 'least developed' countries (that is the poorest, according to the UN [1999]), the comparable figures were from 38 to 52 years. For the developed countries, perhaps a quarter of the population died in the first year of life at the beginning of the century, about 6 per cent by its end.

Improving public health, nutrition and education, the extension of infrastructure and communications as well as technical innovations, capital investment and improved management led to a major increase in the productivity of work. In 1890, the average American worker took an hour to produce the average good, in 2000 7 minutes, and the process of labour involved immensely less effort. Such figures did not measure the extraordinary diversification of the output, nor even greater improvements in quality – at least half the consumption goods of 2000 had not been thought of a century earlier. De Long (2000b: 24) asks:

> How much are the central heating, electric lights, fluoride toothpaste, electric toaster, clothes washing machines, dishwashers, synthetic fibre blend clothes, radios, intercontinental telephones, xerox machines, notebook computers, automobiles and steel-framed skyscrapers that I have used so far today worth – and it is only 10.00am?

De Long computes the decline in labour-time required to make various products; to take only one, a one-speed bicycle, the time taken declined from 266 hours (1895) to 7.2 a century later. By that standard, the productivity of labour had increased 37 times over in the twentieth century (compared to the official figure for real gross domestic product per worker – from $13,700 to $65,540 – at a time when the US labourforce increased from 21.8 million to 142 million). The changes were even more dramatic for developing countries, starting at a much lower level than the US in 1900. In the majority of developing countries, the productivity potential of the average inhabitant was possibly three times that of the average American in 1900. De Long estimates that just over a third of the world's population at the end of the twentieth century lived in countries where the per-capita output fell below that of the US in 1900.

In the longer historical picture, the take-off – propelled by the forced accumulation of the war-making state system – was unmistakeable. Real gross domestic product per-capita changed by perhaps 1 per cent up or down between the eleventh and eighteenth centuries; in the nineteenth century, by possibly 200 per cent; in the twentieth by over 850 per cent. The state obsession with increasing the means to destroy its enemies had, by accident, released a cornucopia.

The majority of people still face a world of what seem to be necessities, even though a world of abundance has in fact arrived. Indeed, the dichotomy is absurd since the target continually moves. Expectations invariably advance ahead of achievements – abundance is constantly turned into scarcity – even though what is now delivered is far in advance of what the rich might have hoped for in the past. The picture is particularly distorted because the figures capture only a minor fragment of improvements. Take, for example, one feature of our environment, the ability to lighten the darkness. William Nordhaus (in Bresnahan and Raff 1997) estimates that the past century has seen a decline in the real price of the provision of light of 10,000 times (compared to the official commodity price of only ten times over). This and countless other improvements are taken for granted, and it is right that that should be so – dissatisfaction is the motor for continual improvement.

The national capital project, driven by the state, immensely enhanced the capacity to produce for those who embarked on the contest of states. In our own times, this included the whole world. But with the process, we have suggested, went the beginning of the end of the old system of competitive national capitals, most marked in the developed countries. Capital escaped to recreate, albeit on a much enhanced scale, a cosmopolitan system beyond the old power of governments. As we have suggested, there were many collisions between capital and state along the way, almost always settled in favour of the state. Indeed, the severity of the Great Depression can be attributed to the willingness of the state to sacrifice the interests of capital (and hence the incomes and employment of the citizens) to the maintenance of its own power.

A cosmopolitan system of capital undermines any sense of what the state regards as in the national interest – to foment a world system to enhance the incomes of the inhabitants of the fragment of the world which the government administers or, in traditional terms, to seize whatever can be seized, and hold it within national boundaries or under national control, a recipe now for economic self-destruction. Interdependence and collaboration are becoming the condition of success. The conditioned reflexes remain askew of the new world, and understandably so, given the length of time national power has existed. As a result, there is great resistance to accepting the new logic and an immense agenda of unfinished business. But the 1960s saw the crossover point from one order to the other in the developed countries, the 1980s – as we shall see – for the developing countries.

Governments retain great resources for destruction, yet they can no longer employ them to force capital back into its national shell. Markets outside the territorial bounds of the state now increasingly determine the capacity for survival of the different governments. Tilly (1993: 247), writing in the early 1990s, notes the same increasing tension, this time in Europe, in

> the shrinking capacity of European States to sustain the dramatic circumspection of capital, labour, goods, services, money and culture that began occurring widely 200 years ago. After two centuries in which they did succeed remarkably in monitoring, capturing and storing resources within well-defined borders, Western States in general are finding it increasingly difficult to maintain control of migrant workers, capital, drugs, technology and money.

6

The Newcomers

INTRODUCTION

The intellectual inheritance of the developing countries after the Second World War was, as we have noted earlier, essentially the agenda of the national capital project – building, as had been undertaken originally in Europe, a self-reliant autonomous national economy with the capacity to defend the new country (in the case of the newly independent countries of Asia and Africa), with the social basis of national unity to support this enterprise. Latin Americans played a key role in launching the programme, backed often by the new UN particularly its Latin American Economic Commission. The elements of the policy package were historically familiar – autarky, state controls of the currency and of imports (protection), large public sectors (or the elimination of the private sector altogether), the banning or tight control of foreign investment; state planning and the physical direction of the economy to force resources out of traditional agriculture and into modern manufacturing (with a stress, for the larger powers, on the development of heavy industry). The only newish element was that the programme was now called socialist. In practice, the agenda was only partially carried out in most places, but it was an intellectual paradigm. Economic development meant supposedly the expansion of domestic incomes and the home market, not 'supplying foreigners', a supposed self-generating pattern of growth. Socially, there was a commensurate general hostility to foreign influences as much as to foreign capital, a stress on national independence in all things. Thus, the developing countries inherited the full package of European economic and political nationalism, the concomitants of a system dedicated to war-making. The programme, as we have seen, took several hundred years to develop in Europe but it now arrived in one complete, as it were, development manual in Asia and Africa. There, the depredations of empire, directed by modern European states, forced the growth of social nationalism at an accelerated pace – but it was by no means the fastest growth of nationalism to be seen in the world.

The background condition for such programmes to be, even in the short term, tolerable was the great boom in the core of the world system between 1947 and 1973, and the expanding demand for imports from the rest of the world. The incomes from expanded export revenues allowed immense strides to be made in building physical and social infrastructure in the developing world and in enhanced capacity in industry (if less consistently in agriculture). For given periods of time, the national economic development project seemed also to promise success – in China's First Five Year Plan (1951–56), and, with lesser effect, in India's Second (1956–61). In both cases, that sudden first surge of growth, despite some impressive achievements, could not be sustained. Furthermore, despite the brave talk of managing without imports ('import-substitution industrialisation'), what growth took place required an increased inflow of imports, and therefore, given the ban on foreign investment and borrowing, increased exports to pay for the imports. To some, that seemed to be a craven surrender to the old economic order – the old colonial export economy.

Given the universal fascination with building an independent national economy, there were few who saw what was already becoming apparent from the late 1950s: the developing economies most successful in terms of growth (if not in building an old-style independent economy) were those that concentrated on exporting, not on limiting imports. The experience seemed to defy the conventional wisdom that developing countries could never export enough to develop their economies, and certainly could not export manufactured goods in the face of the superiority of producers in Europe and North America, commanding the most advanced technology, great concentrations of capital and economies of scale. Export pessimism was universal. Yet Hong Kong, from the early 1950s, showed in textiles, and later garments and many other cheap exports, that this was not so. Taiwan followed in the later 1950s, South Korea from the early 1960s, and Singapore shortly thereafter. What became known as the 'Four Little Tigers' (or the 'Gang of Four') broke not only the myth of export pessimism, in the case of three of them (all except Hong Kong), they married elements of the old nationalist economic model (equally driven by the imperative of creating war-making capacity) and what in the old order had seemed its direct contradiction, the drive to export manufactured goods. This was a major qualification to the European agenda to minimise dependence on the rest of the world.

Three of the Four Little Tigers learned important lessons from Japan and its revival from the catastrophe of the Second World War. If there was a Japanese model of development, it lay in this same marriage of the old project of building an independent national economic power but doing so through exploiting world markets rather than simply developing the domestic market. Those that remained exclusively loyal to the old nationalist project seemed, sooner or later, to enter stagnation. The world conditions which had provided, if not a favourable, at least not an obstructive context for European and Japanese development in the centuries before the Second World War now seemed to force stagnation on those developing countries which tried to follow suit. Even in conditions of extraordinary world boom, the export constraint constantly hobbled the drive to grow (with some notable exceptions in the 1960s, for example Brazil).

THE JAPANESE PHOENIX

As we have seen, the Japanese case demonstrated how effective the mechanism of forced national capital accumulation, driven by the search for war-making capacity, was in the century before 1945. The agenda was not tied to anything peculiarly European. Indeed, in terms of society the Japanese proved themselves considerably more European than the Europeans. Until the 1945 defeat broke the spell, the Japanese ruling regime was able to call on social solidarity and support to an almost unprecedented degree – and to do so in a 'feudal order' without what the Europeans considered the precondition for that commitment, either an 'anti-feudal' revolution and a mass inspiration for collective liberation (as in France in 1789 or Russia in 1917), or significant social reform (as in Germany). On the other hand, Japanese social discipline seemed closer to the Prussian model of the eighteenth century, driven by unremitting terror – which, as we have seen, collapsed under the hammer blows of the Grand Army – rather than inspired by a collective commitment.[1]

War immensely expanded the capacity of the economy of Japan and its empire. But the loss of the war led to a devastation only exceeded by that experienced by Russia. Consider the disastrous output figures for 1947.

The gross domestic product fell to 55 per cent of its former peak of 1941 (and was not restored to that level until 1955) (Hara in Harrison 1998: 225). There were 2.7 million casualties (3–4 per cent of the 1941 population). 80 per cent of the country's shipping fleet was destroyed, virtually all the air power, a quarter of the rollingstock and motor vehicles; 35 per cent of industrial machinery

Japan: production index by selected sectors for 1947 (with, in brackets, the low point of monthly production, 1945–48 inclusive); 1935–1937 = 100.

Sector	Output	Low point and date
Textiles	15.8	(3.9: Jan. 1946)
Chemicals	31.6	(7.7: Aug. 1945)
Iron and steel	10.9	(2.6: Oct. 1945)
Machinery	49.4	(1.3: Sept. 1945)
Coal	65.1	(16.0: Nov. 1945)
Combined figures:		
Mining and Manufacturing:	31.5	(8.5: Aug. 1945)
Consumer goods:	32.1	(11.4: Jan. 1945)
Producer goods:	25.2	(7.7: Sept. 1945)

Source: Japan Ministry of Finance and Bank of Japan, *Statistical Year-Book of Finance and Economy of Japan*, 1948 (Tokyo, Ministry of Finance Printing Office, 1948: 558–59), selected from Moore 1983: 77.

was wrecked, and about 40 per cent of the 65 major cities destroyed (65 per cent in the case of Tokyo, 57 per cent Osaka, 89 per cent Nagoya). About 30 per cent of the population was homeless. The rural standard of living was estimated to be about two thirds of the pre-war level, the urban possibly just over a third. The Tokyo official wholesale price index (1935–37=100) reached 4430 in 1947, the Tokyo blackmarket index for consumer goods 34,925.

The spell was indeed broken, and the country experienced an unprecedented level of revolt – with nearly a quarter of a million workers in dispute, on strike or engaged in the occupation of plants in the last half of 1946 (Moore 1983). Indeed, the dangers of social revolution were probably as important in the minds of the American armed forces in tempering the rigours of the occupation and relaxing the programme of enforced reforms as, subsequently, the need to make Japan an ally in the emerging Cold War with the Soviet Union.

The weakening of the American resolve to recreate Japan so that war would not again occur was evident in the failure to reform industrial ownership. Here, as noted earlier, a corporatist structure, based around the monopoly or cartel core of major industries under the great *zaibatsu* business groups was immensely strengthened by the pre-war drive to war. The occupation forces determined to break up the *zaibatsu* as the allies of the military clique that led Japan to war. The four pre-war 'old' *zaibatsu* (Mitsui, Mitsubishi, Sumitomo, Yasuda), along with six newer ones (Asano, Furukawa, Nissan, Okira, Nomura, Nakajima) had emerged from the hostilities with a greatly strengthened position in the economy. The old four increased their share of investment capital from 10 per cent of the total in 1937 to 25 per cent in 1945, while the ten together controlled just under half the capital in the four major industries (mining, machinery, shipbuilding, chemicals), half that in banking, 60 per cent in insurance and 61 per cent in shipping (Dower 1999: 530). The Supreme Commander of the Allied Powers decided that 325 large corporations should be broken up, but with the onset of the Cold War and the need for a Japanese ally, the number declined to 11 by August 1949. Thus the operational structure of the key sectors of the Japanese economy remained fully appropriate to the restoration of a war economy, or, if for the moment that were not feasible, to a renewed drive for the national capital project.

In conditions of rapid and sustained world growth, Japan had advantages which even exceeded those of Europe. The gap in productivity with the US and with Germany was considerable – in manufacturing, the Japanese level was about 11 per cent of the American (and 35 per cent of the German), while wage rates were 6–7 per cent of the US (and 33 per cent of West Germany). Thus Japan, with an educated and industrially skilled workforce, could pursue a process of sustained 'catching up' – in an Asia where, after the years of war privation, there was an immense unsatisfied demand for goods and very few competitors.

In the 1950s, the gross national product increased by around 10 per cent per year (and in manufacturing by nearly 17 per cent annually). Growth was sustained, in a fearfully poor economy, by extraordinary rates of investment – in manufacturing, investment increased by a third per year between 1954 and 1961. After a slight check to the process in the first half of the 1960s, the Japanese economy then moved into its most rapid phase of growth – gross national product increased by 14 per cent per year in the second half of the 1960s (manufacturing by 16 per cent and investment by 21 per cent).

With a constitutional ban on significant rearmament (let alone the constraints of the opinion of Japan's allies and neighbours), the ruling order turned the pre-war industrial structure to rapid economic growth, within which a national economy was to be built. From the beginning, the government stressed the old national agenda, the core of which was to build heavy industry – iron and steel, shipbuilding, heavy engineering, machinery and petrochemicals: 'the fostering of basic industries which are capital intensive (eg steel, petrochemicals) was planned at a time when labour supply was in excess' (Shinohara 1982: 33). In effect, the strategy maximised the use of Japan's scarce investment resources, and minimised the employment implications for the country's labourforce. The direction of the process was in the hands of the Ministry of International Trade and Industry (MITI) which, in addition to the rebuilding of heavy industry, stressed the creation of high-export industries and those with the greatest implications for the advance of technology (Shinohara 1982: 26).

How was it possible to force this extraordinary pace of growth in conditions of a great scarcity of capital, weak capital markets and continuing social deprivation and unemployment? First, it should be noted that high-growth and rapid modernisation affected only a narrow selection of industries; much of the rest of the economy remained antiquated and protected. For the high growth sector, expansion was driven by the time-honoured processes of forced capital accumulation by the state that we have seen in Europe. Because of the political constraints (and US military protection), however, growth was devoted, for the moment, to the civil economy. The state directed its efforts to supplying capital to its priority industries (neglecting the rest), and to protecting them from risk so that they could expand without restriction. There were two central mechanisms: the state advanced low-cost (that is subsidised) finance for projects selected by MITI in heavy industry and in technical advance. The Ministry of Finance created a Fiscal Investment and Loan Programme to encourage consistent 'over-investment' ('over' by comparison with what might have been assessed on market criteria): an expansion of supply and of capacity independently of demand. Thus, the risks for investors were radically reduced. Furthermore, it was possible to keep dividends low to maximise the funds available for investment – the investor was sacrificed to company expansion. Simultaneously, macro-economic policy was directed to stimulating the highest rate of house-hold savings (channelled through the Post Office) to supply funds for on-lending to the government's favoured clients. By these means, the government in the 1950s supplied 40 per cent of investment in steel, coal, electricity, petro-chemicals, cement and shipping (the state reduction of risk stimulated more than matching private finance).

Simultaneously, the government controlled credit to keep interest rates low and so encourage 'excessive' investment. It ensured that foreign investment was excluded from the capital markets to retain supposedly, in classic style, national control.

The reconstruction of the old corporatist groups – insofar as they needed reconstruction – as instruments of national policy followed from state direction. The reliable owner-manager groups directing the large corporations were allowed – indeed encouraged – to diversify into all key sectors. Business groups and associations now developed to be mutually supportive and quasi-independent of both markets, demand and foreign attempts at takeover – through organising trade within the group at preferential prices, internal finance at preferential interest rates, with risk-free low-cost finance, all ensuring organisational respon-siveness to state direction.

In essence, then, the state created a set of mechanisms which partly detached the scale of investment from demand, with the government bearing the risk of any losses and enforcing a redistribution of resources from consumption to business investment. As a result, market share became the criterion of success, not the rate of return on investment, the profit rate; and government priorities shaped output, rather than demand or consumption.

Such a mechanism worked best with a relatively undifferentiated output (raw materials or simple manufactured goods rather than those with high levels of sophistication or quality). This implied that the method would be more effective in, say, the eighteenth century, but decreasingly so in the twentieth. The more research-and-development input, the more the innovatory character of production, the greater the dependence on the intelligent participation of the worker. This began to be true in the processing industries (cars, machinery, electronic equipment) in the 1960s, and later in the service industries. Then state direction became decreasingly effective. But the mechanism carried Japan into the 1980s, when the economy was arriving at the frontiers of technology.

The most striking contrast with the old war-making economy, however, was also the first symbol of the emerging global economy, the role of exports. The old agenda had laid down the minimisation of external dependence, the self-reliance of the national economy in order to offset the possibility of foreign embargo of supplies. While Japan was not initially as dependent on exports as the Four Little Tigers, in the 1960s it became so. Japan's major exporters were thus obliged to relate increasingly to the demands of competitive markets abroad rather than government priorities, and foreign competitors (with successive international trade rounds) insisted that Japanese exports could only be allowed free of subsidies. Thus trade became a powerful instrument in forcing the reform of the mechanism of forced state-directed growth. What had formerly been a necessary element of the national capital project – for example keeping open unprofitable coal mines to ensure physical self-sufficiency in energy for the war economy, or protecting domestic rice cultivation to guarantee domestic food supplies in the event of war – were now transformed into elements of a 'rent-seeking' economy: keeping mines open to preserve jobs and the position of the mine owners (even though by the late 1990s Japan's domestic fuel was being produced at three times the then world market price [Waelbroeck 1998: 130]) or sustaining rice farming to keep agriculture alive (and, covertly, underpin the rural vote of the ruling Liberal-Democratic Party). The centrality of the drive to build the war economy had slipped away, under the impact of the changed world strategic context, leaving an imperative to economic growth as the means to ensure domestic political support. Even so, at the end of the century Japan still had the second-largest defence programme in the world.

The state proved increasingly incompetent at 'picking winners' the more sophisticated and the more intangible the output became. There were just too many complex innovations to employ bureaucratic means to sift those likely to succeed. MITI gambled on supporting the 'fifth-generation' computer and on artificial intelligence, and missed the desktop personal computer revolution (but Japan's manufacturers, with more dispersed and expert involvement in market trends, did not).

Nevertheless, the Japanese 'economic miracle' seemed to be a striking confirmation of the possibility of forcing accelerated economic growth on a national basis. Initially, Japan's ruling order almost certainly intended this to be the basis for the recreation of a war economy to restore Japan's national position in the world. But the world, as we have seen, radically changed. Economic power on a global, not a national, scale rather than military power on a self-sufficient national economic basis now became the criterion of success. Out of the national project, Japan's government created giant corporations which did indeed attain global reach, but where their origin in a string of islands off the coast of Northeast Asia was becoming, with some exaggeration, all but irrelevant to their world operations.

THE FOUR LITTLE TIGERS

The restoration of the Japanese economy – ultimately to become the second largest in the world – was remarkable, but was seen in developing countries as unique, not affecting the perspective for national economic development. That was changed, however, by the emergence of a group of developing countries, the Four Little Tigers (or, more formally, the newly industrialising countries or NICs) whose strategy was a direct repudiation of the idea that development took place exclusively or mainly on the basis of growth in the domestic market. The four proved to be spectacular exporters and, furthermore, exporters of manufactured goods.

However, three of the four (all except Hong Kong) began with exactly the old agenda – building an independent national economy, the basis for the war-making capacity to support the geopolitical ambitions of the state. They started from a position of the imminent threat of war, and remained permanently threatened by war. Taiwan was created from 1948 as a precarious foothold for the Kuomintang armies, driven off the mainland of China by the People's Liberation Army of the Communist Party. Both governments continued to prepare to invade the other. The continued military support of the US for Taiwan was crucial in protecting it. South Korea was born amid one of the most brutal wars of the post-war period, that in the early 1950s between the US and its allies and North Korea, backed by China and Russia. The new regime remained through the period to the present understandably obsessed with the threat of a resumed invasion by the North. Singapore (like its neighbour Malaysia) was created under the twin threats of being engulfed by Sukarno's Indonesia, by 'Konfrontasi' with the remains of British imperial power in the region, and by domestic revolution. For long, the threat of war remained one which, although not as obvious as in the case of Korea and Taiwan, the leadership of the island-city could not ignore.

Hong Kong was different. The military threat – from the People's Republic of China – was so overwhelming that no one believed it could be resisted, and the British colonial regime therefore kept in the colony armed forces only sufficient for garrisoning the island and guarding its borders. Furthermore, the colonial government had no interest in creating an independent national economy; Hong Kong existed at the outset for the economic purposes of the British Empire, a component in a quasi-cosmopolitan system. It was therefore administered as the nearest approximation to an open, free-trading and free-enterprise market economy that existed in the world. Thus, Hong Kong was most responsive to changes in demand in the world economy, and in particular, to the apparently inexhaustible demand in the developed countries for labour-intensive manufactured goods (initially garments, but then a widening range of goods, leading up to electronic equipment). The scale and structure of the Hong Kong economy was successively transformed by external market demand, not by state demand for war-making capacity. Hong Kong was, as it were, tailor-made for a cosmopolitan economy, without any of the national legacies and ambitions that qualified the aspirations of governments in other countries. It therefore became one of the leading beneficiaries of the process of creating a global economy. As a result, Hong Kong built what was, in traditional terms, a thoroughly 'unbalanced' economy – without a steel industry, without heavy capital goods, without giant petrochemical complexes; for its exports, it relied on importing from wherever was the cheapest source of supply, and was rarely tempted by 'import-substitution': that is economically it was a fragment of a global economy.

For the two larger NICs, Taiwan and South Korea – which began to develop after Hong Kong in the late 1950s and early 1960s – there were thus on offer two models of rapid development: Japan following the old agenda of using the state to force accelerated economic development to create an independent national economy, and Hong Kong pursuing single-mindedly the export of manufactured goods whatever the resulting changes that would be produced in the domestic economy. The first was designed to create the full range of supply industries to support independent military capacity; the other pursued complete integration in a global economy without any attempt at national self-sufficiency.

The choice was easy to make. Japan had already been relatively advanced before the Second World War; it had an experienced – and patriotic – capitalist class and a trained workforce, networks of markets and contacts and a powerful existing industrial base. The three NICs other than Hong Kong had no significant capitalist class. Since all had been colonies, the capitalists had been in the main foreigners – Japanese in the case of Taiwan and South Korea, British in the case of Singapore – and they evacuated the territories with decolonisation (or defeat in the case of the Japanese). In all three cases, the state therefore came to exercise overwhelming domination. It could pursue its own agenda without reference to existing entrenched interests (much as the Soviet Union had done in the 1920s). It thus sought to invent a capitalist class as the instrument of national policy – as did the Tsars in Russia, as we noted earlier in Engels's comment on Russian development. Indeed, Singapore has still hardly created such a class, since its process of development, the most rapid of all the NICs, has been based upon a combination of the state and foreign corporations.

South Korea (like Taiwan) started after the Second World War as a military client state of the US. US aid to South Korea between 1953 and 1960 was equal to 9 per cent of the gross national product, 75 per cent of gross investment (mainly in infrastructure), 70 per cent of the value of imports and fully half of public expenditure. In the late 1950s, Washington began to reduce its aid and encouraged Korea (and Taiwan) to seek to earn export revenues sufficient to finance their imports. Despite the experience of Hong Kong, perhaps no one believed it possible – export pessimism was overwhelming. They were wrong, and export-driven growth attained unprecedented levels.

There is, of the four, no single NIC story, but South Korea, the largest, provides one account of spectacular economic growth in the new global economy. Over half a century, South Korea's economy grew more quickly than that of Japan, starting from a much lower base. In the two decades to 1981, growth of national output never fell below 5 per cent (and in six years was over 10 per cent). In the decade of the 1970s, when the world economy was in recession or stagnation, Korea increased its exports by 18 per cent per year (and in given years by over 50 per cent, and in one, 1973, by 99 per cent). Some of the striking features were that it was not only the capitalist class which was removed with the collapse of the Japanese Empire. The landowners were also eliminated by radical land reform, leaving the state in a position of extraordinarily unrestricted power over society.

As noted earlier, the Korean War was very destructive (with possibly 1.3 million deaths, millions more maimed and missing, costs equivalent to possibly two years of gross domestic product), and bequeathed to the post-war regime an understandable obsession with the possibility of war. The regime thus maintained one of the largest armed forces in the world and one of the largest arms budgets (officially amounting in the 1970s to a third of public spending). The obsession with war shaped initial economic policy, for example in agriculture, to secure self-sufficiency. The government laid down tight regulation of agriculture, making trade in land illegal (and limiting the largest holding to three hectares). It set up a public monopoly in the grain trade in the two decades to the mid-1970s, procuring compulsorily at low fixed prices, half the rice output and most of the barley, a system of requisitions reminiscent of the old Soviet Union or of China.

With state control of finance (banks were nationalised in the early 1960s), patronage, discriminatory taxing and pricing, bribes and bullying, the government forced rapid industrialisation through its favoured client corporations, what became the giant business groups, the *chaebol*. Unlike Japan, the Korean government endeavoured to restrict growth in domestic consumption to force the growth of exports. On the other hand, the *chaebol* were offered loans and incentives, to reduce risk and force exports – with extraordinary success.

In the 1960s, the regime concentrated on forcing the export of light manufactured goods to earn the revenues to make up for the decline in US funding and modernise the economy. Once successful in this, it turned in the 1970s to pursuit of the old national capital agenda, building the core of the war economy in capital-intensive heavy industries: steel, heavy machinery, petrochemicals and downstream chemicals (the aims were embodied in the 1973 Heavy Industries and Chemicals Plan). Investment between 1970 and 1976 increased from 25 to 35 per cent of gross domestic product, four fifths of it to heavy and chemical industries (with 40 per cent of public investment leading the way). The strategy was expensive in resource costs, particularly when the world entered the worst recession since the war, accompanied by major oil price increases (Korea was dependent on imported oil). The government persisted – as so many had persisted before it – regardless of the needs of the rest of the economy or the welfare of the mass of Koreans – and borrowed to keep up the pace.

The dash to achieve a war economy almost overturned the regime. Inflation and a growing balance-of-payments crisis (reflecting expanding imports when Korea's light manufactured exports began to decline because they had become overpriced and under-invested) coincided in October 1979 with the murder of the dictator, General Park. The Koreans rebelled at the sacrifices demanded of them in the interest of state power. The notorious massacre of demonstrators at Kuangju the following year nearly overturned a new military dictator. The government moved quickly to try to reduce what it later called 'excessive government intervention' (the Fifth Plan, 1982–86), restoring the traditional export industries. With the highest per-capita debt in the world, the government was obliged to undertake more wide-ranging reforms in order to secure support from the International Monetary Fund and the World Bank (including, from 1984, the denationalisation of the banks).

The old programme, the national capital agenda as we have called it, was pruned drastically, breaking up the public Korea Heavy Industry and Construction Corporation, leaving only what products could be exported on commercial grounds. In shipbuilding, facing a world market much overburdened with capacity, there was a sharp reduction in the original ambitions. There had, however, been a remarkable success here – the Korean industry (backed by public subsidies) overtook all shipbuilding powers except Japan; for example, in 1973 Swedish shipbuilding output was 230 times that of Korea, but a decade later Korea's was five times that of Sweden, and Korea had accomplished this in a world market that was contracting. The South Korean steel industry expanded output from one million tonnes in 1973 to 12 million in 1984 (with nearly six million tonnes of exports in 1983); the US Secretary of the Treasury, deferring to American steelmakers, was reduced to pleading with the world not to sell the latest steel technology to Posco, the Korean state steel corporation (South Korea possessed little iron ore, coking coal or oil).

The South Korean government's dash for a war economy – like the parallel efforts in Taiwan and Singapore, although not on the same scale – ended in failure. The economies had been created to export to the rest of the world, and reforms to overcome the crisis restored that purpose. The government had been obliged to give up part of the old agenda, but it still strove to create a national economy rather than a component in a global economy. But, as in Japan, the instruments of this policy, the giant corporate business groups, were already operating in a global context, subject to the imperatives of world markets rather than the priorities of the Korean government. Furthermore, the population was not wedded to the old agenda. The revolt of 1980 rumbled on through the decade, forcing wages up and a steady programme of extending civil rights: in sum, a rejection of the austere self-discipline required to build the national war economy. Koreans were going to be neither Prussian nor French.

Taiwan also experienced spectacular rates of growth, based upon the export first of agricultural goods and then manufacturing. Between 1953 and 1985, there were 19 years in which exports grew at an annual rate of 20 per cent or more (and seven of over 40 per cent). For the reasons mentioned, the military priorities of the regime were always foremost;[2] in the 1950s, the regime kept over half a million men under arms (or 14 per cent of the 1950 labourforce, a ratio which if applied to the US would produce armed forces of 32 million); in the 1980s, military spending took 40 per cent of an immensely expanded public budget. As with Korea, the evacuation of the Japanese and a radical land reform, along with, in the Taiwanese case, expropriation of the state by an outside army, lent the state unprecedented power. However, the government did not emulate the Korean development of large business groups. On the contrary, for much of the period, the government held the main industrial sectors – steel, aluminium, petrochemicals, secondary chemicals, synthetic fibres and shipbuilding – in the hands of state-owned corporations. Between 1973 and 1979, the state undertook over half the fixed capital formation through the state banks. The private sector, up to the 1980s, consisted of a mass of relatively small companies; some of these in the 1990s became global corporations, although much less well-known than their Korean equivalents. Again, unlike Korea, Taiwan's great neighbour and rival China succeeded in politically isolating its supposed province in the international context, so it was impossible for the government to borrow on the same scale. It was accordingly much less burdened with debt when the debt crisis afflicted developing countries in the 1980s. In sum, Taiwan followed a similar trajectory to Korea, but without some of the more violent outcomes. It passed through the phases of high growth through the export of light manufactured goods, and tried in the 1970s to build an independent national economy, only to be pulled back by crisis and returned to the role of being a component of a global economy in the 1990s.

Singapore's government, with strong social democratic credentials, was more dominated by state capitalism than any of the other NICs, but this time in alliance with international companies and on the basis, like Hong Kong, of free trade. The state undertook the major investments in the 1960s and 1970s, particularly in heavy industry and transport – in shipbuilding, aircraft and airlines, electrical engineering, munitions, steel, petrochemicals – backed by state financial institutions. Like South Korea and Taiwan, Singapore in the 1970s risked launching a drive to build heavy industries and, like the others, precipitated a major economic crisis that forced the government back to the orientation on exports. Furthermore, unlike the other two, the island city was – like Israel, as we noted earlier – simultaneously a garrison economy and one of the most elaborated welfare states in the developing world, with, for example, a programme of public provision that succeeded in housing the bulk of the population. Like Hong Kong, the government maintained few external trade or financial restrictions, so it combined external freedom with internal quasi-military disciplines and regulations.

South Korea, Taiwan and Singapore were, at the same time as undertaking national economic development, 'transitional economies', with one foot in the old national capital agenda, one in the emerging cosmopolitan economy. Hong Kong was not. By lucky accident it was created as a cosmopolitan economy in itself, integrated from the beginning in global flows of trade and finance. This did not mean it did not suffer from booms and slumps – they were intrinsic to the cosmopolitan economy as much as to a world of national economies – but it had built in the flexibility to accommodate such fluctuations without much 'structural adjustment'.

The trajectory of economic growth of the Four Little Tigers revealed both that a new world economy had emerged, and that many different types of regime were consistent with rapid growth, provided only that they bent all efforts to exploit world markets. Growth was driven thus by changing external demand rather than domestic peculiarities, by the global economy rather than the decisions of government. The longer that process persisted, the more difficult it became to sustain anything like the old national capital project. The spectrum of regimes in Southeast Asia that sought to emulate the NICs – from free-enterprise Philippines to state-directed Vietnam through authoritarian Malaysia and wickedly corrupt Indonesia (under the Suharto family) – showed that, in the circumstances of the 1980s and part of the 1990s, there were many different routes to growth (we will look in a later chapter at what happened when those circumstances no longer occurred). Finally, China, with a Communist regime, made the most remarkable self-transformation on the basis of manufactured exports, and on a such a scale that it affected the world figures for poverty reduction. In the mid-1970s, six out of every ten East Asians were poor; by 1995, two out of every ten. In the two decades to 1990, 175 million Chinese moved out of poverty (40 million Indonesians also did so, though a significant if smaller number moved back in the economic crisis of 1997–98 [Watkins 1998: 29–30]).

Nor, despite the longing to boast in Southeast Asia, was it a peculiarly East or Southeast Asian phenomenon. Mauritius, Sri Lanka, the Dominican Republic, Bangladesh (adding over a million jobs in garment manufacture for exports in the 1980s), Jamaica, Mexico and others all came to discover in time the new world market, began to discover not only that they could export manufactured goods but that there was no inexorable logic which determined that world manufacturing capacity could not move to developing countries.

However, there were severe domestic resistances. The national capital project had two faces: one, the patriotic ambition to build an independent national economy; the other making money through rigging the economy in favour of the minority who benefited, regardless of the cost to the society. The 'rent-seekers' defied the new economic logic and sought to hang on to their jobs or contracts, however utopian the national capital project was becoming. On the other hand, the tolerance required by workforces to make the sacrifices demanded by the old project of national development was increasingly qualified. The strike waves of South Korea – in 1980, 1987, 1993 and so on – the political explosions in the Philippines and Indonesia, the opposition even in authoritarian Malaysia, showed that patience, in the absence of what was seen as justice, was not unlimited. The threat of war no longer cowed populations as it had done in the Japan of the 1930s. The cosmopolitan economy seemed to be resuscitating civil society (a theme we take up later).

In the 1990s, the prospects for development were transformed. India and China had opted for national closure in the 1950s at what now seems immense cost, although at the time it seemed the only option available. The unwinding of those powerful structures took a long time, particularly because they jeopardised so many entrenched interests. In addition, regimes took a long time to recognise that the old agenda not only could not be accomplished, but to pursue it was to inflict severe damage and the possibility of popular revolt. What was needed to secure the enhancement of the welfare of the mass of the population now increasingly diverged from what was required to build a separate developed national economy. The evolution of public policy in the Four Little Tigers showed the pervasive spread of a new global economy, making it steadily more difficult to continue to pursue the old agenda. They – excluding Hong Kong – were thus simultaneously the last of the old order, the war-driven national project, and the first of the new, integration in a global economy. It followed that the state-directed trajectory they pursued could hardly occur again. The global system increasingly made it impossible to pursue the old agenda.

PART III

RESISTANCE TO ENDING THE NATIONAL CAPITAL PROJECT: THREE EPISODES

7

'Structural Adjustment' in the 1980s

INTRODUCTION

The last two chapters describe the period from 1947 to the 1970s as a transition, a bridge between a world credibly described as a political economy, a set of competing national state capitals, to a global economy of competing companies, essentially disciplined not by the demands of the state but by world markets. The outcome of this transition is ultimately still not clear – we cannot predict the impact of systemic crisis, of major war or depression, nor the reaction of states trying to defend their political position by clawing back powers conceded to the world economy, to reaffirm the primacy of political sovereignty. But by the 1980s, other things being equal, it seemed that integration for the developed countries was so far advanced that any attempt at a wholesale retreat would be economically catastrophic and therefore politically disastrous. It certainly does not mean anything like complete integration has been accomplished, and indeed there is enough evidence around of the perpetuation of the old order of national states to support a view that nothing of substance has yet changed and globalisation is no more than a fashionable myth. Nonetheless, other evidence suggests this is not so and a major transition has in substance already been achieved.

The conclusion that nothing has changed partly reflects the fact that the data is collected in national terms, appropriate to the locus of political power in the world and the paymasters of statistical services. 'Globalisation', then, seems to reduce itself to a growth in international trade and capital movements, to the growth of transnational corporations, and the creation of world economic regulating agencies like the IMF (or, some might argue, increased cultural inter-actions between countries). However, few of these elements are new, or if new (like the IMF), of such significance as to constitute a qualitative change. Indeed, the proportion of national output traded internationally or of savings exported as capital flows may indeed be less than in the late nineteenth century (Hirst and Thompson 1999), but these are not key issues. The central element in the change is less susceptible to easy measurement – the predominant role played in the decisions of businessmen, directly or indirectly, by the outcome of global markets.

Such a conception does not turn upon the scale of international transactions, nor upon institutional forms (the multinational corporation), but upon the discipline global markets exercise over hundreds of thousands of small and medium companies (not just the large or the multinational), whether engaged in trade outside or inside their country of operation. A company operating exclusively in Idaho or Uttar Pradesh or the Rand or Tuscany thus reacts to incentives ultimately determined in world markets no less than a major exporter.

Such a system is still imperfectly realised, but we can already begin to glimpse dimly something of its shape and dynamics. These no doubt confused impressions have already had a radical effect on perceptions and reactions. It will be long before integration is realised, since governments are at every stage ambivalent in attitude, constantly tempted (or pushed by the fears of particular lobbies or electorates) to seek to frustrate the trend, to recapture power they feel slipping from their grasp. The choices are difficult. On the one hand, continued integration (and thus a loss of the old forms of sovereignty) seems to be the precondition of economic growth and thus of generating the employment and incomes necessary to secure political survival. On the other, governments try to retain the powers to do something significant to defend their citizens (and affirm the right to national self-determination), to meet the ancient need to protect them against the exploitation of foreigners – and also retain the economic powers to reward friends with privilege and patronage, to buy off lobbies and create loyal clients. The contradiction cannot be overcome while governments are expected to be in command of the economy.

In the next three chapters, we look at cases where resistance to making the transition in part or whole has produced disaster. First, we look at developing countries in general and the factors which forced the transition in the 1980s. Then we examine a not dissimilar case, that of the old Soviet Union and its allies. Finally, we look at the economic crisis of the late 1990s afflicting the high-growth countries of East and Southeast Asia.

DEVELOPING COUNTRIES – A THIRD WORLD?

As we noted earlier, the developing countries – in the 1940s and 1950s, the independent powers of Latin America and the newly independent of Asia; in the 1960s, the newly independent of Sub-Saharan Africa – generally set out to create independent and state-directed national capitals. There was now, as we have seen, a theoretical underpinning to this endeavour – the new field of development economics. It had a variety of intellectual parents – Keynesianism, the experience of the war economies of Europe, of planning in the Soviet Union, and a much older tradition of mercantilism. In sum, this seemed to constitute a clear technical manual to implement the national capital project. European and American advisers often shared the same perspective: the powerful state had the role of creating the new economy. So far as the Great Powers were concerned, the developing countries played so marginal a role in the world economy that whatever policy package they selected had few implications for the rest. In practice, the great boom generated in the developed group ensured buoyant commodity prices for the raw-material exports of developing countries, and thus a tolerance among the dominant governments of the world for the universal fashion of import-substitution industrialisation programmes. However, the failures were already beginning to appear in the late 1950s, just before the new governments of Sub-Saharan Africa set out to assume the immense burden of national industrialisation. They had, courtesy of commodity prices, a decade to go before the crash.

1973–75 saw the most serious world recession since the Second World War (exaggerated for oil importers by a round of major oil price increases), ending a quarter of a century's growth since 1947. Commodity prices crashed. It suddenly jeopardised the whole agenda for the national capital project. This did not immediately affect that small group, the Four Little Tigers, which had created a globally competitive manufacturing industry, and like others they were able to borrow to tide over what was seen as a temporary check to growth. To ward off recession – and protect the national project – many governments tried to finance their economies through increased public spending, sometimes radically expanding the public sector to do so (Little et al. 1993). Almost everywhere budget deficits increased (leading subsequently to chronic inflation). Indira Gandhi in India took over a swath of what were known as 'sick industries' to prevent them failing. To finance the imports required to continue expansion, governments increased their borrowing abroad, especially from international banks awash with petro-dollars as a result of the increase in oil prices. All agreed that the crisis was temporary, so short-term tactics were needed to get through it without major losses so that growth could then be resumed.

It was not to be. At the end of the 1970s, a second major recession occurred in the core of the system, the OECD group – along with a second round of oil price increases, rising interest rates affecting the servicing of cumulative debts, a rising value to the dollar affecting dollar debts. By now, many developing countries had exhausted their reserves, and thus their capacity to borrow. There was no option but, sooner or later, to reform to end or heavily qualify the national capital project.

The signal for the crisis was the 1982 default on its debts of oil exporter Mexico, followed by Brazil, South Africa and many more, suddenly threatening the viability of banks in the developed countries and hence the world monetary system. International lending virtually ceased. Furthermore, the governments of the developed countries, which had also tried to protect their economies by deferring a reaction to the recession, had earlier found themselves obliged to deflate, further cutting the markets for the exports of developing countries. The decade became 'the lost years' for developing countries, years of stagnation or decline. East and Southeast Asia alone seemed capable of sustaining rapid growth.

It would have been theoretically possible for the Great Powers to ignore what was happening in the developing countries and allow them to be bludgeoned by crisis into reform at whatever cost in terms of the welfare of their inhabitants. But the developing countries were becoming economically more important. Defaulting on their debts affected the viability of the banks of the OECD group, and cutting imports affected OECD exports. General economic crisis threatened political instability, with unpredictable outcomes.

This was the background to an unprecedented global attempt to force reform on the developing countries, to force the radical reorganisation of countless national capital projects. Structural-adjustment lending – the condition of lifeline loans from the IMF and the World Bank – was designed not just to stabilise the economies of the borrowers (to cover the twin deficits, on the budget and on the balance of payments), but to undertake the long-term restructuring of national economies and government financing, which in sum accelerated integration into a global system.

The programme of reforms was not just forced on governments (as in Sub-Saharan Africa and parts of Asia and Latin America). Some governments embraced the programme themselves (or felt forced by the changing economic context rather than by the pressures of international agencies), recognising the conditions of future growth. This was true in the developed countries in the 1980s – in Australia, New Zealand and Spain for example. Other important reforms were similarly introduced – for example, the decontrol of financial activity (in the US in the mid-1970s, in Britain from 1979) and its radical liberalisation (what was called the 'big bang' in Britain in 1987); or extensive privatisation of the old public sector, covering not just activities with an obvious commercial viability (manufacturing industries, mining), nor those with traditional military implications (steel, capital goods, airlines, railways, telecommunications, naval and arms production), but traditional public infra-structural services (provision of water, electricity, sewerage, waste disposal). There were also experiments in quasi-private production of educational and health services.

It was a remarkable revolution, the destruction of the old corporatist state economy – the national capital project. The change was undertaken within no more than half a century since policy trends were directly in the opposite direction – to almost the extinction of private activity. Furthermore, the programme was undertaken regardless of the level of development, the income level or the political complexion of the government. It included liberal-conservative regimes (in the US and Britain); leftist-populist-nationalist administrations (Mexico's ruling party, the PRI, under Salinas; Argentina's Peronists under Menem); military regimes (Suharto in Indonesia and Pinochet in Chile in the 1970s); social-democratic governments (New Zealand, Spain, Australia); and, with qualifications, Communist regimes (China, Vietnam, Hungary, Poland). Some attempted to resist or postpone reform – for example Germany, with its 'social market' economy, or France, with traditional *étatisme*. But for the majority, the uniformity of the programme suggested a common source not in national peculiarities but in the emergence of a transformed economic context that obliged all governments to adjust. That is it suggested a new system and a new systemic logic, no less powerful than the old logic of a system of competing war-making states. Indeed, the agencies explicitly promoting the programme (for a time loosely referred to as the 'Washington Consensus [Williamson 1990]), the IMF and the World Bank, appeared less as promoters, more as themselves in the grip of the same obsession as governments. Indeed some suggested that the liberalisation of capital markets, opening them to any borrowers, entailed that there was no further need for a World Bank, and that the IMF should be restricted to short-term emergency help: markets and reformed governments could run the rest.

However, reform exposed a much deeper agenda, a range of 'rigidities' not wished away by simple reform packages. It was one thing for newly indepen-dent governments in Asia and Africa (or old independent governments in Latin America) in the 1950s and 1960s to put in place a structure for the forced development of national capital as the backing for military capacity, without which political independence was seen as illusory. By the time of reform in the 1980s, such programmes had assumed major social weight. Interests had become vested in the project, beneficiaries of the state's diversion of resources from mass consumption to business or government bureaucracy, and could threaten the survival of the government if it persisted in trying to strip them of these privileges. Lobbies for the old agenda existed in the government and in assemblies, linked to segments of business and the cultivators, and worked, often in the name of patriotism, to frustrate or dilute the reform package to substitute unpredictable markets for more predictable political discretion.

The old agenda had, of course, never been free of such considerations. The decisions might be taken in terms of pure national interests, but there were those who lost by such decisions and those who gained: officials of the state, sections of the armed forces, private companies, workforces, often linked to overseas interests and governments, to civil and military aid programmes. All had interests in the contest for power and wealth in selecting one programme rather than another, in one project rather than another, in some technical solutions in place of others. Wherever the discretion of the state was great, necessarily all economic and technical decisions became political. If entrenched interests could not be persuaded that they would not lose, reform could have perverse effects. Structural adjustment got stuck between building the national capital project and opening to global markets, stuck at the point of mere 'rent-seeking' for those in charge. The loss-making industries, under the impact of partial privatisation, plunged into debt as the managers and their allies in the government looted the public assets with impunity, transferring losses to the public sector (to be covered by the government) and profits to the private sector.

Many governments were not persuaded – except under the pressure of crisis – that reform was worth pursuing. By default, the national capital project persisted with all its negative effects in the new world context. Take as an example the evolution of policy in Mexico. From the 1930s, successive governments pursued protected industrialisation with a large public sector, and the world boom in the post-war world sustained respectable growth. The active principle of the national capital project was a fierce nationalism (reactive to the long-standing careless imperialism of Washington). Successive governments accepted that it was utopian to seek to rival the US in war-making capacity. However, in the 1960s close proximity to its northern neighbour still reshaped the Mexican economy towards the export of labour-intensive manufactured goods, as was occurring at the same time in the case of the Asian NICs. By 1975, half Mexico's exports were manufactured goods (Harris 1993). Shortly thereafter, however, major new oil deposits were discovered, and this windfall, perversely, provided the basis for a redoubled drive to complete the national capital project (through the development of, among other things, the steel and capital-goods industries). At that time, the majority of leading forecasters were predicting continuing oil price rises through the 1980s, and on this basis Mexico borrowed massively to invest in oil and other parts of the public sector. Oil revenues from the state-owned oil monopoly flowed through state expenditure into the domestic economy, creating a boom which quickly swallowed the manufactured goods which would otherwise have been exported. By the end of the 1970s, Mexico had returned to where it had been before the 1960s, an exporter of raw materials, pre-eminently oil. The collapse, as we have seen, came in 1982 when Mexico was overwhelmed by its debts (Mexicans endeavoured to move between $30 and $60 billion out of the country to escape a feared devaluation) and defaulted.

In the following decade, the economy slowly recovered, led now once again by manufactured exports. The economy had become two separate components: the main economy, the object of government policy and the strategy of building a national economy, and a border region, outside Mexican customs control and open to free trade with the rest of the world. The collapse of the peso radically reduced prices in this second component, leading to a remarkably sustained boom (while the main economy stagnated). Manufacturing employment in the border region in production for export (in factories known as *maquiladores*), mainly to the US, grew from 120,000 in 1982 to 600,000 a decade later. Meanwhile, structural adjustment in the rest of the economy slowly dismantled the old national capital project and thus began to remove the difference with the border region, a process superseded then by an agreement with the US on free trade (NAFTA). The old fortresses of the public sector (steel, chemicals, fertilisers, telecommunications, airlines) were privatised. Even the two icons of the old project, both begun in the late 1930s by the legendary nationalist President Cárdenas, the nationalised oil industry and radical land redistribution, were reformed. It was a programme that could scarcely have been conceived a decade earlier. Whereas in 1979 Mexican businessmen joined the opposition to the country joining GATT (what became the World Trade Organisation) in defence of the old protected national economy, a decade later they were strongly in support of joining – Mexican business had turned from the national economy to world markets.

It was not the end of the story – there is no end. In 1994, at the end of a presidential period, there was another flight of capital, another collapse of the peso and another financial rescue. Officially, national output fell by 40 per cent. But it was an astonishingly brief check: within a year the economy was growing again, Mexican funds flowed back. Within an extraordinarily short time, the losses had been made up, so much so that the crisis seemed to be a statistical illusion. The reforms, including the demolition of the national capital project, had created an economy flexible enough not to end booms and slumps but to cope with fluctuating world markets without long-term damage.

SUB-SAHARAN AFRICA

Sub-Saharan Africa became a byword for the disasters both of globalisation and of imposed structural adjustment. It was indeed the change in the world context, globalisation, which produced the severity of the crisis. But it could only have been so severe because the regimes involved were so late to change and so unwilling to abandon the national capital project. There were, however, also special features: at the time that independence came to many of the countries of Sub-Saharan Africa it was one of the worse-endowed of the developing regions in terms of education and skills. In most cases, it had been colonised last by the Europeans, and expatriates continued to man the key points of many economies – for example the Zambian copper mines and the railways which carried the copper. If exports failed, the expatriates could not be paid, the mines and railways could not be maintained, and the economy came to a halt.

As we have noted, the 1960s were, for the developed countries, a time of transition to a global economy. The costs of building from scratch a protected independent national economy was about to become increasingly high, even while the NICs of Asia were stumbling upon extraordinary growth through manufactured exports. The African countries, like most of the world, failed to learn from East Asia how the world economy had changed direction, so missing the opportunity, insofar as it was practicable, to exploit that change. The results were dire – in the three decades after 1960, Asian NIC per-capita incomes increased (in real terms) from $1300 to $5000 (or nearly 400 per cent), African ones from $800 to $900 (or 13 per cent) (Easterly and Levine 1995: 27). The wasted years meant hideously wasted lives, wracked by a crisis of the state, at its worst in persistent civil war.

The costs of import-substitution industrialisation were especially high in Africa in terms, paradoxically, of increased dependence on imports. Industrialisation entailed increased imports of industrial machinery, raw materials and energy, and so increased vulnerability to anything that affected the capacity to earn foreign exchange through exports or to borrow. In the 1980s, external revenues dried up and the industrialisation process was wrecked – economies seemed to reach such a low ebb (with a flight of skilled labour)that many could hardly conceive of revival.

One country with a sufficient level of development – and highly competitive exports – to make the transition from the old closed national economy to an open one was South Africa. But it was trapped in an even more destructive version of the national capital project, married to an inheritance of British colonial racism, Apartheid. The war drive was less governed by rivalry with its neighbours (who were, in relative military and economic terms, puny), and more by a war on the black majority of the population, linked to the hysterias of the Cold War. Historically, the white workforce was heavily dependent on employment in the great structures of the state and public corporations, so the national capital project was also the central pillar of the social order. The exporters who made the model economically possible, the miners and farmers, depended on a mass of unskilled black workers (indeed conditions in the mines were so bad that South Africans avoided jobs there, making the mines dependent upon immigrant contract labour). But the world economy changed, pushing farmers and mine-owners to demand progressively higher labour productivity if they were to compete in world markets – and that required a settled, not a migrant, labourforce, and an educated one. Apartheid, designed to supply migrant unskilled workers from the 'homelands' ('bantustans') became increasingly a restriction on the economy (part of the argument in Lipton 1985). Economic reform, adjusting the economy to the new world order, thus became impossible – without a break with the old political order, Apartheid.

In Sub-Saharan Africa, pursuit of the national capital project led to an economic structure which taxed exporters (on raw materials) to finance imports to produce manufactured goods which were unsaleable except in the closed domestic economy (often the output had 'negative value-added' – that is the cost of the imported inputs was higher than the price of the finished output). State trading monopolies which enforced this regime opened the way for spectacular corruption. If world prices were higher than that offered exporters, farmers shifted cultivation to non-export crops or, like the diamond miners, smuggled the output out of the country. Governments recognised the problem but too often could not change the system without alienating supporters. They were restricted to denouncing 'unpatriotic' exporters. Zambia, for example, went further and nationalised the copper mines to take over the profits of the mining companies. But when world copper prices declined, the government found that not only were there no profits, the mines needed to be subsidised – out of taxes on the rest of the population – to prevent the political threat of layoffs, and the expatriate engineers could not be paid (so they left the country). As a result, it could not undertake investment in the mines, nor even basic maintenance, thus jeopardising the very existence of the industry. The same thing happened to the railways that carried the copper exports to the port. The catastrophe was compounded. As export revenues shrank, imported medicines disappeared from pharmacies, threatening the survival of young and old. Other governments just failed to maintain existing infrastructure. Tanzania's roads deteriorated to the point where truck owners complained that the cost of road damage to trucks going to the villages to collect the maize crop exceeded the profits earned in selling maize – so the domestic food distribution system was threatened. With the second round of oil price increases (1979/80), the government proposed to reopen donkey farms as an alternative form of transport. Zaire was an even more extreme case – by the early 1990s, under a tenth of the roads inherited at the time of independence remained operational; the country was consuming its capital stock even before civil war made a disastrous situation even worse.

The ruin of countries demoralised civil services (especially when governments curbed public expenditure in conditions of high inflation by holding down civil-service pay). Those with skills left for better-paid private work or emigrated; those without started private businesses from their government offices, plunging into corruption. Aids seemed only to be the final judgement of God on a disastrous record.

The country with the oil and gas resources to protect itself from the ruin, Nigeria, was plagued with successive gangs of a military mafia, squandering revenues on useless projects (the famous catastrophic steel mill, a new capital at Abuja) or salting them away in overseas bank accounts. The national capital project had had, whatever its economic merits in contemporary conditions, an honourable past, but all that was now lost in pure corruption. Yet corruption was only a symptom of exhaustion, of demoralisation, of the collapse of a vision of national development, made worse by the factional fighting over who could capture the trough of rent-seeking. Civil war was only the final sign of the failure to build an effective state of any kind, let alone one set upon the archaic agenda of building a self-sufficient national economy. The national capital project disintegrated into rent-seeking, and thus political paralysis.

THE TRANSITION OF THE 1980s

Despite the severity of the crisis in Sub-Saharan Africa, the shift in orientation by governments towards the new economy accelerated in the 1980s. There were some key changes. The liberalisation of capital markets led to unprecedented short-term international movements of capital, in scale now larger than the value of trade. When there were partly closed national economies, countries were in the main dependent on domestic savings to build the capital stock, and as a result developing countries were 'capital-scarce'. With mobile world capital flows, all countries had in principle access to a common pool of global resources – provided a country's credit was 'sound' (that is government policy followed the particular international precepts of sound finance). Thus, again, governments were obliged to adopt a common range of domestic and external policies if they wished to borrow from world capital markets.

The then current set of negotiations on trade relationships under the GATT, known as the Uruguay Round, was the first round of trade talks opened to developing countries. The talks included – again for the first time – some of the sectors of most entrenched protectionism in the developed countries: agriculture (crucial, as we have seen, for self-sufficiency in the old war-making economy) and textiles and garments (supposedly to protect employment in a sector where developing countries had the greatest comparative advantage). Trade talks were thus a key arena for the continued defence or reform of the old capital project in the developed countries. The Uruguay Round also showed another major change. Developing countries had hitherto resisted trade liberalisation (championed by the developed countries) in the interests of defending their attempts to develop their national capital projects. Now positions were reversed as developing countries came to recognise how important it was for them to keep open access to markets in North America, Europe and Japan, whereas the developed countries were apparently treating further liberalisation with growing reluctance. The round also introduced the issue of the liberalisation of tradeable services, a topic we return to later.

The 1986 Plaza Agreement to realign the currencies of East Asia – to eliminate what was seen as the under-valuation of the currencies there – also had important effects in terms of the global integration of the region. The increase in the value of the Japanese yen now came to exaggerate the effect of the high domestic costs of Japanese manufacturing, accelerating the diaspora of Japanese manufacturing plants, particularly to Southeast Asia. In the first half of the 1990s, Japanese investment in Southeast Asia increased three times over, and Japanese subsidiaries there became important exporters back to Japan. South Korea and Taiwan were not far behind. Again, currency realignment exaggerated domestic costs and encouraged the emigration of plants, again to Southeast Asia but also to the Caribbean, Mexico and China. The *chaebol* began to create much more extensive global manufacturing networks. At the same time, high labour costs in Japan, Korea and Taiwan stimulated legal and illegal immigration. The globalisation of capital was being accompanied by the globalisation of labour.

Countries did not, of course, move in unison. Indeed each country was unique in its relationship to the world economy, unique in its history and political order, in the external crises which forced reform, in the leadership which had to decide whether to reform or not. Thus, the 'Swedish model' resisted the full programme of reform for a long period. After 60 years in office and the creation of what was seen as, in welfare terms, one of the most successful national capital projects – the Swedish Social Democrats faced a long-term decline in the growth of the economy and of incomes. In the first three years of the 1990s, national output declined by 5 per cent (industrial output by 13 per cent, capital formation by 12 per cent) and the rate of unemployment grew by over 14 per cent. The business class began to threaten to leave the country unless the burden of taxation could be reduced – and the economy opened up (Lindbeck 1994; Herekson et al. 1994; Rosen 1995).

The process of creating a new world economy out of the independent national parts was not, despite the opinion of economic advisers and international institutions like the IMF, the pursuit of an intellectual agenda, nor usually the result of conviction so much as continual adjustment to changes in the world economy. It was a process driven by markets, generating crises or opportunities to which governments were obliged to respond. Reform was thus simultaneously a response to new systemic imperatives and itself strengthening the emergence of a new system. Companies were even less susceptible to arguments. They reacted to changed incentives by changing their behaviour, and in doing so, changing the world without being aware of the outcome. The implications of the process were equally opaque, so that exaggerated fears and hopes were both often equally disconnected with what turned out to be the reality. The World Bank, along with most other official aid agencies, thought that once the incentives of markets were restored through the reform of government policy, growth would be swiftly resumed in Sub-Saharan Africa or the Soviet Union. Only one or two years would be needed to achieve this turnaround. The economic calculation omitted social structures, the entrenched position of beneficiaries of the old order, rent-seekers, the lack of reliable laws and legal systems, of ownership rights and much more. The reforms were resisted, and even when formally implemented, done so patchily or in the letter, not the spirit. But even if implemented without the other conditions, they could exaggerate the disasters. What had appeared to require one or two years turned out to need one or two decades, years of apparently endless misery for many people that could undermine any political order.

Structural adjustment then moved on. It was no longer just a question of reforming public finances and the external economic regime. Now macro-economic reform, to be effective, required political reform. There was a new political agenda, the resuscitation or creation of civil society and representative government, of transparent and accountable administration, of human rights and decentralisation. If economic reform had constituted an unprecedented general interference in the prerogatives of sovereign governments by aid donors, political interference in what used to be peoples' right to choose what kind of government and order under which they wished to live was also strikingly novel. The newly invented 'international community' had, it seemed, appropriated unilaterally rights to decide how all people should live in the new global economy.

The 1980s then represented for the developing countries the decade of transition, from one systemic imperative to another. Economic crisis – and in particular the debt crisis – forced the new agenda upon them. Many did not accept the transition, and those that could afford to do so continued to seek to defend parts of the old order of sovereignty (especially apparent for those powers possessing nuclear weapons). But all made some adjustment – from maintaining closed economies and controlled currencies to opening up and managing floating currencies; from seeking self-sufficiency and limiting imports to promoting exports (and so dependence on external markets); from favouring state or local ownership (and being hostile to foreign ownership) to wooing foreign capital. They did it often with great reluctance, under the spur of external economic threat. But all imbibed from the emerging climate of opinion the ubiquitous notion of 'sound policy'.

The aim of policy could no longer be taken for granted, the very definition of 'economic development' was transformed. It had formerly been to create an independent economy. It now came to mean to achieve a given standard of living for the inhabitants – and with a growing emphasis on the amelioration, reduction or eradication of poverty. And when it worked, the new world economy seemed capable of delivering the standard of living far faster than ever before. It was also far quicker to move from exporting light manufactured goods to exporting capital goods. And quicker to create multinational corporations. This was most obvious with the NICs – and especially with South Korea's famous *chaebol*, whose names – Hyundai, Samsung, LGS, Daewoo – became in a handful of years as famous as their long-established American, European or Japanese rivals. But it was also true of poorer countries – almost from the beginning, China's leading state-owned enterprises became capital exporters, buying their way into foreign subsidiaries or joint ventures in New York, Paris or London. Indeed, the measure of national power was now becoming not domestic assets, certainly not size of armies, but how far the country was a home to global corporations, to a share of the cosmopolitan order.

Thus, the disasters of Sub-Saharan Africa were not simply the result of errors of government (as the international agencies said), nor of unfavourable commodity markets abroad (as the African governments said), but of a fundamental change in the nature of the system and therefore the prospects for local growth. The old strategies, like the old objectives, had become not just redundant, but positively destructive.

8

The Collapse of the Soviet Union

The purposes of men, especially in a revolution, are so numerous, so varied, and so contradictory that their complex interaction produces results that no one intended or could foresee

Gordon Wood (1973: 129)

To revive Russia without the army and apart from the army is impossible. The army – this is the living personification of the official being of Russia.

Peter Struve in Odom (1998: 388)

'the car does not drive at all in the direction the driver steers it'

V. I. Lenin (1923/1974: 490)

THE REVOLUTION

Peter the Great began the long process of fashioning Tsarist Russia as a proto-typical military state, with a supportive 'national capital project'. He emulated, as we have noted earlier, his Swedish rivals, and later on Prussia, to create not just armed forces but a society shaped to produce and support his armed forces, backed by an appropriate educational system for its officers, a peasantry habituated to deliver up its sons to military service, a state-developed industrial system to supply weapons, ships and military provisions. In March 1917, as Odom notes (1998: 388), it was to the army Chief of Staff, not to the parliamentary assembly, the Duma, that Tsar Nicholas II tendered his resignation as supreme ruler of all the Russias.

The past does not determine the present, but it offers facilitating conditions, reflexes, a set of familiar predispositions. Those predispositions interacted with the necessities of the years in which the Soviet Union was born. The 1917 revolution was the child of world war, born in conditions of war, its infancy nurtured in the bitter and pitiless conditions of the Civil War – with terrible famine along the Volga and in the Ukraine. With hardly a pause, the new Soviet Union was obliged to secure its own defence, to enter the inter-war competition of the Great Powers, culminating in the Second World War. That in turn proved to be but the prelude to a Cold War and the threat of a Third World War. Thus the Soviet Union was created at a time of the most extreme systemic disciplines, and if there were predispositions, it was least defended against their influence.

The irony would not have been lost on the revolution's intellectual progenitor, Karl Marx, for the inspiration of the Bolsheviks had been the search for a world at peace and without frontiers, unified by a world working class that had conquered nationality. Yet he himself remained fascinated with exactly the centralisation and 'socialisation' which were such important parts of an economy refashioned for war. Lenin was consistent: 'socialism is merely the next step forward from state-capitalist monopoly' (Lockwood 2000: 58).

The reality was of active Soviet participation in a system of competing and war-making states. Here the ethics of sacrifice and collective struggle that were the supposed marks of the socialist movement were transposed into those of military devotion, painfully illustrated in the period of 'war communism', the most extreme junction of two apparently contradictory ethics of self-sacrifice – to communism and to war (since the majority of Party members in 1923 had been recruited after the revolution, Civil War was the founding experience of their party membership). Trotsky, as Commissar for War, called for the militarisation of labour, and Lenin repeated the call for the conscription of labour and for labour armies, 'the practical realisation of socialist and communist labour'. The Party cadres were the soldiers of revolution, and for them no sacrifices were disallowed in the class war, now become the war to defend the state. The collective way of life – free barrack accommodation, food supplies in collective canteens, a common uniform, marches and banners – all confused the socialist and the military: if the cadre felt he or she was responding to the one, and it was counter-system, he or she was in all likelihood obeying the second, ancient and familiar – and systemic. When Lenin praised the *subbotniks*[1] – the new Communist man whose fanatical dedication tolerated no constraints – and, years later, Mao rediscovered the idea in the turmoil of the Great Leap Forward, both were identifying an ethic more commonly associated with the heroism of war, of military orders of society. Mao's commune peasants hated the communal canteens. Lenin might embrace scientific management, Taylorism in the factories (itself so close to the logic of large – and Prussian – field armies) as the swiftest means to accelerate the transition to socialism, but Western trade unionists hated it as the epitome of exploitation, and Soviet workers might equally have seen it as the means to turn factories into Prussian garrisons, to institute a regime of terror as the main instrument of factory and social discipline.

It is, of course, not possible to determine how much of the new Soviet order was the working out of those historic military dispositions of Tsarism, interacting with the systemic disciplines of the state-system, or how much was entailed by the sheer extremities of the situation. Long ago, Chamberlin (1935/1965: 81) saw Soviet terror as entailed by the immediate condition of Russia:

> no government could have survived in Russia in these years without the use of terrorism … The national morale was completely shattered by the World War. No one, except under extreme compulsion, was willing to perform any State obligation. The old order had simply crumbled away; a new order, with new habits and standards of conduct, had not been yet formed; and very often the only way in which a governmental representative, whether he was a Bolshevik commissar or a White officer, could get his order obeyed was by flourishing a revolver.

Yet the tactics impelled by the needs of survival fitted into a particular mode in which the difference between the ethics and tactics of war and 'building socialism' became perilously opaque.

Perhaps the experience of the Civil War and war communism could have been absorbed without permanently scarring the new Soviet society in the years that followed, the time of the more relaxed New Economic Policy (NEP), if the external context had been different. But Moscow determined to return to participation in the world system of states at the 1923 Rapallo conference, and to do so as a Great Power, albeit an impoverished one. By this means, it accepted the imperative – in conditions of a wrecked economy and great poverty – to expand its defence capacity, to create an industrial and agricultural base appropriate to such an expansion, and to institute that pitiless administrative and political order appropriate to the reign of terror to achieve these ends. As Stalin (1933/1940: 47) put it in the 1933 planning aims,

> to create in the country all the necessary technical and economic prerequisites for increasing to the utmost the defence capacity of the country to enable it to organise determined resistance to any and every attempt at military intervention from outside, to any and every military attack from without.

The agenda could not be accomplished swiftly; the political faction fights of the 1920s, partly in defence of the old agenda of revolution, were a continuing distraction. But, embodying the national instincts of the new cadre of the party, rather than what were now seen as the internationalist daydreams of the old cadre, the full logic emerged – breakneck industrialisation (with priority to defence and heavy industry),[2] the ransacking of agriculture to ensure guaranteed control of food supplies (and to keep up the export of agricultural goods to sustain imports for industrialisation, the price of which was another terrible famine in the Ukraine), and the maintenance of a state of permanent emergency, punctuated by terrifying purges that despatched troops of bewildered loyalists, as well as rebels, to the concentration camps. The revolution had cleared away all those social interests, land and capital, which might have resisted the process; the working class had been decimated or absorbed into the bureaucracy. As in the cases of South Korea and Taiwan later, the state in Russia exercised unprecedented dominance.

The Soviet Union's pursuit of industrialisation and militarisation could now be pursued without attention to cost or to the damage inflicted on the mass of Russians. It was here that the agenda of what became known as 'economic development' was fashioned, bequeathed to a host of others after the Second World War, with its peculiar stultifying emphasis on the source of military goods, heavy industry.[3] All sacrifices were now the mark of the singular heroism of the new society and the new Communist Man; each phase was a step along the road to the 'construction of socialism'. Engels might have thought in the 1870s that the European ruling orders exploited society without any restraint simply to support the drive to militarism, but these earlier cases were puny beside the obsessions of the Soviet leadership. The ancient mechanism to transfer resources from consumption to accumulation was now so purified through the elimination of the intermediate class of private capitalists that it seemed specially designed to fit the systemic logic of war-making states, to be more perfect than even Frederick the Great's Prussia. Of course, it was a myth. The lack of capitalists fatally undermined the capacity to accumulate capital. Thus, the resources to be ransacked by the state to sustain the drive to war, even if the process could have overcome the absorptive incapacity and chaos of the bureaucracy, was much smaller than had been available to Western Europe, let alone North America.

However, foreign observers were rarely able to see these qualifications. For them, very often, the formal structure seemed, even for those for whom Bolshevism was anathema, the perfection of the national capital project, a 'new civilisation' as the British Fabians Sidney and Beatrice Webb (Webb 1935) put it. Like the Soviet Union, armies presented themselves as models of disinterested but decisive efficiency, when in reality bureaucratic chaos, duplication and often corruption was the reality. In the case of the Soviet Union in the 1930s, only the operation of the opposite of planning, arbitrary terror, could keep the system in movement – and only the immense sacrifices of the Soviet people could ensure positive outcomes. While Stalin lived, it was his peculiar function to keep the bureaucracy in constant movement, to prevent it settling into the routines of administration and institutionalised rent-seeking.

WORLD WAR

The Second World War was the supreme test of the order that Stalin and his followers had put in place. Despite the immense waste and the appalling errors, the Soviet Union has the leading claim to have won the war. But it was a close-run thing. Just as the towns and cities of Prussia greeted Napoleon as a liberator, indicting the rule of terror of the Junkers, the 'Prussian system', so the peasants and citizens of the Ukraine greeted the German armies with flowers. Several hundred thousand Soviet troops agreed to fight for the Nazis. The Soviet system failed as resoundingly as the Prussian had done. However, unlike Napoleon, who could present his armies as liberating, the terror unleashed by the Nazis, the SS and security police with the aim of 'ethnically cleansing' the Ukraine, exterminating or enslaving the population in order to settle German farmers (to achieve the aims of the *grossraumwirtschaft*), left Ukrainians and Russians with no exit. It forced them back into the extraordinary sacrifices of Stalin's Great Patriotic War as the only option. It was understandable that all those who after 1945 returned from being prisoners of war of the Germans, perhaps expecting gratitude from the regime for their sacrifices, were arrested as deserters and traitors, and went to fill the regime's immense prisons, the Gulag.

The war, as we have seen, devastated the country. If the USSR attained 35 per cent of the US per-capita output in 1938, despite the heroic efforts made to expand production for war in the years to 1945, the country could attain only 30 per cent of the American level in 1950, and 33 per cent 37 years later (1987) (Harrison 1998: 34). Yet what had the destruction of a generation been for? Only two years after the triumphs of victory, Washington and Moscow returned to preparing for the next war, hot or cold. In doing so, the Kremlin committed itself to a contest with an economy many times larger than its own in terms of ability to achieve and maintain military superiority. The miracle is that the Soviet Union was able to do this for 40 years before finally imploding. It is amazing that the final crisis took so long, that the peoples of the Soviet Union tolerated their ruling order's continuing demands for sacrifice for four further decades.

Yet, as with the Webbs in the 1930s, the inner reality of the regime defied scepticism. New governments in developing countries saw only the model of the national capital project. Soviet Russia had, by its own efforts, been able to cross the barrier from being a developing country to being developed, had been able to build the means to become militarily a Great Power, to defeat Nazi Germany and go on to match the US in technology, in nuclear weapons, missiles and satellites: 'socialism' worked. Furthermore, it seemed, while the standard of living might be lower, the conditions of life were more equal and more secure with a guaranteed supply of housing, healthcare and education.

THE WAR ECONOMY

Yet all the components – the appearance of equality and security, albeit at a low level – were linked to the military dominance, much greater after the Second World War than before. A minimum level of welfare was required to sustain the army at rest. But the central rationale remained military – as Berliner (1988: 162) puts it, writing in the mid-1980s:

> If we are to capture the aims of the Soviet ... elite, then we must accord first place to military defence, and derivatively to heavy industry, as the aim of economic development ... the military and heavy industry attainments of the advanced capitalist countries are the principal goal towards which development has been directed.

The core of the Soviet economy was an immense military-industrial system, statistically unrecorded (in a supposedly planned economy) even in the directing centre of the regime. Demand for military production determined the size and output of the rest of the economy. The central allocation system dealt in physical quantities without reference to relative costs or scarcities, according highest priority to the political agenda of defence strategy. Indeed, to raise questions about the allocation of resources between, say, civil and military purposes, as happened in the 1980s, was to be guilty of both immorality and high treason – issues of national security, matters supposedly connected to the very existence of the Soviet Union, were outside the discussions even of the central leadership.

Through all the years, no military budget was prepared, let alone published until 1989 when Gorbachev – to the outrage of the military – forced his planners to try to prepare a set of guesstimates (even then, no real prices were employed to assess the relative burden on the Soviet economy). The innovation encouraged others. The Institute of Economic Forecasting (Academy of Sciences) approached the analysis through the Machine Building and Metal Working Sectors of the economy on the basis of 1988 official data (at world prices), and reached an estimate that between 62 and 63 per cent of national output went to meet military needs, 32 per cent to investment goods, and 5–6 per cent to consumer goods (in Gaddy 1996: 13n.). Nearly two thirds of the industry, the central core of the economy, was directly linked to military demands, and possibly more indirectly (through 'investment goods'). In absolute terms, the scale was immense – on some accounts, the Soviet defence sector was four times larger than that of the US, and we must suppose that it had to be so to make up for the glaring differences in productivity and ensure the significant margin of superiority that the military planners regarded as necessary.

State demand and the supposed economies of scale made defence enterprises the largest, covering 1100 industrial groups and 920 research and development institutes. It included the largest of all, the Nizhny Tagil Urals plant, employing over 40,000 workers. The senior managers of such enterprises carried immense political weight as members of the upper echelons of the party and the government, as did the military itself.

MILITARY PLANNING OF THE CIVIL ECONOMY

Frunze replaced Trotsky as Commissar for War in 1921, and the ending of the Civil War allowed military planners to consider what kind of civil economy was needed to sustain an adequate scale of military preparedness. It was the same preoccupation as that which concerned the German High Command in the demilitarised years of the Weimar Republic, a concern officially, as we have seen, headed by Colonel Georg Thomas. In Moscow, it was laid down that military-industrial requirements entailed reshaping the civil apparat of the state to ensure, in the event of war, a 'total societal and military mobilisation' (Odom 1998: 431–32). This led to the creation of a State Council of Labour and Defence, and continuing debate on how much of the economy should be directed to weapon production. Tukhachevsky pressed the case for massive defence construction, but this only won Stalin's approval after the war scare of 1927. In the chaotic conditions of Russia in the inter-war years, it was the most the regime could achieve to increase the output of military goods rather than reshaping the whole economy.

The hard lessons learned in the Second World War – in losses and shortages of supply – led to the creation of a new school of 'military economics'. The most influential theorist here was Colonel Andrei N. Lagovsky. He endeavoured to identify the implications for the civil economy of the demands of modern warfare in his *Strategy and Economics* of 1957 (Gaddy 1996: 35–40). Lagovsky cited a set of figures to illustrate the immense increase over time in the demand for military goods, in this case, artillery ammunition: in the Austro-Hungarian War of 1866, the Prussian military used 40 rounds of shells per artillery piece; in the Franco–Prussian War, four years later, 190 rounds were used; in the Russo–Japanese war of 1905, the Russians used 720 rounds; in World War I, in

1914, the Russian military planners anticipated using 1000 rounds, the total for the duration of the war being put at some 7 million rounds. In fact, the armed forces used 55 million rounds; in World War II, the Russian forces used 17 million rounds per month, rising dramatically in 1944 and 1945. The exponential increases when generalised to all fields of military equipment implied spectacular demands on the capacity of the civil economy, without which wars would be lost.

From this calculation, Lagovsky drew strategic economic conclusions. Immense stockpiles of weapons and ammunition were required well before hostilities began. The industrial structure must maintain extraordinary levels of spare capacity which could be brought into production when needed. The design of all relevant civilian output must be inspected by military experts to ensure that it could be employed immediately, or swiftly converted, for military purposes, regardless of the needs of civilian consumption. Raw materials must be stockpiled on a commensurate scale to ensure a rapid and sustained expansion of output. Industry supplying the armed forces must be protected from destruction from the air by being relocated away from the western industrial heartlands of Russia to the east, to and beyond the Ural Mountains.

Lagovsky offered calculations to illustrate the scale of requirements. If an airforce of 10,000 planes was seen as the minimum necessary, and the average life of an aircraft in war was six months, the aircraft construction industry must have the capacity to produce 20,000 aircraft per year. To ensure this required equivalent stocks of raw materials and parts, as well as manufacturing and mining capacity upstream capable of sustaining supplies. More generally, stocks of raw materials must permit factories to continue to produce without re-supply for between four and six months. If the planned output was to be 30,000 tanks annually, then the stocks of materials required in tank production must be capable of supporting, without early replenishment, an output of 10–15,000 tanks per year.

A military inspectorate would be needed to supervise all units producing civilian goods of military relevance – tractors, trucks, mobile power stations, aircraft, ships etc. The inspectors would need powers to order changes in design to meet military requirements. This recommendation was one of the sources of the disastrous design of much Soviet output – goods of a weight that showed no concern for fuel consumption, or of a durability far beyond any normal period of use.

Later definitions of Soviet military strategy – for example Sokolovski's *Military Strategy* (1962 ed. in Odom 1998: 44) – reinforced this position. Nuclear weapons were now officially identified as tactical weapons which would be used to blast through NATO defence lines on the European front. This would allow

Soviet forces to race through the gaps to the Atlantic (originally set to take two months, but later two to three weeks). It followed that the vehicle stock required to accomplish this (and replace losses) became immense.

Fortunately for the people of the Soviet Union, the programme was never put fully into operation. But enough of it was accomplished to mark Soviet industry – with vast overcapacity and immense stocks of raw materials and finished products. It was, by any ordinary standards, immensely wasteful. Given the dynamic changes in technology constantly occurring, it was also futile, since current stocks were constantly becoming obsolete and having to be written off – so the struggle to keep up usable stocks became an endless and enormously extravagant operation.

Military preoccupations also gave to Soviet society a military character – from the vast barrack-like blocks of public housing, the regimentation of social life and its closure to interactions with people abroad, morning reveille, youth brigades marching, red banners tossing in the wind, to tasks on the 'production front', 'storming' road construction or dam building and so on. Society was an army in waiting, but always in a state of military preparedness.

REFORM

A war-making state requires, at least occasionally, a war to sustain the validity of the sacrifices demanded of the citizens. The Second World War established the state of permanent emergency in this respect, revived by the Korean War and by successive crises with the US. But it had declining effect, especially after the death of Stalin, when the regime of fear within the bureaucracy could no longer be politically sustained. Indeed, the end of the General Secretary removed the lynchpin of the system. There were even threats of popular rebellion, especially in the Eastern European satellites. It was the role of Khrushchev to start the process of dismantling the old order, his most dramatic step in this direction being his speech to the 20th Congress of the Communist Party (1956), which, for the first time acknowledged some of Stalin's 'excesses'.

However, the underlying problem grew increasingly severe – the civil economy was barely able to support the demands of the military-industrial complex. Furthermore, times had changed, and Soviet leaders were obliged to pay increasing attention to the state of popular opinion. It was the established wisdom that the long-term survival of the Soviet order and its reputation abroad required increased popular consumption, a significant improvement in the quality of life. Yet how to reconcile the two divergent aims? The new leadership experimented with reforms – for example the Liberman reforms of the late

1950s to empower and reward managers to encourage them to compete. But nothing could be implemented which affected the power and position of the bureaucracy. The Soviet regime was now ensnared in the paralysis of official-dom. The effort required to combat or bypass the officials now was of a scale, it was thought, to risk the stability of the order.

Meanwhile, there was growth and some improvement in the levels of consumption, although at a declining rate. The grain harvest, for example, stagnated through much of the 1960s and 1970s, despite receiving a growing volume of plan resources. In the mid-1970s, under Brezhnev, there was a time when disarmament agreements with Washington seemed to bring the promise of a possible decline in military spending, but the armed forces were strongly opposed to any relaxation. An increase in world oil prices stimulated arms purchases by the oil-producing countries, and this seemed to vindicate the existing scale of military spending.

By the early 1980s, the problem could no longer be avoided by the leadership. The speed with which the world economy was advancing ahead of the Soviet Union could no longer be concealed. The whole vindication of the war economy – that it was the most efficient method to deliver the greatest quantity and the best quality of the means to make war – was under threat. What was the point of 60 years sacrifice to create the Soviet Union if, at the end, even in the capacity to fight the Soviet performance was deteriorating? Even what had been achieved had been immensely wasteful – the Soviet Union had been obliged to mobilise three to four times the scale of capital investment used in the US to produce a far smaller output of undoubtedly inferior quality. The picture was far worse in terms of what most people judged such matters by – the shortages of consumer goods, even bread, and the quality of most non-military manu-factured goods. The population was, by turns, cynical or hostile. Furthermore, everything became even worse when the leadership allowed itself to be drawn into a war in Afghanistan – the effect on Soviet society being not unlike that of the Vietnam War upon Americans. A new President of the US, Ronald Reagan, then seemed to promise another gigantic increase in defence spending through his Strategic Defence Initiative (SDI) – or 'Star Wars' – programme to defend the US from missile attack.

This was the context in which a new leadership came to power with a mandate, insofar as 'mandates' could be said to exist, for reform – to upgrade the military capacity and improve the standard of living. But Soviet society had changed so much that the reform impetus no longer broke instantly upon the obdurate resistance of the established order, Party and State, nor was shattered in collision with the systemic imperative of military defence at any cost. Gorbachev was able to introduce a radical recognition of a new reality, a new systemic imperative – national competitive status in the world, he said, now turned upon economic strength, not military capacity. 'We are encircled,' he declared in May 1986, mimicking Stalin's famous phrase about 'capitalist encirclement', 'not by invincible armies but by superior economies' (Gaddy 1996: 53). If the aim of the old order had been war-making capacity and therefore economic development to achieve this, economic development was now becoming an end in itself.

However, throwing resources at the problem had consistently failed. Each increase in investment produced a decreasing growth in output, and made no improvement in quality, so that there was increasing production of defective or unusable products. Gorbachev and his advisers were struck, as many had been earlier, by the contrast in quality between military and civilian output (Gaddy 1996: 49):

> 'I can understand the consumer,' he meditated in the autumn of 1985, 'who simply cannot grasp why we are able to produce space ships and nuclear-powered vessels, at the same time that we turn out defective household appliances, shoes or clothing. This is hurting us not only materially, but morally and politically as well.

He attributed the difference to the closer military inspection of goods in production, and consequently transferred Defence Ministry directors into civil production departments and military quality control officers into the factories. The rejection rate of goods soared – and workers threatened strike action because their annual bonuses were cut. The scheme was scrapped.

There were various experiments, each seeming to lead back to the opposition of the central apparat, the great central ministries and the central control institutions of the Party. It was here that all reform was neutralised. Gorbachev began to seek to decentralise powers away from the centre, to dismantle the central planning directorate. The measures did nothing for the quantity or quality of output, but it did begin to weaken central direction.

THE END OF THE WAR ECONOMY

By the end of 1988, Gorbachev was coming to confront the fact that the core of the problem of Soviet economic reform was itself the war economy and the entrenched position of the armed forces in overall policy-making. He had, as Odom (1998: 235) observes, come to see that 'The very essence of the Soviet economy was its war mobilising character'.

He then – most remarkably in retrospect – took steps to defy the systemic logic in which he had been raised and trained. Without informing the High Command, he announced major cuts in the size of the armed forces (it was not at all clear that he could in practice implement such reductions); the withdrawal of a significant body of forces from Eastern Europe and the eastern Soviet Union (facing China); and the beginning of a campaign to convert much more military industry to civil production. Simultaneously, he moved to reform trade relationships between the members of the Eastern Bloc trading system, Comecon or CMEA, so that, in particular, Soviet exports of oil and gas to its allies could be charged at prices increasingly close to those in world markets (in effect moving towards ending these major subsidies to its allies). Enhanced oil revenues could allow increased Soviet imports and hence both the upgrading of equipment of Soviet industry and improvements in popular consumption. But cheap oil, justified on military grounds, was one of the few things holding the alliance together, and the reform was effectively the beginning of the end of both CMEA and the Warsaw Pact.

Gorbachev had indeed begun to remove some of the key obstacles to reform, to begin to defy the systemic logic. But he was doing it without replacing the central control mechanism, let alone establishing market allocation mechanisms. He seems not have envisaged the chaos that was likely to follow from this failure, a chaos compounded in the country at large by his anti-alcohol campaign. He balked at the idea of introducing markets, but moved on to some measure of 'co-operativisation' – at least for new retail services – as a way to improve the supply of basic consumer goods. Meanwhile, the context was itself not static – as Finance Minister Pavlov put it in Trud at the end of 1990 (Lockwood 2000: 125): 'You can argue whether or not we are prepared for the transition to the market … but the reality is that the market is already imperiously intruding into our life. More than 60 per cent of prices are not under the control of the State.'

Successive crises, mutually reinforcing, now began to unravel the Soviet economy – the failure of any central allocation mechanism, the demoralisation of the central Party cadre and the military leadership, pressure from the Republics and provinces for much greater freedom, and the collapse of the CMEA trading system (and the immense implications of the end of Soviet subsidies). It was not helped by a recession in Russia's export markets in Europe. There was a flight of capital, undermining the currency and the financial system. The linkages of the domestic economy failed, leaving a primitive barter system and a criminal nexus controlling the key sectors.

The political scene was not static while Gorbachev experimented with reform. If he was willing to sacrifice the Eastern Bloc, CMEA and the Warsaw Pact to liberate the Soviet Union from the system and remain in power, Boris Yeltsin, his Party colleague in the Russian component of the USSR was willing to undercut him and sacrifice the Soviet Union itself, the Communist Party and a much larger part of the military establishment to come to power in the Russian Federation. Yeltsin was elected President of Russia, and in alliance with the other republics of the Soviet Union, to universal astonishment, brought the union to an end, leaving Gorbachev without a state. Furthermore, Yeltsin's 1992 defence budget cut spending by two thirds – 'the world's largest and arguably most powerful military machine melted like spring ice' (Odom 1998: ix).

The speed with which the old order unravelled was extraordinary. Few had anticipated that it was so vulnerable. Indeed, few detected that the system of war-making states had grown, unseen over the years, to a point of such enervation that it could permit the Soviet Union to make such a dramatic attempt to escape a logic which for so many decades had imposed such harsh burdens upon the Soviet peoples. The speed had made it impossible to prepare a transition. Structural adjustment in Sub-Saharan Africa had been a smoothly directed process by comparison. As a result, the economic crisis in Russia and its now independent former associates was as severe as any economic crisis recorded. The collapse of the military-industrial core imposed a massive implosion upon the national economy. Between 70 and 80 per cent of the defence sector was located in the Russian Federation – in terms of number of enterprises, volume of output and share of employment. Much of the rest was based in the Ukraine and Belarus, where the economic crisis was equally severe. If the 1980s were a 'lost decade' in the adjusting developing world, the 1990s were even more so for what had once been the 'centrally planned economies'.

The enterprise managers, now stripped of the controlling hand of the Party and the central ministries, by default inherited the major part of the economy and, as a result, assumed heightened political importance. They now resisted attempts to reduce their position, and carried on production to underpin that power – but without paying bills. Inter-enterprise arrears soared (by mid-1992, arrears were equal to 78 per cent of Russia's gross domestic product); loans from state banks were not serviced, nor the principal repaid; taxes were not paid (or were paid in kind); and often the workforce was not paid (or the lucky ones were paid in kind). Schleifer and Boycko (1994: 75), writing before 1994, observed that

> Most enterprises continue to be unchallenged by the old management teams … their management is principally dedicated to preserving the traditional production lines, which may have no markets, as their core activity. In many cases, enterprise managers have consolidated control by buying shares in the aftermarket, and are simply killing time, hoping for a miracle (and credits).

The problem was at its most extreme in the military industries. By 1995, over 200 of the largest defence complexes were insolvent, kept in operation only by government transfusions. And in terms of the state-owned enterprises as a whole, average labour productivity, 30 per cent of the American level in 1991, had sunk to 19 per cent by 1997.

Nimble managers tried to make what they could out of stealing the assets that had fallen into their hands, transferring any profits to their private companies and abroad (courtesy of IMF credits) and moving losses the other way (through overpricing sales to their public-sector operations, or underpricing sales in the opposite direction). The state now had little power even to monitor what was happening. Three major lobbies – agriculture, fuel and energy, defence – exercised great pressure on central government to protect their position. A symbol of the new order was perhaps the emergence of Viktor Chernomyrdin, for a time one of Yeltsin's Prime Ministers, former chief executive of the giant natural gas corporation Gazprom, and chief shareholder; he was instrumental in protecting Gazprom from paying taxes on its enormous operations, thus exaggerating the fiscal crisis of the state.

Out of the chaos emerged great public–private baronies, protected by their own security forces, blocking or reshaping all reform proposals to conform with their own interests. Three quarters of the first phase of privatisation were 'closed subscriptions' – that is effectively takeovers by existing managers. After sale, 70 per cent of the assets remained in the same hands (with an additional 16 per cent being vested in the local authority where the corporation operated). In effect, the state bribed the 'stakeholders' to accept the change. Sutela (1994: 418) explains: 'to ensure speedy privatisation … breaking the ownership position of the branch Ministries was the overwhelming priority if the irreversibility of the transition was to be ensured … the speed deemed necessary could not be attained without bribing the insiders'.

When England's Henry VIII nationalised the land of the Church of Rome in the sixteenth century, he used this treasure chest as bribes to create a new group of landowners with a vested interest in his settlement and the status quo; Yeltsin did much the same, distributing with great speed at low cost much of the state industrial property of Russia – assets worth possibly $50 to $60 billion were sold for $1.5 billion.

Slowly, new business groups emerged, combining former state assets, new banks, new private business, with overseas subsidiaries, often with a foothold in the media and close links to parts of the government, sections of the Duma, and the criminal fraternities – 'a capitalist economy,' as Martin Wolf (*Financial Times*, 30 June 1999) puts it, 'more ruthless, more corrupt and more unequal than anything even (Lenin) could have imagined'. The diversified structures allowed swift defence against negative circumstances – a currency crisis in August 1998 led to $136 billion leaving the country, precipitating Moscow into default on its debts and a freeze on bank credits and dollar holdings. By September, the gross domestic product had officially fallen by 10 per cent on a year earlier, and imports by 45 per cent. Since 1991, output had fallen by 40 per cent and employment by a quarter. Of course, all the new activities – private, those in services and the small-scale sector – were always undercounted, but even so the 1990s were catastrophic. Of the 27 countries of the world which experienced a decline in income in the 1990s, 21 were in the former Eastern Bloc.

The costs to the inhabitants were severe. In 1999, 30 per cent of the population was said to have slipped below the official monthly subsistence level. Internal differences widened dramatically – between pensioners (whose pensions were either not paid or paid in kind) and the young who embraced the new opportunities, between Moscow, where life for many was vastly improved, and the provinces, the isolated industrial towns where the one large factory had closed, mining settlements in the Arctic where miners were not paid for six months at a stretch, to the villages, now forced back into the Tsarist nineteenth century. In 1999, the Red Cross reported that in the district of Chukotka the average expectation of life (at birth) had fallen to about 34 in the 1990s, a level close to that in the developing world half a century ago. It was notorious that the national figure for men had fallen from 65 to 58 years, that is worse than many developing countries.

The destruction of the war economy – and the devastation of the old national capital project – did not create an efficient market economy (or it has not done so yet). The reform process itself bankrupted the economy, or rather transferred what was of value to new oligarchs, watched over by a weak state. The transition from the old order to the new was ambushed, caught in the middle at a rent-seeking stage (Harris and Lockwood 1997).

A NEW WORLD ORDER

The collapse of the Soviet Union was the most dramatic signal of the emergence of a new world system. It had been the centre of an international war-making group with eight members. With the change, its allies in Eastern Europe, Cuba and Vietnam became free-standing, and the old group of eight produced 27 new countries. As surprising as the disintegration of the group was, it was equally surprising how quickly the heirs were absorbed into the world. The sheer novelty wore off with extraordinary speed. The steely facade of Soviet military power, for so long taken for granted as part of the natural order of things, disappeared so quickly that it became difficult for the participants to remember what it had been like, let alone the passions and fears that had gone into its making.

The economic damage seemed hardly supportable. The plants, it was reasoned, as in a Western slump remained intact even if unused; could they not be put back to production? More thoughtful observers noted that China had not suffered in making the transition (Nolan 1995), nor had Vietnam. Yet there was little equivalence. The old Soviet Union had been one of the two greatest powers in the world, and its military economy by far the largest (in terms of employment and output). By comparison, China was still puny, and it still had to face the reforms that had been accomplished in Russia. Russia was a very special case.

Each country was, in some sense, a special case, and declined to different degrees, and recovered similarly. By 1997, real output in the old CMEA group had reached or exceeded the level of 1989. Poland, Slovakia, and outside the CMEA group Slovenia, seemed to have recovered and significantly grown. Hungary, the Baltic states and the Czech Republic were also beginning to grow once again. Few of these declined as far as Russia, the Ukraine and Belarus, and none became blocked in a similar politico-economic paralysis to these three. But then these had constituted the old order war-making economy for 70 years; it was hardly surprising that they should be resistant to simple reform. Indeed the error of Western advisers was to think that simple reform, the 'freeing of markets', would swiftly lead to growth. Consider the combined wisdom of the IMF, the World Bank, the OECD and the EBRD in 1990 at the prelude of the process: 'A recovery from the reduced level of output should be able to get underway within two years or so ... Further, strong growth of output and rising living standards could be expected for the remainder of the decade and beyond' (IMF et al. 1990: 18–19).

In sum, then, systemic rivalries in Europe reshaped the revolutionary regime of 1917 into yet another national war-making competitor. 'Building socialism' was one of the most purified forms of the national capital project to back that war-making. The transformation, under the same rhetoric, betrayed socialists round the world. Closure of the country was a fundamental part of the exercise, closure in order to focus more sharply continuing hostility towards the rest of the world. The Second World War was the test which, despite an initial disastrous failure, finally ended as a triumph for the Soviet order. After the war, there were other triumphs as the Soviet Union seemed to be capable, with ease, of surpassing each new innovation in the US. Yet it was in the national capital project that the system failed. Output could be produced but not rising productivity – so that sustaining war parity with NATO took an exponentially increasing volume of resources, threatening the economic ruin of the Soviet people.

Gorbachev identified the central problem correctly and pursued disarmament with the US in order to undertake reform. Already the world had changed enough to allow him to risk such a giant leap out of the old necessities. Yet reform directed to end part of the war-making drive in fact removed the lynchpin of the system. The Soviet Union fell apart. Only a return to Russian nationalism could hold together part of the historic territories of the Tsars. Not even that could stave off a monumental economic decline – Russian output sank to a level

80 per cent of India's, 36 per cent of China's, 45 per cent of Brazil's, 89 per cent of Mexico's (World Bank 1999: 230–31). Russia did globalise – its mafia were to be found in Cyprus, London, Miami and many other places.

The implications for the world at large were perhaps even greater. The end of the Cold War released the world from a thraldom which had lasted for the lifetime of most of the world's leaders. The enforced unities of position divided in entirely new ways and rivalries. The signal of the end of the system of war-making allowed serious discussions of what had seemed to be entirely dead issues, for example disarmament. International agencies now began to seek to force general disarmament on all. So quick were people to forget how dangerous things had been that many thought the dangers of the world had not been reduced; but substantially reduced they had been by the standards of the old order.

9

Economic Crisis in Asia

INTRODUCTION

The NICs were earlier described as the last of the old agenda, building a national economy as backing for military capacity, and the first of the new, building a prosperous fragment of a world economy through exploiting global markets. But the drive to build national power, as opposed to seeking to raise local incomes and employment by whatever means were to hand, created a peculiar economic and social structure, one with interests vested in, or entirely dependent on, the persistence of the national project. This degree of rigidity, of, as it were, pre-emptive claims on the economy, collided with the flexibility required to adjust to a world economy of continuous change and innovation. The greater the degree of integration with the world, the more the requirement that each government allow the continued change in domestic institutions and structures – even down to the physical forms of the economy (for example the layout of cities) – if the employment and wealth of the inhabitants were to be protected or advanced.

Through this account, a variety of different types of modern state in the period of transition between the two orders of world economy have been identified, some of them moving from one type to another. First is the survival of the old war-making state, autarkic, closed, focussed on creating a fully diversified economy to support military capacity. In reality, there are no cases in the world today which correspond to the full agenda of the old order of the world economy and the prototype war-making state, but for some periods North Korea, Belarus

189

or Burma (Myanmar) might be thought to be the closest approximations (Cuba has moved much further along the reform spectrum). Second are those states which employed external markets and – to a controlled degree – foreign capital to create a national capital, a set of locally based corporations covering part of the range of world output. Three types can be distinguished here. The first is those states which developed global corporations which in turn came to exercise such political dominance at home that they tended to overshadow the government. In effect, local companies were externally interlocked with a cosmopolitan environment, but retained a protected home base (within which the government continued to offer singular privileges) – we have noted the example of South Korea here. The second is those which promoted local companies in order to monopolise the domestic market, excluding foreign competitors. The individuals composing the government in turn received major financial benefits, and specific economic interests received government favour – this is a rent-seeking state. The case earned the name 'crony capitalism' among journalists. We have seen examples in Russia, but Indonesia and the Philippines also became notorious in this respect. Finally, there is the market-facilitating state, where the government imposes no particular economic plan, although it may engage in encouraging some and discouraging other activities without seeking either to protect any, to ensure low-cost finance or divert orders to selected companies; great emphasis is placed on economic management and the provision of physical and social infrastructure. Both Hong Kong continuously and Singapore after the 1980s would constitute the closest examples.

The first case, such an important mechanism for the historical development of the currently developed countries, is decreasingly tolerable in the new world economy. Countries moved along the spectrum, pushed by systemic imperatives – in the form of economic crisis and domestic challenges – and in moving combined elements from each type. The degree to which governments could move, however, depended, at least in the short term, on the degree of flexibility, how far entrenched interests blocked movement. As we have seen in Russia, the new order that emerged from the wreckage of the old economy allowed only changes which perpetuated or enhanced its position, regardless of the position of the mass of the population.

Flexibility was tested by the reaction of government and a national economy to externally generated crisis. Reform did not mean the end of economic fluctuations, but an enhancement of the capacity to respond to it. We have noted earlier the remarkable difference in Mexico's reaction to the crises of 1982 and of 1994/95. In the second case, despite what seemed initially a catastrophic slump, the economy had, through a decade of reform, attained sufficient flexibility to rebound within a year. By contrast, crisis in Russia, in parts of Sub-Saharan

Africa and, as we shall see, Japan, dragged on for a decade or more. By this criterion, others of the Asian high-growth economies were also models of flexibility – South Korea, for example, moved from a year of strong contraction, 1998 (–6 per cent in national output), to growth of nearly 11 per cent a year later (with industrial production increasing 30 per cent); others, less dramatically, also made what seemed on the surface strong recoveries – Thailand (from –9 per cent), Malaysia (–7.5 per cent) and Indonesia (–14 per cent). Appearances were, as we shall see, misleading.

The economic crisis of the Southeast and East Asian economies in 1997–98 revealed for the first time the structures that had been employed to propel extraordinary growth. However, the countries were very different: being geographically close did not make a standard case. We look at a small selection of some of the more important cases, starting with overwhelmingly the largest economy of the region, Japan (the second-largest economy in the world with, at its peak, a product equal to three quarters of that of the US).

JAPAN IN CRISIS

The mechanism by which government and business propelled extraordinary growth in Japan turned out to be, with slowing growth in the early 1980s and the collapse of a spectacular boom later the same decade, an equally impressive means to enforce long-term stagnation. The accumulation of debt now became a means not of providing a springboard for future growth, but a dead weight preventing growth. The government which had been a key means to ensure the growth of a selected group of industries in the past now failed to find the political courage to permit the bankruptcies which would cut debt, cut the bad debts and change the management of the banks and large companies, to restore profit levels – or make returns on capital, rather than market share, the most important criterion of success. The political nexus which had before been the consensus to support growth now produced immobility that held the Japanese economy in a state of stagnation for a decade.

The alliance of state and business tolerated companies which concealed a level of debt which elsewhere would have led to either radical reform or bankruptcy. The debts accumulated in the boom of the 1980s had originally been in part guaranteed by holdings of land and equity valued at inflated prices. Land prices fell by nearly 80 per cent after the recession, and equity declined sharply with the collapse of prices on the stock exchange (Japan's share of world stock-market value, 42 per cent in 1990, was barely 10 per cent in 1998). In the recession that followed, most of those in the list of Japan's leading non-financial companies, the Nikkei 300, failed to cover the costs of their capital, so debts – either of the companies or of their banks – continued to drift upwards. The collapse of values meant that Japan's share of the world's largest companies in 1990 shrank to almost nothing – Nippon Telegraph and Telephone, the world's largest company at the beginning of the decade (with assets valued at $119 billion), was no longer in the top 20 by 1999; a complete newcomer, Microsoft, entered the list with assets of $318 billion.

The government's approach was, despite its own heavy indebtedness, to protect what was left of the national capital project by preventing companies going bankrupt in the belief that growth would soon be resumed and the debts thereby covered. Its approach was two-fold: major public works spending to stimulate the economy, and a major programme of underpinning the banks financially. In the first case, the funds were directed at public infrastructure, benefiting the construction companies who were important patrons of the ruling Liberal Democratic Party, and leading to notorious oversupply of highways, tunnels, dams and so on. However, the construction industry – with six million employees – was so burdened with prior debt that the new work did little more than keep construction companies afloat. The expenditure, despite its apparent size, barely lifted the economy. Financing the banks was also a problem, particularly because of the political opposition to bailing out those whose rash decisions had produced the problems. The banks, in addition, were again so heavily burdened with debts (despite major bad debt write offs) that they could not resume new lending on a significant scale, although for much of the 1990s they allowed their favoured clients to continue turning over a growing volume of debt. In 1997 the onset of the financial crisis in Southeast Asia led to a run on Korean banks, which in turn obliged the Japanese banks to call in loans to them. This added new edge to long-run stagnation.

The government was finally forced in 1997 to allow some significant bankruptcies. Sanyo Securities (with debts three times those declared by the company) was allowed to go under, followed by Yamaichi Securities (the largest financial collapse in Japanese history to that time), having concealed the scale of its debts for seven years, since the end of the boom, with the complicity of the Ministry of Finance. Yamaichi's creditors had assumed that ultimately the government would prevent a failure. It was also assumed that the group, the *keiretsu*, of which Yamaichi was a member (and which included Hitachi, Nissan, Sapporo Breweries, Canon, Marubeni and 57 others) would not allow it to fold, but the debts of the group banker, Fuji (kept afloat by the Bank of Japan) made that impossible. Fuji Bank merged with two others and withdrew entirely from the *keiretsu*. Thus the sheer economic attrition of the years was not only eroding the old relationship of business to the state, and so undermining what was left of the national capital project, it was also subverting the old group system of mutual support.

In 1998, the government set up a Financial Reconstruction Commission (backed by ¥70 trillion in funding) to oversee the absorption of the debts by 2001. This did no more than reduce the level of bankruptcies. The conditions for funding were permissive, and did not involve radical reforms of the banks, closures or mergers. Lending relieved pressures on the borrowers, and hence their clients, without forcing reform. The Bank of Japan accepted, in return for the loans, corporate securities, and as a result came to hold 40 per cent of out-standing paper – the scheme was a kind of creeping nationalisation.

The process of reform was so hesitant and half-hearted that the damage grew steadily worse. For example, it was not until October 1998 that banks were obliged to disclose bad loans in subsidiaries not completely owned by them; when the banks protested, the measure was postponed until 1999. The govern-ment moved only with difficulty both because of the instability of the factions within the ruling party and because of the need to carry important lobbies – of which the banks were one. We have noted the position of the construction industry as another. Farmers were another important source of votes – rural constituencies had three times the electoral weight of urban areas. The subsidies to agriculture and the external tariff against imports were two offers to keep rural support – even though this kept the domestic price of rice at three times the American level (and beef five times) – to the loss of the Japanese poor.

The turnaround was agonisingly slow. What was lacking in firm govern-ment was hardly made up for by rhetoric: the perpetual reiteration of 'tough measures' to deal with bad debts. By early 2001, they were put at ¥34 trillion or, at the official exchange rate, £203 billion, but a later estimate of the outstanding loans of Japanese banks put the total at ¥455 trillion (or £2585 billion), with ¥83 trillion 'non-performing'. To write off such debts, the government calculated, would increase unemployment by 0.5 per cent and reduce the growth rate of the gross domestic product by 1.5 per cent.

However, there were signs of change. Take, for example, Nissan Motors, Japan's second-largest makers of vehicles. Like other major companies, the huge expansion of the second half of the 1980s left it, in the downturn, with much over-capacity and debts of possibly $30 billion (in 1997) at just the time when its associated financial institutions, the Fuji Bank and the Yasuda Trust, were pulling out of obligations to the *keiretsu*. The debts made Nissan vulnerable to takeover, and Renault was able to build up a controlling interest, putting in one of its executives, Carlos Ghosni, to run the firm. He instituted cuts of 21,000 in direct employment (including the closure of five factories in Japan), and cut through the corporate networks of the company to its suppliers and associates (in many of which Nissan held shares), reducing suppliers, it is said, from 1394 to 4.

Thus, foreign ownership – 'distressed asset sales' – was one way of achieving reform: an enforced cosmopolitanisation through foreign ownership and foreign management. In the last three years of the century, it is estimated (and much of the detail of deals was secret) that US banks and investment funds bought up companies in Japan at heavily discounted prices (at perhaps 7 to 10 per cent of face values). The means by which the US government salvaged something from the financial crisis of the savings and loan banks in the early 1990s were imported to Japan. The crunch often came suddenly in some cases. Sogo, a major super-market chain with 10,000 employees (and, it is said, the same number of suppliers) was in heavy debt (¥1.87 trillion) to a financial institution purchased by an American company which refused to accept the debts and passed them back to the government; political opposition made it impossible for the govern-ment to cover the debts and it was obliged to allow the company to go bankrupt, the largest non-financial collapse to that time.

Other reforms were being slowly introduced or forced on companies. The lack of new bank finance or internally generated funds compelled companies to issue new shares – in 1999, the value of equity issues reached a new record of ¥4.5 trillion (the former peak, in the boom year of 1990, was ¥3.4 trillion). Wider share ownership allowed both increased foreign intervention and much greater outside supervision of companies. New shareholders, foreigners or investors drawn from outside the ranks of the old keiretsu companies, were likely to press for maximising profits rather than borrowing to extend market share. In the mid-1990s, the return on capital (operating surplus over asset value) in Japan was 3.9 per cent, compared to 9 per cent in the US. Outside shareholders – and the company's need to sustain its share prices – forced greater transparency and the exposure of real balance sheets. New accountancy rules banned the use of historic values to assess the now collapsed value of a company, to prevent the burial of losses in the accounts of subsidiaries or other outlets not recorded in company balance sheets. Increasing deregulation allowed outside competition to break, for example, existing controls in the wholesale and retail trades, and thence into the rest of the relatively closed base of the economy.

There was also the emergence of new sectors, unencumbered by historic debts. New banks opened for lending. Small service companies, particularly in information and digital technology, boomed for a time alongside the major sector of stagnant business. With growth, as in Russia, such activities might eventually supersede the old economy. But it was a very slow process, punctuated often by other major company collapses, especially where new rules transformed a company's position. For example, Tomen, a second-tier trading house, discovered under the new accounting rules that it was bankrupt with debts of ¥407 billion. Some commentators estimated that if the large land and property holdings were revalued at current prices (rather than those of the late 1980s), perhaps 40 per cent of companies might be found bankrupt.

Much manufacturing and many financial companies were, in any case, global operations, at work in all major centres. Although their Japanese base was no doubt important – especially access to Japanese savings – they had a cosmo-politan existence that did not depend on Japan (unlike, say, the construction industry, retail and wholesale trade, agriculture). As we have noted, high domestic costs had long encouraged the migration of capital so that Japanese companies escaped the tribulations of stagnation at home.

Dismantling the remnants of the old national capital project, however, still had far to go. Much of the economy still operated in the old mode – for example, 1595 agricultural and fishing co-operative banks, 322 credit unions (only 12 of which were legally required to publish accounts). Even in the public domain, there were dark shadows. When Kyoto Miyako foundered in 1999, its debts were claimed to be ¥6.1 billion, but subsequent enquiry showed them to be 11 times larger.

At the centre of the problem was the state, the nexus of bureaucracy, of the Liberal Democratic Party and its clients, of major corporations and banks, the core of the national capital project and now under determined attack by the new global order. It was here that politics created immobilism. There was even open resistance to reform – in the autumn of 1999, members of the Liberal Democratic Party set up a campaign to fight deregulation on the grounds that this damaged small and medium-sized enterprises. But Japan was too large a component of the world economy, its major companies too deeply embedded in the cosmo-politan order, to escape reform. It was no longer feasible to exploit world markets while protecting a major part of its domestic economy.

SOUTH KOREA: THE GIANT *CHAEBOL* – WITH FEET OF CLAY

South Korea was a very much smaller economy than Japan, even though, through its spectacular growth process (with an average growth rate of between 8 and 9 per cent per year for close on three decades), by the 1990s it had become among the dozen largest economies in the world. The central drive up to the 1990s had been the same kind of amended national capital project as in Japan, with the state using cheap investment to force companies to expand market share rather than maximise profits, but it was much more consistently focussed on exploiting world markets to force that growth (Korea's domestic market was very much smaller, and for long the government, in the interests of forcing exports, constrained the growth of domestic consumption). The result, as in Japan, was the creation of a group of giant global corporations, groups of companies, protected from foreign takeover or shareholder intervention by family networks of control and government collusion. As in Japan, government and business were captive to the political illusion that size was a measure of market strength. It was assumed, again as in Japan, that the *chaebol* were too big to be allowed to fail, that they had an informal sovereign guarantee (that is the state would and could ultimately prevent them failing). In the hectic process of growth, government and bank financial support allowed the accumulation of loans which almost inevitably turned into bad debts, but which it was expected would automatically be rolled over by further growth. It also allowed the *chaebol* to employ their privileged protected status at home to spread into an immense range of diversified activities – the easiest method to increase the volume of profits was to expand the volume of business, not to increase the rate of profit per unit of output. By 1997, the five leading *chaebol* held 37 per cent of national sales, produced 44 per cent of Korea's exports, and operated in 140 different sectors.

The crisis of 1997/98 began with a government-initiated boom to escape the recession of the first half of the 1990s. However, factors were operating to limit this surge of growth. As noted earlier, the Plaza Agreement revalued exchange alignments. This revealed how high, relatively, were Korea's labour costs (from 1987, after years of wage repression, workers began to catch up with their phenomenal earlier increases in productivity, pushing up wages by around 15 per cent per year). An appreciating dollar, to which the Korean won was tied, exaggerated the process. In addition, a major devaluation of the Chinese RMB undercut Korean export prices. In 1996, the semiconductor market collapsed (with a 70 per cent decline in the profits of Korean exporters), followed by a slackening in some of Korea's other export markets – in shipbuilding, steel, chemicals. The stock market fell precipitately, and the government unofficially asked the banks to support share prices by refraining from selling equity holdings in other companies. The *chaebol*, to protect continued growth of output in the face of slackening demand, increased borrowing. But the banks were increasingly reluctant to risk further advances, so companies borrowed abroad, where interest rates were lower. Opaque accounting – alongside apparent continued growth in the overall economy and a hectic boom in the region – for a time misled the lenders, eager to get a stake in Korea's economy.

As the boom continued, short-term borrowing increased dramatically. The cumulative volume reached a level 14 times the government's official reserves (in fact the opaque accounts ensured that debts were underestimated – in 1997, short-term debts were officially put at $65 billion when they were in fact over $100 billion). Stock exchanges and exchange rates began to weaken in Southeast Asia as lenders became suddenly fearful at the scale of debts and possible devaluations which would undercut their loans. Korean banks tried to pull in their loans to Southeast Asian banks (put at $16–20 billion) – as Japanese banks were seeking the return of their loans to Korean banks (equivalent to 35 per cent of Japan's short-term lending). Korean reserves shrank alarmingly – $1 billion a day – increasing the panic. In the end, the government could not hold the value of the currency, and was forced to allow it to float, at which point the dollar value of debts soared, and the banking system was faced with bankruptcy.

Some of the warning signals were clear well in advance but ignored in favour of continuing to try to perpetuate growth. Thus, when Thailand led the way into the regional crisis, Korea's Hanbo Steel failed with debts of $6 billion, despite the efforts of government and banks to keep it afloat. In the following two years, over a dozen of the 64 *chaebol* failed.

But the system of cheap loans – with government support – was not stopped, allowing big companies to continue borrowing in order to expand output and continue diversification. For the top 30 *chaebol*, the ratio of their debt to equity, 400 per cent in 1996, grew to 800 per cent by 1998 (compared to US equivalents of some 70 per cent). When the assets of the failed *chaebol* came on the market, the existing groups were able to increase their debts to buy them. Thus Daewoo, whose debts (said to be $80 billion) were ultimately to sink the group in the world's largest corporate bankruptcy to that time, was able to purchase Ssang Yong Motors in late 1998. Hyundai, with 1998 debts six times the group's equity, was able to borrow to buy Kia Motors as well as an oil refinery, two fund management groups, a semiconductor firm, and to launch a life insurance corporation.

A new President, Kim Dae-jung, drawn from outside the group that had long controlled power, came to office in 1998 with what appeared to be a strong reform package. However, with the *chaebol*, he tended to rely on the old format of seeking to issue instructions to the *chaebol* – for example, to cut their debt-to-equity ratios to 200 per cent. He took some steps to open the domestic market, to begin the privatisation of state-owned enterprises, to block the continued *chaebol* borrowing, to force greater dependence on equity (and shareholders' supervisory powers), to introduce international accountancy systems, to strengthen supervision, and, in order to try to reduce family control, to ban cross-shareholdings within corporate groups. He also tried to force the *chaebol* to reduce their continuing diversification.

The *chaebol*, however, were not to be defeated so easily, and with global assets could indeed defend themselves against mere national power. Thus the Hyundai group did indeed lower its debt-to-equity ratio – by issuing shares to members of the Hyundai group (so preserving the position of the family of the founder, Chung Ju-yung), not by reducing its debts. The biggest purchaser was Hyundai Construction (the parent company of the group), but it faced its own problems of debt and a slack construction market. Companies were spun off from the group, under Chung's sons, but this did not strengthen the parent company, whose failure could wreck at least two other heavily indebted members of the group, Hyundai Securities and Hyundai Electronics.

Hyundai also offered to reduce diversification by cutting the number of subsidiaries from 79 to 26, concentrating on only five specialised fields. In practice, four subsidiaries were closed, eight sold, with promises to sell 13 others. The group continued to expand.

The *chaebol* generally started taking over or initiating financial institutions to escape the government ban on bank funding for loss-making operations. By 1999, the five largest *chaebol* had acquired 39 financial firms (investment banks, insurance companies, fund managers). While the government was trying to force specialisation, the *chaebol* financial institutions were employed in share dealing to change the financial weight of group members – Hyundai Securities was accused of using group funds to raise the value of Hyundai Electronics in order to induce the government to select it as the chosen instrument for Korea's efforts in the sector.

The risks were palpable, as shown in the collapse of the Daewoo group, the second-largest group in Korea (with a group output equivalent to 5 per cent of Korea's national output) – with 30 subsidiaries operating in 26 different industries. Creditors – mainly state-run banks – organised a debt-restructuring programme in 1999, but did not institute serious reform (the trade union opposition to job losses also influenced the government's seriousness). Without this, it proved difficult to sell the assets. One of the main casualties of this was the debt-ridden Daewoo Motors, which, along with Hyundai Construction, played such a crucial role that any failure could have had immense ramifications.

Unlike Japan, Korea resumed rapid growth with astonishing speed – it seemed as if reform was irrelevant. However, this was something of a misfortune, since the economy still remained highly vulnerable to future shocks. The government set up a fund to relieve 17 commercial banks, nationalising the largest to protect them from bankruptcy, but the sums were exhausted by the spring of 2000. Some efforts were made to force bank mergers so that the weaker could be relieved, but the stronger banks resisted; foreign banks were unwilling to take over the loss-makers without the government assuming responsibility for the debts. On the other hand, the government could not privatise the publicly owned banks without risking the survival of the 70 or so *chaebol*.

The secret of Korea's extraordinary growth over the preceding three decades had been the exploitation of world markets, but that in its turn involved increasing obligations to integrate Korea with the world system, to abandon any separate national capital project. Structural crisis was the result of the failure to adjust in time – a crisis which forced reform on terms driven by global markets, even if those global markets were expressed through the interests of rival companies and governments. The government continued to try to compromise, protecting as much of the bankrupt corporations as possible. When the government endeavoured to organise a rescue plan for the *chaebol* by buying part of their debts, it was the US government, lobbied by US Micron Technologies, which protested that this would be to give subsidies to its rival, Hyundai Electronics (the world's largest producer of memory chips).

For the moment, Korea was protected by the rapid return of growth, which removed the immediate pressure for reform. Unemployment was cut and the country's reserves pushed up from $8 billion in 1998 to $63 billion late in 1999. But the twin struggles remained – of the Korean government to master the *chaebol* at home, and of global markets to remove the privileged home status of the *chaebol*, to make sure the level playing field extended right into the heart of the Korean economy. The new systemic imperatives would not be held at bay to suit the convenience of the government.

CHINA: THE FUTURE BEHEMOTH?

China, like Korea earlier, benefited from combining many of the direct controls of the old project with the exploitation of external markets. In particular, controls on the currency (and the lack of a significant integration of domestic and external financial markets) damped down the tendency for the regional crisis to be imported. Unofficially, there was still a flight of capital – an estimated $35–45 billion was transferred out of the country, largely by large Chinese corporations – but the government was able to ward off any process by which it was forced to devalue. The reserves remained high – possibly $140 billion – and the trade surplus, of around $50 billion, strong.

However, in structural terms China was even more vulnerable to slump than many of the far smaller economies of Southeast Asia. The most extreme measure of this was the 370,000 companies of the state-owned sector. Producing most of the country's industrial output and employing most of the urban workforce two decades ago, its rate of growth had been so poor as to reduce it to about a third by the year 2000. Over the same period, the losses officially increased 20 times over – the ratio of debt to equity increased between 1988 and 1995 from 82 to

570 per cent (the debt measure is almost certainly an underestimate, since again the accounting system is opaque).

The government made continual modest attempts at reform, but as we saw earlier in Russia reform very often made the position worse. For a period it allowed managers to raid the assets of the corporations for which they were responsible while laying off millions of workers (or putting them on *xia* gang, allowing them not to come to work while paying them a nominal retainer). The state sector for much of the period absorbed the bulk of finance on preferential terms from the state banks. A decentralisation of political responsibility for the state-owned enterprises vested provincial party leaders with the power to develop their own 'provincial capital project', and forced local banks to finance 'their' enterprises, to refrain from pressing for loans to be serviced if this might jeopardise the survival of the firm. Companies were able to evade paying taxes (paid in China to local authorities, agents for the central government but with a strong interest in the survival of local employers), avoid paying other state-owned enterprises, even in some cases avoid paying their workers. Shrewd company managers exploited the access to low-interest state funds and savings on current expenditure to develop – illegally – commercial lending at market interest rates to those outside the state-owned system, the town and village enterprises, to finance their own private initiatives, to speculate, even to export funds to Hong Kong and then reinvest them in China to benefit from the privileges attached to 'foreign' investment. Again, as in Russia, through inter-enterprise sales and transactions, profits were transferred from the state-owned to the private sector, losses transferred in the opposite direction. Many of the worst offenders were net 'destroyers of wealth' – that is, it would be cheaper for them to continue to pay their workers while shutting down all activity.

Reform exaggerated the endemic problems of corruption, particularly with a much weaker central control and competing provincial authorities. As in Russia, the 'rent-seeking state' was the direct result of reform, but unlike Russia this situation could not paralyse the entire social order. The government could therefore more directly attack some aspects of corruption – in the first half of 1999, corruption was officially estimated at some 120 billion yuan (equal to $14.4 billion, or about a fifth of central government tax revenues). Official secrecy, the opacity of accounts, the interest of different sections of the political leadership in protecting the assets controlled by them all conspired to minimise this figure, so what occurred in Indonesia or the Philippines as 'cronyism' might have been much larger in China.

Officially, the reluctance to press reform more vigorously has been a fear of rapid increases in unemployment. But managers have often sacked large numbers of workers, although there is little comprehensive information on the effect of this. Some of the worst conditions afflict the heart of the old national capital project, the heavy industrial regions of the Northeast. One study plotted the advance of unemployment in Liaoning province from 1995, when the figure was 329,000; 800,000 (late 1996); 1.8 million (late 1997); 2.2 million (late 1998). Out of an official workforce of 12 million, this would represent a rate of unemployment of 18 per cent. Of course this would be a misleading calculation, since the real Chinese economy is outside most of the official data, so we have no guide as to how many are in secure unrecorded jobs. But whatever the reality, sporadic strikes, occupations, demonstrations and petition campaigns showed that the workforce was not at all at one with national policy.

By 2000, the cumulative debts of the state-owned companies – excluding the over-valuation of assets, the increase in unsaleable stocks and liabilities – had possibly come to equal half China's domestic product, and the total debts of the entire state sector may have equalled the value of the national output. The bad debts of the four state banks (which provide about four fifths of lending to state-owned enterprises) is put at 30–40 per cent of national output. In an effort to give some measure of help to the banks, four asset management companies (AMCs) were created to swap debts for equity, with the aim of saving some 600 companies by early 2000. But AMCs had access to only $45 billion and no power to change managers or reorganise companies (that power was reserved to the central government under the State Economic and Trading Commission, threading its way through a political minefield).

Reforms, as in Japan and Korea, slowly percolated. China sustained relatively high rates of growth throughout the 1990s, so the pressure was less severe. Bankruptcies increased, and in a celebrated case in 1998 the government demonstrated that even state-owned enterprises might lack any sovereign guarantee when it allowed the bankruptcy of the Guangdong Investment and Industry Company, followed shortly thereafter by the Hainan Development Bank.

In sum, then, China's spectacular growth trajectory, with dramatic effects in terms of the brute scale of poverty in the country, had been purchased through maintaining or balancing between the contradiction of a national capital project (supporting a significant war-making capacity) and measures of global integration which brought high growth. The more important the Chinese economy becomes, the more straddling both alternatives will become insupportable, the more powerful the forces eroding both the project and the unreformed political structure. The politics of the country at present block any attempt at incremental change, and so render the country peculiarly vulnerable to a severe crisis of adjustment.

THE SUCCESSES

The Asian crisis was by no means universal in the region. At least five cases were virtually unscathed: Australia, Taiwan (both growing by 4–5 per cent through the last half of the 1990s), Vietnam, Singapore and the Philippines. Taiwan is particularly interesting, since, as a case, it seems to contradict the central thrust of the argument presented here. Development was propelled, as we noted earlier, by the drive for military capacity, and in many ways the Taiwanese state was a classic example of what we have called the war-making state, inventing from scratch an indigenous capitalist class, albeit one always firmly subordinate to the tasks of the state.

Paradoxically, it was precisely the clarity of the national capital project which saved the state in the crisis. The development of heavy industry, the 'strategic core' of the economy (to employ the terms appropriate to the old agenda), remained in state hands, while the private sector – from the point of view of the state's military agenda of low priority – remained relatively neglected. Private business, unlike the situation in Korea and Japan, was relatively small-scale. The size of the largest Taiwanese company is about one sixteenth of its Korean equivalent, and one eightieth of its Japanese. There were a few globally famous brand names (Acer was one), but Taiwanese companies specialised more in producing parts for the finished output of companies abroad than branded finished products.

The banks were generally retained in private hands, but lent mainly to the state-owned enterprises on commercial grounds. As a result, there was relatively little bad debt (1.5 per cent of asset values in 1997, compared to 60 per cent in Indonesia). Small and medium-sized businesses were obliged to borrow outside the banking system, on the 'kerb market' or from relatives at relatively high cost, as the result of which loans were repaid swiftly. Debt was not allowed to accumulate (the ratio of debt to equity in Taiwan was about 30 per cent in the late 1990s, compared, say, to Indonesia's 400 per cent).

The tightly restricted financial markets – and the lack of sovereign guarantees for private companies – ensured that Taiwanese companies were much less concerned with expanding market share, more with profit per unit of output. In 1997, for example, the average rate of return in Taiwan's electronic equipment industry was 23 per cent, compared to under 10 per cent in Korea and Japan. Furthermore, the temptation to go for growth because borrowed funds were cheap and easily available was curbed. Companies could not afford the risk of creating excess capacity because the costs of borrowing were so high. In sum, the private economy was created in a way that equipped it for incremental adjustment in relation to changes in external demand, without those rigidities that magnified the effect of shocks.

The flexibility of the economy was further illustrated in the ease with which it became globally spread. In the 1990s, 80,000 Taiwanese companies started overseas operations, half of them in China (producing, some said, a third of China's exports), and perhaps half in Southeast Asia. Over half the computer parts and electronic equipment made by Taiwanese firms was manufactured outside the island. It was a mark of how far the national capital project had faded that Taiwanese capital was so deeply embedded in the economy of its most important enemy, China.

However, the economy still had problems with the national capital project. The privatisation of the state sector continued, but slowly. The government was not averse to promoting a national champion in banking to keep at bay foreign rivals. The defence programme entailed a chronic budget deficit and a significant public debt. The government retained informal control of the exchange rate, and placed restrictions on foreign capital buying more than 3 per cent of the assets of the stock exchange. But there were no global corporations, no national champions with a call on government finance, no accumulation of debts. Indeed, externally, Taiwan's political isolation as the result of the hostility of Beijing entailed that it could not for long maintain a balance-of-payments deficit, nor borrow extensively abroad (so the external debt in 1997 was of the order of $250 million). Furthermore, insecurity led to the accumulation of major reserves – by 1997, at $84 billion, the third-largest in the world. The regional crisis wiped out a fifth of the value of the stock exchange (compared to between 50 and 80 per cent elsewhere) and possibly cut the rate of growth to its lowest for five years (at 5 per cent), but in comparison to the other countries of the region the economy did not crash.

In sum, Taiwan's peculiar characteristics did not allow it to escape the regional recession altogether, but made it a mild decline. There are still numerous reforms required – as in virtually all countries, including those in Europe and North America – but the structure was flexible enough, it seems, to make possible incremental change rather than violent restructuring.

THE REGIONAL CRISIS

The themes we have noted in the earlier cases recurred through many of the countries of Southeast Asia – the implicit sovereign guarantee to companies favoured by the government, borrowing abroad with fixed exchange rates, the concealed accumulation of debts in the banking and corporate economy. In some cases, the problems were exaggerated by spectacular infrastructure investments – new cities, railways, highways, power stations, dams; in some, by gross corruption

– for example the favours shown to the children of President Suharto in Indonesia; in some, by efforts by governments to liberalise the financial economy without structural reform. In Hong Kong's case, its rigidity was not in the structure of the economy, or any national capital project, but in defending a fixed exchange rate (tied to the dollar), linked to Beijing's interest in not allowing a devaluation of the yuan, which was thought likely if the Hong Kong dollar was devalued.

The social effects were often severe, although not as bad as thought likely at the time. Possibly the worst affected was Indonesia, where official poverty increased from 11 per cent of the population in 1996 to between 14 and 20 per cent two years later (but not the 40 per cent of some forecasts). Real salaries were said, in the crisis, to have declined by 30 per cent, and household consumption by 24 per cent. But more important, the country remained mired in political paralysis, despite the overthrow of Suharto and the introduction of a new 'uncontrolled' electoral system. And only with time did the crimes of the old regime emerge – that, for example, the $15 billion advanced to private banks to salvage the financial system had been misappropriated for other purposes, two thirds of it taken to support the five banks owned by friends or relatives of the former president.

Events in Indonesia, however, were only one of the more obvious revelations of the return of civil society in formerly authoritarian regimes, and of a much more dedicated popular hostility to corruption and the rent-seeking state. The Philippines was even more dramatic, with two successful popular coups against corruption. Corruption was not seen as the almost inevitable by-product of the discretionary powers of the state, which pursuit of the national capital project implied. Rather the attack on corruption was seen as an important step towards rethinking the role of the state in terms of popular welfare rather than economic nationalism.

There are, however, many more battles to be fought before the world and the peoples of Southeast and East Asia can defend themselves against the predatory states and their allies in national capital. The economic disarmament of states is a long-drawn-out affair in all parts of the world. What was shown in Southeast Asia was not that the spectacular growth of the countries concerned was some kind of mirage – a 'bubble' in the dismissive phrase of the time – but it was not invulnerable to the normal booms and slumps of the system. Indeed, almost everywhere in the region, incomes were significantly higher than they had been a decade earlier, let alone two decades before. What was also shown was that in the midst of a supposed free-market-driven growth process, governments had not relinquished entirely the project of building an independent national capitalism.

PART IV

THE NEW
WORLD ORDER

10

Governance

INTRODUCTION

In the context of the old agenda of nation-states, global economic integration raises difficult problems of regulation and representation. The new system seems to undermine the old conception not only of national sovereignty, but with it democratic control, hence eroding the traditional legitimation of the order. It is often quite difficult to think about these trends – if trends they are – simply because our minds are so grounded in the idea of a world composed exclusively of states, of unitary territorial authorities, brooking no independent role for sub-national or supranational agencies. Many of the elements of the old order of warring states are still around us to validate the idea that nothing of substance has changed. Indeed, in the developing countries the order often appears entirely unchanged, with, in some cases, military regimes forcing national unity around the old project of trying to build a national capitalism directed by the state.

It is useful, initially, to rehearse some of the key features of the old conception of the state and the state system as a measure of what is changing.

The world's population and capital are supposedly divided into discrete national shares, with none left outside, distributed between geographical patches which exhaust the land surface – and part of the seas – of the world. Each territorial patch is managed exclusively by one centralised authority, directing at the same time both the domestic political order, a separate economy, the formation and operation of the legal system, possessing a monopoly of the legitimate use of violence within the territory, and traditionally the authority to define unilaterally the moral order within its domain (what forms of behaviour, and in some cases thought, are morally or culturally acceptable).

The unification of the domestic order – political, economic, social – requires a degree of relative isolation from the rest of the world. The assumption is that the local share of population and capital is relatively immobile. In the economy, exports are no more than what is left over after domestic consumption has been met; imports are insignificant, and there is no significant role for foreign capital in the domestic economy. This relative closure of the national unit is the obverse of the external rivalries which constitute the global system of states. Only states have legitimacy in the world context as agencies of rivalry and of violence. Whereas within national boundaries the state supposedly has total sovereignty, externally its sovereignty turns upon its recognition by the other states. Although this is not independent of the condition of the domestic order, it does not depend upon it – demonstrated authority, not the degree to which the government represents the inhabitants, is the criterion for recognition. Recognition by other states is an acknowledgement that none can legitimately interfere in the domestic affairs of a recognised state. But externally, supposedly, there are only a limited number of moral or legal constraints on the actions of the state (for example agreements with other states).

The power of the state is territorially bounded, and controlling those boundaries – who and what goods and people, and, in some cases what ideas should be permitted to cross – is therefore symbolically fundamental to its power. Internally, it is equally important for the state to control the creation and provision of information, a power that matches its capacity to protect its secrets, the right to exclude both citizens and the rest of the world from knowing its affairs. States, thus reserve the right to invent the facts, to lie or issue misinformation in the interests of defending what the state alone is permitted to define as its security.

The state requires, and in practice in time secures, an extraordinary, indeed, bizarre, level of obedience in its citizenry, even in, as we have seen, the most extreme and testing conditions. The whole idea of a separate civil society came to seem slightly absurd when, despite all the horrors inflicted on, for example, the German or Russian population there were no significant rebellions against the Nazis or the Communists. The very idea that states represent their citizens seems equally absurd – citizens seem more like pliant instruments of states. Furthermore, the prototype personality of the citizen and the tasks required of him or her seems itself created by the interests of the state – most explicit in the idea in Russia of the 'good Communist', but with paler imitations in the 'true American'. In the era of world war, the masculine personality is reshaped to the taciturnity of the warrior (compared to the garrulity of our own times).

The reduction of civil society is matched by the extraordinary domination of the state bureaucracy, permeating the whole of society, with a privileged status accorded its concerns, its moral infallibility and its self-adulation. Even when everyone knows it to be corrupt and self-seeking, it alone supposedly represents the only common good, the only morally pre-eminent non-sectional interest (defined relative to the capitalists as 'non-profit-making'). Marx splendidly exposes the absurd self-adulation and hypocrisy of the class of capitalists, but this is more than matched by state officials. In Stalin's Russia, the bureaucracy ruled supreme even as Stalin's scourges reached deep into its existence. Its collective interest, framed by systemic imperatives, existed independently of the private interests of individual officials.

One of the possible implications of the system needs to be noted in passing: the organisation of classes. Marx identifies the emergence of industry and the division of labour this produces as defining two new clusters of power in society, grouped round the classes of employers and of workers. Further, he distinguishes the existence of these groups as existing 'in themselves' (that is as groups defined by their objective relationship to each other and to society at large) and 'for themselves' (that is with a subjective awareness of their existence as a class and a perception of a common class interest). In this second sense, the self-awareness, such as it occurs historically, is possible only in a struggle between classes for power, a power which is embodied in the state. Thus the class system in Marx presupposes a single centre of power, the modern state. One can hardly conceive of a unified class structure without implying both a bounded territorial unit and a central pivot of power, control of which is the target of the struggle of classes. The point will become relevant to the later discussion of what possibilities emerge in a world moving to integration, to an unbounded system.

These features of the modern state are deliberately exaggerated to highlight the contrast with what is emerging. Insofar as they existed in practice, it was a quite extraordinary system, forcing domestic 'homogeneity' at the cost of enhancing external differences. In practice, the features could hardly exist for any length of time without breakdown, without the unruly characteristics of real people, if not rebelling, wrinkling the appearance of uniformity, even if only in a secret world. Eccentricities were matters of shame and public criticism; people deliberately suppressed individualism or even evidence of 'heterogeneity' (a foreign grandparent, say; this was even true in the US, Canada or Australia, countries of immigrants, until relatively late). The amazing history of the suppression of homosexuality – and the fantasy horrors attributed to it – is only one thread in what we might call the natural totalitarianism of the modern state.

The erosion of this order has been slow, slow enough to undermine the old political and moral agendas without people being easily aware of the process.

However, it has led to sporadic confusion as familiar landmarks fade, or moral icons become meaningless. Whereas once it was inconceivable that states might weaken, that an alternative order might arise – that was a fantasy reserved for the anarchist margins of society – in our own times at least a discussion has begun. And events – ending the thraldom of civil society to the all-powerful state – move even faster than the discussion. Charles Tilly, writing in the early 1990s, dares to note the paradox: 'States may be following the old routine by which an institution falls into ruin just as it becomes complete. In the meantime, nevertheless, States remain so dominant that anyone who dreams of a Stateless world seems a heedless visionary' (1993: 225).

GLOBALISATION

The old order fashioned economies according to political geography, according to the interests of states, not according to global markets. It was never true that this could be undertaken independently of the rest of the world, but the myth that this was possible inspired many national projects. Insofar as the state's economic role weakens, a new market-driven economic geography will tend to supersede the political ordering of the terrain. It follows that the perimeter of political management, the administrative reach of governments, no longer encompasses the decisive economic variables. Markets determined outside the national borders of any particular economy are coming to dominate domestic activity. Government economic policy becomes of relatively declining importance among the factors deciding the material position of the citizens – and even then the preparation and operation of policy require continual collaboration and co-ordination with other governments and agencies. States are still large economic actors in their own right, and they have great powers to facilitate or frustrate markets, but this is a very much more limited role than that of exercising an economic sovereignty.

The decline in the economic power of states (although that power was never as great as was thought) sets limits to what are thought of as the powers of democracy. In the old agenda, in systems of popular representation, parties competed for the responsibility of enhancing, protecting or restoring the material position of the population. But if the power to influence events here is declining, then political parties are obliged to promise things that are not within their power to deliver (for example a significant reduction in unemployment). The alternative – to confess that the determination of the level of employment or unemployment is beyond the power of government – is to court political suicide. Even if a political leader's confession of policy impotence in this respect is accepted, it undermines one of the main incentives to vote at all, and hence the very legitimacy of government itself.

The situation is saved for the moment by the limited extent of globalisation. The European Union, the most advanced attempt at economic integration, is still far from economic fusion – that is where the logic of external market imperatives, rather than state interests, determines the geography of economic activity. The partial character of the domestic integration can be seen in comparison with large territorial – and properly 'fused' – economies like the US, Russia and Canada (equally large economies like China, India and Brazil still have major internal differentiations, perpetuated by quasi-federal administrative arrangements). The next level of integration, the Atlantic and Pacific regions, is, in comparative terms, still far from even the European model. Much of Africa, the Middle East and parts of Asia remain firmly part of the old order, in which economy and polity are supposedly equally subject to the sovereign state (even where the bureaucracy is incapable of exercising such power).

Even in the present heartlands of the world economy, in the developed countries, integration is notoriously uneven. The continual squabbles of governments over trade, with more or less shamefaced cheating on the spirit of agreed rules, the continued preoccupation with 'our' companies and 'our' capital, all suggest that despite declarations to the contrary governments maintain a stubborn, if not particularly coherent, resistance to globalisation. All adhere at some level to a version of the need to enhance national economic power, even at the cost of the welfare of their citizens, let alone the wellbeing of the world at large. Thus, for example, the European Union notoriously spends $75 billion annually protecting agriculture, to the considerable damage not only of the interests of farmers in the US, Canada, Australia, New Zealand and in many developing countries, but also to the mass of consumers in Europe – especially Europe's poor – who pay significantly higher than necessary prices for what they eat. Or the US government sporadically bans the takeover of US companies by foreign interests 'in the interests of national security'.

Globalisation is thus still limited – political geography still matters a great deal and is a primary preoccupation of governments. Global networks of economic interaction are laid, as it were, on top of this pattern of national economies. Millions of small producers respond to incentives generated in world markets, but the instrument they see is a local buyer or seller, and the political context for the transaction seems to them still decisive. Multinational companies may pursue global strategies, even though the local variant of this will relate closely to the government of the area in which they operate, but many remain tied to one national home market, employ in the higher managerial positions staff from one nationality etc. The virtual multinational remains still marginal – where a group of workers interact on the Web to produce a saleable product without any of the participants or the buyers knowing or caring where the others are geographically; location, the essence of the state, has become entirely irrelevant to this activity. And in terms of the world's workforce, national protectionism is still, at least in theory, absolute; each country here is still a citadel, armed to repel boarders and imprison inhabitants. There is a growing world of legal migrant labour, especially for professional and technical staff, and a clandestine world of unskilled migrant labour, constituting a kind of global apartheid, but it is still, relative to the world's workforce, small.

In social and political terms, the world is still very much a national one – as the contents of national news media show. At best the world is 'cosmopolitanised'. The local still takes precedence in the creation of identity, in marriages and upbringing, even when the world of work goes far beyond this. But the trend is towards something different, an order in which the problems of governance, of democratic control, of legitimacy and of the protection of populations against the ravages of markets become severe. The questions are large, and the answers here inevitably no more than suggestions of direction: speculative, partial, tentative – and messy.

WAR AND THE STATE

The rationale of the state in the old order, its central concern, was with the capacity to make war (or to defend itself). In the former European system, this was matched by a supposed 'balance of power' between states which, as we have seen, failed both before the power of France under Napoleon and of Germany, once united. The melancholy results in the twentieth century were two world wars.

However, this apparently inescapable system, leading inevitably to ever more destructive war, broke down after the Second World War. One sign of this was that issues of European territory – as, for example, the bloody dispute over Alsace-Lorraine or the former lands of East Prussia – came to play almost no role in the relationships between the Great Powers. Insofar as imperialism meant the acquisition of political control of territory outside the existing domains, it died. The drive was, as we have seen, still important in Nazi Germany's assault on the Soviet Union and the expropriation of the Ukraine, but even then the idea was archaic – as represented in Hitler's fantasy of happy German peasant families tilling the Ukrainian soil, guarded along the eastern marches by the stern warriors of the Teutonic Order. Some ancient territorial issues persisted within countries – between the Flemish and the Walloons in Belgium, the Basque separatists in Spain etc; the British continued to fight for three decades to hold

Northern Ireland, but the British cabinet debated whether it should be abandoned, and the British and Irish populations expressed a consistent stolid, if occasionally irritated, indifference. Decentralisation of the UK brought the possibility of the secession of Scotland, but no one believed that, in that event, the British army would fight to hold the rebels (as would certainly have occurred half a century earlier). And if Scotland goes, what is to stop Wales – or Quebec, or Catalonia, or the Basque country, or Brittany, or Bavaria, or Sicily? With economic fusion, political fission becomes for the first time feasible, perhaps even impelled, without any implication of the need for war to hold together recalcitrant provinces. If the old Czechoslovakia could separate without violence, why not many more nations?

The evolution qualifies claims to absolute sovereignty. One of the most important of these is the insistence that no state has the right to interfere in the domestic concerns of another. But the old separation of domestic and external becomes increasingly blurred. The European Union proved to be a highly developed mechanism for continual mutual interferences in other states' 'domestic affairs' – from the size of a sausage or the definition of 'chocolate' to the tolerable level of a budget deficit or the rate of inflation – to the intense irritation of those who continued to feel sovereignty should be inviolable. In Kosovo, the right of the Serbian government (outside the European Union) to slaughter part of its own citizenry with impunity was hideously rejected by NATO.

The conditioned reflexes of the old order lead some to see all this as no more than swapping one sovereignty, the national, for another, the European. Brussels is, on this account, set upon creating a new giant sovereign state, the United States of Europe to match the United States of America. But such aspirations seem remote from reality – an invented fear to activate the old conditioned reflexes of the defence of the old nationalities. After the period of scandals of the European Commission, national governments resumed their entrenched powers to define and determine the key issues. With the continued decentralisation of powers to the states in the US, it seems more likely that the US and Europe will converge on a similar point, much looser federations or associations. In the case of the US, the arrival of more countries – in Latin America – using the US dollar as their currency, or through sets of bilateral linkages (with Japan, with Israel), association might be extended to even looser affiliates. On the periphery of Europe, similar looser associations – of the Mediterranean countries, of the ACP – spread relationships far round the world. Thus Brussels and Washington would become, in essence, the centres of clusters, fading through different kinds of relationships to a remote periphery without clear boundary, a model quite unlike the old order of centralised national states. It will prove exceptionally frustrating for those of the old school, demanding unequivocally delineated power, but would have been quite familiar to the ruling orders prior to the rise of the modern state.

In the military field, there was also a remarkable reversal of the old order. The US and the Soviet Union maintained for some three decades some kind of stable order by agreeing not to defend themselves against long range nuclear weapons, a system appropriately named MAD (or mutually assured destruction), in order to reassure each that their power to deter remained with their stable vulnerability. Within that, there was steady progress to end secrecy, to reveal what armaments each possessed, first in order to assure the other that there were no nasty surprises which warranted a pre-emptive strike, then to secure agreement for mutual disarmament. Under the 1972 Anti-Ballistic Missile Treaty, the signatories renounced a missile shield to protect themselves on the assumption that any such attack would evoke such a massive counter-attack that they would be destroyed. The old world of complete secrecy over national arms stocks was replaced by one in which each military leadership was invited to inspect the weapon stocks of the enemy. Transparency was now the essence of adequate defence for the leading powers, to end the possibility of bluff and of an 'accidental' war. NATO obliged its members to display their cards, to end any risk of poker games. The Conventional Weapons in Europe Treaty committed signatories to register the quantity, type and location of all heavy weapons and permit their inspection, prior to a programme of their progressive reduction and destruction. It led the way to the attempt to formulate similar principles for the world – and Saddam Hussein's reluctance to accept this major interference in Iraqi sovereignty perpetuated the long misery of the Iraqi people.

Just as in trade and capital movements, the new military order emerges fitfully in response to particular crises and challenges. Enough of the old persists to pretend that nothing has changed, and the old unbridled egotism of states, the drive to war and empire, persists, albeit at some covert level. This simplification is a comfort in a world of growing complexity where it is increasingly difficult to identify an unequivocal 'national interest'. The era of world war has, like empire, gone, but that does not stop either Great Power rivalries or exceedingly vicious local wars. There is an almost universal decline in military spending (with, for given periods, important exceptions, especially in East and South Asia and the Middle East), particularly relative to the growth of national output.

The productivity of the war economies has now become spectacular – the US created a stock of 70,000 nuclear warheads and bombs, enough to destroy the world several times over. The peak American stock, 30,000, came in the early 1960s; in Russia, in the early 1980s, at 45,000. Furthermore, so immense has become the productivity of the overall American economy that the burden of defence inevitably declines – spectacular increases in output and quality are possible with a declining share of gross domestic product.

Under the impact of the so-called 'war on terrorism' (following the 11 September 2001 destruction of New York's twin trade towers and the assault on the Pentagon in Washington), US defence spending – running at about $325 billion – is projected to increase to $360 billion by 2007 (and there is talk of $400 billion). This compares to the last peak, in 1987 under President Reagan, of $360 billion. However, as a proportion of gross domestic product, defence continued to decline – under Reagan it exceeded 6 per cent, with a low point of 3 per cent in 2000. After 11 September, it has risen to 3.5 per cent.

But there is no rest in the arms industries. The technology of armaments, as in manufacturing, requires increasing imports by all (and therefore increasing exports). Just as each country's civil output requires growing collaboration with sources of production abroad, so even the old stronghold of self-sufficiency, war capacity, requires collaborative efforts with potential enemies as much as with friends.

The other side of the coin to increased dependence on imports is increased arms exports by the main producers. Arms exports are completely contrary to the old agenda – except supplies to safe allies. But the arms industries, faced with shrinking budgets, are obliged to sell to potential enemies to justify the scale of their establishment (although the value of official arms exports is still only around 7 per cent of arms spending, or $719 billion in 1999 at 1995 prices). Arms become just another commodity export (although peculiarly entwined with official subsidies, protection and promotion).

The advance in technology produces perverse results in relative power. On the one hand, the increasing political opposition to any casualties from the armies of the Great Powers – revealed in the Vietnam War, but then more strikingly during the US participation in later wars – is made possible by, and stimulates the search for, accurate weapons, launched remotely (and often unpiloted), rather than ground troops. The accuracy of the weapons is required to avoid what in the old order was a positive virtue, the killing of civilians, 'collateral damage' (in the Newspeak of the times), now also politically unacceptable. On the other hand, the new technology, despite the prohibitions in the arms trade, allows poorer countries to import or develop secretly the parts to make weapons, tipping them now not necessarily with nuclear warheads but with the means of biological or chemical warfare. The economically weak – facing the devaluation of their military strength in large mass but ill-educated armies by the employment of advanced airborne weapons – are thus rearmed with a few powerful weapons to intimidate the great. In the nightmares of the Pentagon, the slings of the Davids can still smite the Goliaths. It is reasoned that if during the Vietnam

War with the US, Hanoi had been able to reach Los Angeles with one germ-warfare missile head, the balance of power between the two adversaries would have been altered. It is this new problem which has led the US to propose ending its agreement with Russia and to remove the constraints on building an anti-missile defence shield for America to offset the problem of the one missile (it will not of course stop the determined terrorist wreaking havoc on an American city). Some see this as fundamentally affecting the balance of military power, starting a new arms race. But there are now no serious competitors with the US, and there are unlikely to be any for decades. The Chinese and Russians might bluster, the Europeans drag their feet, but the threat of a new arms race is an idle one; the heart has gone out of the world, if not the local, contest. Implicitly, the majority accept a division of labour in which Washington shoulders the bulk of world military spending.

It is the persistence of those peculiarly vicious local wars, more devastating in destruction now with the sophistication of weaponry, that strikingly high-lights the peace between the Great Powers, as well as the spreading network of international laws, regulation and inspection. It also shows a changed agenda – most (but not all) military interventions are not by one state or another to advance their power and influence, but by collectives to establish order. There are still some of the old kind – the French in Africa, the British in the Falklands and Sierra Leone, the US in Granada, but they are increasingly marginal. More generally, conflicts are being regulated by treaty. The regime of regulation lacks any consistent military power to enforce it – the model of national law, enforced by the police powers of physical coercion. But it is nonetheless surprisingly effective in the majority of cases, even if it is quite ineffective for determined rebels.

The spread of the UN blue berets – at their peak 78,000 troops (in 1993), with a trough of 12,000 (in 1999) – was an index of symbolic enforcement, backed sporadically by the awful terrors of a Desert Storm or by a NATO in Kosovo. The wars are overwhelmingly concentrated in the poorest countries, where the ferocious struggle to create modern states produces the same conflicts as before, but now with modern weapons. All agree that the conflicts are appalling, but there is no 'international community' yet with common criteria as the basis for consistent united intervention. The politics of the UN Security Council make many interventions impossible. In full-scale war, as between Iraq and Iran, no power dare risk intervention, other than by covertly arming those they consider less dangerous (as the US and UK helped to arm Iraq against Iran). And in the worst case of humanitarian crisis, genocide in Rwanda in 1994 (where, it is said, the killing rate was five times that in the Nazi death camps half a century earlier), all except France dodged the issue; and France was late and its motives suspect. In other cases, intervention by a local power made matters worse – as when India intervened in the Sri Lanka civil war, the US in Somalia, the Soviet Union in Afghanistan, Nigeria in Sierra Leone.

Nonetheless, with all the inconsistencies, failures and inadequacies, it is not impossible to have some modest optimism that the world is now, for the first time, set upon a process which ultimately can bring the elimination of war – if none of the accidents along the way destroy it first. The systemic drive to auto-destruction appears to have substantially weakened. By far the greatest military power in the world is unwilling to play the role of world policeman, and usually unwilling to allow others to combine for the same role. Washington refuses to pay its debts to the UN, and for long refused to allow its troops, as part of an international force, to be commanded by a foreigner. Congress remains ambivalent between the supposed historic interests of the US and the needs of the new world order (and supposes there is conflict between these two aims) – which led the Senate, for example, to reject the 1996 Test Ban Treaty in 1999 (although the US government refrains from tests). In a world economy which dissolves national drives to self-sufficiency, which forces collaboration between companies in different countries, as much in defence as elsewhere, Washington tries to block the logic, to force companies back into a clear nationality. Thales (the former Thomson-CSF) established a joint venture with Raytheon of the US, but was not thereby allowed to escape being French when it came to tendering for US defence contracts. Northrup-Grumman, a giant US defence company, needed European contracts and research results, but its collaboration with the Franco-German EADs did not open US defence contracts to the Europeans. The formerly British BAE Systems operated as a US company – and got a foothold in the mainly American Joint Strike Fighter project – but it was not allowed to aspire to the privileges of being American. Nonetheless, Lockheed's participation in the Joint Strike Fighter project required subcontracts with 300 partners in 62 countries – like it or not, it was a global project.

Washington plays the role in the world of a kind of Holy Roman Emperor in medieval Europe. But the American President cannot espouse appropriate traditions of universalism without risking his political support at home – the under 5 per cent of the world's people who are American thus exercise disproportionate influence. American presidents are obliged to try to behave as if they are solely responsible for this 5 per cent, for a narrow national self-interest, though, as they well know, they are also responsible for the world at large. Thus, under President Bush, there are on the one hand irritable displays of perverse unilateralism, on the other covert collaboration, the condition of American survival in an interdependent world. The global role is underlined by the disproportionate American share of the world's armaments (with an even greater share of the technically advanced weaponry) – US military spending is now greater in total than the expenditure of the next eight powers. It is a great temptation to Washington to rattle swords in place of employing other elements of foreign policy, and there seem to be some in the administration who see the present military lead as a window of opportunity – with a pre-emptive US military strike on all the supposed enemies of the US could not the world be rendered safe for US interests in the next half century? Wiser heads recognise the illusion. Enemies will be created by such an approach faster than they can be put down – force creates counter-force. In any case, the shiny weapons are an illusion – without the power to put men (and women) on the ground, to remake Baghdad, control cannot be exercised at a height of 35,000 feet (or now with unmanned aircraft, at 65,000 feet). The defeats are there – from Vietnam to Somalia – to illustrate the illusion of military power, and the new precision weaponry is as much of a fantasy as the new economy of the recent boom. If Washington is unwilling to risk the loss of American lives, it becomes overwhelmingly dependent on its allies to reform regimes – and hence has to return to the politics of persuasion and collaboration.

However, outside the geographical sphere of the Great Powers, what are for the moment the integrating heartlands of the world order, there is much less change. Latin America seems well on the way to emulating what is happening in the Atlantic region (and entertaining what is, by the standards of the past, an astonishing collaboration with 'American imperialism' in the initiative for the Americas), and ASEAN in Southeast Asia is, despite the historic rivalries, following a similar direction. But in Sub-Saharan Africa, the wreckage of states and the continuity of war and civil war suggest a world where it would be a step forward to create modern states, not to unwind them. Here not only is there no advance, there is a terrible retreat. To restrict one's view to Africa is certainly to encourage no optimism about the future. More threatening to the world order, however, are the two giant Great Powers, China and India, firmly committed to the old agenda of the modern state, with insoluble territorial disputes and claims. Both these are making major and sustained increases in defence spending, both in mutual rivalry and to challenge the US.

If the modern state has lost its systemic drive to war, what has replaced it? Rivalry remains the principle of any state, particularly now in the economic field – the management of the national economy in relationship to external events is thought to be decisive for domestic political stability. There is still fierce competition, if not in armaments, then in education, research, sport, culture, the quality of infrastructure and of life. Furthermore, domestic political management has become an obsession of governments as fierce as the old obsessions with war, a constant preoccupation with winning elections, managing crises that might deflect political support, being seen everywhere to claim responsibility for national triumphs and blame foreigners for national defeats. It is here that the plethora of trivialities, of gossip, of hourly disasters and victories, seems to swamp all other issues. And yet, regardless of the popular illusion that political discretion creates the world, inexorably world markets, step by step, are adjusting political behaviour and responses, creating, all unseen, a new world order. It remains vital for the legitimacy of government that people believe that political discretion can determine outcomes, that political will, not markets, decides events.

CIVIL GOVERNANCE

It is not just world markets that are reshaping sovereignty. Sovereign government is being undermined from different directions – both in terms of supranational and sub-national governance. Here it is not a question of alternative sovereignties at a different level so much as a dilution and dispersion of power. The alternative is thus not world government, which has always been a utopian aim, but the dispersal of powers in an immense network of dense regulation, directed by hundreds of different specialised agencies (including in some cases national governments), often operating with the common agreement of governments rather than with the power to force conformity or punish disobedience. Each national state increasingly sees it as part of its interests to interfere in the domestic affairs of other states – whether to defend, say, intellectual property rights in China (to stop the piracy of videos, for example), reorganise the retail trade of Japan, stop American farmers using genetically modified crops or reorganise domestic aviation.

The patterns of regulation are often quite unseen by the majority of people. Many are conscious of some measure of global regulation through the better-known agencies – the UN, WTO, IMF, World Bank, OECD or the Bank of International Settlements. Some of these agencies (IMF, World Bank), as conditions of their loans, try to enforce on developing countries a standard pattern of domestic economic management, even to the point of trying to reduce national military spending in favour of social budgets, or create representative voting systems, transparency of government, or enforce recognition of rights to form political parties and allow a free press, and introduce respect for civil rights; in essence, to radically reduce the discretionary powers of government. Most bilateral aid programmes do the same kind of thing, so that in sum there is considerable cumulative pressure to conform to a single political, social and economic agenda. Thus attempts are being made to reshape the states of the world to fit a particular model, a model which facilitates the operation of world markets and the integration of the system, and which creates government less as simply representative of given populations, more as brokers between the domestic and the external, between populations and the world at large. However, this is not some kind of deliberate conspiracy by international agencies, for other governments institute the same agenda spontaneously, in response to world events rather than the pressure of those agencies. On the contrary, if one believes in conspiracies it is more plausible to see the agencies as being in the grip of world markets in forcing one agenda.

Furthermore, there are an increasing number of regional regulatory bodies, particularly in the economic field – for example NAFTA, ASEAN, Mercosur. Half the 153 regional trade agreements signed in the last half of the twentieth century were concluded in the 1990s. Perhaps some of them are a response to the declining power of governments as the result of multilateral agreements, since regional pacts restore the continuing supervisory role of administrations. They tend to concern only trade. Despite some geographical romanticism, the regional pacts do not simplify the complexities of world power into sets of 'blocs' – even with the three most famous, the European Union, NAFTA and the Asia-Pacific, only the Union constitutes in economic terms anything like a bloc.

On the other hand, regional trade pacts add to the confusion between national orders of regulation and global imperatives. Thus, the 'rules of origin' under US regulations decree that Mexican computers, under NAFTA, can enter the US without tariffs – provided they do not include parts made outside the NAFTA area (which leads to higher prices being paid by US consumers). Bangladesh garment exports are forbidden to use cheap high-quality fabric imports if they are to enter Europe (again, European consumers are obliged to pay more as a result). Imports to the US of 'Italian' silk scarves were reclassified as 'Chinese' because they employ silk made in China, and so on. Archaic rules thus allow states to try to force the world economy back into national patches constructed for the purposes of governments, sacrificing both the benefits of global integration and low prices for their own consumers in the interests of particular lobbies.

There are many other agencies which try to legislate or enforce rules on the world. It was New York state, not the US government, which assumed the responsibility for seeking compensation for Jews of German origin who had lost assets in Swiss or German banks during World War II. California tried to force the disclosure of the global income of Shell International as a means to tax its Californian earnings. On the other hand, national governments increasingly become instruments for the enforcement of international law. In one of the more prominent cases, the British High Court was required to rule on the liability for punishment of Chile's former dictator General Pinochet (and had difficulty finding a local law on which to indict him). The same court awarded

Kuwait $1 billion dollars damages against Iraqi Airlines (a state-owned enterprise and therefore supposedly covered by the protection of Iraqi sovereignty) for expropriating ten aircraft and spares from Kuwait Airlines during the Gulf War. Iraq claimed unsuccessfully that Kuwait had not at that time had an independent existence, being then part of Iraq, and therefore the dispute was a 'domestic' matter. The court's decision – for Kuwait – implied that all governments were under an obligation to seize aircraft of Iraqi Airlines if they landed in their territories as compensation to Kuwait.

Furthermore, there are many more specialised regulatory agencies at the international level in specialised sectors – bankers regulate world banking, accountants world accountancy, all in order to regulate their members in the interests of their global reputation. Groups of multinational corporations similarly try to establish codes of behaviour in the interests of the reputation of all. Others police the system – NGOs, the media, investigative journalists. Indeed, in comparison with, say, the nineteenth century, the world is already comprehensively 'governed'. Governance in the world does not eliminate abuses or crime any more than laws within one national jurisdiction eliminate abuses. The lack of a global police force to enforce regulation is less important where offending firms can be forced out of the system at large and into the jurisdiction of one government with an enforcing police presence.

Management of the national economy poses some of the more severe problems. The unwinding of the national capital project and global integration allows parts of the economy to escape the state and its efforts to raise taxation, whether by going offshore for the rich or, for the less rich or even the poor, simply slipping below the threshold of the statistical system to become part of a black, a shadow, a clandestine or informal economy. In the first case, multinational corporations organise the distribution of their global income so that it appears in countries with low-tax regimes – corporate tax yields accordingly shrink; before 1940, federal corporation tax in the US generated about a third of tax revenues, but in the mid-1990s, 12 per cent (in Britain, the yield was heading towards zero). Individuals with access to foreign centres try to do the same. In the old order of economies, it seemed easy to identify where a company or an individual undertook their transactions and were therefore liable to tax, but now global companies and transactions blur this simplicity. Already by the late 1980s, nearly a third of the profits of US-based international companies were derived from tax havens (Hines and Rice 1994).

In the second case, it appears that everywhere the part of the economy which misses the data-collection system is expanding – although guesses as to its size rest entirely upon the assumptions made. One estimate for the world (Friedrich Schneider, in *The Economist*, 28 August 1999: 67) – including both the unrecorded and the criminal – puts it at some $9 trillion, equivalent to nearly a quarter of the world's output (or roughly the size of the US output). In the developed countries, the estimate ranges from 10 to nearly 30 per cent (in Greece, Spain, Belgium and, famously, Italy). In developing countries, estimates ranged up to 70 per cent of the official economy in Nigeria and Thailand – and in other cases, such as Pakistan or the city of Lima, up to 60 per cent. In terms of employment, estimates are even higher – nearly half the Italian workforce is unrecorded (and 22 per cent in Germany). Thus a major part of the world economy escapes being recorded, badly throwing out official estimates.

The arrival of the internet and of global e-commerce much exaggerates the problems. In the fiscal sense, taxpayers can escape any location, making it impossible for the tax official to attribute liability. Sales tax is severely threatened: 'A consumer in Essex [in Britain] could download software made in Seattle, marketed via a website in Australia, and delivered by a server located in the Bahamas. Where should this transaction be taxed?' (Leadbeater 1998: 22).

Government efforts to escape the problem raise major political issues. If capital, companies and the rich become mobile and thereby escape tax liability, governments are driven to maintain their income by taxing more heavily the immobile – land, property, offices, roads (and road pricing) and the immobile workforce. Even the tax on property and offices is dangerous, since it can force the concern also to go offshore – or, in the case of land, use land elsewhere. Increasing the tax on immobile workers threatens to increase labour costs, tending to drive jobs out of the country. All this follows on the state seeking to protect its fiscal position intact – at a cost to the taxpayers – while global economic integration removes its power to make capital captive.

The immobility of government is thus forcing reform, undermining the old kind of state and its supposed bedrock in an immobile population and a patch of territory. If countries are to become no more than junctions in flows, who is to have the obligation to pay for government, and who the right to create and supervise government? Those born there, those who live there, those who use the facilities located there, those who are passing through?

CORPORATIONS AND GOVERNANCE

Important issues of regulation arise in the case of large international companies. In a global economy, corporations can escape government regulation, a problem most clearly illustrated, as we have seen, in the difficulties governments have in identifying the size and distribution of the global income of corporations in order to tax it. The problem is made worse where some governments, eager to attract foreign capital, operate a lax or opaque system of accounting and regulation.

However, the picture is not quite as stark as it seems. Companies are increasingly subject to exposure by international trade unions and NGOs, some of them with international networks extensive enough to monitor multinational operations. They can and do impose sanctions in the largest markets where the company operates (not necessarily where the company abuses its position). Sanctions on Union Carbide's appalling disaster in Bhopal in India were felt most severely in its main markets in the US, and would have been magnified if the Government of India had allowed the case against the company to have been heard before American courts. Insofar as Shell Petroleum was complicit in repression by the Nigerian military regime in the river provinces, sanctions operated against Shell in its main markets and affected its world reputation. Multinational corporations have grown increasingly sensitive to their vulnerability in this respect, and have tried to protect themselves by, for example, trying to co-opt critics into company consultation mechanisms, operating with a single global standard of safety, paying higher wages than local companies as a means of diverting criticism etc. Of course, there are companies that do not do this and persist in not doing so as long as they are not exposed, so there are no grounds for complacency in this respect. On the other hand, the regulation of small companies is a much more severe problem – as represented by the operations of smaller US companies in the Mexican border region, but this is a problem of small companies, not of foreign capital, and depends on the government's strength and willingness to act to ensure compliance with the regulations.

At the moment, foreign firms are increasing their share of the economy of many countries. However, 'foreign' here may not indicate a large world operation, but rather a medium company with only one or two foreign locations. It is not clear that the very large multinational corporation is set to survive, let alone play such a prominent role in the world economy. Large national corporations are a product of the old state agenda, facilitated and protected by a powerful government. The significance of such companies is not their economic strength, but their political muscle in lobbying governments. In the period after the Second World War, American large companies returned to internationalising their operations from the 1950s, with the beginning of the liberalisation of trade and capital movements. But with the emergence of serious foreign competition in their home market, many were forced to begin radical restructuring. In some cases, they almost failed – General Motors, cosseted by the US government in its heyday as the largest company in the world, floundered for several decades after it found itself in a global market. Governments have, for long periods, patronised large companies as instruments of the national capital project, as political champions of national prestige. However, in an open economy, to maintain such rigid structures becomes expensive to a government – even if it is tolerated by its competitors.

The speed of change, the intensity of competition, fluctuations in world markets and the conditions of innovation seem to require a flexibility that is difficult if not impossible to attain in a very large centralised company – without government privileges. It is this market logic which seems to be forcing large companies to concentrate on their core business, to specialise, to spin off subsidiaries and outsource supplies and, if required, downsize or create, at most, clusters of specialised companies. In the more extreme cases, corporations have been broken up. As we have seen, South Korea's relatively closed market encouraged the *chaebol* to diversify far beyond their original specialisation – and liberalisation forces specialisation: the bankruptcy of Daewoo and the severe difficulties of other major corporations, not least the leader, Hyundai, show the price of resisting too long. A case study of this process is also provided by South Africa. In the heyday of the old regime, large local corporations could invest abroad only with great difficulty, but were protected against import competition at home. As a result, they diversified at home (Anglo American, the largest, and a mining corporation, moved into making an immense range of things – from cars to paper, fruit juice, wine etc). Opening up the economy exposed these peripheral activities to international competition, so they were dropped. As Anglo American moved its stock-exchange base to London, to the world – along with South African Breweries (with 98 per cent of the South African market for beer), the metals group Billiton, Sappi paper-makers, and possibly Barlow, the industrial conglomerate, Old Mutual insurance, and Gold Fields – all were required to restructure to concentrate on their core specialisation. It now appears that a closed and protective state is the precondition for stable monopoly or a diversified monopolistic group.

Perhaps the same trend explains some of the scattered evidence of a decline in business concentration – despite the headline news of mergers and business acquisitions. Take, for example, the world car-manufacturing industry. In 1969, the three largest companies (all three American: General Motors, Ford, Chrysler) made half the world's output; by the mid-1990s, it was down to a third – and the Japanese company, Toyota, had replaced Chrysler as the third. In 1969, there were nine companies producing over one million vehicles annually (and together making 84 per cent of world output); in 1996, 14, including some complete newcomers, for example Suzuki and Hyundai, that produced no cars in 1969 (and the largest nine now produced only 66 per cent of world output). It seems that sheer size, the economies of scale – as represented in General Motors – is no longer a competitive advantage. Nor does size exclude the possibility of newcomers, or save the established producers (such as British Leyland).

However, for the moment large companies are still very prominent in the world economy, and new ones are created constantly (although we have no way of assessing the relative concentration involved, since many of the millions of small companies are not recorded). The economies of scale, like the patronage of states, may have declining effects, but this has not prevented the swift emergence of companies like Microsoft. However, just as IBM's domination of the field of computer manufacture proved vulnerable, so also it is the relatively swift turn-over of companies which is impressive, especially in the most dynamic sectors. Without state protection – a closed or semi-closed domestic market – it is most difficult for a company persistently to capture the innovations which make for future temporary domination of the market. Sheer size may thus become a temporary phenomenon, and perhaps even a mark of high vulnerability.

If size is becoming counter-productive, why do companies merge or acquire others with such frequency? Business behaviour in this respect appears to be perverse. In examining 168 acquisitions and mergers between 1979 and 1990, Mark Scrivener (1997/2000) shows that in two thirds of the cases the acquisition reduced the value of the company making the bid. Shareholders in the bidding company lost through paying more for the company acquired than the market valuation, and few ever made up the loss. In some cases, the acquisition was a disaster. For example, the insurance company Conseco purchased Green Tree Financial for $6.4 billion in 1998, as the result of which Conseco share value fell from $58 to $12 up to the time when Conseco tried to sell Green Tree. Or again, Quaker Oats paid $1.7 billion for the drinks firm Snapple in 1994, and three years later was forced to sell it at a loss of $1.4 billion. Similarly, Sony paid $3.4 billion for Columbia Pictures in 1989, and sold it, much chastened, five years later at a loss of $3.2 billion. A different study, of the oil industry (HSBC 2001) argues that the recent mergers in the industry have not increased profitability or productivity, nor reduced costs nor facilitated undertaking major projects (all arguments used by oil companies to justify acquisitions) – they may indeed only have opened the way for smaller and more nimble companies to attack the position of the large. Warren Buffet, the American expert on share values, comments (in Skapinker, *Financial Times*, 12 April 2000) that many companies who want to acquire others see themselves as princesses whose kisses will turn toads into handsome princes. 'Many managerial princesses remain serenely confident about the future potency of their kisses, even after their corporate backyards are knee deep in unresponsive toads.'

Many different motives explain these major errors of judgement – including the search for prestige by the businessmen concerned. However, one of them may be that in the old state agenda access to government was crucial to business success, and the strength of access varied with the size of company – the bigger the company, the greater its political capacity to win concessions and protect itself from competition. Now, however, it seems that mere size may be of declining significance in an open world economy – indeed size may be a disability. Furthermore, insofar as there are real economic advantages of size – in, for example, reducing the risks of major research spending – they can be achieved far more cheaply and with much less risk through outsourcing, strategic alliances, networks. An emerging form of business organisation is the elaborate network or association of small companies. For example, Hong Kong's Li and Fung, with a very small central staff to manage logistics, finance, design and transport, links 1500 independent companies in 23 countries, with one and a half million employees, to produce to order a wide range of consumer goods.

However, governments are still tempted to pay to support their national champions, to protect them against the competition of foreigners. This is most clear-cut in the military sector, but occurs in many other areas of supposed concern for 'national security'. The US government, as we have seen, does not accept that there are companies without nationality, and forces firms that wish to tender for US defence contracts to become 'American' (yet simultaneously US defence companies are having software written in a dozen countries). Similar fears spread much more widely – the FBI raised the issue of Deutsche Telecom acquiring the US VoiceStream; or Japan's NTT bidding for Verio; or the Dutch ASM Lithography seeking to buy the electronic chip manufacturer Silicon Valley Group (since one of its subsidiaries supplied components to defence equipment). Other industries are affected – for example US airlines, television companies, fishing fleets. The old national capital agenda continues a half life, even when the project as a whole has died. The continuing attempt is brave since, in reality, it is increasingly difficult to say what nationality – in any effective sense – major companies retain.

Governments also tolerate or promote legal arrangements to prevent foreign companies acquiring 'their' companies, to exclude foreign capital. We have noted such provisions in Japan, Korea and Taiwan. The German government tolerates – or actively supports – provisions whereby only a handful of institutional shareholders control major companies, and are committed to preventing takeovers. It is said that 89 per cent of listed companies have a single shareholder with a quarter or more of the equity. In France, there is a continuing battle to open up ownership, to prevent, for example, Société Generale's practice of limiting any individual shareholder voting power to no more than 15 per cent of the whole, regardless of the size of ownership stake. Such mechanisms not only deny the company significant foreign investment, and this is becoming increasingly expensive; they also keep out foreign management and innovation to upgrade company performance. Furthermore, tolerant large shareholders have allowed companies to pursue the strategies of managers rather than shareholders, of growth rather than profitability, a direction which, as we have seen in the case of Japan, ultimately renders companies highly vulnerable, if not to foreign take-over, then to collapse in a recession.

Cross-shareholdings between big companies, as we have seen in the Japanese and Korean cases, is another mechanism for keeping foreigners out (and fortifying the position of the insiders). Sometimes, there are special rules to skew the company board's voting power – the Swedish holding group, Investor, holds only 2.7 per cent of the capital of Ericsson but, under the company rules, exercises 22 per cent of the voting strength. However, such arrangements are often not impregnable. The Vodafone-Mannesman outcome shows that shareholder power is emerging, and if the returns from holding a company's shares are too low, investors will be disloyal and sell out to whoever makes an offer. Inter-company shareholdings are declining throughout Europe, and the mass of shareholders becoming increasingly critical of company managers (not least of their pay levels and awards). The process is facilitated by the privatisation of state assets, opening new fields of investment, but also by the vast growth in the number of shareholders – by the end of the twentieth century, the number of shareholders in Europe overtook, for the first time, the number of trade unionists.

Furthermore, cross-border mergers remain relatively rare. When they occur, they seem often to become national, even if they lose their original base; a famous example here is the company Bata, which lost its base in Czechoslovakia in the 1948 Communist takeover, but remains Czech in culture. The merger of Daimler-Benz and Chrysler seems to have produced a German company; that of Pharmacia and Upjohn in pharmaceuticals in 1995 a US company, ultimately taken over by Monsanto of the US. Thus it seems that the culture of companies resists genuine globalism within the company, even if the operations are indeed global.

In sum, the trends in business suggest that forms of regulation are emerging which can be effective, provided governments really do abandon the old national capital project – but without adopting the half-way house of cronyism, favouring the friends of the President. However, the effectiveness of regulation ultimately relies on self-regulation (in the interests of protecting the company's continuing capacity to operate), regulation through associations of competitors, suppliers and buyers (as occurs in the oil industry), through government and inter-national inspectorates (as with agencies of the UN), monitored by independent agencies, NGOs and so on, but ultimately backed by government sanctions. In practice, there is no shortage at all of dense networks of regulation for large prominent global corporations, but there is little regulation for the immense mass of small local companies (many of them unrecorded) where the worst problems of pay and conditions occur.

A WORLD OF NGO

Possibly the most extraordinary change in the political landscape in the past 30 years has been the growth and development of NGOs. It is as if the ending of the thraldom of the war-making state and the state system has liberated civil society. The diversity, the numbers, the range of issues are so great that it is impossible to discuss the phenomenon in general, only to note the astonishing difference with the period that went before, when the 'official' virtually mono-polised the stage. By now, NGOs are so large, as a group that they have become significant employers in a number of countries – providing jobs, it is said, for 12 per cent of the labourforce in the Netherlands, 8 per cent in the US, 6 per cent in Britain. OECD estimates that NGOs in 1997 raised directly $5.5 billion from private donors; international NGOs managed annually funds larger than those delivered by the UN system or loaned by the World Bank, or equal to about a fifth of all aid flows to Africa.

The diversity of sizes is immense – from large multinational concerns (Action Aid, Care, Save the Children, Christian Aid, Oxfam, MSF) to tiny groups, based on a group of streets, houses or apartments. The diversity of purposes is even wider – from the establishment of democracy, the conquest of poverty, the liberation of women or the defence of the environment to the provision of emergency relief, of technical advice, of monitoring or inspection services, of research and publications or even delivery of a local service, improvement in a housing scheme, drilling of a well or creation of a pilot cultivation scheme. Many replace govern-ments in important functions (and governments increasingly employ them in specialised roles), although many can only ultimately survive with government.

Some have been developed in response to the availability of aid funds. Some are virtually private businesses, some compete with business. Some developed as authoritarian regimes decayed – the civic associations in the declining years of South African Apartheid, the Comités do Base under the weakening Brazilian military rule in the 1970s. On the margins, they fade into more traditional organ-isations which have often existed throughout the last period – trade unions, political campaigns, business associations, religious organisations, co-operatives, youth and women's voluntary organisations, sports or cultural clubs. They over-lap with straightforward lobbies – of farmers, teachers, cyclists, cities. There were said to operate in Brussels in the early 1990s 3000 or so special interests, officially represented to the European Union, employing about 10,000 people.

The numbers have become immense. The 1995 UN Commission on Global Governance enumerated nearly 29,000 international NGOs. In each country, there are many more – perhaps two million in the US; possibly one million in India; maybe 100,000 in Eastern Europe (created between 1988 and 1995), and

65,000 in Russia. In a typical African country, van de Walle (*Financial Times,* 19 August 1999) reports, with 30–40 aid donors, 75–125 foreign NGOs manage 1000 or so projects, employing between 800 and 1000 foreigners and an unknown majority of local people.

NGOs span the political spectrum, although all are to some degree meant to be militantly non-political (to protect the monopoly of politics by established parties and reassure donors that they have no political axe to grind), but they cannot fail to be concerned with power, and generally slanted to the left. If there were a predominant political view – and if this were conscious – it would probably be a species of conservative anarchism, more consistent with the mutual co-operation of Kropotkin than the Deed of Bakunin. Some NGOs reject the state and official society; others deal in the fashionable triad, government–private business–NGOs. However, in practice all must be to some degree political.

In the international sphere, this has become explicit in converting technical or expert conferences into high political events (these are discussed later) – from the 1992 Earth Summit (where NGO pressure was important in pushing governments to act on greenhouse gases) through a series of UN global conferences in the 1990s. NGOs organised a 'swarm' at the World Bank meeting to mark its fiftieth anniversary; the Bank responded by inviting into its deliberations a selection of NGOs on a permanently consultative basis (specialists from over 70 NGOs now work, it is said, in Bank field offices), with over half its projects including NGO representatives. The UN had a much longer record of consultation – by the mid-1990s, some 1500 NGOs were accredited for consultation to the UNDP. A coalition of NGOs helped sink the OECD Multilateral Agreement on Investment (to harmonise international rules on foreign investment), although a change of position by the French government was also crucial (Henderson 1999). Another coalition successfully campaigned to get governments committed to the cancellation of the debts of the poorest developing countries. Late in 1999, NGOs – with American trade unions – helped to force the abandonment of the WTO's attempt to initiate a new round of trade talks, and in 2000 unsuccessful attempts were made to force the ending of joint IMF–World Bank meetings in Washington and Prague.

These are the high agenda of global action, as much symbolic as effective. But there are also effective single-issue campaigns – to end nuclear testing, to outlaw the use of landmines, to end whaling. Some impressive campaigns have been fought against companies – forcing some out of South Africa in protest at apartheid (those who left included Shell, BP, Rio Tinto Zinc, Disney, Reebok, Nike, Starbucks) and out of Myanmar in protest at the suppression of the opposition (companies evacuating included Levi Strauss, Macy's, Liz Claiborne, Eddie Bauer, Pepsi, Texaco). Others targeted particular companies: Nike shoes (as a protest at conditions in shoe factories making these shoes in Vietnam and Indonesia); or Nestlé baby milk (in protest at it being forced on the poorest developing countries); or Monsanto (for its attempts to monopolise seed technology); or Shell (for involvement in the Nigerian military repression of people in the Nigerian southwest); or Australia's BHP for polluting the rivers of Papua New Guinea; or De Beers for trading in diamonds from war zones that might finance the fighting (De Beers pulled out of Angola, ended purchases in Congo and Guinea, and committed itself to make no purchases in war zones, particularly Sierra Leone); and there are many more. Companies increasingly strive to demonstrate that they are beyond reproach. Thus Nike bravely commissioned an independent report on conditions among its subcontractors which revealed that many of the strong criticisms of the contracted firms were correct – and Nike accepted the report, promising to seek to rectify conditions.

This is an impressive record by voluntary organisations, whether right or wrong, for a new level of action, one which for the first time focusses on the appropriate global level. There are inevitably problems. One is seen most sharply in the competitive scramble to seize the opportunity of an emergency to build an organisation – for example in Goma in Rwanda following the massacre of the Hutus. In Tirana in the spring of 1999, with the flight of the Kosovan Albanians, 200 groups arrived to offer relief; the Red Cross was sufficiently horrified at the unseemly competition for press attention that it tried to launch a code of conduct to derecognise interlopers (70 groups and 142 governments signed up). Errors are made through the excessive enthusiasm of the ignorant – operating sterilisation clinics in poor areas, buying slaves in southern Sudan (and so stimulating the supply), feeding warring soldiers or guerrillas or fuelling black markets rather than getting food to the starving. But the errors are probably no worse than those made by official agencies (who may simply have a greater capacity to hide those errors).

Others worry about the relationship of NGOs to democracy – national government is elected, NGOs self-selected. NGOs cannot claim to represent populations, but they can claim – if they wish to be successful – to embody important interests and action. Furthermore, they vastly increase the extent of popular participation and knowledge in key issues; even if the results are partial, they are generally superior to the funereal silence which states impose when left to themselves. But the simplicity of single issues allows the collaboration of contradictory interests – for example, of American trade unions that oppose imports from developing countries and those that deplore the restrictions imposed by governments in developed countries on imports from developing countries, both united in opposing the World Trade Organisation. The alliance of convenience allows governments to escape responsibility by blaming the NGOs for, for example, the cancellation of the WTO discussions when it is the result of official stalemate or paralysis.

Despite the scale of this political intervention, others worry that only under the old agenda, the state order, can people be properly protected. Many trade unions in the developed world, seem to agree, having been through a period of severe decline. In Europe, Waddington and Hoffman (2001) report that trade unions have failed to escape from the decline in their traditional sectors of support – male-dominated and ageing, full-time permanent manufacturing employment in large factories or in the public sector; leaving on one side young and women workers, in flexible employment, in service production and small-scale units. The unions, it seems, are the product of the old statist economy, and are declining with it. Almost everywhere trade-union membership continues to shrink, although not necessarily as sharply as in France – from 21 per cent of the workforce 30 years ago to 8 per cent in the late 1990s. The best unions try to recycle themselves as personal-service organisations rather than collective bargainers, as proto-NGOs with a broader political remit.

Who is to protect workers if the state's power and the trade unions decay together? 'No individual State,' Tilly (1995: 21) observes, 'will have the power to enforce workers' rights in the fluid world that is emerging'. Manuel Castells (I 1996: 475) is even more gloomy – on the one hand, 'networks converge towards a meta-network of capital that integrates capitalist interests at the global level and across sectors and realms of activity ... [while] Labor is disaggregated in its performance, fragmented in its organisation, diversified in its existence, divided in its collective action'. Is the gloom justified? In fact, the decline of the state does not necessarily affect its capacity for regulation within its sphere of responsibility, and at the global level, as we have seen, international NGOs have been more effective in achieving specific goals than traditional trade unions. Indeed, in many cases governments restrict the capacity of worker organisations to employ their strength to achieve improvements – in the interests of managing inflation, public sectors or the operation of the rest of the economy. Hence the decline of the power of the state can increase the reliance of workers on their own resources to defend their rights. The old agenda saw the state as the guarantor of popular welfare, and the unions depended upon that; the new returns to a much older agenda of self-reliance.

The development of influence is perhaps more effective than actual enforcement. Companies react early to avoid a damning report. Governments might protest that an Amnesty or Human Rights report is a tissue of invention, but often adjust behaviour to try to avoid a second denunciation. The British government was enraged at reports of the oppressive behaviour of the Royal Ulster Constabulary and the army in Northern Ireland under the Prevention of

Terrorism Act, but it also changed official behaviour. Thus it would be wrong to scorn such efforts because they lack the power of official sanctions; often they are slowly creating a new culture in which governments and companies feel obliged to behave in ways which protect their reputation. Despite the Rwandas, the Kosovos, the Angolas, the Cambodias, a culture is slowly being developed to bind the mighty Goliaths of government and corporations. To achieve this requires continuing efforts, sustained by the capacity of NGOs to raise more of the rising incomes of people to embody an emerging popular conscience.

DECENTRALISATION

If the old war-making state – and the system which created and maintained it – is in long-term decline, the centralised governmental order which sustained it cannot also escape radical reform. As we have seen, to attain the flexibility required to survive in an open world economy, large companies are obliged to transform their structures; so also national governments are forced into long processes of self-reform, of experiment and innovation to find structures flexible enough to respond sensitively to the continual reshaping forces – and the sudden shocks – of the world economy. After an immensely long period of an apparently inexorable drive to centralisation, to a dogmatic and irreversible extension of direct public rule of parts of the economy and of society, suddenly the structures appear to go into reverse – to the privatisation of the public sector, the sub-mission of parts of the public domain to the regime of autonomous cost-centres or to actual or quasi-profit-making, to independent trusts, to offloading public responsibilities on NGOs, private firms or coalitions of interests (including universities, trade unions, associations), and to the decentralisation of govern-ment itself. It is, in the long historical picture, an extraordinary reversal of trends.

A key part of the change is, as we have noted, the removal of the systemic imperative to war. This is assisted by the lack of a major economic crisis of the order of the inter-war Great Depression, although that in its turn itself might justifiably be attributed also to the decline of the war-making state; in the inter-war depression, governments sacrificed their populations to the maintenance of national power. The removal of the systemic drive permits – indeed encourages – the vast growth of the NGO sector as well as a decline in the secrecy of the state. The two factors lead to a remarkable increase in public transparency – and the exposure of the economic failures of state operations, the sheer waste of unaccountable discretionary public spending. The old war economies produced immense waste, nowhere so impressively as in the former Soviet Union, but occurring in all the leading states, particularly in the gambles of industrial policy.

In the old agenda, what began as a response to the necessities of defence became part of the habituated practices of government, the routines of secrecy, which then in turn provided the cover for favours to friends and clients, the cronies of the state and its officials. Exposure encourages much greater electoral pressure, as expressed in the competition between, and promises made by, political parties, for reductions in taxation, for cuts in public activity. This is also increased by the decline in another component of the old national capital project, hostility to foreign capital; tax levels are seen now as an element encouraging or discouraging foreign investment and so economic growth, and hence the incomes of the workforce at large.

The change in direction and scale of the public domain is hardly reflected in the statistical measures of the government sector. Public spending as a proportion of gross domestic product in 1913 ranged between 6 and 17 per cent for the Great Powers; it was around 32 per cent for the OECD group by 1970 (with at the top of the then range 65 per cent in Sweden, 54 per cent in France). Even in the heyday of the downsizing of government in the 1990s, the share changed only marginally – in France, for example, from 55 to 54 per cent, or in Germany from 49.5 to 47.7 per cent. But the content of the spending was radically altered, with an immense increase in transfer payments between sections of the population, as opposed to the direct financing of the state's activities.

The fashion for administrative and financial decentralisation swept the governments of the world in a most remarkable fashion. Part of this is purely verbal, to deflect criticism, but much of it has more substance. The Indian case is interesting here. For much of the period since Indian independence, the state has driven to concentrate activities in its own hands, with a large public sector in most modern activities (especially manufacturing, banking and insurance, transport). However, under Prime Minister Rajiv Gandhi, before his murder, a significant attempt was made to decentralise power; the grounds for doing so were attributed to the Prime Minister's inference from the break-up of the old Soviet Union – either India decentralised or it would also break up. Thus the reform was proposed not on the relative merits of different forms of administration, but as a question of the survival of the existing political order – a shift from the old systemic imperative to the new, from centralisation to flexibility.

At the other extreme, post-1949 China has always been more decentralised than its parallels in the Eastern Bloc. In the 1990s, provincial power had become so strong that the country seemed almost a federation, despite the rhetoric of the central government. As we noted earlier, the role of the centre declined in financial terms remarkably, and despite efforts to reverse the process Beijing seems politically unable to do so.

Whatever the local reasons offered for decentralisation, reform came to encompass many of the governments of the world. The US government cut its direct funding to state and local tiers of government while increasing the dispersal of responsibilities. The French government, famous historically for the degree of Parisian centralisation, made major efforts (in 1982, 1986 and 1996) to disperse powers and responsibilities to 22 regions, to larger cities and towns, enhancing local autonomy and initiative. In Britain, after a phase of increased centralisation in the 1980s as a means to increase central control of spending, the same trend occurred, most famously in the creation of new assemblies and powers for Scotland, Wales and Northern Ireland, new powers to city mayors. Spain experienced one of the most radical decentralisations, restoring the provinces and turning the country into a quasi-federation. Europe of the regions encourages both increased degrees of political (and cultural) separation, and new transnational alliances and coalitions – the coalition, for example, of Rhône-Alpes, Lombardy, Catalonia and Baden-Württemberg, or of various European cities.

In sum then, the old idea of government is fading into the vaguer notion of governance, a coalition of forces managing a cluster of activities. This is not, as we noted earlier, a transfer of the old concentration of sovereignty in the hands of the state so much as a dispersal of powers along with a blurring of the distinction between official or public agencies and unofficial ones. Along with increased transparency of government, there is increasing opacity in the exercise of power, increasing complexity. Each participant is intimately familiar with his or her corner, the distribution of responsibilities and obligations, but it is increasingly difficult to portray the system as whole, particularly because of the lag of old concepts. Old simplifications fade without being replaced by comparable simplicities.

STATES AND THE GLOBAL ECONOMY

The end of the Soviet Union and the old Eastern Bloc revealed that a new world order was emerging, that it had been growing and developing under the cover of the Cold War, but unseen since the threat of world war concealed the processes in what seemed to be merely a continuation of the old agenda. What is extraordinary is how a cluster of events in such a short space of time could reveal such a dramatic change in the world polity. Instead of the primacy of the old war-making state, a new agenda for the internal organisation of government, democracy, is being promoted on all sides – and the system now confers legitimacy on governments insofar as they accept this agenda. Furthermore, the aims of the agenda are themselves emerging. Regimes elected by limited or unlimited suffrage covered 6 of the 43 recognised states in 1900, 37 of the 121 countries of the world in 1980 (including 35 per cent of the world's population) and 117 of the 193 countries in 1998 (or 54 per cent of the world's people).

Democracy might spread, but the decline of a single concentration of power, the state, to be democratically supervised, undermines its legitimacy. The dispersal of power to include a widening range of organisations, NGOs, trade unions, private companies etc not included in the overview of democracy promises an immense increase in participation and consultation at the cost of democratic control. The old idea of the individual combining with others through a majority vote to embody a general will to check the state gives way to a much more opaque picture of competing lobbies without the possibility of a general will.

However, the emerging world order might be formally more responsive to popular demands, but the maintenance of order itself, the policing of the world, is fragile and erratic. The 'international community', such as it is, failed in Rwanda, in Somalia and other parts of Sub-Saharan Africa, in the Balkans and elsewhere. It cannot end the disputes in Palestine, in Kashmir, in Tibet and many other places. Those with the power to intervene are suspect as merely national competitors, seeking to advance simply national interests, and there is sometimes enough truth in the charge to make it stick. Governments remain ambivalent between the old and the new agendas, between the old national capital project and the interests of the peoples of the world. Nor do the Great Powers accord enough power to the blue berets to maintain order. Thus, peace turns upon negotiation, arms-length management, with rare displays of awesome brute strength – as in Kosovo – to stiffen the authority of the negotiators. For those accustomed to an order maintained within national states it can only seem weak and ineffective.

The ambivalence of governments changes only slowly, and as a result elements of the national capital project continue, even if now less securely embedded in the war-making drive. National economic development – meaning the creation of an independent national economy – has still a half-life in many developing countries. The Europeans continue, from time to time, to promote national industrial champions, to protect agriculture (and dump cheap agricultural exports abroad, wrecking the markets for other exporters) and so on; Washington rarely resists stroking selected lobbies, again protecting selected sectors, all this without noting the continued military rivalries in South and East Asia, in the Middle East, and the ferocious civil wars of Africa. It remains systemically true that all will make some attempt to defend themselves while any power remains armed. While the US maintains its gigantic military cluster at the centre of its activity – with a commitment to continue to upgrade it – all feel obliged to make some gesture at self-defence, even if the nature of weaponry now makes any modern defence impossible.

A COSMOPOLITAN BOURGEOISIE?

The social formations (to employ an old-fashioned term) appropriate to the old agenda of national states also fade. As noted earlier, the classes of the old society, in industrial countries, pre-eminently capital and labour, were defined by the central principle of national power, the state. With the dispersal of power, it is difficult to see the persistence of these political entities, even though relationships, often of conflict, persist and will certainly continue between employers and workers. Global integration does not lead to a simple transfer of concepts from the national to the world level, but rather the dissolution of the national entities. While class struggles may and almost certainly will persist, they are not simply transferable to the world level since there is no equivalent cluster of global power, a world government, and there seems no realistic possibility of such an eventuality

It follows that if there is a new global class running the world, it is – in Marx's terms – a 'class in itself' (that is a group that can be defined objectively) – the managers and owners of multinational enterprises, of international official and unofficial agencies, and the managers of each state (with one foot in each camp, national and global). It is, however, not possible to see it as potentially a 'class for itself', a group with a perception of a common interest, since that would presuppose effective agencies of a global sovereignty, an idea that makes no sense, since sovereignty presupposes a plurality of sovereignties. Thus the idea of a cosmopolitan bourgeoisie may imply the existence of people of a similar style of life, a similar relationship to the world, but not a group that can rule the world on a single agenda.

The emergence more clearly of a class of people who run or deal with parts of the world is apparent, but it is also clear that in general they strongly retain a geographically specific sense of identity (even if they do not pursue interests linked to that territory) – they are 'Chinese' or 'German' or 'Korean'. It seems hardly feasible that these national – or local – identities will fade as quickly as national economies, even though the experience of people extends to many other places. However, this may be put too strongly; we need only remind ourselves how far the fierce religious identities of sixteenth-century Europe have faded to suggest that once the war-making state is disarmed this may also occur with national identities. This will not, however, end other collective identities, communal or religious, or perhaps more local identities, of a city or a province. Before the rise of the national modern state, there were many such identities which did not coincide with national power, some of which survived the whole period of national power – gypsies, Jews, Armenians, Lebanese. There were also famous cosmopolitan families, for example the Rothschilds, the ancestors of the Aga Khan; and famous migrant communities, from the Normans to the Huguenots. We have already mentioned the two trading-banking communities, associated with two cities in the Sind of pre-British and British India, one sustaining a business network throughout Central Asia, the other a trading network throughout the world, and both surviving British India and the subsequent period of India and Pakistan (Markovits 2000).

On the other hand, the degree to which existing national identities are operational in the emerging cosmopolitan world of business – that is to inform, influence or direct operational decisions – is very variable. A large-scale survey (nearly 12,000 responses in 25 countries) in the early 1990s (Kantor 1991) of businessmen, to assess how far the global economy was producing a global culture and a decline in patriotism, found that at that time most older industrial corporations in Europe were least attached to their national markets, protectionism and local suppliers; only a quarter cared more about their country's success, than their company's performance. The most nationalist were then businessmen from Korea, Hungary, Mexico, India and the US. Such a survey, as much as anything, measures the confidence of businessmen at the moment at which they are interviewed, so not a great deal of significance can be attached to the results. A survey of American businessmen after the long period of growth in the US economy of the 1990s might produce very different results.

On the other hand, not only are foreign managers increasingly employed abroad – Britain's largest corporations frequently employ them – there is also a small class of genuinely cosmopolitan businessmen. Take for example Carlos Ghosni of Renault, and currently chief of Japan's second-largest vehicle manufacturing company, Nissan: in his words, he is Lebanese by origin, Brazilian by birth, French by nationality and Japanese by adoption. Or Sarkis Kalyandjian of GKN – Armenian by origin, French by birth, American by nationality, British by employer, with a home in Germany. There are no doubt many more whose way of life allows them the privilege to choose their national identity or to choose none at all.

In addition, modern management training is helping to create a common cosmopolitan business culture, as are periods of service in international organisations for members of national governments. There is a reverse flow of, for example, former high officials of international organisations – for example the IMF or the World Bank – to become, say, ministers of finance in national governments. Thus a global cadre is being created with a common discipline and culture, a sort of global civil service which staffs national administrations.

The hint of a global social order is embedded in Marx's view of a world capitalism. But, like the socialists generally, Marx underestimated the systemic imperative of the state order and overestimated the capacity of its opponents, on their own, to overcome it. Accordingly, many of his followers failed to see the transformation of the Soviet Union, under the impact of the systemic competition of states, into, at least formally, a more purified form of war-making state. The immense efforts of the Soviet state to develop the national capacity to wage war was thus presented as 'building socialism', and the flimsy significance of the distinction between what was publicly and what privately owned turned into a major ideology to justify all the sacrifices required of the first. The perspective of universal collective self-liberation disappeared in an even more grotesque tyranny, the military serfdom of the 'Marxist-Leninist State'.

The world today is one which, compared to that of Marx, has already gone far beyond the 'realm of necessity' to that of abundance. Despite the immensity of the numbers of those who are poor, the conquest of poverty is within our grasp. The state national capital project was, in retrospect, a diversionary episode in the long endeavour to end poverty, but perhaps one that was required to break the political obstacles to rapid growth – even if nationally organised growth creates just those immense distinctions between rich and poor countries which mark our times. Global integration carries with it the promise of defeating poverty by weakening the state, weakening that systemic drive which enforces social differentiation as well as war.

11

The Unfinished Agenda

PROTECTING NATIONAL CAPITALISM

Globalisation is still very partial and uneven. Even where it is most advanced, in Europe, there are still endless battles between governments to secure some advantage or to defend part of the old agenda. The issues are usually buried in the detail, not exposed in broad strategies. Hence, to identify them sometimes requires pursuit into the tedious complications of issues. Not only are there sectors of the new agenda that are excluded from consideration, there are major topics – such as labour – where national protectionism has, if anything, grown more severe during the period of global integration.

In trade, the area in which globalisation was originally most advanced, the disputes – particularly between Brussels and Washington – never ceased. Despite the logic of the economists – that it is an unequivocal advantage to countries to open their borders unilaterally to imports without seeking parallel concessions from trade partners – governments continued to insist on making access to their home market a privilege only conceded in response to a matching privilege by the trade partner. Trade remains, even if in a qualified fashion, an instrument of state power and of the ancient rivalries.

In agriculture, one of the last areas to be touched by international negotiations on trade liberalisation, this is peculiarly true. Originally, governments protected agriculture – and massively so – to ensure self-sufficiency in foodstuffs and agricultural raw materials in the event of war (and an enemy imposition of a trade boycott or attacks on international supply lines). Protection was imposed regardless of cost – and in particular of cost to domestic consumers, particularly the poor (spending a higher proportion of their income on foodstuffs). The case slid imperceptibly into a different one – protecting farmers was protecting a rural way of life as a general amenity to the urban (and rural) population, discouraging the 'drift to the cities', and – an unspoken agenda item, particularly in the case of conservative parties – a means to try to secure the rural vote (particularly where, as so often, rural constituencies were electorally over-weighted). A key component in the old war-economy agenda thus smudged into one of political rent-seeking lobbies. The Europeans – and the Japanese and others – still exercise much ingenuity in trying to pretend that agriculture should be a special case, not subject to the harsh imperatives of free markets; this entails that their own citizens should be obliged to pay more for food, and that more efficient foreign farmers be deprived of markets. Cultivation is in this case supposedly a culturally valuable way of life (even if most people do not want to do it as anything more than a hobby), and has special relevance for the environment and for leisure. Thus, a formerly productive sector has been nudged into being more like a park or a museum (as indeed happened to former mines and ancient factories). Despite subsidies, what is left of the agricultural population continues to vote with their feet and move to the cities, or at least to non-farming jobs. The leading competitive agricultural exporters – the US, Canada, Australia, Argentina – understandably regard these arguments as shameless special pleading to defend an uncompetitive industry at the cost of the consumers of the world. However, even the free traders subsidise – it is a matter of degree. The highest subsidy to farmers (1996–97) occurs in Switzerland – at nearly $35,000 per farmer annually; in Norway it is over $30,000; in Korea and Japan $23,000 (by comparison, the European Union paid the average farmer $17,000, the US, $15,000). In the advanced countries, three quarters of the value of rice production is government support (over-weighted by the extraordinary position of Japan), over half of milk production, a third of beef, veal and wheat.

All governments compromise in other ways on the question of free trade in agriculture. The US government, harried by congressmen from farming states, offered, for example, emergency compensation for low prices and drought relief in 1999, and was not at all averse to banning imports in 'anti-dumping' actions (afflicting, for example, lamb imports from New Zealand and Australia, sugar from Australia and elsewhere), to the cost of American consumers. But this is relatively slight compared to the obstinate durability of Europe's Common Agriculture Policy. The systems of subsidy invariably seem to accrue to the benefit of the largest farmers, dealers and food manufacturers – and certainly do not at all end the failure of small farmers and the drift from the land.

The bigger farmers are also going global, legally or not – German farmers move to Poland to farm, American farmers moved to Mexico and Central America, some British farmers to Hungary – in order to export back to the old home market. The question of what agricultural exports are 'Polish' or 'German', 'Mexican' or 'American' becomes obscure – or simply arbitrary.

Furthermore, while charges and counter-charges on cheating on trade rules thunder and echo across the Atlantic, it is developing-countries who have more substantive grievances on trade in general. The developed, it is said, forced the developing to open their markets while keeping their own still protected, particularly where developing country exporters are competitive – in unsubsidised agricultural goods, in textiles and clothing, shoes etc. One source estimates that developed country tariffs on manufacturing imports from developing countries are four times higher than imports from other developed countries (the UN Conference on Trade and Development calculates that with open markets in the developed countries the developing countries would be able to increase exports to the value of $700 billion by 2005). The developing countries complain also that they do not have the political muscle of the developed countries to prosecute their interests – within, for example, the WTO. Only with this can they combat additional means of US protectionism – banning imports on grounds of, for example, damaging the environment or not conforming to given labour standards.

Within the developed countries, other lobbies exercise a peculiar power, far greater than the size of the industry might suggest. American steel-makers are notorious in this respect. Those who purchase steel demand cheaper steel imports in order to be competitive in manufactured exports (and against manufactured imports). They complain through the American Institute for International Steel (AIIS) that the big steel corporations lobby and bribe Congress (and offer jobs to former government officials) to block cheaper imports, at a cost of $150 billion to American steel users – 'No other industry,' the AIIS report maintained, 'has so thoroughly fooled the American public into allowing its taking of their wealth and its stifling of free market competition' (*Financial Times*, 16 June 2000).

Trade is only the issue that receives most publicity. But the reform agenda, driven by the interests of the rival powers, is never restricted to this. It ranges widely and unpredictably – from the allocation of landing slots at Heathrow airport, subsidies to the aircraft industry, issues of what should be allowed to remain in the public sector, how Japan should organise its retail trade, the powers of German or French shareholders, the right of American farmers to use genetically modified seeds, and so on. Germany's state banks and state savings banks advance cheap loans, guaranteed by the government, giving them therefore a competitive advantage over foreign banks. This advantage should be eliminated in order to create, a favourite phrase, 'a level playing field'. Indeed, banking in many countries seems to attain something of the status once enjoyed by heavy industry as fundamental to national sovereignty – governments are dedicated to preventing them falling into foreign hands. Thus the Portuguese moved to block a Spanish takeover bid for the country's third-largest bank. The French warned off foreign bankers from making a bid for a major French bank (as a result, Deutsche Bank started opening retail branches in France). The British government expressed anxiety even at the takeover of one of the big four British banks by a supposedly British-controlled but Hong Kong-based bank, the Hong Kong and Shanghai Banking Corporation.

Despite the changed context, many governments remain enamoured with large companies, supposedly owned by their nationals. The French government has something of a reputation for blocking takeovers in 'strategic' industries, and as a result French companies have been able to make more bids for foreign companies abroad than foreign companies are able to buy companies operating in France. As a further result, French companies are denied the benefits of foreign management reforming and enhancing their competitive strength – to the loss of the French economy. In defence-related industries, the French government tried to prevent links with US companies (but failed where French private companies were concerned). The German Chancellor made half-hearted attempts to frustrate a bid by 'British' Vodafone for 'German' Mannesman – and failed.

Even in non-'strategic' industries, discreet government manipulation sometimes tries to exclude the foreigner. Thus the French supported a merger of French supermarket chains Carrefour and Promodés to keep out foreign rivals (and exclude, above all, the mighty Walmart of the US). The Italian government welcomed the bid by Olivetti for Telecom Italia to keep out the aliens, and the British government tried to ensure that Rover Group remained British by putting it in the hands of the unrelated British Aerospace (the attempt failed and Rover went to 'the Germans', BMW). The efforts are expensive and slightly risible since nationality has already become ambiguous – as we noted earlier, 60 per cent of the ownership of Nokia, supposedly a Finnish company, was vested in the US (although whether the owners were 'American' – whatever that equivocal term might mean – is not clear).

Foreign investment and management play a key role in the process of spreading the reform experience of other countries – as much French experience in the US as vice versa. It helps the shift away from national conglomerates to multinational specialised corporations. Despite efforts to discourage foreigners, by the end of the 1990s, a third of the stock of leading French companies was held by investors in the US and Britain, and some 40 per cent of the Milan stock exchange turnover. And despite the entertaining pretensions of government to protect the exclusive national identity of capital – the last remnants of the national capital project – the differences between foreign and national are becoming increasingly blurred.

Nonetheless, even in the prototype of economic fusion, the European Union, governments are far from relinquishing the contest for economic dominance (even if military dominance, the former aim of economic power, has almost disappeared). The rivalry is underpinned by the continuing inertia of spatial distributions, the geographical clustering that is the result of the long period of state domination and economically restrictive boundaries, as well as the continued persistence, as we have seen, of the social significance of nationality. This is equally true in North America, within a mainly single language area. John Helliwell (1998) shows that, seven years after the conclusion of the NAFTA, an average Canadian province is still 12 times more likely to trade goods, and 40 times more likely to trade services, with another Canadian province than with an American state (allowing for size and distance). Migrants are 100 times more likely to move within Canada than to the US. In a similar way, Americans still hold 90 per cent of their wealth in US-based firms (although this is to say nothing of where US-based firms undertook the bulk of their transactions); in Japan, the equivalent figure is 98 per cent. The national identification of capital by some important measures is still very much alive and well.

THE OPPOSITION

'Mark it down. This last great date of the Twentieth Century – November 30th, 1999 – the Battle of Seattle, the day the people got tired of having to work a second job while fighting off the collection agents and decided it was time the pie was shared with the people who baked it' – *Michael Moore's Newsletter*, 7 December 1999.

The ambivalence of government towards a reduction in the discretionary power to shape the domestic economy – in return for continued economic growth – fits the contradictory nature of its interests. As we have noted, on the one hand its claim on the vote and popular support requires that it be seen to possess power to shape the economic events vital for the material existence of its citizens; on the other, it needs to accommodate the influences of global markets to ensure employment and growth. Given the long history of institutionalised xenophobia that is the psychic underpinning of state sovereignty, the second imperative may well appear to the population as betraying the nation. The government also continues to have a need to escape responsibility by blaming the evil disposition of foreigners for whatever goes wrong.

It is therefore hardly surprising that 'globalisation' – whatever that slippery word means to people – has become a focus for opposition, even though, as we have seen, it is still limited in effect. Present ills are seen as unprecedented (that is, they did not occur under the old 'pre-global' order) and therefore should be blamed on whatever is new, and globalisation is the current fashion for the new. Since governments are also not averse to saying that they have been forced to unpopular courses of action, against their best instincts, the case that government and people are together victims of hostile foreigners attains some plausibility (so the attack on globalisation becomes a special version of the ancient sport of blaming foreigners). Popular opinion finds it easier to blame people and their deliberate intentions – as opposed to abstractions like world markets which lack 'intentions' – globalisation tends to be reduced to the actions of particular institutions, multinational corporations, the WTO, the IMF, the World Bank, or even particular individuals, like Georg Soros or Rupert Murdoch.

Some criticisms of the new world order involve issues of substance – that globalisation has increased poverty and income inequality, has led to a deterioration in the environment, a liquidation of cultures and the capacity of nations to be self-governing. Overall the case is that globalisation has shifted power from the popular majority to a minority of multinational corporations and international agencies.

Few of the charges can be made to stick, not least because globalisation itself is often used in a way too vague to establish its causal role. But the case, or different aspects of it, has fuelled, as we have seen, a new and impressive global opposition which is itself a remarkable accomplishment. It unites contradictory elements – from old-fashioned nationalists, defending the old protectionist war-making state to those who embrace globalisation but want to reshape its direction – from trade unionists opposing imports, governments defending the absolute prerogatives of sovereignty, to a multitude of environmentalists, to those who accurately identify the gross inequality of the system in its treatment of developing countries, to old fashioned right-wing populists like Ross Perot, Pat Buchanan or Sir James Goldsmith.

What can be said of the charges? Has globalisation increased world poverty? The numbers who are poor have increased and seem to be increasing, even though the proportion of the world's population that is poor is decreasing. The decline in the proportion is largely due to what has happened in the biggest countries – China, India, Indonesia etc. In the case of China, with a remarkable and sustained expansion, led by exports and an inflow of foreign capital, the changes have been dramatic – between 1987 and 1996, the number of Chinese living on one dollar a day declined by 93 million (or 30.7 per cent), and on two dollars a day by nearly 125 million (or 17 per cent). The economic crisis of 1997–98 in Southeast Asia increased the number of poor but without at all reversing the overall decline.

The great concentrations of poverty – in south Asia and Sub-Saharan Africa – have much worsened over the past two decades, but this can hardly be attributed to two measures of globalisation: greater external trade or the arrival of greater foreign capital. On the contrary, these two regions are marked out by the lack of integration in the world economy – in striking contrast to the position of China.

Has globalisation increased income inequality? Household income inequality at the global level is a hideously complicated matter to identify reliably, so people tend to rest content with inequality between countries (given the differences in population size, comparing China to, say, Belgium is an absurd exercise). Here the long-term picture is clear – a staggering increase in inequality. Pritchett (1997) calculates that in 1870, Britain and the US together had a per-capita income nine times that of the poorest countries of the world; in 1990, the US had an average per-capita income 45 times that of Chad or Ethiopia, the world's poorest. In 1870, the world's richest 17 countries had income per head two-and-a-half times that of the rest of the world; in 1990, four-and-a-half times.

In the immediate past, there seems also to have been increases in income inequality. Can they be attributed to greater interaction with the rest of the world? The former US presidential candidate Ross Perot certainly thought so when he said that NAFTA would lead to a 'great sucking sound' as jobs were pulled out of the US and into Mexico. An immense economic literature has grown up seeking to prove or disprove that, for example, US income inequality trends are caused by increases in imports from developing countries. The case cannot be established beyond dispute – particularly because American imports from the developing countries are still such a small share of the US economy.

The technical debate is remote from popular fears. Those fears are perhaps closer to the argument of Rodrik (1997), who says that globalisation extends the US labour market to include much of the rest of the world, and so the opportunities of American employers to use labour of different skills and to escape the social costs of employment. The result is, he says, increased burdens on employed workers, instability in earnings and hours, and reduced bargaining power. However, the effects are interwoven with a changed structure of the economy (whether related to globalisation or not) – increased temporary and part-time work, self-employment, more frequent job changes, more home working, greater opportunities and uncertainties. In fact, if true, it is a return to the earlier conditions of work, albeit at very much higher incomes than in the past. The shifts in the balance of class power over wages and conditions, it is argued, undermine what is seen as the post-Second World War bargain in which the workers conceded peace on the shop floor in return for security of pay.

In fact, so radical has been the increase in incomes in the developed countries that these have masked increases in inequality. The changes in developing countries are even more dramatic, since they start from a much lower base point. In the developing countries, the average expectation of life was possibly not much over 32 in 1950, but around 65 in the 1990s. And that change is for a vastly increased total population. Infant mortality figures for the under-fives in low-income countries fell from 175 in 1980 to 113 in 1996 (and in middle income countries from 85 to 43).

In sum, then, on the income figures, poverty has increased, most alarmingly in Africa; income inequality has increased in the developed countries and between countries. But still consumption continues to improve sufficiently for most measures of demographic mass welfare to improve. There are some alarming exceptions in the countries of the former Soviet Union and parts of Sub-Saharan Africa (the World Health Organisation estimates life expectancy in Zambia at 30.3; in Malawi at 29.4; in Niger at 29.1; in Sierra Leone at 25.9).

But the links to globalisation – increased trade and capital movements – are not at all clear. The evidence rather suggests that where developing countries could and did 'globalise', they were able to reduce poverty far more rapidly than where they could not – or chose not to. Indeed, in the most robust case globalisation seems to benefit the poor most in low stages of development and to do so without increasing inequality; crises do not afflict the poor disproportionately (Dollar and Kraay 2000).

On the other contentions, the evidence is similarly miserably inconclusive. In some parts of the world the environment has drastically deteriorated as the result of the expansion in manufactured output and the transport to deliver it in trade. The big industrial cities of China, India or Brazil are notorious examples of the results. However, in the cities of the developed countries there has been a fairly continuous improvement in the quality of air, watercourses and soil. In the worst cases, public exposure – particularly by NGOs – is slowly having some effect in cleaning up polluting processes or restoring the natural habitat. There are many disasters still to come in the struggle to achieve a clean environment, but there does not seem an alternative route to tackle the issues without denying (if anyone had the power so to deny) the developing countries the same rights to develop as the developed.

The arrival of modern manufacturing in much of the world is threatening environments – but in the best cases it is also leading to a massive improvement in living conditions and the productivity of workers and their families. The factory conditions are frequently appalling, but allow improvements that would formerly have been thought utopian. Furthermore, contrary to the position of, say, European factory conditions in the nineteenth century, there are now strong forces campaigning to improve conditions – as the work of NGOs in, for example, Nike shoe factories in Korea and Indonesia demonstrate. That campaign has led to a transformation in the attitude of the company itself – and the beginnings of a wider change in public perception of what is tolerable. What would be absurd is to suggest an end to manufacturing – and to global trade – in order to curb bad conditions and wages. That would be suicidal.

Are cultures under threat from globalisation? There seem to be as many arguments for as against on this. On the one hand, the appearance of MacDonalds hamburger restaurants in many cities, the spread of Coca Cola or Pepsi Cola, seen as the symbols of a threat to local cultures, can equally be seen as the forces of progress – in terms of speed and cleanliness of provision – or as forces stimulating the redevelopment of local cuisine as a primary means to beat off the competition (for an example, see Chase 1994: 73–86, on the effect of MacDonald's on Istanbul's cooking). If economic fusion allows and may even promote political fission, it may equally promote cultural variety, new cultures with new territorial units. At present, there seems no more threat involved in the spread of MacDonald's than there is in the dispersal of Chinese or Thai or Korean restaurants – neither politics nor cultural homogenisation follow from adventurous eating habits.

There are many more problems attached to a global order administered by national states than can be examined here. One has already been touched upon – the escape from local taxation of mobile factors, individuals or companies. The implicit threat is that governments will become dependent on the least mobile elements of the citizenry, the mass of the local workforce, the poorest, allowing the richest and most mobile to escape to whatever haven offers the lowest tax burden; as a result, the people left behind have an even stronger incentive to emigrate to the shadow economy at home. The issue relates to government efforts to alleviate poverty and achieve greater measures of equality through the redistribution of income from rich to poor. Governments have increased the scope of collaboration with each other, forced offshore financial centres towards greater transparency, but they have been most reluctant to concede the measure of sovereignty which might be required to create global fiscal agencies to detect and track income flows. Sooner or later, however, some such system will be needed if mobile sources of tax are to be captured. But this is no argument for trying to restore a world of closed national economies just for the convenience of government revenue raising – and sacrificing the possibilities of much greater growth in wealth as a result.

Finally, there are the larger issues of democratic self-government implicit in the undermining of sovereignty. At the moment, the immense increase in participation, embodied in the work of NGOs, is not an alternative to the old theory of democracy, majority rule within one territorial unit. The NGOs are self-appointed, select their own agenda and, provided that they can raise the means to finance themselves, choose their own campaigns. They have become a vital element in shaping and educating opinion, in monitoring and evaluating what happens, but there is no assurance that their agenda reflects the priorities of majorities. Nonetheless, the NGOs, with all their internal differences, constitute not only all that is left of a fundamental critique of modern society, but also the beginnings of a global political forum that reaches well beyond the conventional circle of world power and influence. They are an embodiment of a new global civil society with growing power to influence events and institutions. The electorates of the old national states may still go through the procedures of majority voting – albeit with a decline in mass political involvement and the membership of political parties – but they have little power of expression at a global level. For the moment, the NGOs almost alone carry that responsibility and are among the few organisations which link a base in the population to world events.

Has the new global order disenfranchised the population? Power has rarely been vested in majorities, and democracy is a very recent phenomenon in most parts of the world. The overall drift of events seems to be towards greater democratisation, not away from a past state of better representation. The deprivation of power, if such it is, is not of electorates but of states few of which were democratic in the past. The new international regulatory authorities – the WTO, IMF (like the World Bank, primarily a funding organisation) – wield relatively little power compared to the scale of world markets, and are directly under the control of governments, so they can hardly be seen as independent sources of action or influence in the world. They are creatures of the most powerful national governments rather than having a life of their own.

In sum, it seems, the world has more popular participation today than ever before. This, however, is not at all the same as the power to control markets. Here the problem is not that one group of players – whether international agencies or multinational corporations – has the power to direct the world economy in its own interest, but that there is ultimately no way of controlling the outcome of markets except by abolishing them. Even if this were remotely feasible, it raises problems of a greater order of magnitude.

THE STATE

a perfection of planned layout is achieved only by institutions on the point of collapse

C. Northcote Parkinson 1957: 60

States may be following the old routine by which an institution falls into ruin just as it becomes complete. In the meantime, nevertheless, States remain so dominant that anyone who dreams of a Stateless world seems a heedless visionary

Charles Tilly 1990: 4

The state remains of decisive importance in the world economy, both as an economic agent in its own right, as vital in the administration and management of the territorial units of the world, and indeed as the instrument – through international negotiation and agreement – of global integration. However, patterns of regulation, sub- and supranational, official and unofficial, already snare governments in webs of obligation, collaboration and duty far beyond those owed to their population. Yet the world talk – newspapers, broadcasts, conferences – still pre-eminently concerns the interests of states (even if disguised in the clothing of countries or nations), and individuals are predominantly shaped by one national identity, embodying a relationship to one state.

There are, of course, many variations. The nature of different states reveals the layered history of the modern world. The richest states are most embedded in, most constrained by, the global networks of which they are a part. There are still systemic rivalries, but for the richest not now – leaving aside the US – pre-eminently in war-making capacity, but rather relative economic standing.

Where the old system of competing national sovereignties still seems basically intact is among the leading developing countries – China, India, Egypt and so on. The old agenda of state rivalry persists: in war-making capacity; in the prickly defence of the absolute rights of sovereignty; even in the continued ferocious armed claims to territory, at home or abroad. However, even here, the contest has become partly detached from the old agenda of the national capital project. It is clear that economic growth depends upon an open economy; and economic closure is disastrous. As a result, the webs of international collaboration and obligation overlay the old sovereignties. Regional trade federations – ASEAN, Mercosur – bind the smaller powers into quasi-economic federations.

Yet further out from the core zones, the world of international integration seems a fantasy. In parts of Sub-Saharan Africa – as in Colombia and Algeria – states are only imperfectly realised, constantly fading into competing factions, into mutual slaughter. In the old Congo, rival African foreign powers contest for territory and raw materials as fiercely as the old imperialist powers once competed to carve out enclaves in China or Africa. Sovereignty here is still an aspiration, a hoped-for future rather than a relic of the past. What the still unrevised history books approvingly record as 'nation-building' or 'state-building' (bludgeoning the opposition into obedience) still remains to be accomplished.

Yet states, even the best organised, are everywhere ambivalent, wobbling between accepting and resisting integration. Even where much of the priority that used to be attached to the old war-making state project has gone, some continue to oblige their young men (and sometimes now young women) to do a period of service in the armed forces – to 'educate young men in what is needed for the nation' as the German government recently put it. Hardly anyone now remembers why it is the army which is supposed to instil this peculiar devotion; why not agricultural work? The ethic and the reality have come apart, and it will take a long time for a new reality to create an ethic anything like as strong as the old one.

THE WAR-MAKING STATE

> Capitalist society is unthinkable without armaments, and it is unthinkable without war
>
> Nicolai Bukharin 1917/1972: 169

> At last, the time has come when serious and lasting war must disappear completely among the human elite
>
> Auguste Comte IV 1842: 239

> the more completely capitalist, the structure and attitude of a nation, the more pacifist – and the more prone to count the costs of war – we observe it to be
>
> Joseph Schumpeter 1943/1994: 28–29

> Despite confusion and uncertainty, it seems just possible to glimpse the emerging outline of a world without war
>
> John Keegan 1993: 58

The origins of the modern state and of sovereignty lie in a war-making system, and the unwinding of that system has removed the old systemic necessities – creating new ones. Yet governments seem to cling to many of the elements of the old agenda, even while other signs reveal decisive change.

The decline in defence spending

At a global level, the decline in military spending – at least in declared official terms – is small and uncertain, but nonetheless taking place. Between 1985 and 1990, spending fell by about 1.3 per cent (of gross world product) annually, and in the following decade by 1.2 per cent. By 1996, the world total – $811 billion – was the lowest since 1966 (and 40 per cent below the peak spending year of 1987). Employment in arms manufacture is said to have declined from 17.5 million in 1987 to 11.1 million in 1995.

There was great variation: 90 governments cut spending in the 1990s, 40 maintained or increased it. In the case of the largest military power, the US, with some 35 per cent of the world total, the decline was more dramatic. For the Europeans, the decline was even sharper – by 5 per cent per year over the past five years – increasing their dependence on the US. But elsewhere, as we have seen, regional arms races persisted vigorously – as in South and East Asia, in the Middle East.

Disarmament

The proliferation of modern weapons, particularly nuclear ones, also continued. Thirty-five non-NATO members acquired missiles, 18 of them with the capacity to install nuclear, biological or chemical warheads. However, the disarmament of the two leading military powers more than offset this in terms of the world's stock of weaponry. The US claimed that its stockpile of usable weapons was cut between the early 1960s and 1997 by 70 per cent (with a further 9 per cent cut scheduled by 2001, and 9 per cent again by 2003). The cuts in the larger old Soviet stockpile were bigger to reach the same size of reserves as the American. Thus the world process is not simply one of disarmament, but one of a declining concentration of weaponry, and increasing dispersal. Furthermore, arms spending continues to be needed to upgrade weapons systems, their accuracy and lethal capacity, regardless of shrinking numbers. Technologies continue to be transformed and require continual upgrading of stocks – for example, currently in remote-sensing or precision-guided weaponry, new systems of communication and networking etc. The world remains a dangerous place.

Collaboration

We have noted earlier in the context of Europe's past traditions, the exceptional character of the Cold War in sustaining NATO (and to a lesser extent the Warsaw Pact) as military federations, with a single command structure and common weapons systems. Military interventions of the old style continue – where a single power acts in pursuit of what are thought of as national interests – but decreasingly so. The trend is towards collaborative action in the supposed interest of 'the international community'. As we have seen, the decline in military spending entails that collaboration often depends on US military might – 13 governments participated in the NATO bombing of Serbia, but 70 per cent of the firepower was American. In the old order this would have been seen as action by Washington under the disguise of a collaborative alliance; in the new, the alliance is real enough and Washington cannot act without it. More commonly, collaboration takes place under UN auspices – the most extreme form of the use of national forces for completely 'non-national' purposes. Some of the more old-style modern states are also important contributors to global military collaboration, as in the case of India.

The contraction in defence spending enforces new types of discipline. It leads to increased concentration in a handful of large defence corporations – in the US case, Lockheed Martin, Boeing, Raytheon, Northrup Grumman (with a reduction in employment from the 3.9 million of 1987 to 2.1 million 11 years later). Of the leading 20 defence corporations in the world, 11 are American (making two thirds of the combined revenues of the 20), four French, two British, with one each in Germany, Italy and Japan. The decline in spending forces companies both to export (in an industry where supply is traditionally limited to one buyer and under strict controls) and to collaborate with companies in other countries. Governments have long employed arms supplies to bind political allies in dependence, but now, arms are used to try to tie buyers to one supply – that is simply as ordinary civil exports. There are paradoxical leftovers of the old agenda – a third of British export credit is employed to finance arms exports, which constitute under 2 per cent of British exports.

Governments which anticipate large weapon requirements usually insist on the creation of local manufacturing capacity, and this further intensifies international collaboration and dispersal. Collaboration is also spread through technical co-operation, licensing, co-development to defray the extraordinary costs, subcontracting, joint ventures and minority stakes on foreign companies. Defence production is thus dragged from its secretive national origins into the daylight of normal civil production through international networks of supply. Even in the case of the US, with some of the more strict limits on international collaboration, budgetary pressure forces collaboration – for example Lockheed Martin licenses South Korean companies to manufacture the F-16 aircraft, developing other collaborative manufacturing sources in Taiwan, Australia, Russia, Argentina and Europe. As we have seen, however, the efforts of the Pentagon to retain core manufacturing in the US (and in the hands of unequivocally American nationals) constrains the working out of the new market logic and accordingly raises costs, which in turn collides with the need to stay within lowered budgets. One short-term remedy is to defeat the spirit if not the letter of the law. The need to keep weapons purchases in the hands of Americans is met in foreign-owned companies by creating proxy boards of management composed of US nationals, approved by the Pentagon, and restricting the role of foreign managers. Other lesser powers cannot afford to be so squeamish and rely on imports, often from the US. Europe imports six times as much weaponry from the US as it is allowed to export to the US, which in turn encourages the Europeans to seek to develop their own capacity and protect it. US companies then press Washington to open the US weapons market to European imports in order to offset the European tendency to close its markets to US imports – and allow US companies to set up capacity in Europe to supply the Europeans. Thus the market mechanisms – along with the budgetary pressures on governments – subvert the old agenda of national self-sufficiency in weaponry manufacture. In the end, arms production will also follow the logic of globalisation.

In Europe itself, the old conditioned reflexes of national power inhibit collaboration. Private weapons-manufacturing companies in Britain and Germany find it difficult to collaborate with state-owned companies in France. Paris identifies the political interest of Europe as pursuing a defence programme independently of the more advanced Americans. Market logic goes in the opposite direction, in favour of transatlantic collaboration rather than duplicating capacity – as with Britain's GEC or British Aerospace or Germany's Dasa-Daimler (and indeed the French private corporation Thomson, in alliance with US Raytheon). Again, the development of international specialisation – and thus interdependence – is in continual collision with the old orthodoxies of national military independence.

Commercialisation

Declining budgets force outsourcing to secure economies of scale and thus a global arms industry supplying many buyers rather than simply one national power. Weaponry is thus becoming only another form of commercial production. In an analogous way, the decline in publicly maintained armed forces is more than matched by the growth in private security forces for civil policing.

The defence industries of North America and Europe may be privatised and commercialised, but in a number of important developing countries – where, at least on the surface, it seems that the old nationally independent defence agenda remains intact – armed forces themselves are partially privatised. Consider the case of China with, in employment terms, the largest defence manufacturing sector in the world (employing perhaps three million in over one thousand factories). Much of the defence industries also manufacture goods for the civil markets to offset high costs (as occurred, as we noted earlier, in the old Soviet Union). The civil share in defence-industry output has grown continuously through the period of reform, from under 10 per cent of total output in 1979 to over 76 per cent by 1995 (Berthélemy and Deger 1995: 10). Furthermore, the armed forces sponsor their own complex of commercial companies – known as 'bureaucratic entrepreneurship' – to offset reductions in public military spending (and provide retirement jobs for ex-servicemen). At its peak, the army operated possibly 20,000 enterprises, some among the largest in the country: China Northern Industries Corporation (Norinco); China State Shipbuilding Corporation (CSTC); China Electronic Import–Export Corporation (Chinatrex); China Nuclear Energy Industries Corporation; China Great Wall Industrial Corporation; China National Aero-Technology Import–Export Corporation (CATIC); China Poly Group; Xinxing Corporation; and many others. It is estimated that the military-owned industries contributed to the costs of the armed forces in the early 1990s some two to three times the official defence budget. The government became aware of the anomaly – armed forces, supposedly the instrument of national policy, were financing themselves independently of their supposed masters in government, from their own market activities (albeit with a privileged political, and therefore financial, position). In mid-1998, the armed forces were ordered to dispose of these operations. But there is no evidence of a major unloading of these companies, nor a commensurate increase in the defence budget to make up for the loss of the enterprises (nor a radical cut in the scale of armed forces to compensate for a drastic reduction in income).

A parallel phenomenon occurs in Indonesia, again to make up for declining defence spending. Here, foundations, sponsored and controlled by different armed services, operate enterprises in the civilian economy. In this way, army groups operate companies in hotels, property, plantations, fisheries, banks, airlines, timber, construction, pharmaceutical products, metals, tourism and insurance (with a total asset value in 1995, it is said, of $8 billion). The navy – with some 70 companies – operates trading co-operatives, petrochemicals, shipping, vehicle imports, banking and films, and the airforce runs operations in banking, air cargo, air services and trade. These business empires are encouraged by military and political patronage and by privileged access to finance and raw materials; the interests were interwoven with those, in the old regime, of the Suharto family, with state corporations and other private groups. Similar instances have been noted in Thailand and Pakistan. Thus, if, in the English proverb, he who pays the piper calls the tune, in these cases the armed forces become both piper and patron.

Armies as commercial enterprises (devoted not to fighting as mercenaries but to ordinary commercial transactions, with a sideline in creating war capacity) are far removed from the old national war-making state or the national capital project. The phenomenon is close to what we identified in the discussion of Russia as the rent-seeking state, the use of public privilege to make private profits – or a blurring of the distinction. Corruption replaces the old prickly aggressiveness of the sovereign state.

Thus, despite the appearance of a third world still trapped in the old order of competing militarised states, the old agenda has already been subverted. This

has forced both integration, collaboration and a sapping of military preparedness even in those areas where many of the old issues seem to remain as dangerous
and intractable as ever. The technology of warfare today makes fighting more
destructive than ever before, and if local wars persist – as in the case of the
Iraq–Iran War – the scale of devastation is extreme. But the possibility of world
war grows increasingly remote, and with it the systemic imperatives of war-
making states.

THE LAST FRONTIERS?

The measures of partial integration of the world economy seem yet to affect the
workers of the world. Indeed, in the last third of the twentieth century, when
globalisation accelerated, the legal isolation of national populations seemed to
grow more extreme. The pressures against this have been significant. Each time
part of the world economy booms, the geographical redistribution of part of the
world's workers cannot be contained. In the long American boom of the 1990s,
a continued inflow of legal and illegal workers was required to support the growth
of the economy, and yet at the same time border controls became very much
more intensive, intimidating and costly. Domestic populations that publicly grieve
for disasters in faraway places tolerate a condition of semi-warfare along the
borders, with deaths and disabilities inflicted on those foolish enough to try to
cross without the requisite papers.

The warfare against unskilled illegal migrants co-exists with increasing trans-
border movement of the skilled, professional and some legal unskilled. There
are businessmen, consultants and the executives of international companies and
agencies (with their families, which settle where a parent is sent to work); selected
classes of skilled (medical doctors, nurses, university teachers, airline pilots, software programmers); contract workers (maids, seamen, construction and shop
workers); temporary and seasonal workers (in agriculture, in construction);
cross-border commuters (especially between Mexico and the US, or Poland and
Germany). Finally there are the rising numbers of refugees, driven out by the
implosion of one or other state. It is hardly to be wondered that government
claims that immigration has finally ceased are so vividly contradicted by the
growing cosmopolitanism of the great cities of North America, Japan and Europe
and the reduction in some areas of the original native population to a minority
(for example Los Angeles County in the coming decade; Texas and California
by 2020).

The movement of people seems a clear measure of globalisation, but it
conceals more radical changes. Take, for example, California's Silicon Valley, the

symbol of America's technical superiority. More than a third of the labourforce are Asian immigrants (as opposed to US-born Asians), and they retain important links with their countries of origin – both in terms of the supply of hardware components and software as well as of technical staff. Indeed, the Valley is rather more the centre of a global network than an American phenomenon. Its technical position cannot not be separated from that global role and reduced simply to the US. Border controls on the movement of parts, people, finance or ideas would be exceptionally damaging.

Yet governments seem everywhere to strengthen the fortifications against newcomers, so much so that it seems inconceivable that they will go into reverse, let alone return to the position in most countries before the First World War, with virtually universal freedom to move and work. The result of the controls is the creation of a major global economic sector, those facilitating illegal movement – from those recruiting in the source areas to those placing workers in the destinations, the financiers and brokers, providers of transit papers and false passports, of guides and transport, of safe houses and food supplies, and so on. Furthermore, so tight are the controls on borders now that it is virtually impossible for genuine refugees to gain admission to a country except illegally. The industry has many patrons, is truly global, and in addition facilitates some of the worst kinds of abuses – in the trafficking of women and children, of slave labour, of narcotics, arms and stolen goods.

Thus globalisation is in practice already operating in the labour market, even if possibly half the international movement of workers is clandestine. Governments have so far managed to live with the contradiction – the need, on the one hand, for a continuing flow of workers into and out of the economy and, on the other, the need to ensure a clearly demarcated settled population as the foundation of sovereignty. But there are signs that the contradiction is going to become insupportable. The first indication of the breakdown is the crumbling of the existing immigration control system – led by the move in the US to recruit scarce skilled labour (particularly software programmers for Silicon Valley). Canada and Australia have moved in parallel. Singapore, Korea and Japan have also shifted to active recruitment. Finally, Germany, Britain, Ireland and other European countries reversed what seemed policies cast in concrete and joined the competition. However, governments would not trust employers to recruit the workers they required. Governments retain the right to choose the immigrants on the basis of estimated demand for workers – even though governments no longer claim to be able to predict any other elements of the modern economy. And it concerns only categories of scarce skills, with the overt purpose of fishing for the best talents in developing countries. However, other factors are pushing for a more generalised relaxation of controls on the migration of the unskilled, for an ending of the system of international apartheid where the skilled are free to move, the unskilled, like medieval serfs, are tied to the soil of the place where they were born.

On the question of ageing, the developed countries – followed shortly by China and the NICs – face a set of intractable economic problems arising from the prospect of a declining size of national population, a more rapid decline in the number of workers and an increasing number of aged people, many of whom are living far longer than ever before. Implicitly, the world workforce is being redistributed away from the developed countries towards the developing. Thus, in the last 15 years of the twentieth century, the developed countries increased their population by about 14 per cent, compared to an equivalent figure in developing countries of 103 per cent; the working population (aged 15–65) increased by 6 and 130 per cent; and the young population (aged 20-40) by minus 10 per cent and 108 per cent. Over the next half century, those aged 60 or more will increase from around 600 million to two billion.

There are already grave shortages of unskilled workers and domestic craftsmen in developed countries. It is seen most clearly in recruitment to hospitals, public transport, hotels and restaurants, agriculture, construction, home services, childcare and so on. Indeed the caring services, particularly for the aged and disabled, in many developed countries are already staffed by first-generation immigrants.

The simple numbers of people available understate the problem. Simultaneously, the workers of the developed countries are working less. Education and training take an increasing proportion of working life. Early retirement shortens the working life, and older workers find it increasingly difficult to stay in work (and employers avoid the additional costs of older workers, particularly in manufacturing). The working year and week have contracted – in 1900, the average British worker worked 2700 hours annually; in the 1990s between 1400 and 1800. The average worker now spends only half his or her life in work. Without counteracting changes, OECD estimates that the change in the ratio of the pensioned to those of working age will, by 2040, cut living standards by 23 per cent in Japan, by 18 per cent in Europe, and by 10 per cent in the US.

In a single world economy, none of this would matter any more than within a country – the ageing of the inhabitants of one locality while those of another remain young is not a matter of any particular concern. But while each government is concerned only to manage its national territory and the human resources it possesses, the issue becomes a severe problem. Governments try numerous remedies. For example, some have extended the age of retirement (or abolished it) or offered incentives to non-working women to enter the workforce but without significant results. The aged are unwilling to work at the wage on offer, and employers unwilling to invest to ensure that productivity does not fall by employing the elderly. Automation offers another escape – and the Japanese have put most resources into robotics. But this affects only one range of activity (pre-eminently routine manufacturing), and is expensive. Ageing increases the demand for labour-intensive services (particularly in caring and nursing), and it is difficult to imagine that automation would either substitute for human caring or be affordable for the majority.

The shortage of young workers is likely to affect manufacturing most directly, accelerating the process of the relocation of capacity to where the workers are, in developing countries. But the problems do not stop here – consider recruitment to the armed forces, the heart of the old state. A shortage of workers will bid up the price of work, making it impossibly expensive to use scarce workers in the military. It is possible here that automation – as with pilotless aircraft and precision weaponry – will radically reduce the number of troops required. But the occupation of territory still requires substantial manpower. Perhaps the developed countries will return to the mercenary armies of history, recruited in developing countries or, as with current UN missions, will come to rely increasingly on the armies of the developing countries. In any event, the outcome seems to doom much of what is left of the old war-making state, the link between mass military recruitment of citizens and the foundations of sovereignty.

Governments have yet to explore in any depth the possibilities of the aged retiring to developing countries, but it is to be expected that private developers will become engaged here. At the moment, US insurance companies do allow cover to be extended to Americans retiring in Mexico or Central America. A Japanese scheme to develop in developing countries 'silver cities', colonies of aged Japanese, foundered, it seems, because of the unwillingness of the aged to live too far from families and friends. But with a further cheapening of air fares (and reduction in travel time), this might become more feasible, although the costs are likely to make it prohibitive for the majority of the elderly.

None of this touches on the problem that has received most attention – the decline in the workforce relative to the pensioned. In Germany, one of the more extreme cases, those aged 65 or more are projected to become equal to half the active population over the next three decades – put crudely, two workers will be required to support one elderly dependent. The cost of keeping benefits to the aged stable is expected to increase from 19 to 28 per cent of the average wage, and of health and welfare contributions from 14 to 23 per cent, or a total deduction from the average wage of 51 per cent. It is little wonder that the debate surrounding social security and pensions is becoming so fierce and insoluble.

Could relaxed immigration controls offset the decline in the size of the labourforce? It would seem, on its own, unlikely, although it might be a contribution to a remedy. Take one of the more extreme cases: for the population of Germany to be kept stable in the first half of this century it would need, on present UN projections, immigration of the order of 487,000 annually, and for the European Union 1.6 million annually. But to keep the ratio of pensioners to workers stable would need immigration of 3.6 million per year, and 13.5 million annually for the European Union. As proportions these are not impossible, but as political options, in the current climate of opinion, they seem unfeasible – even if such numbers can be found outside Europe and induced to migrate annually. Furthermore, the calculations cannot accommodate future unanticipated changes in the structure of the labour market and therefore other unexpected shortages.

A greater problem faces governments trying accurately to identify the need for workers. It is agreed generally that it cannot be done with any reliability. The labour market is likely to work most inefficiently if it remains a government pre-rogative to decide who is to work and who not. The argument is thus about the free movement of workers to respond to job opportunities, rather than the widening of government recruitment efforts. Without controls, not only can companies recruit and workers respond to vacancies without the immense inefficiencies and costs of bureaucratic controls, but also workers can freely return home as they wish – without having to choose between the stark alternatives of staying at home or permanent exile. Then some combination of increased immigration of workers, increased emigration of the aged, increased automation and alternative financial bases for pension plans might offer some hope of effective remedies.

Liberalising world trade in services

Services have become the basic activity of the modern economy, with manu-facturing tending to follow agriculture and mining into relative insignificance. Unlike the arms-length relationship between buyer and seller in commodity trade, trade in many services requires the seller to move to the buyer or vice versa – in home visits by doctors, the first; in tourism, the second. Satellite technology is easing some of these requirements – software programmers in Bangalore work for clients in California; Hollywood's Walt Disney cartoons are drawn in Manila. But this is still limited; more commonly, providers or consumers of services internationally must cross borders, and this has implications for international migration. Many services cannot be relocated elsewhere – as was once noted, the dustbins of Munich cannot be emptied in Istanbul.

In the Uruguay Round of trade talks, under what used to be GATT, internationally tradeable services were for the first time considered. The US representatives pressed the leading developing countries to liberalise their imports from the US of banking, insurance, shipping and computer technology – that is, pressed for American managers and experts in these fields to set up operations and work in developing countries. The response was that this was possible, provided the developed countries in turn liberalised their imports of services from developing countries in those areas where they were strong – in effect, allowing service companies and workers to enter countries for work in, for example, cleaning and hospital services, construction, hotels and restaurants, retail and wholesale trade. The issue was unresolved and passed on to GATT's successor, the WTO.

The pressure here is in terms of costs. In developed countries, the continuing upgrading of the educational level of the workforce leaves whole sectors of the economy without staff – the grave shortage of unskilled labour mentioned earlier. The advance of average wages makes it increasingly expensive to provide basic and other labour-intensive services, a process for reasons already mentioned which will be greatly exaggerated by the ageing of the population.

On the model of the liberalisation of commodity trade, this would imply that countries would move towards opening opportunities for such services to global tendering – for contracts, for example, to clean London's streets, operate the hospital laundries of New York, to build highways and bridges. Such arrangements already exist for offshore activities – for construction work in the Middle East, to staff international shipping or free-trade zones. Thus the technology to organise such contract labour is already in place for major projects. The only obstacle is the commitment of governments in developed countries to immigration controls.

If these two factors – ageing on the one hand, the expansion of tradeable services on the other – can force a change in immigration controls, then there would be yet another important positive outcome. The flow of worker remittances from the developed to the developing countries could become economically significant as a means to speed development and the reduction of poverty in the rest of the world. More important still with free movement, to come and to go, the transfer of skills and experience could be much enhanced, in turn accelerating development in the developing countries.

EVENTS AND MEANING

> Wittgenstein ... imagined some leaves blown about by the wind and saying, 'Now I'll go this way ... now I'll go that way', as the wind blew them
>
> G. E. M. Anscombe 1957: 6

> theory is always proposing hypotheses of such a degree of fineness that data cannot seriously test them, verify them or improve them ... The result is that we pretend to

answer questions far beyond the capacity of our observational material to provide credible and reliable evidence. Having gone so far, we find ourselves forced to pretend to believe the answer we get

Robert Solow 1993: 47

This account has described, from a particular perspective, a selection of historical events to illustrate a theme, but the events only make sense as part of intellectual history, the account of ideas, theories, policies, ideologies: the reasons for, the reaction to and interpretation of those events. The story is of the creation of a system, within which each fashioned political entity carved out, created and dominated a peculiar national economy. Driven by the needs of systemic warfare, states created the means to raise the resources to wage war, and in doing so also created not only the centralised structures of power, a centralised morality that superseded other systems of morality (and concealed the immorality of the state itself), but a national society, a nation, a culture and language, an entity symbolised in a selection from the cultural lumber of preceding peoples (and superseding or contradicting alternative symbols of identity). That process created minorities as political entities, to be 'homogenised' by force, driven out or liquidated. It was as much an intellectual exercise as anything else – and the decline of the state is as much a decline of an ideology as an actual diminution of public authority.

The process – the rise to dominance of the national state – affected each branch of concern with the central preoccupations of society. Take, for example, the evolution of that social concern with the relationship between the state and the economy, economics. By the standards of social science, the subject has developed with unusual rigour, a rigour purchased at the cost of any relationship to history – or indeed society. Economists are thus the 'innocents' of the social sciences, reflecting unreflectively the predominant or emerging concerns of the state with an uncritical simplicity that is normally clouded with the richness of reality. The model is assumed to be valid regardless of time and place, and history must therefore be excluded – in the movement from mercantilism, the open doctrine of the primacy of state interests; to classical economics, paralleling the free-trade era – and cosmopolitanism – of the period of British world dominance; to the return to mercantilism in the inter-war years, the assumed predominance of states and policy over markets, embodied most vividly in the new branch of the economics of development; to neo-classical economics and the return – on a much grander scale – of the open global economy. These intellectually wrenching changes – from one position to, apparently, its diametric opposite – have been achieved with astonishingly little self-consciousness, and few lessons learned about the sociology of economic knowledge.

A quite contrasting intellectual tradition, only touched upon here, is in military theory, the tactics and strategy of waging war, and more important, of the social and economic preconditions of waging war. We earlier underlined the contrast between the development of armies in the seventeenth century as military machines composed of paid and well-armed drilled mercenaries and professionals (as in the succeeding cases of Sweden, Russia and, most famously, Prussia), or as a citizen army of dedicated believers, with a commitment (as in the English Civil War) to a religious position or passionate loyalty to a secular state (as in the American War of Independence). In the second case, the relationship to civil society and the economy was transformed, and the constraints on war-making capacity immensely relieved. In Napoleon, the two threads came together, and it was Clausewitz's genius to draw out the implications of this – a committed war-making nation, willing to make any sacrifice in the cause of national interests. Industrialisation and the militarised organisation of society preoccupied the century that followed, culminating in the melancholy grandeur of the First World War, supposedly the first total war. There was more to come – the further militarised organisation of the civil economy in time of peace, for inter-war Germany and after the Second World War for the Soviet Union. With the benefit of hindsight, we can see that in the post-war period the Soviet Union far overshot the mark; the world was already being turned in a quite different direction, away from total war and back to the small professional army, away from the simplicities of national interests to the collaboration of the 'international community'.

However, much the most dramatic transitions occurred in politics. There the phases of state policy are rarely the result of intellectual conviction, more often simply the culmination of pragmatic adjustments to what are seen as necessities or 'common sense'. Theory catches up after events, rather than leading them. It is this that produced the paradoxes – that in the Europe of the nineteenth century it was the right-wing defenders of established society who rejoiced in a powerful state and rejected the market; the left-wing Liberal and socialist who called for free trade or the subordination of the state to civil society (or the working class). In the inter-war years of the twentieth century, both became committed to state power, to planning and large public sectors, doctrines described as corporatism on one side of politics, socialism on the other. Politics was the prime mover of states, not economics or markets. The statist orthodoxy became almost complete in the organisation of the war economies of the Second World War and as a model was bequeathed to the developing countries. The state, not private business, was to develop the new nations – until, from the 1970s, the whole intellectual apparatus began to crumble.

All the utopian schemes of the nineteenth century were eaten away by the rising power of the state. The agitators on the Left became actors, speaking lines impelled by systemic necessities of the state system while believing that they were the voices of liberation. The anarchists were thus correct. But in opposing the state per se, they rendered themselves irrelevant to events. The Marxists, social democratic and Communist, chose to use the state, but in doing so, became captive to it and to the systemic logic which governed its reactions. Between the options of irrelevance and being captive there seemed little room to manoeuvre until the shift towards the weakening of the state, the liberation of society from the terrible thraldom of the war economy and the old state system.

Marx was a great centraliser, and in that respect is one of the prophets of the centralised national state, even if he married that conception to its opposite, universal self-liberation. He also produced the idea, as fantastic as that of Hegel's notion of the unseen Spirit of Reason creating a perfect world, that it was businessmen who, also unseen, directed the state. Yet capital was only one of the raw materials of state action. In this error, he failed to see that the systemic order of states was, in his terms, a world ruling class, extending its rule ultimately to all corners of the world. Like his ruling classes, its role was initially immensely productive in forcing the accumulation of capital, albeit constrained to a national basis. Indeed, without the active role of the state it is difficult to see how the modern world with its extraordinary levels of productivity – and its capacity to feed vastly more people than ever before – could have been created. The process involved, as we have seen, regimes of extraordinary oppression and a continuing story of revolts, revolutions, executions and prisons. But by the twentieth century, the state system's central drive to destruction begins to overtake its capacity to force the growth of the economy – 40 years of Cold War with a world teetering on the brink of nuclear self-destruction is the most vivid index of the failure of the old order. In Marx's classic phrase, the old ruling class of states had become a 'fetter on production', a source of destruction rather than growth. It is doubtful if unrestricted markets could do worse in running the world than the states of the First and Second World Wars.

Even so, in a world of combined and uneven development, the state project continued temporarily to have an important role in one part of the world. States in some of the developing countries were still able for a time to persist in accelerated accumulation on a national basis. That role is now, however, increasingly exhausted, and the state in its old form emerges as essentially a parasitic formation. For states to persist in the old agenda now involves sacrificing the growth of the consumption of the population at large and the reduction of poverty. We can now see that the Great Depression was as bad as it was because states endeavoured to protect themselves at the cost of the employment and incomes of their citizens.

There are, as we have seen, many battles to come in the reform of the state, and war remains a continuing threat, even if now increasingly on the margins of the system. Governments fight stubborn rearguard actions to defend their privileged position. Like any decaying ruling order, they will seek to cling to power to the end. Not all, fortunately, are willing to persist so far as Hitler, willing the destruction of Germany if Germans failed him in his project, or of the Soviet leadership, coming perilously close to self-destruction rather than concede serious reform. But equally, few will give up without a fight. However, the war is lost simply because capital has escaped and there is no way in which it can be recaptured – for governments even to pay for their minimal activities, they must do a deal with the world at large. In fact, the issue is no longer that of defending the old sovereignties, since that role is dispersing over many other agencies, but of retaining some measure of public management.

Now, from Marx's perspective, we have the paradox of the 'withering away of the State' – in his terms, its reduction to the administration of things – without the abolition of capitalism and of markets. Indeed, we can now see the further paradox – if capitalism and markets were abolished, this would only profoundly expand the power of the state. Thus, it is only now that we can see the real 'bourgeois revolution', the establishment of the power of world markets and of businessmen over the states of the world. That power is embodied in markets, the unknown – and unintended – outcome of market transactions, not in the creation of a world political class of capitalists.

The productivity of the world now puts it within our grasp to end poverty, to make the conditions of all consistent with the best. Here the old agenda of the socialists remains – the attempt to secure a measure of collective mastery of the means by which people ensure their material survival. Yet before that we need to establish a world in which all who want to work can do so. At the moment, states lock up their populations and deny the right to work to those outside. Sovereignty is still embodied in a captive and immobile citizenry, but the theory and the practice is under threat. To allow people to move and work freely where they will requires a degree of trust between peoples which is the precise opposite to that resentful and angry xenophobia which has hitherto been the glue of national sovereignty. No one, half a century ago, would have thought such trust was possible in trade, but it is being achieved, and the radical decline in the war ethic makes it possible to hope for just such a change in the migration of labour.

Globalisation offers an immense vision of hope for the world – to escape from the domination of states and their preoccupation simply with national power and, in the past, war. Without those burdens, much more of the product of labour can go back to the labourer and into expanding the means to achieve future output. Not only can world incomes grow far faster in an economically integrated system, growing wealth and the ending of the national constraints on people's behaviour has the power to release very much more human creativity.

Notes on the Text

Notes on Preface

1   Jim Higgins has kindly pointed out to me that the Kidron/Cliff thesis originated in six articles on the 'Permanent War Economy' by T. N. Vance in *New International* (New York) in 1951.

Notes on Chapter 2

1   For example, the Bible records from a very early date (perhaps between the thirteenth and eighth centuries BC) the availability of rare imports – in this case, from what is now Yemen and Sri Lanka. Of course, these precious items could have been inserted in the text much later. The Book of Exodus (30; 23) records the instructions to Moses as follows: 'Take thou also unto thee principal spices of pure myrrh, five hundred shekels, and of sweet cinnamon ... and of sweet calamus ... and of cassis'.

2   Pliny the Elder (23–72AD), one of the first recorded mercantilists, grumbled that 'By the lowest reckoning, India, China and the Arabian Peninsula take from our empire 100 million sestercies every year – that is the sum which our luxuries and our women cost us; for what fraction of these imports, I ask you, now goes to the gods or to the power of the lower world?' – *Natural History* (1998) XII 84: 717.

3   There are strong accusations that the work is a forgery since the editor, David Selbourne, has not produced the original manuscript. However, having examined the charges in some detail, it seems to me they are largely circumstantial, and less persuasive than the equally circumstantial evidence of authenticity, particularly given the careful and knowledgeable refutation of the allegations by Professor Wang Lianmao, Director of the Quangzhou Maritime Museum, in the Chinese journal, *Maritime History Studies* (as translated by the original publisher, Little, Brown).

Notes on Chapter 3

1   Schurmann (1974: 132) draws out a related logic: 'War creates, intensifies and consolidates distinctions between human entities like nations. Exchange has the opposite effect – it constantly breaks down distinctions and creates larger and ever more encompassing systems'.

2   The form identified here is that of an historical prototype – it might be argued as we do elsewhere here that many states today are 'postmodern': the 'modern State' is already an historical phenomenon.

3   Two hundred years later, Schurmann (1974: 430) made a similar point about the US armed forces: 'The military services are the closest thing we have in America to the communist parties of the socialist countries – being an elite cadre, immensely centralised and entrusted with the highest social purpose of the nation – and occasionally operating outside the law'.

4   Tilly (in Evans et al. 1985) notes that this brings the role of government close to that of the racketeers: 'To the extent that the threats against which a government protects its citizens are imaginary or are the consequence of its own activities, the government has an organised protection racket. Since governments themselves commonly simulate, stimulate or even fabricate threats of external war, and since the repressive and extractive activities of government often constitute the largest threats to the livelihood of its own citizens, many governments operate in essentially the same way as the racketeers.'

5   Marx reiterates the same point in discussing the regime of Napoleon III in France: 'The army is no longer to maintain the rule of one part of the people over another part of the people. The army is to maintain its own rule, personated by its own dynasty, over the French people in general. It is to represent the State in antagonism to the society' (Draper I 1977: 454–55)

6   A point made about the German Social Democrats before the First World War by Hintze (1906/1975: 10): 'Social Democracy which in principle is against everything connected with militarism, not only owes to it the discipline on which its party organisation largely rests, but also in its ideology for the future, it has unconsciously adopted a good measure of the coercion of the individual by the community which comes from the Prussian military State'.

7   Schmitt (1963: 49–50; in Poggi 1978: 9) observes that 'There is no goal so rational, no norm so right, no programme so exemplary, no social ideal so attractive, no legitimacy or legality so compelling as to justify men's killing one another ... A war does not make sense by virtue of being fought for ideals or over rights, but by virtue of being fought against an actual foe.'

Notes on Chapter 4

1   Of course, there were many other views, from outright pacifism to indifference or rage. The socialists rightly saw war as destroying them by swamping their domestic challenge in the external conflict. Consider the gloom of August Bebel, leader of the Reichstag Social Democrats (Reichstag Protokol 268: 7730C-D, 1911 – in Volker and Kitchen 1981: 31): 'Then the great general march will be undertaken in Europe, in which 16 to 18 million men, the blossoming male youth of the different nations, equipped with the best murder weapons, will turn against one another as enemies in the field ... The twilight of the gods of the bourgeois world is in prospect ... '

2   Much of the material in this section is drawn from Milward (1977).

Notes on Chapter 5

1   Raising messianic hopes of the arrival of abundance. Consider the meditation of
     C.A.R. Crosland (1956), seeking to update the idea of socialism: 'It will really not
     much matter in a decade from now whether we plan to produce rather more of this
     or less of that ... the level of material welfare will soon be such that marginal changes
     in the allocation of resources will make little difference to anyone's contentment'.
2   Latin America, being a set of countries that had achieved their independence in the
     nineteenth century, had not at this date decided if it was part of the Third World.

Notes on Chapter 6

1   Yet despite many qualifications to the official picture, the basic commitment,
     seems fairly firm. Dower (1999: 22) is somewhat scornful, rather than impressed,
     by that commitment: 'Japanese died in hopeless suicide charges, starved to death
     in the field, killed their own wounded rather than let them fall into enemy hands,
     and murdered their civilian compatriots in places such as Saipan and Okinawa.
     They watched helplessly as fire bombs destroyed their cities – all the while listening
     to their leaders natter on about how it might be necessary for the "hundred
     million" all to die "like shattered jewels" ... In China alone, perhaps 15 million
     people died. The Japanese lost nearly three million ...' But was it so different from
     Germany during the Second World War?
2   Amsden (1985: 78) is one of the few observers to note the transition from a military
     to a civil economy in the following – but not entirely convincing – terms: 'the reality
     of economic development itself both seduced the military away from its initial
     orientation, and changed its position within the State apparatus, which freed up
     the process of capital accumulation still further'.

Notes on Chapter 8

1   *Subbotnik* was derived from a word meaning 'those who work on Saturdays
     without pay'.
2   The Polish economist Oscar Lange (1957: 15–16) noted the links between indus-
     trialisation and war: 'Socialist industrialisation and particularly very rapid
     industrialisation which was necessary in the first socialist countries, particularly
     in the Soviet Union, as a political requirement of national defence ... requires
     centralised disposal of resources ... essentially it can be described as a *sui generis*
     war economy'.
3   It often took a long time for economists in the successor Stalinist states to see this
     distortion. Three Chinese economists, writing in 1994, observe that 'many authors
     equate this distorted policy environment and the administrative controls [in
     China] as socialism ... However ... we find that the rationale for the existence of
     these policies and controls was not "socialism". Rather, the distorted macro policy

environment and planned allocation system arose because of the adoption of a heavy industry oriented strategy in a capital-scarce economy. All the socialist economies…adopted the same development strategy, probably under the influence of Stalin' (Lin et al. 1994: 11n.).

References and Sources

Abdulgani, Roeslan (1981): *The Bandung Connection: the Asia-Africa Conference in Bandung in 1955*, transl. Molly Bondan, Gunung Agung: Singapore.

Abelshauser, Werner (1998): 'Germany: guns, butter and economic miracles', in Harrison (1998: 122–76).

Abu-Lughod, Janet L. (1989): *Before European Hegemony: the World System, AD 1250-1350*, Oxford University Press: New York.

Ackroyd, Peter (2000): *London: The Biography*, Chatto and Windus: London.

Aghassian, Michel and Keram Kévonian (1987): 'Le commerce arménian dans l'océan Indien aux XVIIe et XVIIIe', in J. Aubin and D. Lombard (eds): *Marchands et Hommes d'Affaires asiatiques dans l'océan Indian et la mer de Chine*, XIII-Xxe, Guibert: Paris.

Aguis, Dionisius and Ian Richard Nelton (1997): *Across the Medieval Frontier: Trade, Politics and Religion, 650-1450*, International Medieval Research I, Turnhaut: Brepolo.

Airaldi, Gabriella (1997): 'The Genovese Art of Warfare', in Aguis and Nelton: 132–90.

Amsden, Alice (1985): 'The State and Taiwan', in Peter Evans et al. (eds): *Bringing the State...*, op. cit.

Anderson, Perry (1974): *Lineages of the Absolutist State*, New Left Books: London.

Anscombe, G.E.M. (1957): *Intentions*, Clarendon Press: Oxford.

Atkinson, Anthony B. (1999): 'Is rising inequality inevitable? A critique of the Transatlantic Consensus', WIDER Annual Lecture 3, United Nations University/World Institute of Development Economics Research: Helsinki, November.

Bairoch, P. (1982): 'International Industrialisation Levels from 1750 to 1980', *Journal of European Economic History* 2: 268–333.

— (1989): 'European Trade Policy, 1815-1914', in P. Matthias and S. Pollard (eds), *Cambridge Economic History of Europe*, VII, Cambridge University Press: Cambridge.

Baldwin, Richard E. and Philippe Martin (1999): *Two Waves of Globalisation: Superficial Similarities, Fundamental Differences*, National Bureau of Economic Research (Working Paper 6904): Cambridge MA.

Balogh, Thomas (1949): *Dollar Crisis: Causes and Cure*, Blackwell: Oxford.

Baran, Paul A. and Paul M. Sweezy (1966): *Monopoly Capitalism*, Monthly Review Press: New York and London.

Bardhan, Pranap (1984): *The Political Economy of Development in India*, Blackwell: Oxford.

Barendse, R.J. (1998): *The Arabian Seas, 1640-1700*, Research School CNWS, Leiden University: Leiden.

— (1999): *Arabian Seas in the Eighteenth Century*, International Institute of Asian Studies, Leiden University: Leiden

Barnett, Michael N. (1992): *Confronting the Costs of War: Military Power, State and Society in Egypt and Israel*, Princeton University Press: Princeton NJ.

Bederman, Gail (1995): *Manliness and Civilisation: a Cultural History of Gender and Race in the United States, 1880-1917*, University of Chicago Press: Chicago IL.

Berger, Suzanne (1981): *Organised Interests in Western Europe: Pluralism, Corporatism and the Transformation of Politics*, Cambridge University Press: Cambridge.

Berle, A.A. (1960): *Power without Property*, Sidgwick and Jackson: London.

Berliner, Joseph S.(1988): *Soviet Industry from Stalin to Gorbachev*, Cornell University Press: Ithaca NY.

Berthélemy, Jean-Claude and Saadet Deger (1995): *Conversion of Military Industries in China*, Development Centre, OECD: Paris.

Bisson, T.A. (1945): *Japan's War Economy*, Institute of Pacific Relations/Macmillan: New York.

Black, Jeremy (1994): *European Warfare, 1660-1815*, UCL Press: London.

Blasi, Joseph R., Maya Kroumova and Douglas Kruse (1997): *Kremlin Capitalism: Privatisation of the Russian Economy*, Cornell University Press: Ithaca NY and London.

Blume, W. von (1899/1930): *Die Grundlagen unserer Wehrkraft*, Ernst Siegfried Mittler und Sohn: Berlin.

Borjas, George, Richard Freeman and Lawrence Katz (1992): 'On the labor market effects of immigration and trade', in George Borjas and Richard Freeman, *Immigration and the Workforce*, University of Chicago Press: Chicago IL.

Böhning, W.R. (1972): 'The social and occupational apprenticeship of Mediterranean migrant workers in Germany', in Massimo Livi Bacci (ed.), *The Demographic and Social Patterns of Emigration from the Southern European Countries*, Universitá di Firenze: Florence.

Borjas, George and Valerie Ramey (1995): 'Foreign competition, market power and wage inequality', *Quarterly Journal of Economics*, 110/4, November: 1075–110.

Borrell, Brent and Lionel Hubbard (2000): 'Global economic effects of the European Union Common Agricultural Policy', *Journal of the Institute of Economic Affairs*, 20 February.

Bose, S. (1990) (ed.): *South Asia and World Capitalism*, Oxford University Press: Delhi.

Brady, R.A. (1943): *Business as a System of Power*, Columbia University Press: New York.

— (1950): *Britain in Crisis*, Columbia University Press: New York.

Bramson, Leon and George W. Goethals (1968) (eds): *War: Studies from Psychology, Sociology and Anthropology* (revised), Basic Books: New York and London.

Braudel, Fernand (1982/84): *Civilisation and Capitalism, 15th–18th centuries*: vol. II: *The Wheels of Commerce*; vol. III: *The Perspective of the World*, Fontana Press edition: London.

Bresnahan, Timothy and Daniel Raff (1997) (eds): *The Economics of New Goods*, University of Chicago: Chicago IL.

Brookings Institution (1997): *Atomic Audit: The Costs and Consequences of US Nuclear Weapons, 1940-95*, US Nuclear Weapons Costs Study Project (USNWCSP), Brookings: Washington DC.

Brown, R.A. (1972): *The Origins of Modern Europe*, Allen and Unwin: London

Brummett, Palmira (1994): *Ottoman Seapower and Levantine Diplomacy in the Age of Discovery*, State University of New York Press: Albany NY.

Bukharin, Nicolai (1917/1972): *Imperialism and World Economy*, with an introduction by V.I. Lenin, Merlin Press edition: London.

Bulatao, Rudolfo, Eduard Bes, Patience W. Stephens and My T. Vu (1990): *World Population Projections, 1989-90, Short and Long Term Estimates, 1989/90 ed.*, World Bank: Washington DC.

Bullock, Alan (1952): *Hitler: A Study in Tyranny*, Harper: New York.

Burnham, James (1945): *The Managerial Revolution*, Penguin: London.

Carr, William (1972): *Arms, Autarky and Aggression: A Study in German Foreign Policy, 1933-1939*, Edward Arnold: London.

Carroll, A.B. (1968): *Design for Total War: Arms and Economics in the Third Reich*, Mouton: The Hague.

Casson, Lionel (1964): *The Ancient Mariners: Seafarers and Sea Fighters of the Mediterranean in Ancient Times*, Macmillan: New York.

Castells, Manuel (1996): *The Rise of the Network Society, I (The Information Age: Economy, Society and Culture)*, Blackwell: Oxford.

Chamberlin, William Henry (1935/1965): *The Russian Revolution, 1917-1921*, 2 vols, 1935, Grosset and Dunlop: New York.

Chase, Holly (1994): 'The Meyhane or McDonald's? Changes in eating habits and the evolution of fast food in Istanbul', in Sami Zubaida and Richard Tapper (eds): *Culinary Cultures of the Middle East*, I.B. Tauris: London, 73–86.

Chaudhuri, K.N. (1966): 'India's foreign trade and the cessation of the East India Company's Trading Activities, 1828-40', *Economic History Review*, 19 (2): 345–63.

— (1978): *The Trading World of Asia and the English East India Company, 1660-1760*, Cambridge University Press: Cambridge.

— (1985): *Trade and Civilisation in the Indian Ocean: An Economic History from the rise of Islam to 1750*, Cambridge University Press: Cambridge.

— (1990): *Asia before Europe: Economy and Civilisation of the Indian Ocean from the Rise of Islam to 1750*, Cambridge University Press: Cambridge.

Clark, George (1958): *War and Society in the Seventeenth Century*, Cambridge University Press: Cambridge.

Clausewitz, Carl von (1968): *On War*, ed. Anatole Rapaport, Penguin ed.: London.

— (1993): *On War*, ed. and transl. Michael Howard and Peter Paret, Everyman: London.

Coelho, Phillip R.P. (1973): 'The profitability of imperialism: the British experience in the West Indes, 1768-1772', *Explorations in Economic History* 10: 253–80.

Coleman, D.C. and Eli Hekscher (1957): 'The idea of mercantilism', *Scandinavian Economic History Review*, v/i.

Commander, Simon, Fabrizio Coricelli and Karston Stalhr (1991): *Employment in the Transition to a Market Economy*, Working Paper 736, Economic Development Institute, World Bank: Washington DC.

Comte, Auguste (1842): *Cours de philosophie positif*, Entrente: Paris, IV.

Cooper, Robert (1996): *The Post-Modern State and the World Order*, Demos: London.

Corvisier, André (1979): *Armies and Societies in Europe, 1494-1789*, transl. Abigail L. Siddall, Indiana University Press: Bloomington IN and London.

Craig, Gordon A. (1955): *The Politics of the Prussian Army, 1640-1945*, Oxford University Press: London.

Croft, N.F.R. (1982): *British Economic Growth during the Industrial Revolution*, Clarendon: Oxford.

Crosland, C.A.R. (1956): *The Future of Socialism*, Cape: London.

Curtin, Philip D. (1984): *Cross-cultural Trade in World History, Studies in Comparative World History*, Cambridge University Press: Cambridge.

D'Ancona, Jacob (1997): *The City of Light*, ed. and transl. David Selburne, Little, Brown and Company: London.

Dale, Boisso, Showna Grosskopf and Kathy Hayes (1996): *The Response of Local Governments to Reagan-Bush Fiscal Federalism*, Federal Reserve Bank of Dallas, Research Dept., Working Paper 96-04: Houston, May.

Das Gupta, Ashin (1967): *Malabar in Indian Trade, 1740-1800*, Cambridge University Press: Cambridge.

Das Gupta, Ashin and M.N. Pearson (1987) (eds): *India and the Indian Ocean, 1500-1800*, Oxford University Press: Calcutta.

Davis, L.E. and R.A. Huttenbeck (1986): *Mammon and the Pursuit of Empire: The Political Economy of British Imperialism, 1860-1912*, Cambridge University Press: Cambridge.

Davis, Ralph (1973): *The Rise of the Atlantic Economies*, World University/Weidenfeld: London.

Deist, Wilhelm (1981): *The Wehrmacht and German Rearmament*, St Antony's College and Macmillan: London.

Deist, Wilhelm, Manfred Messerschmitt, Hans-Erich Volkman and Wolfram Weller (1990): *Germany and the Second World War*, transl. P.S. Falla, Dean S. McMurry and Ewald Osers, 2 vols, Research Institute for Military History, Freiburg, Clarendon Press: Oxford.

De Long, J. Bradford (1998): *Estimating World Gross Domestic Product, 1 million BC-present*, http://econ167.Berkeley.EDU/TCEH/1998_Draft/World_GDP/

— (2000a): *The Shape of Twentieth Century Economic History*, Working Paper 7569, National Bureau of Economic Research: Cambridge MA, February.

— (2000b): *Cornucopia: the Pace of Economic Growth in the Twentieth Century*, Working Paper 7602, National Bureau of Economic Research: Cambridge MA, March.

De Ste.Croix, G.E.M. (1981): *The Class Struggle in the Ancient Greek World*, Duckworth: London.

De Vries, Jan (1976): *The Economy of Europe in an Age of Crisis, 1600-1750*, Cambridge University Press: Cambridge.

Diakonoff, I.M. (1992), 'The Naval Power and Trade of Tyre', *Israel Exploration Journal* 42/3-4: 168–93.

Dickson, P.G.M. (1967): *The Financial Revolution in England: A Study in the Development of Public Credit, 1688-1756*, Cambridge University Press: Cambridge.

Dollar, David and Aart Kraay (2000): *Growth is Good for the Poor*, Development Research Group, World Bank: Washington DC, March.

Dorn, Walter (1963): *Competiton for Empire*, Harper: New York.

Dower, John W. (1999): *Embracing Defeat: Japan in the Wake of World War II*, Norton: New York.

Draper, Hal (1977): *Karl Marx's Theory of Revolution: State and Bureaucracy*, vol. I, Monthly Review Press: New York and London.

Drucker, Peter (1943): *The Future of Industrial Man: A Conservative Approach*, Heinemann: London.

— (1946): *The Concept of the Corporation*, Beacon edition (1960): Boston MA.

Duffy, Michael (1980) (ed.): *The Military Revolution and the State, 1500-1800, Exeter Studies in History 1*, University of Exeter: Exeter.

Easterly, William and Ross Levine (1995): *Africa's Growth Tragedy: A Retrospect, 1960-1989*, Policy Research Working Paper 1503, World Bank: Washington DC, Aug.

Eberhard, Wolfram (1977): *A History of China* (4th ed.), Routledge Kegan Paul: London.

Ebrey, Patricia Buckley (1996): *China, Cambridge Illustrated History*, Cambridge University Press: Cambridge.

Ehrenreich, Barbara (1997): *Blood Rites: Origins and History of the Passions of War*, Virago: London.

Ellis, John (1974): *Armies in Revolution*, Oxford University Press; New York.

Ellman, Michael and Robert Scharrenborg (1998): 'The Russian economic crisis', *Economic and Political Weekly*, Bombay, 26 December: 3317–22.

Engels, F. E. (1887/1990): 'Introduction (To Sigismund Borkheim's pamphlet In Memory of the German Blood-and-Thunder Patriots, 1806-1807)', in *Collected Works of Karl Marx and Friedrich Engels (1882-1889)*, vol. XXVI, Lawrence and Wishart: London.

— (1890/1990): 'The foreign policy of Russian Tsardom', in *ibid*, vol. XXVII: 11–49.

Ertman, Thomas (1997): *Birth of Leviathan: Building States and Regimes in Medieval and Early Modern Europe*, Cambridge University Press: Cambridge.

Evans, Peter, Dietrich Rueschemeyer and Theda Skocpol (1985) (eds): *Bringing the State Back In*, Cambridge University Press: Cambridge.

Ferguson, Niall (1998): *The Pity of War*, Penguin Books: London.

Firth, C.H. (1912): *Cromwell's Army* (2nd ed.), C. Hirst: London.

Flink, James J. (1975): *The Car Culture*, MIT Press: Cambridge MA.

Foot, M.R.D. (1973) (ed.): *War and Society: Historical Essays in Honour and Memory of J.R. Western, 1928-1971*, Paul Elek: London.

Frank, Raymond (1958): *War and Industrial Society*, Oxford University Press: London.

Freeman, R.B., Birgitta Swedenborg and Robert Topel (1995): *Reforming the Welfare State: Economic Troubles in Sweden's Welfare State*, Occasional Paper 69, National Bureau of Economic Research-SNS project: Stockholm, January.

Gaddy, Clifford C. (1996): *The Price of the Past: Russia's Struggle with the Legacy of a Militarized Economy*, Brookings Institution Press: Washington DC.

Galbraith, J.K. (1967): *The New Industrial State*, Hamish Hamilton: London.

Garnsey, Peter, Keith Hopkins and C.R. Whittaker (1983): *Trade in the Ancient Economy*, Chatto and Windus/Hogarth Press: London.

Gaxotte, L. (1942): *Frederick the Great*, Yale University Press: New Haven CT.

Gernet, Jacques (1996): *A History of Chinese Civilisation* (2nd ed.), Cambridge University Press: Cambridge.

Gershenkron, Alexander (1970): *Europe in the Russian Mirror: Four Lectures in Economic History*, Cambridge University Press: Cambridge.

Gilpin, Robert (1981): *War and Change in World Politics*, Cambridge University Press: Cambridge.

Goitien, S.D. (1967): *A Mediterranean Society: The Jewish Communities of the Arab World as Portrayed in the Documents of the Cairo Geniza:* vol. I: *Economic Foundations;* vol. II: *Community*, University of California: Berkeley and Los Angeles CA.

Glover, I.D. (1990): *Early Trade between India and South East Asia: A Link in the Development of a World Trading System* (2nd ed.), Centre for South East Asian Studies, University of Hull: Hull.

Goldin, Claudia and Robert A. Margo (1992): 'The great compression: the wage structure of the United States in mid-century', *Quarterly Journal of Economics*, 107/1, February: 1–35.

Gollwitzer, H. (1969): *Europe in the Age of Imperialism, 1870-1914*, Oxford University Press: London.

Goubert, P. (1973): *L'Ancien Regime*, II, Sohne: Paris.

Grant, Wyn, Jan Nekkers and Frans vam Waarden (1991): *Organising Business for War: Corporatist Economic Organisation during the Second World War*, Berg: New York and Oxford.

Guy, Arthur (1951): *The War Business*, John Layne: London.

Habib, Irfan (1991): 'Merchant communities in precolonial India', in Tracy (1990) (ed.): 361–99.

Hamilton, Earl J. (1950): *Origin and Growth of the National Debt in France and England*, Studi in onori di Gino Luzzato, Giuffre: Milan, II.

Hale, J.R. (1985): *War and Society in Renaissance Europe, 1450-1620*, Leicester University Press/Fontana: London.

Hall, John (1986): *Powers and Liberties*, Penguin: London.

Hanna, Nelly (1998): *Making Big Money in 1600: the Life and Times of Isma'il Abu Taqiyya, Egyptian Merchant*, American University in Cairo: Cairo.

Hara, Akira (1998): 'Japan: guns before rice', in Harrison (1998): 224–67.

Harris, Nigel (1972): *Competition and the Corporate Society: British Conservatives, the State and Industry, 1945-1964*, Methuen: London.

— (1983): *Of Bread and Guns: The World Economy in Crisis*, Penguin: London.

— (1985): *The end of the Third World: Newly Industrializing Countries and the decline of an ideology*, I.B. Tauris/Penguin: London.

— (1993): 'Mexican trade and Mexico-US economic relations', in Neil Harvey (ed.), *Mexico: Dilemmas or Transition*, Institute of Latin American Studies/British Academy Press: London and New York, 151–71.

— (1996): 'Preferring the lie', *Economic and Political Weekly*, Bombay, 24–31 August: 2301–6.

Harris, Nigel and David Lockwood (1997): 'The War-making State and privatisation,' *Journal of Development Studies*, 33/5, June: 597–634.

Harris, W. (1979): *War and Imperialism in Republican Rome*, Oxford University Press: London.

Harrison, Mark (1998) (ed.): *The Economics of World War II: Six Great Powers in International Comparison*, Cambridge University Press: Cambridge.

Harrison, Mark (1998): 'The Soviet Union: the defeated victor', in Harrison (1998): 268–301.

Harrod, R.F. (1951): *The life of John Maynard Keynes*, Harcourt Brace: New York.

Hawley, E.W. (1966): *The New Deal and the Problem of Monopoly*, Princeton University Press: Princeton NJ.

Hayes, Peter (2001): *Industry and Ideology: I.G.Farben in the Nazi Era* (2nd ed.), Cambridge University Press: Cambridge.

Heinl, Colonel Robert D. Jr (1971): 'The collapse of the armed forces', *Armed Forces Journal*, 7 June, reproduced in Marvin Gettleman et al., *Vietnam and America: A Documented History*, Grove Press: New York, 1995: 327.

Held, D. (1985) (ed.): *States and Societies*, Blackwell: Oxford.

Helliwell, John (1998): *How Much do National Borders Matter?*, Brookings Institution Press: Washington DC.

Henderson, David (1999): *The MAI Affair: a Story and its Lessons*, Royal Institute of Affairs and others: London.

Herekson, Magnus, Lars Jonurg and Joakim Stymme (1994): *Economic Growth and the Swedish Model*, Working Paper 19, Stockholm School of Economics: Stockholm, May.

Herz, John H. (1957): *The Nation-State and the Crisis of World Politics: Essays in International Politics in the Twentieth Century*, McKay: New York.

Hibbert, Christopher (1979): *The Rise and Fall of the House of Medici*, Lane, 1974, Penguin: London.

Hilferding, Rudolf (1910/1981): *Finance Capital: A Study of the Latest Phase of Capitalist Development*, ed. and intr. Tom Bottomore, from translations by Morris Watnick and Sam Gordon, Routledge and Kegan Paul: London.

Hines, James and Eric M. Rice (1994): 'Fiscal Paradise: Tax Havens and American Business', *Quarterly Journal of Economics*, CIX: 149–82.

Hintze, Otto (1975): *The Historical Essays of Otto Hintze*, ed. Felix Gilbert with assistance of Robert M. Berdell, Oxford University Press: New York.

Hirschfeld, Gerhard and Lothar Kettenacker (1981): *The 'Fuhrer State': Myth and Reality, Studies on the structure and politics of the Third Reich*, Klett-Cotta: Stuttgart.

Hirst, Paul and Grahame Thompson (1999): *Globalization in Question*, Polity Press: Cambridge.

Hitler, Adolf (1943): *Mein Kampf*, transl. James Murphy, Hurst and Blackett: London.

Hobsbawm, Eric (1968): *Industry and Empire: An Economic History of Britain since 1750*, Weidenfeld and Nicholson: London.

— (1994): *Age of Extremes: The Short Twentieth Century, 1914-1991*, Abacus: London.

Hopkins, A.G. (1973): *An Economic History of West Africa*, Longman: London.

Howard, Michael (1976): *War in European History*, Oxford University Press: London.

HSBC (Hong Kong and Shanghai Banking Corporation) (2001): *Integrated Oil and Gas – Exploding the Myth*, HSBC: London.

Hummel, D. and R. Stern (1994): 'Evolving Patterns of North American Merchandise Trade and Foreign Direct Investment, 1960-1990', *World Economy* 17: 2–39.

IMF-World Bank-OECD-EBRD (1990): *The Economy of the USSR*, World Bank: Washington DC.

Irwin, D. (1996): *Against the Tide: An Intellectual History of Free Trade*, Princeton University Press: Princeton NJ.

Islamoglu-Iran, Huri (1987) (ed.): *The Ottoman Empire and the World Economy*, Cambridge University Press: Cambridge.

Issawi, Charles (1963): *Egypt in Revolution: an Economic Analysis*, Royal Institute of International Affairs and Oxford University Press: London.

Jackson, Peter and Lawrence Lockhart (1986) (eds): *The Timurid and Safavid Periods*, vol. VI, *The Cambridge History of Iran*, Cambridge University Press: Cambridge.

Jenkins, Roy (1969): *Asquith: Portrait of a Man and an Era*, Collins: London.

Jobson, José and De Andrade Arruga (1991): 'Colonies as mercantile investment: the Luso-Brazilian Empire, 1500-1808', in Tracy (1991): 360–72.

Johnson, John J. (1962) (ed.): *The Role of the Military in Underdeveloped Countries*, Princeton University Press: Princeton NJ.

— (1964): *The Military and Society in Latin America*, Stanford, University Press: Stanford CA.

Jones, Charles A. (1987): *International Business in the Nineteenth Century: the Rise and Fall of a Cosmopolitan Bourgeoisie*, Wheatsheaf Books: Brighton.

Jones, D.W. (1988): *War and Economy in the Age of William III and Marlborough*, Blackwell: Oxford.

Kantor, Rosabeth Moss (1991): 'Transcending business boundaries: 12,000 world managers view change', *Harvard Business Review*, May–June: 151–64.

Kaplan, Lawrence (1977) (ed.): *The American Revolution and 'A candid world'*, Americana *Diplomatic History*, Kent State University Press: Kent, OH.

Katzenstein, Peter J. (1985): *Small States in World Markets: Industrial Policy in Europe*, Cornell University Press: Ithaca NY.

Keegan, John (1993): *A History of Warfare*, Hutchinson: London.

Kershaw, Ian (2000): *Hitler: Nemesis, 1936-1945*, vol. II, Allen Lane, Penguin Press: London.

Keynes, J.M. (1925): *The Economic Consequences of Mr Churchill*, Hogarth Press: London.

— (1924) 'The End of laissez-faire', Sidney Ball Lecture, Oxford, November, Hogarth Press: London, included in *Essays in Persuasion*, Macmillan: London; (1972) *Collected Works of John Maynard Keynes*, Macmillan-St Martin's Press for the Royal Economic Society.

Kindleberger, C. (1996): *Manias, Panics and Crashes*, Wiley: New York.

King, Blair and M.N. Pearson (1979) (eds): *The Age of Partnership: Europeans in Asia before European Domination*, East-West Center: Honolulu HI.

Kramer, Stephen D. (1978): *Defending the National Interest: Raw Materials Investment and US Foreign Policy*, Princeton University Press: Princeton NJ.

Kropotkin, Peter (1902): *Mutual Aid*, McClure, Phillips & Co.: New York.

Krugman, Paul (1994): *Past and Present Causes of High Unemployment; Reducing Unemployment: Current Issues and Policy Options*, Federal Reserve Bank of Kansas: Kansas City KS.

Kuczynski, Jurgen (1972): *Klassen und Klassenkampfe im imperialistischen Deutschland in der BRD*, Schmidt: Frankfurt-am-Main.

Kuznets, Simon (1965): *Economic Growth and Structure: Selected Essays*, Heinemann: London.

Kynaston, David: *The City of London* (1994): vol. I: *A World of its Own, 1815–1890*; (1995): vol. II: *Golden Years, 1890–1914*; (1999): vol. III: *Illusions of Gold, 1914–1945*; Chatto and Windus: London.

Lall, Deepak (n.d.): *The Political Economy of the Predatory State*, UCL Dept of Political Economy, Discussion Paper 84-12, UCL: London.

Landes, D. (1969): *The Unbound Prometheus*, Cambridge University Press: Cambridge.

Lane, F.C. (1995): *Venetian Ships and Shipbuilders of the Renaissance*, John Hopkins University Press: Baltimore MD.

Lange, Oscar (1957): *The Political Economy of Socialism*, State Publishing House: Warsaw.

Lardy, Nicholas (1998): *China's Unfinished Economic Revolution*, Brookings Institution Press: Washington DC.

Lasswell, Harold D. (1940): 'The garrison state', *American Journal of Sociology* XLVI: 455–68.

Laurent, Henri (1935): *Un grand commerce d'exportation au moyen age: la draperie des Pay-Bas, in France dans les pays méditerranéans (XIIe-Xve siècle)*, E. Droz: Liège-Paris.

Lawrence, Robert Z. (1994): 'Trade, multinationals and labour', in Philip Lowe and Jacqueline Dwyer (eds), *International Integration of the Australian Economy (Proceedings of a Conference)*, Economic Group, Reserve Bank of Australia: Sydney.

Lawrence, Robert Z. (1996): *Single world, divided nations? International trade and OECD labor markets*, OECD: Paris.

Leadbeater, Charles (1998): 'Goodbye, Inland Revenue', *New Statesman*, 3 July.

Leamer, E. (1994): *Trade, Wages and Revolving Door Ideas,* National Bureau of Economic Research, Working Paper 4716: Chicago IL.

Leitz, C.M. (1998): 'Arms exports from the Third Reich, 1933-1939: the example of Krupp', *Economic History Review* LI: 133–54.

Lendbeck, Assar et al. (1994): *Turning Sweden Round*, MIT Press: Cambridge MA.

Lenin, V.I. (1917/1974): 'Imperialism, the Highest Stage of Capitalism', republished in *V.I.Lenin: Collected Works*, vol. XXII: 185–304, Progress Publishers: Moscow.

— 'Better Fewer, But Better', in *V.I. Lenin: Collected Works*, vol. XXXIII (August 1921–March 1923), Progress Publishers: Moscow.

Lewis, John P. (1964): *Quiet Crisis in India: Economic Development and American Policy*, Doubleday: New York.

Lewy, Hildegard (1971): *Assyria, 2600-1816 BC, Cambridge Ancient History* (3rd ed.), Cambridge University Press: Cambridge.

Lin, Justin Yifu, Fang Cai and Zhou Li (1994): *China's Economic Reforms: Pointers for Other Economies in Transition*, Policy Research Working Papers 1310, World Bank: Washington DC.

Lindbeck, Assar et al. (1994): *Turning Sweden Round*, MIT Press: Cambridge MA.

Lipton, Merle (1985): *Capitalism and Apartheid, South Africa 1910-84*, Gower/Maurice Temple Smith: Aldershot.

Little, I.M.D., Richard Cooper, W.Max Corden and Sarath Rajapatirana (1993): *Boom, Crisis and Adjustment: The Macro Economic Experience of Developing Countries*, World Bank: Oxford University Press: New York.

Lloyd, C.M.H. (1924): *Experiments in State Control*, Blackett: London.

Lockwood, David (2000): *The Destruction of the Soviet Union: A Study in Globalization*, Macmillan Press: Houndmills.

Lottman, Herbert R. (1995): *Return of the Rothschilds: the Great Banking Dynasty through two Turbulent Centuries*, I.B. Tauris: London.

Macdonald, Brian R. (1982): 'The importance of Attic pottery to Corinth and the question of trade during the Peloponnesian War', *Journal of Hellenic Studies* 102.

Machiavelli, Niccolo (1952): *The Prince*, transl. Luigi Ricci, New American Library, Mentor: New York.

MacFarquhar, Roderick (1997): *The Origins of the Cultural Revolution: 3. The coming of the Cataclysm, 1961-1966*, Royal Institute of International Affairs and Oxford University Press and Columbia University Press: London and New York.

MacIntyre, D. (1979): *The Great War: Causes and Consequences*, Glasgow University Press: Glasgow.

Macmillan, Harold (1938): *The Middle Way: A Study of the Problem of Economic and Social Progress in a Free and Democratic Society*, Macmillan: London.

Maddison, Angus (1995): *Monitoring the World Economy, 1820-1992*, OECD: Paris.

Mankiw, N. Gregory (1995): *The Growth of Nations*, Discussion Paper 1731, Harvard Institute of Economic Research: Cambridge MA.

Mann, Michael (1988): *States, War and Capitalism: Studies in Political Sociology*, Blackwell: Oxford.

— (1990) (ed.): *The Rise and Fall of the Nation State*, Blackwell: Oxford.

Markovits, Claude (2000): *The Global World of Indian Merchants, 1750-1947: Traders of Sind from Bukhara to Panama: Cambridge Studies in History and Society*, Cambridge University Press: Cambridge.

Marx, Karl (1996) (ed.): *Capital*, vol. I, *Collected Works* 35, Lawrence and Wishart: London.

Mason, E. S. (1959) (ed.): *The Corporation in Modern Society*, Harvard University Press: Cambridge MA.

Mason, Tim (1966): 'Politics and economics in National Socialist Germany', *Das Argument* 41, December: 165–95.

— (1981): 'Intention and explanation: a current controversy about the interpretation of National Socialism', in Hirschfeld and Kattenacker, op. cit.

— (1993): *Social Policy in the Third Reich: The Working Class and the National Community*, transl. Jim Broadwin, ed. Jane Caplan, Oxford University Press: Oxford.

— (1995): *Nazism, Fascism and the Working Class, Essays*, Cambridge University Press: Cambridge.

Mathew, Gervase (1963): 'The East African coast until the coming of the Portuguese', in Roland Oliver and Gervase Mathew (eds), *The History of East Africa*, vol. I, Clarendon: Oxford.

McCloskey, Donald (1981): *Enterprise and Trade in Victorian Britain*, Allen and Unwin: London.

Migdal, S. (1988): *Strong Societies and Weak States: State-Society Relations and State Capabilities in the Third World*, Princeton University Press: Princeton NJ.

Milward, Alan S. (1977): *War, Economy and Society, 1939-1945*, Allen Lane: London.

— (1981):' The Reichsmark Bloc and the International Economy', in Hirschfeld and Kettenacker: 377.

Minchinton, W. E. (1987): *The Growth of English Trade in the Seventeenth and Eighteenth Centuries*, University Paperback (Debates in Economic History), Methuen: London.

Mohan, Rakesh and Vandana Aggarwal (1990): 'Commands and Controls: Planning for Indian Industrial Development, 1951-1990', Paper, Conference on Indian Planning, Delhi, 19–21 April.

Moore, Joe (1983): *Japanese Workers and the Struggle for Power, 1945-1947*, University of Wisconsin Press: Madison WI.

Moore, Karl and David Lewis (1999): *Birth of the Multinational: 2000 Years of Ancient Business History – from Ashur to Augustus*, Copenhagen Business School Press: Copenhagen.

Morishima, Michio (1982): *Why has Japan 'Succeeded'? Western Technology and the Japanese Ethos*, Cambridge University Press: London.

Murphy, K. and F. Welch (1993): 'Inequality and real wages', *American Economic Review* 83 (2): 104–9.

Murray, John J. (1972): *Amsterdam in the Age of Rembrandt*, David and Charles: Newton Abbot (UK).

Nathan, Otto (in collaboration with Milton Friedmann) (1944): *The Nazi Economic System*, Duke University Press: Durham NC.

Nef, John U. (1950): *War and Human Progress: An Essay on the Rise of Industrial Civilisation*, Routledge, Kegan-Paul: London.

Nkrumah, Kwame (1961): *Hands of Africa!*, Kwabena Omusu-Ayem: Accra.

Nolan, Peter (1995): *China's rise, Russia's Fall: Politics, Economics and Planning in the Transition from Stalinism*, Macmillan Press: Houndsmills and London.

North, Douglas (1981): *Structure and Change in Economic History*, Norton: London.

O'Brien, Patrick K. (1988): 'The costs and benefits of British imperialism, 1846-1914', *Past and Present: A Journal of Historical Studies* 120, August: 163–200.

— (1990): 'The imperial component in the decline of the British economy before 1914', in Mann (1990): 12–46.

O'Rourke, Kevin and Jeffrey Williamson (2000): *Globalisation and History: The Evolution of a Nineteenth Century Atlantic Economy*, MIT Press, London.

Odom, William E. (1998): *The Collapse of the Soviet Military*, Yale University Press: New Haven CT and London.

OECD (1994): *The OECD Jobs Study: Unemployment in the OECD area, 1950-95*, OECD: Paris.

Okun, Arthur (1970): *The Political Economy of Prosperity*, Brookings: Washington DC.

Olsen, Mancur (1993): 'Autocracy, democracy and prosperity', in Richard Zeckhauser (ed.), *Strategy and Choice*, MIT Press: Cambridge MA.

Origo, Iris (1957): *The Merchant of Prato*, Cape: London.

Orlin, L. (1970): *Assyrian Colonies in Cappadocia*, Mouton: The Hague.

Overy, R. J. (1994): *War and Economy in the Third Reich*, Clarendon: Oxford.

Parker, Geoffrey (1988): *The Military Revolution: Military Innovation and the Rise of the West, 1500-1800*, Cambridge University Press: Cambridge.

— (1991): 'Europe in the wider world, 500-1750: the military balance', in Tracy (1991): 161–228.

Parker, G. and L.M. Smith (1978): *The General Crisis of the Seventeenth Century*, Routledge: London.

Parkinson, C. Northcote (1957): *Parkinson's Law and Other Studies in Administration*, Houghton Mifflin: Boston MA.

Perham, M. (1956): *Lugard: the Years of Adventure, 1886-1898*, vol. I, Allen and Unwin: London.

Pliny the Elder (1998) (ed.): *Natural History*, transl. H. Rackham, Loeb Classical Library: Cambridge MA.

Poggi, Gianfranco (1978): *The Development of the Modern State: A Sociological Introduction,* Hutchinson University Library: London

Pollet, Gilbert (1987) (ed.): *India and the Ancient World: History, Trade and Culture before AD 650,* Orientalia Lovaniensia Analecta 25, Dept. Oriëntalistiek, Leuven.

Pomeranz, Kenneth and Steven Topik (1999) (eds): *The World that Trade Created, Society, Culture and the World Economy: 1400 to the Present,* M.E.Sharpe: Amonk NY and London.

Porter, Michael (1990): *The Competitive Advantage of Nations,* Macmillan Press: London.

Pritchett, Lant (1997): 'Divergence Big Time', *Journal of Economic Perspectives,* 11/3, Summer: 3–18.

Pullan, Brian (1968) (ed.): *Crisis and Change in the Venetian Economy in the Sixteenth and Seventeenth Centuries,* Methuen: London

Putnam, Robert, Susan Pharr and Russell Dalton (2000): *What is troubling the Trilateral Democracies?,* Princeton University Press: Princeton NJ.

Ramaswamy, Ramana (1993): *Structural crisis in the Swedish Economy,* Paper 93/18, IMF Series on Policy Analysis and Assessment, IMF: Washington DC.

Reader, John (1998): *Africa: A Biography of the Continent,* Penguin, London.

Redfield, James (1986): 'The development of the market in ancient Greece', in B.L. Anderson and A.J.H. Latham (eds), *The Market in History,* Croom Helm: London.

Reid, Anthony (1993): *South East Asia in the Age of Commerce, 1450-1680,* vol. II: *Expansion and Crisis,* Yale University Press: New Haven Conn.

Ritter, Gerhard (1969): *The Sword and the Sceptre: The Problem of Militarism in Germany: The Prussian Tradition, 1740-1890,* vol. 1, University of Florida Press: Miami FL.

Robinson, Francis (1996) (ed.): *Cambridge Illustrated History of the Islamic World,* Cambridge University Press: Cambridge.

Robinson, William I. and Jerry Harris (2000): 'Towards a global ruling class: globalisation and the transnational capitalist class', *Science and Society* 64/1, Spring: 11–55.

Rodrik, Dani (1997): *Has Globalisation Gone too Far?,* Institute of International Economics: Washington DC, March.

Rosen, Sherwin (1995): *Public employment and the Welfare State in Sweden,* National Bureau of Economic Research, Occasional Paper 61: Chicago, January.

Rosenberg, Hans (1958): *Bureaucracy, Aristocracy and Autocracy: The Prussian Experience, 1660-1815,* Harvard University Press: Cambridge MA.

Rostovtzeff, M. (1926/1957): *Social and Economic History of the Roman Empire,* 2nd ed., (2 vols), 2nd ed. rev. P.M. Fraser, Oxford University Press: London.

Rothenberg, G.E. (1980): *The Art of Warfare in the Age of Napoleon,* Indiana University Press: Bloomington IN.

Ruben, I.I. (1979): *A History of Economic Thought,* Ink Links: London.

Rubinstein, Nicolai (1968) (ed.): *Florentine Studies: Politics and Society in Renaissance Florence,* Faber and Faber: London.

Rudolph, Lloyd I. and Suzanne Halber (1987): *In Pursuit of Lakshmi: the Political Economy of the Indian State,* University of Chicago Press: Chicago IL.

Rueff, Marc (1983): *The Well-ordered Police State: Social and Institutional Change through Law in the Germanies and Russia, 1600-1800,* Yale University Press: New Haven CT and London.

Runciman, Steven (1952): 'Byzantine Trade and Industry', in M.Postan and E.E.Rich (eds), *Cambridge Economic History of Europe*, vol. II: *Trade and Industry in the Middle Ages*, Cambridge University Press: London, 86–118.

Samuelson, Paul A. (1948): 'International trade and the equalization of factor prices', *Economic Journal* 58: 163–84.

— (1949): 'International factor prices once again', *Economic Journal* 59: 181–97.

Sansom, G.B. (1950): *The Western World and Japan*, Routledge: London.

Schleifer, Andrei and Maxim Boycko (1994): 'Next steps in privatisation: six major challenges', in Ira W. Lieberman and John Nellis (eds): *Russia: Creating Private Enterprise and Efficient Markets*, World Bank: Washington DC.

Schmoller, Gustav F. Von (1931): *The Mercantile System and its Historical Significance* (1884 transl. from German), Reprints of Economic Classics, Evans: New York.

Schumpeter, Joseph A.(1943/1994): *Capitalism, Socialism and Democracy*, Routledge ed.: London.

— (1927/1958): *Imperialism. Social Classes, Two Essays*, Meridian: New York.

Schurmann, Franz (1974): *The Logic of World Power: An Inquiry into the Origins, Currents and Contradictions of World Politics*, Pantheon: London.

Schweitzer, Arthur (1964): *Big Business in the Third Reich*, Eyre and Spottiswoode: London.

Sereny, Gitta (1996): *Albert Speer: His Battle with Truth*, Picador: London.

Shaw, Martin (1984) (ed.): *War, State and Society*, Macmillan: London.

Sherwood, R.B. (1965): 'The wealth of Jamaica in the Eighteenth Century', *Economic History Review* 28: 292–311.

— (1969): 'The plantation revolution and the industrial revolution', *Caribbean Studies* 9.

— (1970): *The Development of the Plantation to 1750: An Era of West Indian Prosperity, 1750-1755*, West Indian University Press: Barbados and London.

Shinohara, Miyohei (1982): *Industrial Growth, Trade and Dynamic Patterns in the Japanese Economy*, University of Tokyo Press: Tokyo.

Shleifer, Andrei and Robert W. Vishny (1998): *The Grabbing Hand: Government Pathologies and Their Cures*, Harvard University Press: Cambridge MA.

Shleifer, Andrei and Maxim Boycko (1994): 'Next Steps in Privatization: Six Major Challenges', in Ira W. Lieberman and John Nellis (eds): *Russia: Creating Private Enterprise and Efficient Markets*, World Bank, Washington DC, 75–86.

Shonfield, Andrew (1965): *Modern Capitalism: the changing balance of public and private power*, Royal Institute of International Affairs/Oxford University Press: London.

Simmel, Bernard (1981): *Marxism and the Science of War*, Oxford University Press: Oxford.

Sirower, Mark L. (1997): *The Synergy Trap*, Simon and Schuster: New York.

Skidelsky, Robert (1992): *John Maynard Keynes: II: The Economist as Saviour, 1920-37*, Macmillan: London.

Skocpol, Theda (1979): *States and Social Revolutions: a Comparative Analysis of France, Russia and China*, Cambridge University Press: Cambridge.

Solimano, Andres (1992): *After Socialism and Dirigisme: Which Way?*, Policy Research Working Paper 981, World Bank: Washington DC.

Sombart, Werner (1913): *Krieg und Kapitalismus, Studien zur Entwicklungsgeschichte des modernen Kapitalismus' Wirtschaft*, Dunker und Humbold EA: Leipzig.

Solow, Robert (1993): 'How economic ideas turn to mush', in D.C. Colander and A. Coats (eds), *The spread of Economic Ideas*, Cambridge University Press: Cambridge.

Spruyt, Hendrik (1994): *The Sovereign State and its Competitors: an Analysis of Systems Change, Studies in International History and Politics*, Princeton University Press: Princeton NJ.

Stachura, Peter D. (1983) (ed.): *The Nazi Machtergreifung*, Allen and Unwin: London.

Stalin, Josef (1940): 'Tasks of Planning, Report to the 6th Central Committee meeting', in *Problems of Leninism* (11th ed.), Peoples' Publishing House: Moscow.

Stalker, Peter (2000): *Beyond Krismon: the social legacy of Indonesia's Financial Crisis*, UNICEF (Innocenti Insight): Florence, December.

Stepan, Alfred (1978): *The State and Society: Peru in Comparative Perspective*, Princeton University Press: Princeton NJ.

Stern, Walter M. (1960/1961): 'Wehrwirtschaft: a German contribution to economics', *Economic History Review* 13/2: 270–81.

Stolper, Wolfgang and Paul A. Samuelson (1941): 'Protection and real wages', *Review of Economic Studies*, November: 58–73.

Stone, Lawrence (1965): *Social Change and Revolution in England, 1540-1640*, C. Hirst: London.

Sugar, Peter F. (1971): 'The Ottoman 'Political Prisoners' on the Western Borders of the Empire in the Sixteenth and Seventeenth Centuries', *Études Balkaniques* 2.

Sutela, Pekka (1994): 'Insider privatization in Russia: Speculations on systemic change', *Europe-Asia Studies* 46/3.

Tallett, Frank (1992): *War and Society in Early Modern Europe, 1495-1715*, Routledge: London.

Taylor, Robert H. (1987): *The State in Burma*, C. Hurst/Orient Longman: London.

Temin, Peter (1991): 'Soviet and Nazi economic planning in the 1930s', *Economic History Review* XLIV: 573–93.

Thomas, R.P. (1968): 'The sugar colonies of the old Empire: profit or loss for Great Britain?', *Economic History Review* 21: 30–45.

Thompson, Leonard (1990): *A History of South Africa*, Yale University Press, New Haven CT.

Tilly, Charles (1975) (ed.): *The Formation of Nation States in Western Europe*, Princeton University Press: Princeton NJ.

— (1981): *As Sociology Meets History*, Academic Press: New York.

— (1990): *Coercion, Capital and European States, AD 990-1990, Studies in Social Discontinuity*, Blackwell: Oxford.

— (1993): *European Revolutions, 1492-1992*, Blackwell: Oxford.

— (1995): 'Globalisation threaten's labor's rights', *International Labor and Working Class History* 47, Spring: 1–23.

Tracy, James D. (1990) (ed.): *The Rise of the Merchant Empires*, Cambridge University Press: Cambridge.

— (1991) (ed.): *The Political Economy of Merchant Empires*, Cambridge University Press: Cambridge.

Tuchman, Barbara (1989): *A Distant Mirror: The Calamitous Fourteenth Century*, Macmillan: London.

Turner, Henry Ashby Jr (1985): *German Big Business and the Rise of Hitler*, Oxford University Press: New York.

Twitchett, Denis (1983): *Printing and Publishing in Medieval China*, Wynkyn de Worde Society: London.

United Nations (1999): *The Human Development Report 1999*, UN–Oxford University Press: New York.

Vagts, Alfred (1959): *A History of Militarism: Civil and Military* (2nd ed.), Columbia University Press: New York,

Van Creveld, Martin (1977): *Supplying War: Logistics from Wallerstein to Patten*, Cambridge University Press: London.

— (1991): *The Transformation of War*, Free Press: New York.

— (1996): 'The fate of the State: Parameters of the US Army', *War College Quarterly*, XXVI/I, Spring.

Volker, R. Berghahn and Martin Kitchen (1981) (eds): *Germany in the Age of Total War*, Croom Helm: London.

Waddington, Jeremy and Reiner Hoffman (2001): *Trade Unions in Europe: Challenges and Searching for Solutions*, European Trade Union Institute: Brussels.

Wallerstein, Immanuel (1997): 'Merchant, Dutch or Historical Capitalism?', *Review* 20/2, Spring: 253–4.

Watkins, K. (1998): *Economic Growth with Equity: Lessons from East Asia*, Oxfam Publications: Oxford.

Waelbroeck, Jan (1998): *Half a century of Development Economics*, Policy Research Working Paper 1925, World Bank: Washington DC.

Weber, Max (1922/1948): 'Structures of Power', in H. H. Gerth and C. Wright Mills (transl. and ed.), *From Max Weber: Essays in Sociology*, Routledge and Kegan Paul: London, 159–79.

Webb, Sidney and Beatrice (1935): *Soviet Communism: A New Civilisation*, Longmans, Green: London.

Weighley, Russell F. (1996): *The Age of Battles: The Quest for Decisive Warfare from Breitenfeld to Waterloo*, Indiana University Press: Bloomington IN and London.

Weiss, Linda and John H. Hobson (1995): *States and Economic Development: a Comparative History Analysis*, Polity Press: London.

Williamson, Jeffrey (1996): *Globalization and Inequality Then and Now: The Late Nineteenth Century and Late Twentieth Centuries Compared*, National Bureau of Economic Research, Working Paper 5491: Cambridge MA.

Williamson, John (1990): *Latin American Adjustment: How Much has Happened?*, Institute of International Economics: Washington DC.

— (1994) (ed.): *The Political Economy of Policy Reform*, Institute for International Economics: Washington DC.

Wilson, C.H. (1967): 'Trade, Society and the State', in E.E. Rich and C.H. Wilson, *Cambridge Economic History of Europe, IV, The economy of expanding Europe in the Sixteenth and Seventeenth Centuries*, Cambridge University Press: London: 487–576.

Wolf, Eric (1997) (ed.): *Europe and the People without History*, University of California Press: Berkeley and Los Angeles CA.

Wolf, John B. (1951): *The Emergence of the Great Powers, 1685-1715*, Oxford University Press: New York.

Wood, Adrian (1994): *North-South Trade: Employment and Inequality*, Clarendon Press: Oxford.

Wood, Gordon (1973): 'The American Revolution', in Lawrence Kaplan, op. cit.

Woodward, Mary (2000) (ed.): *Exceptional Returns: The Economic Value of America's Investment in Medical Research*, Lasker Charitable Trust: New York.

World Bank (1989): *International Migration and International Trade*, by Sharon Stanton Russell and Michael Teitelbaum, World Bank: Washington DC.

— (1997): *The World Development Report 1997: The State in a Changing World*, World Bank/Oxford University Press: New York.

— (1999): *World Development Report 1999/2000*, World Bank: Washington DC.

— (2000): *Global Economic Prospects for Developing Countries: 2000*, World Bank: Washington DC.

Wright, Quincy (1942): *A Study of War*, University of Chicago Press/Phoenix Books: Chicago IL.

Zarnowitz, V. (1972) (ed.): *The Business Cycle Today*, National Bureau of Economic Research/Columbia University Press: New York.

Zubaida, Sami (1999): 'Cosmopolitanism in the Middle East: History and Prospects', in Roel Meijer (ed.), *Cosmopolitanism, Identity and Authenticity in the Middle East*, Curzon: London.

Index